A History of Mindfulness

Also by Bhikkhu Sujato through Santipada

Sects & Sectarianism
How tranquillity worsted insight in the Pali canon

Beginnings
There comes a time when the world ends...

Bhikkhuni Vinaya Studies
Research & reflections on monastic discipline for Buddhist nuns

A Swift Pair of Messengers
Calm and insight in the Buddha's words

Dreams of Bhaddā
Sex. Murder. Betrayal. Enlightenment. The story of a Buddhist nun.

White Bones Red Rot Black Snakes
A Buddhist mythology of the feminine

SANTIPADA is a non-profit Buddhist publisher. These and many other works are available in a variety of paper and digital formats.

http://santipada.org

A History of Mindfulness

How insight worsted tranquillity in the Satipaṭṭhāna Sutta

BHIKKHU SUJATO

SANTIPADA

SANTIPADA
Buddhism as if life matters

Originally published by The Corporate Body of the Buddha Education Foundation, Taiwan, 2005.
This revised edition published in 2012 by Santipada.
Printed and distributed by Lulu.com.

ISBN: 978-1-921842-09-2

Typeset in Gentium using LuaTeX.

Contents

List of Tables

There's no jhāna for one without wisdom;
No wisdom for one without jhāna.
But for one with both jhāna and wisdom,
Nibbana truly is near.

—THE BUDDHA, DHAMMAPADA 372

FOREWORD: THE VIPASSANANĀVĀDĀ

THE PURPOSE OF THIS BOOK is to analyze the textual sources of 20th century Theravāda meditation theory. The focus is on the prime source works for what I call the *vipassanāvāda*, the 'vipassanā-doctrine'. This is a special interpretation of some central meditation concepts that has become the *de facto* orthodoxy in Theravāda Buddhism, although not without controversy. The term *vipassanāvāda* is useful in that the Pali suffix *-vāda* points to the importance of the *theory* on which the practices are based. More than that, the same suffix comes to mean not just a doctrine, but also the school that follows the doctrine. This is all too appropriate in the current case, since 'vipassanā' has come, rather strangely, to be used as if it refers to an actual school of Buddhism (rather than an aspect of meditation cultivated in all schools).[1]

2 The key points of the vipassanāvāda are reiterated countless times in almost every book on 20th century Theravāda meditation, so here I will sum up briefly. The Buddha taught two systems of meditation, samatha and vipassanā. Samatha was taught before the Buddha (so is not really Buddhist), it is dangerous (because one can easily get attached to the bliss), and it is unnecessary (because vipassanā alone can develop the access samādhi necessary to suppress the hindrances). Vipassanā is the true key to liberation taught by the Buddha. This method was pre-eminently taught in the Satipaṭṭhāna Sutta, the most important discourse taught by the

---

[1] There is a precedent in the case of the Chinese Chan school (Zen in Japanese), which is derived from the Sanskrit *dhyāna* (Pali *jhāna*), which here just means 'meditation'.

Buddha on meditation and on practice in everyday life. The essence of this practice is the moment-to-moment awareness of the rise and fall of all mind-body phenomena. Thus satipaṭṭhāna and vipassanā are virtually synonyms.

3 Not all modern meditation traditions accept this dichotomy of samatha and vipassanā. For example, the teachers of the Thai forest tradition often emphasize the complementariness, rather than the division, of samatha and vipassanā. The late Thai meditation master Ajahn Chah, for example, once said that in samatha, you sit down cross legged, close your eyes, watch your breath, and make the mind peaceful. But vipassanā, now, that's something quite different. In vipassanā, you sit down cross legged, close your eyes, watch your breath, make the mind peaceful, and then you know: 'It's not a sure thing!'

4 I have always felt that in this approach to meditation there was a strong affinity between the Suttas and the teachings of the forest masters. In this work I demonstrate from a scholarly point of view the same truths expressed with such pith and authority by masters like Ajahn Chah.

5 In 2000 I wrote *A Swift Pair of Messengers*, emphasizing the harmony and complementariness of samatha and vipassanā. There, I discussed at some length the treatment of satipaṭṭhāna in the early Suttas, focusing on the Satipaṭṭhāna Sutta. The purpose was to show that satipaṭṭhāna, far from being a distinctive or separate way of practice, was embedded both deeply and broadly in the meaning of the early Suttas and could neither be understood nor practiced outside of this context.

6 Nearing the end of that project I came across an article by Richard Gombrich entitled 'Retracing an Ancient Debate: How Insight Worsted Concentration in the Pali Canon'.[2] Although only partially convinced by his arguments, I was intrigued by his idea—that the shift in emphasis from samādhi to vipassanā, so obvious in later Theravāda, could be traced to editorial changes made within the period of compilation of the Pali Nikāyas. It jolted some memories of a few loose ends left dangling in my study of satipaṭṭhāna. I decided to tug on those strands of thought, and to my amazement the whole Satipaṭṭhāna Sutta started to unravel before

---

[2] GOMBRICH.

my eyes. This is the story of how the Satipaṭṭhāna Sutta was woven, how it unravels, and how this affects our understanding of Dhamma-Vinaya.

7 The significance of such a historical approach to the teachings is still largely unrecognised among practicing Buddhists. In fact, our normal approach to the teachings is the very opposite of historical. An aspiring meditator first learns from the lips of a teacher whose words as they utter them must be the very latest formulation of the topic. Then they might go back to read some of the works of well-known contemporary teachers. Since devotees usually have faith that their teacher (or the teacher's teacher) was enlightened, they assume, often without reflection, that the teachings must be in accord with the Buddha. Finally, if they are really dedicated, they may go back to read 'the' Satipaṭṭhāna Sutta. Once they come to the text itself, they are already pre-programmed to read the text in a certain way. It takes guts to question one's teachers; and it takes not just guts, but time and effort to question intelligently.

8 Apart from 'the' Satipaṭṭhāna Sutta, the other discourses on satipaṭṭhāna, since they are so much shorter, are usually ignored under the assumption that they add little new. Even the best of the scholars who have studied satipaṭṭhāna from a historical perspective, such as Warder, Gethin, and Anālayo, have treated the Satipaṭṭhāna Sutta as primary and the shorter discourses as supplements.

9 So now I would like to reverse that procedure. Our first step must be to forget all we've learnt about satipaṭṭhāna, and to start again from the bottom up. A basic principle of the historical method is that simpler teachings tend to be earlier and hence are likely to be more authentic—we must start with the bricks before we can build a house. It is the shorter, more basic, passages that are the most fundamental presentation of satipaṭṭhāna. The longer texts are an elaboration. We do not assume that shorter is always earlier, but we take this as a guiding principle whose implications we can follow through.

10 This stratification, it should be noted, does not claim to be able to decide which teachings were genuinely spoken by the Buddha. He himself would likely have given the same teachings initially in simple form, then later expanded on various details. But the universal testimony of the traditions is that the texts as we have them today were assembled in their present form

after the Buddha's passing away; so the rational approach is to consider the texts as the outcome of an evolutionary process.

11 Those who disagree with this approach usually do so because they have faith that all of the teachings in the Suttas were literally spoken by the Buddha, or they doubt the possibility of meaningful historical reconstruction due to the unreliability of the sources or the uncertainty of the method. I believe the first position is too credulous and the second too sceptical. In any case, regardless of the historical situation, it is surely sensible to learn the Dhamma by starting with the simple teachings and working up to the complex.

12 So we should start by identifying the smallest, simplest units of meaning used to describe satipaṭṭhāna. These are the basic terms and phrases common to all descriptions of satipaṭṭhāna in all the schools. It makes sense to start with the Buddha's first sermon. This raises an interesting question. This sermon is for the group of five monks, who were, at the time, non-Buddhist ascetics. However, the text refers to mindfulness as if it assumes the audience would know what it means. Mahāsi Sayadaw noticed this, and felt that the discourse should have originally included a more detailed explanation of satipaṭṭhāna. But I felt this was unlikely, for the Saccavibhaṅga Sutta, which explicitly explains the Dhammacakkappavattana Sutta 'in detail', includes the standard satipaṭṭhāna formula in this detailed expansion. What need for such an expansion if the formula was there in the original? The conclusion is inescapable: the Dhammacakkappavattana Sutta assumes that the five monks already knew what mindfulness was, and so mindfulness was a pre-Buddhist practice. To check this I had to examine more closely the accounts of pre-Buddhist meditation found in both the Buddhist and non-Buddhist texts.

13 I was first alerted to the idea of historical change in the Satipaṭṭhāna Sutta by A.K. Warder, who refers to versions of the Satipaṭṭhāna Sutta in ancient Chinese translations. After recording the major differences he notes in connection with the contemplation of dhammas that 'the original text simply opposed these good principles [awakening-factors] to the obstacles.'[3] It is through such seemingly innocuous remarks that I have become aware of the truly momentous significance of the comparative study of

[3] WARDER, pg. 86.

the Nikāyas and Āgamas. While the Theravāda Nikāyas will forever remain our primary source for exploration of pre-sectarian Buddhism, the Āgamas of the contemporary Sarvāstivāda, Dharmaguptaka, and other schools, which are preserved in ancient translations in the Chinese canon, provide an essential and underutilised check on the Pali. As the Encyclopaedia of Buddhism puts it: 'In our days it is impossible for any scholar to refer to early Buddhism unless he pays due regard to the comparative study of the southern and northern traditions.' This study will show that the early Nikāyas/Āgamas are not a mined out field whose treasures are all safely housed in the later compendiums.

14 In the Nikāyas/Āgamas it is obvious that no one text presents an all encompassing, definitive exposition, so each text must be considered in relation to the collection as a whole. This raises questions of the overall structure and organization of the canon. I began to suspect that the shorter texts in the Saṁyutta may preserve an earlier perspective on satipaṭṭhāna, a perspective that in some respects was better reflected in the Chinese versions of the Satipaṭṭhāna Sutta than in the Pali. My suspicions were further aroused by a comment by Bhikkhu Varado on the laxity of the compilers of the Abhidhamma Vibhaṅga in omitting much of the material from the Satipaṭṭhāna Sutta. Maybe, I wrote back, they weren't lax at all—maybe the Satipaṭṭhāna Sutta had not been written when the relevant portions of the Vibhaṅga were compiled. (I later found out that I was not the first to raise this question.) This suggested that I should take account of the early Abhidhamma texts as well as the Suttas, overcoming, in part, my prejudice that the Abhidhamma was a late and sterile body of sectarian dogmas. And then, if the early Abhidhamma period overlapped with the composition of the Satipaṭṭhāna Sutta, it seemed likely that sectarian agendas would be involved in the settling of the final text. This called for a closer examination of the ways the emerging sectarian disputes found expression in the early texts. It then seemed appropriate to extend the survey to the later commentarial period, to try to gain a deeper insight into the ways the traditions adapted satipaṭṭhāna to their own particular perspective on the Dhamma, and to bridge the gap between the Buddha's time and our own.

15 To make use of the material on satipaṭṭhāna translated in Chinese, I had to improve my own understanding of the Āgamas and other early Buddhist sources outside the Pali. When examining and comparing these collections, with their very strong connections but also real and persistent differences, there is a strong need for a resolution, like the feeling in music that comes when two notes are very close together, but not quite: they yearn to become one. At this time I was fortunate enough to get to know Roderick Bucknell. Informed by his comparative work on the structure of the early scriptures, I have tried to clarify the relations between the various types and strata of texts in the early canon, and have formulated this as the GIST. This theory suggests a specific relationship and hierarchy of texts in the existing canons, a relationship that reflects both the doctrinal importance and the historical provenance.

16 I realized that the methodology that I had been using in studying satipaṭṭhāna followed closely the outlines of the GIST. No doubt my belief that this approach had been fruitful in the context of satipaṭṭhāna prepared me to accept that it could be extended to a general interpretive theory. So I decided to include a presentation of the GIST together with the study on satipaṭṭhāna, although here the general theory is presented first. These two parts substantially reinforce each other. The study of satipaṭṭhāna provides a detailed examination of an important doctrine along the lines suggested by the GIST. It exemplifies the method, providing additional evidence for the basic principles of the GIST, and showing that the GIST produces meaningful and useful results. Despite this, however, the two parts are not mutually dependent. If my analysis of satipaṭṭhāna turns out to be misguided, this weakens but does not destroy the evidence in support of the GIST. Likewise, if the GIST is felt to be unacceptable, this weakens but does not destroy the evidence in support of the analysis of satipaṭṭhāna. To some degree, the two studies may be considered independently; but taken together they are more meaningful.

17 We are not embarking on a search for certainty. As long as we stay in the realm of concepts our ideas can only ever approximate the truth. What is important is that we are moving in the right direction, moving away from confusion towards clarity, away from dogmatism towards inquiry. Each of the criteria employed in historical criticism when taken individually is

an imperfect tool. But they are synergistic: where several criteria agree, the concurrence multiplies our confidence in our conclusions—the whole is greater than the sum of the parts. So it is imperative to use as wide a variety of criteria as possible, sensitively appraise the reliability of each criterion in the relevant context, remain alive to any contrary indications, and make our conclusions no more certain than the evidence warrants.

18 I have tried to make matters no more technical and specialized than necessary, without sacrificing precision. The translations are from various sources. Research was carried out in many places—monasteries, libraries, Buddhist centres, internet—and I am not able to standardize or to check all the references. Special thanks are due to Bhikkhu Fa Qing, who gave much of his time to help me explore some arcane corners of the Chinese canon, and to Roderick Bucknell for much illuminating information and challenging ideas. It is to Rod that I owe most of the detailed information on such texts as the Dharmaskandha, Śāriputrābhidharma, Kāyagatāsmṛti Sūtra, and much else. Towards the end of this project, I began a correspondence with Venerable Anālayo, who helped me get a handle on reading the Chinese canon.

19 I have tried to maintain consistency of renderings of technical terms, and have sometimes taken the liberty of bringing the renderings in quoted passages into line with the main text. Since the Pali canon is the backbone of this work, and since I am more familiar with Pali, I have rendered almost all Indian words in their Pali rather than Sanskrit form. Exceptions include proper names and terms that are unknown in Pali in the relevant meaning.

20 A peculiar difficulty of this work is that it discusses several texts with confusingly similar titles. I have tried to minimize confusion by spelling out names and affiliations of texts mostly in full.

21 It is common practice among scholars to refer to the texts by their language, as for example the 'Pali Majjhima Nikāya' and the 'Chinese Madhyama Āgama'. This conveys the entirely misleading impression that the Āgamas, and indeed all the Indian Buddhist texts that happen to be available to us in Chinese translation, are in some sense 'Chinese'. We might as well refer to the 'English Majjhima Nikāya' simply because we happen to be reading an English translation. What matters is the meaning; and this is more significantly affected by the redactors' doctrinal perspectives

than by their language. It is therefore preferable to classify texts according to school whenever possible. It is, of course, still necessary to refer to the 'Chinese canon', since those texts stem from many schools, and the collection as a whole is a Chinese artefact.

22 I have tried to give references to all known versions of a particular text, which usually means the Pali and the Chinese version. Readers should be aware that this refers to a text identified as cognate[4] in available concordances. It does not imply that the particular term, phrase, or idea under discussion is found in all versions. I have, however, checked as many significant references as possible, and have indicated relevant differences.

23 Historical criticism is not *nice*. This study may sometimes appear more surgical than inspirational. Relentless analysis can seem opposed to faith. But this need not be so; the Buddha regarded reason as the foundation of true faith. One who has true faith in the Dhamma would surely not fear that mere literary criticism could destroy the teachings. And is it not just fear that makes us want to protect one's sacred scriptures, to enshrine them on a pedestal, to lock them safely away in a gorgeous chest on one's shrine, safe from any impious inquiry? Thankfully such fear, while certainly not absent, does not predominate in contemporary Buddhist circles. And our findings, no matter how cruelly we wield the scalpel, don't affect the fundamentals. There is a massive agreement among the early sources as to the central teachings—not just the ideas and principles, but the specific texts and formulations as well. The discrepancies we shall notice in our explorations undermine not these fundamentals, but certain implications and trends discernable in the arrangement and emphasis of the developed formulations. Even here the differences, to begin with, are slight and few in number. So it is my intention, not to raise doubts, but to encourage the maturing of faith.

---

[4] The term 'cognate' literally means 'born together', and is used in etymology of words that are believed to derive from a common ancestor. Some scholars prefer to use words such as 'parallel' or 'counterpart' to refer to the suttas found in Pali and Chinese versions, since these terms do not imply any particular theory as to the relations between the texts in question. However, I am quite comfortable with 'cognate', since I believe that in most cases the theory that similar suttas derive from a common ancestor is the most rational.

PART ONE

THE GIST: THE HIDDEN STRUCTURE OF THE DHAMMA

Friends, just as the footprint of any creature that walks can be placed within an elephant's footprint, and so the elephant's footprint is declared the chief of them because of its great size—so too, all skilful principles can be included within the four noble truths.

—THE BUDDHA, MAHĀ HATTHIPADOPAMA SUTTA

Chapter 1

THE MEANING OF 'BUDDHA'

BUDDHA.

2 It is said that even to hear this word is precious beyond reckoning. Through countless aeons, beings fall into ruin since they are denied the opportunity of hearing it. Finally, after an incalculably long time, the Enlightened One arises in the world and the word 'Buddha' is heard, like a shower of rain in the parched desert. When the merchant Anāthapiṇḍika heard this word he was overwhelmed—his hair stood on end, he could not sleep at night, his heart leapt up with a strange exultation. In the millennia since the Buddha's time, this word has developed a unique aura, a spiritual charisma that lends unparalleled prestige to the religious communities and institutions that proclaim their allegiance to his liberating teaching. We are the spiritual heirs of that great being, that man of flesh and blood who walked the rich soil of the Ganges plain nearly 2500 years ago.

3 The very words we use to speak about Dhamma, including this word 'Buddha', are bound and limited by the Indo-Aryan culture in which the young Siddhattha Gotama grew up. An etymologist might say that '*buddha*' derives from an ancient Indo-European root, whose basic meaning is to 'wake up', and which has several cognates with related meanings in contemporary European languages. A grammarian could tell us that it is a past participle formed from a verbal stem. A philosopher of language might find it significant that the past participle, which is unusually common in Buddhist languages, denotes the arrival at or emergence into a certain

condition, rather than an eternal, timeless state of being. A historian of religion could tell us that the title 'Buddha' is used to denote an enlightened or consummate being in several religions, such as Jainism and Brahmanism, as well as Buddhism. A meditation teacher,on the other hand, might emphasize how 'Buddha' refers to the intrinsic quality of awareness. And so on. All of these aspects inform and condition the resonance of the word 'Buddha'; they are part of the meaning of the word 'Buddha'.

4 It is the shared allegiance to this 'Buddha' that defines the Buddhist religion. All forms of Buddhism, from the Buddha himself down through all the schools, have acknowledged two facets, or rather phases, in arriving at true wisdom. First comes hearing the teachings, the words of truth that ultimately stem from the Buddha himself; and second is the application, investigation, and verification of those teachings in our own immediate experience. In the beginning we merely hear the Buddha teach us of the four noble truths—suffering, the cause of suffering, the end of suffering, and the way of practice leading to the end of suffering—then we look into our own minds. 'Yes!' we realize. 'There it is, right there! My own attachments, stupidity, and hatred causing this welling up of suffering and anguish in my heart, and making me speak and act in harmful, foolish ways, imposing my own pain on others.'

5 So this inseparable pair, the theory and the practice of Buddhism, each balancing and informing the other. Theory without practice becomes a mere intellectual mind game; while practice without theory tends to drift without direction, or rather, directed by the personal delusions of the individual. It should hardly need restating that all Buddhists of all times agree that intellectual knowledge of the Dhamma is insufficient. Intellectual knowledge, due to the ripples in awareness stirred up by the activity of thinking, must disturb clarity of understanding, and deep insight arises only when the mind is still and silent. But intellectual knowledge has its uses; it is not a problem in and of itself. It only becomes a problem when we mistake our intellectual knowledge for the truth, our opinions for reality. Then opinion becomes conceit, and we easily succumb to a spiritual arrogance that is very hard to cure. But a skilful meditator, alert to the distorting potential of ideas and preconceptions, learns to engage fully in the present moment, seeing the impermanence and emptiness of thought,

and growing wise in the ways that, at the most fundamental levels of consciousness, even the most sublime and refined mental constructs limit the power of awareness.

6 Consider the training of a musician. Perhaps one has been inspired by some great composer or player to take up an instrument. But how to start? I remember one time in a music shop when a student walked in and said he wanted to sound like Mark Knopfler, who was at the time the most popular guitar player, famed for his delicate and emotive melodic phrasing. Unfazed, the shop owner sold the student a $30 fuzz box, and he walked out a happy man. Sadly, it's not that easy. In reality, we must spend many hours learning to read music off a page, stark black and white dots and lines that share nothing of the warmth and colour that was our inspiration. Taking up our instrument, there are countless hours of scales, exercises, and trivial studies to be mastered before anything vaguely approaching 'music' is heard. But once the technique is mastered, it must be left behind. There is nothing worse than hearing a musician egotistically showing off his technical skill. All the technique, the study, the practice, must be forgotten as the artist immerses himself in the art that is created there in the present moment; but that present moment is only made possible by the previous study and application. In this way, the experience of the past creates the magic of the present.

1.1 The Ambiguity of Tradition

7 It is implicit in the claim to be a 'Buddhist' that one believes that the Dhamma descends from the Buddha himself through the transmission of his teachings by the traditions. We must take this claim seriously. As a monk I am aware that, in a very real sense, I am the material as well as the spiritual heir of the Buddha. Faithful Buddhists offer me rice and curries, just as in the past the people of India offered Siddhattha Gotama rice and curries, because they take me for a genuine follower, a 'Son of the Sakyan'. It would be insincere, even fraudulent, for me to eat that alms food while at the same time believing, practicing, or teaching things that I knew that Siddhattha Gotama would not agree with.

8 This raises some interesting, and challenging, problems. It is obvious that the existing cultures that all claim to be 'Buddhist' vary widely in their beliefs and practices. Often these are just cultural variations as the Dhamma-Vinaya adapted itself to time and place. Taiwanese Buddhists do their chanting in Mandarin, while Thai Buddhists do theirs in Pali; no one makes a big deal of such things. After all, the Buddha himself urged his followers to learn the Dhamma in their own language, and not to insist on local dialects.

9 However, other aspects of cultural Buddhism are deeply opposed to the Dhamma. A disturbing example of this is the use of Buddhist language and concepts to justify war, which has blighted many Buddhist countries. This is no innocuous cultural adaptation, but a complete perversion of the Buddha's teachings.

10 Such uncomfortable facts demand that we stop and examine the traditions more closely. It is simply not good enough to accept with unexamined trust the myths, the stories, and the dogmas of the schools. As people who have a commitment to understanding and practicing the liberating message of the Sakyan Sage, there is an obligation to honestly enquire as to what, exactly, our Teacher taught. We know that the traditions went wrong in some cases. But these clear, unambiguous examples are in the minority. There is a wealth of other teachings presented to us by the schools, some of which differ from each other in the letter; and we need something better than blind faith before we can intelligently conclude whether they do, or do not, also differ in the meaning.

11 All existing schools of Buddhism share a large mass of teachings in common, and yet also include a large mass of divergent teachings. There is no doubt that the founders and developers of the various schools believed that there were genuine, meaningful doctrinal differences between the schools. All the schools agree that they disagree. This is amply demonstrated by the large quantity of polemical material filling the shelves of Buddhist canons. And, by and large, the schools also agree on what they disagree about. A text of the Theravāda school might allege that the 'person' doctrine of the Puggalavāda school contradicts the teaching of not-self; while the texts of the Puggalavāda will vigorously argue that the teaching of the 'person' is in fact the correct way to interpret not-self. Given this situation,

it would seem a trifle rash to claim, as some modernist Buddhists do, that there are no differences, or that the differences are not significant. What is needed is not such bland platitudes but an improved methodology, a way of approaching the teachings that is derived, not from the perspective or doctrines of any particular school, but from a sensitive evaluation of the textual tradition as lived by Buddhists. Yin Shun, the renowned scholar monk of modern Taiwanese Buddhism, expressed a similar sentiment in his autobiography.

> 12 Although 'non-dispute' is good, expediently-rendered syncretism that does not know where and why the disparities are could be far-fetched, too general, and vague.
>
> 13 To understand the origin and transformations of the Buddha Dharma within certain temporal and spatial contexts in the actual world gradually became the principle of my quest for the Buddha Dharma.

1.2 The Death of Myth

14 It is a striking feature, common to all the schools, that they feel the need to justify their particular doctrines mythologically—this is what all religions do. For 2500 years, Buddhism has been constantly changing, adapting, evolving; yet the myths of the schools insist that the Dhamma remains the same. Thus the Theravāda insists that the Theravāda Abhidhamma was taught by the Buddha in Tāvatiṁsa heaven during his seventh rains retreat. The Mahāyāna claims that the Mahāyāna sūtras were written down in the time of the Buddha, preserved in the dragon world under the sea, then retrieved by Nāgārjuna 500 years later. Zen claims authority from an esoteric oral transmission outside the scriptures descended from Mahā Kassapa, symbolized by the smile of Mahā Kassapa when the Buddha held up a lotus. All of these are myths, and do not deserve serious consideration as explanations of historical truth. Their purpose, as myths, is not to elucidate facts, but to authorize religious convictions. They tell us, not how the teachings came to be, but how the devotees felt about them. In this way, myth offers an irreplaceable complement to history, and should never be disregarded. What I am criticizing here is not myth as myth, but myth as history: the naïve fallacy of insisting that the stories of the traditions are

factual. The myths stand as a flagrant denial of impermanence, and so a sub-theme of this work is to notice the poignant irony of how the very effort to preserve the teachings, so that 'the true Dhamma may last a long time', tends towards a reification of time.

15 One of the great lessons of history, perhaps *the* great lesson, is that reason displaces myth. There is something about the human mind that cannot continue to believe in a mythic explanation for what can be understood through reason. Mythic explanations fulfill a purpose; they create a sense of meaning and communal identity that is gratifying and self affirming. But reason too is a positive force, since it assumes that the human mind is capable of approaching truth. As rational explanations for religious claims are progressively advanced, it becomes more and more wearying to sustain two incompatible belief structures side by side. The myths fall into disuse. Being no longer inherently convincing, they become redundant and eventually pass away. This is the inexorable tide of time.

16 When the modern historical study of Buddhism began in the mid-19th century there was, as a result of these competing mythologies (not to mention the even more misleading Hindu myths), considerable confusion as to the historical picture. In a burst of rationalist enthusiasm, scholars were prepared to question whether the myths had any factual basis at all. Was there any historical connection between the different religions practiced in far separated places like Sri Lanka, Tibet, and Japan? Did the Buddha really exist? Was he just a sun-god? Was he an Ethiopian prophet? What did he teach? Can we know? Which traditions are most reliable (or least unreliable)? Since the traditions had been largely separated due to the forces of history—especially the destruction of Buddhism in India—they had little information about each other, and each asserted its own primacy. Each school preserved its traditions in vast collections of abstruse volumes of hard to read manuscripts in wildly different languages (Chinese, Tibetan, Pali, and other Indian languages such as Sanskrit). But gradually the evidence was assembled. The traditions were compared; archeological findings confirmed key facts. 1500 year-old Sri Lankan chronicles mention the names of the monks Kassapa, Majjhima, and Durabhisara sent in the Aśokan period as missionaries from Vidisa to the Himalayas; a stupa was excavated in Vidisa and the names of these monks were found there, in-

scribed in letters dating close to the Aśokan era, and recording that they were the teachers of the Himalayas.[1] By the beginning of the 20th century, in works by such scholars as T.W. Rhys Davies, whose writings retain their value today, accurate outlines were drawn. There was still debate in the early half of the 20th century, though, as evidence was still being accumulated, new texts were edited, and new studies done.

17 However, as early as 1882 a scholar called Samuel Beal published a series of lectures titled *Buddhist Literature in China*. This included information on the process of translating into Chinese, as well as sample translations from some of the main strata of Buddhist texts—the early Suttas, the Jātakas, and a Mahāyāna text. He stated the following:

> 18 The Parinibbāna, the Brahmajāla, the Sigalovada, the Dhammacakka, the Kasi-Bhāradvadja, the Mahāmangala; all these I have found and compared with translations from the Pali, and find that in the main they are identical. I do not say literally the same; they differ in minor points, but are identical in plot and all important details. And when the Vinaya and Āgama collections are thoroughly examined, I can have little doubt we shall find most if not all the Pali suttas in a Chinese form.[2]

19 Over a century later, the thorough comparative study urged by Beal is still wanting. However, some progress has been made. In 1908 a Japanese scholar named M. Anesaki published his 'The Four Buddhist Āgamas in Chinese: A concordance of their parts and of the corresponding counterparts in the Pali Nikāyas'.[3] This was followed in 1929 by Chizen Akanuma's *The Comparative Catalogue of Chinese Āgamas and Pali Nikāyas*,[4] a comprehensive catalogue of all known existing early discourses in Pali and Chinese, as well as the few texts available in Tibetan and Sanskrit. These findings were incorporated in full scale historical studies such as Étienne Lamotte's *History of Indian Buddhism* and A.K. Warder's *Indian Buddhism*. These studies have largely confirmed Beal's initial hypothesis—the Chinese Āgamas and the Pali Nikāyas are virtually identical in doctrine. They are two varying recensions of the same set of texts. These texts—popularly referred to simply

[1] See FRAUWALLNER 1956; recently corrected by WILLIS. Also see WYNNE.
[2] BEAL, pg. xii.
[3] ANESAKI.
[4] AKANUMA. An updated version of Akanuma's tables is at www.suttacentral.net.

as 'the Suttas'—were assembled by the first generations of the Buddha's followers, before the period of sectarian divisions. They are presectarian Buddhism. Although they are usually considered to be 'Theravāda' teachings, this is not so. The scholar David Kalupahana went so far as to declare that there is not one word of Theravāda in the Pali Nikāyas (although I think this is a slight exaggeration.) The contributions of the schools are mostly limited to fixing the final arrangement of the texts and standardizing the dialect. Interpolations of sectarian ideas are few and usually readily recognizable. Lamotte comments:

20 However, with the exception of the Mahāyanist interpolations in the Ekottara, which are easily discernable, the variations in question [between the Nikāyas and Āgamas] affect hardly anything save the method of expression or the arrangement of the subjects. The doctrinal basis common to the Nikāyas and Āgamas is remarkably uniform. Preserved and transmitted by the schools, the sūtras do not, however, constitute scholastic documents, but are the common heritage of all the sects.[5]

21 All other texts, including the Jātakas, the Abhidhammas of the various schools, the Mahāyāna sūtras, and so on, were written later. Relatively few of these teachings are held in common between the schools; that is, they are sectarian Buddhism. Through the lens of historical criticism, the broad picture of the emergence and development of these teachings can be traced quite clearly, both in the internal dynamics of doctrinal evolution and in Buddhism's response to the changing cultural, social, and religious environment. There is no evidence that the special doctrines of these texts—that is, the doctrines not also found in the early Suttas—derives from the Buddha. Rather, these texts should be regarded as the answers given by teachers of old to the question: 'What does Buddhism mean for us?' Each succeeding generation must undertake the delicate task of hermeneutics, the reacculturation of the Dhamma in time and place. And we, in our own tumultuous times, so different from those of any Buddhist era or culture of the past, must find our own answers. From this perspective, the teachings of the schools offer invaluable lessons, a wealth of precedent passed down to us by our ancestors in faith.

---

[5] LAMOTTE, pg. 156.

22 Understanding the historical basis of Buddhism provides a meaningful foundation for appreciating the common ground of the schools. The traditional myths of the origin of the Buddhist texts serve the polemic, divisive purpose of authenticating the particular doctrinal positions of the schools. This is not to denigrate the important religious role that myths play in Buddhism; on the contrary, we will see that the Buddhist scriptures have always been embedded in spiritual narrative, which breathes life into the teachings. Our purpose is not to criticize the schools, but to distinguish the essential from the inessential.

Chapter 2

THE GIST 1—THREE STRATA OF EARLY TEXTS

WHAT IS THE GIST? It is a general hypothesis on the origin and development of the Buddhist texts. Seeing the need for a handy name for this idea, I originally thought, with tongue securely in cheek, of following the example of the physicists and calling it the 'Grand Unified Sutta Theory'. But the acronym 'GUST' sounded like a lot of hot air, so I thought of the 'General Integrated Sutta Theory': the GIST. Which is, of course, exactly what we're after. We seek a tool with which we can reliably prune away the masses of accretions that fill Buddhist libraries and arrive, as nearly as possible, at the teachings of the Master himself. Even if we limit our inquiry to the early Suttas and Vinaya we are still presented with a vast array of teachings, some obviously post-dating the Buddha. There have been several more or less successful attempts to distil this matter into various strata. The most important advance in this regard has been the collation of the Pali Nikāyas with the Chinese Āgamas. This takes us back to around a hundred years after the Buddha's death. But we are still faced with a mass of discourses with no apparent way to go further back. The GIST attempts to penetrate even further, to within the lifetime of the Buddha.

2 The GIST is 'General' because it encompasses the entire gamut of extant early scriptures, that is, the Suttas, Vinayas, and Abhidhammas of all the schools preserved in Pali, Chinese, and various Indic dialects. It is 'Inte-

grated' because it offers a synoptic presentation of the essential relations between these texts. It deals with 'Suttas' not just in the obvious sense that the Sutta Piṭaka contains the most important teachings, but because it suggests a revaluation of the meaning of the word 'sutta' in the earliest texts. For this reason we will not follow the usual practice of referring to any text in the Sutta Piṭaka as a 'sutta', but will use more neutral terms such as 'discourse', reserving '*sutta*' in italics for the special meaning that the term carried in earlier usage. We will, however, continue to use 'Sutta' with a capital to refer to the early texts in general as contrasted with the Abhidhamma and other later works.

3 And finally, the GIST is a 'Theory' because it is not certain. No theory can ever fully capture the truth. I think a successful theory is, firstly, one that addresses a genuine problem, secondly, explains a variety of facts in a way that is at least as plausible as any alternative, and thirdly, is suggestive of further inquiry. Although the GIST is only a new born child taking its first tottering steps, it still satisfies these standards.

4 There is a serious issue at stake: how do we relate the Pali and Chinese collections together, beyond merely stating that they share many similar texts? We must try to investigate the similarities and differences more systematically, and a promising avenue for doing that is to use the structural principles spoken of within the texts themselves.

5 As for alternatives, there is no space here to evaluate all the theories that have been proposed for the origin and development of the canon. However, I believe the current theories do not sufficiently acknowledge the influence of the structure of the Dhamma itself on the structure of the canon. The early discourses are methodical and symmetrical, and there is a glaring discrepancy between the balanced architecture of the teachings themselves and the sprawling collections within which the teachings are housed.

6 As for the third standard, the GIST offers a clear, simple, systematic method for approaching any study of the fundamental teachings of Buddhism. Rather than pulling passages, ideas, or quotes from here and there to back up one's own argument, the GIST suggests a clear hierarchy of significance within the early scriptures. In the second part of this work I undertake such an inquiry in the subject of satipaṭṭhāna.

7 The GIST was sparked by the findings of the renowned Taiwanese scholar monk Yin Shun, who himself relied on earlier Japanese and Taiwanese research, none of which is widely known in English speaking circles. I haven't read Yin Shun's works directly; my information comes from the summary of Yin Shun's work in Choong Mun-keat's *The Fundamental Teachings of Early Buddhism*, and through conversations with and the writings of Roderick Bucknell. Although Yin Shun's insights sparked off the GIST, here the theory is developed significantly further. I will, therefore, not present Yin Shun's findings to start with, but will outline the GIST in my own way and present Yin Shun's contributions at the appropriate places. While Yin Shun argued back from later texts to establish the early, I will leap over the Buddha's lifetime and approach the Buddha's teachings by drifting downstream on the river of time.

8 The GIST asks three questions. Firstly, what are the earliest texts? This question is applied to three historical strata: the first discourses, the first collection of discourses, and the first Abhidhamma. The three strata are each established independently; that is, we do not rely on our identification of the earliest discourses in order to establish the earliest collection, and we do not rely on either of these to establish the earliest Abhidhamma. Rather, to establish each layer we use two basic criteria: the concordance of the texts and the testimony of the tradition. An important confirmation for the validity of these criteria is the elegance of the results. This becomes apparent when we answer the second question: how are the three strata related to each other? And the third question is: how are the three strata related to the rest of the Nikāyas/ Āgamas? The results of this inquiry, I might mention in advance, are entirely mundane; so mundane, in fact, that they could easily be dismissed as merely stating the obvious. But what is important here is not so much the conclusions as the method; we are trying to put on a more sound basis what, up till now, has been largely a matter of subjective opinion.

2.1 Before the Buddha

9 We should start by considering possible pre-Buddhist models for the Buddhist scriptures. It is apparent that new literary compositions in any

culture are powerfully influenced by the literary forms that are available in that culture. It is therefore likely that the organization of the earliest stratum of Buddhist scriptures would have been primarily influenced by pre-Buddhist models. Subsequent strata would, of course, be primarily influenced by the earlier Buddhist models. If, therefore, we find evidence of Buddhist textual structures that are derived from pre-Buddhist models, this suggests that these structures are not merely early, but the earliest.

10 The only literary tradition mentioned in the early discourses is the Brahmanical tradition of the three Vedas and various auxiliary works. These obviously played a dominant role in the cultural/spiritual/literary milieu in which the Buddhist texts were formed. There are some obvious connections between the literary style of the Buddhist texts and the Vedas—especially in the poetic forms—but I don't know of any attempt to relate the overall structure of the Buddhist texts to the Vedas. This is, no doubt, because the structure of the existent canons bears little obvious relation to the Vedas. But let us revisit this question to see if the Vedas might have influenced an earlier organizing principle.

11 The three Vedas are the Ṛg, Sāman, and Yajur. (The fourth Veda in the later Brahmanical tradition, the Atharva, is mentioned in the early Buddhist texts but was evidently extra-canonical at the time.) The Ṛg Veda is by far the most important. It is a very ancient (1500 BCE?) collection of around 10 000 devotional and liturgical verses. One of the classification systems of the Ṛg is in *vaggas*, groups of about ten lines of verse. The *vagga* of ten suttas went on to become one of the most basic building blocks in organizing the Buddhist scriptures. The Sāman is largely a collection of hymns taken from the Ṛg. Even though all the Vedas contain verse, the Sāman is the songbook par excellence; its students were the *chandogyas* ('versifiers'). Alone of the Vedas the Yajur contains prose as well as verse; it focuses mainly on the sacrifice. So we have one central work and two supplements.

12 This triune form is probably of religious significance, reflecting the Trinities of deities found so commonly in antiquity. The Trinity usually consists, not of three equal partners, but of one presiding deity (god or goddess) who manifests in the world through the medium of two lesser deities: the One becoming Two, the Two becoming many. The 'threeness' of the Vedas

is multiplied in later lists of the extended Vedic literature mentioned in the Pali tradition, where we find both a sixfold and a twelvefold classification. Various parts of the Vedic literature are referred to as *aṅgas*, 'sections', and we find the terms 'Vedanta' and 'Vedaṅga'. We may also note that the familiar term *sutta*, which in Buddhism usually refers to any discourse, in Brahmanical usage means specifically a short, basic doctrinal statement, which is treated as a basis for elaboration and commentary.

13 Several of these formal elements are also found in the Jain scriptures. Although Jainism is an older religion than Buddhism, the Buddhist texts do not mention any Jain texts existing at the time of the Buddha, and the Jains themselves agree that their scriptures were formalized much later. However they clearly contain early elements, and it is possible that early features of the Jain texts that are still evident in the existing texts may have exerted some influence on the formation of the Buddhist texts, although it is more likely that the influence was the other way around. The Jains acknowledge a list of fourteen *purvas* ('previous') that are now lost, and twelve aṅgas, eleven of which still exist. One of these aṅgas is called *prasnavyākaraṇa*, which means 'Questions & Answers'. In addition they have twelve *upangas*, 'auxiliary sections'. It is evident that for both the Vedic and the Jain traditions the term 'aṅga' referred to specific texts that were organized in groups of multiples of three. The Ājīvakas, another non-orthodox sect, are said in the Jain sūtras to have possessed prognostic scriptures consisting of aṅgas, in this case eight in number. Also note that Jains, like the Brahmans, use the word *sutta* for brief doctrinal aphorisms, although like the Buddhists they also use it as a term for the doctrinal texts in general. For now, we can tuck all these points away in a corner of our minds for later reference.

2.2 The First Discourses

14 Now let us turn to the Buddhist texts. How to identify the earliest discourses? As mentioned above, one of the most powerful tools used by scholars to identify early texts is the concordance of the traditions. In Buddhism this study, so far as it has happened at all, has focussed on the concordance between the texts preserved by the different schismatic schools. But, of

course, what matters is not schism as such, but divergence into different textual lineages. There is abundant evidence of a significant degree of separation and specialization of textual study even within the Buddha's own lifetime, long before any schism. This is the most fundamental division of the teachings in all schools and traditions: Dhamma and Vinaya. The texts refer to groups of monks who specialize in one or the other of these areas of study. They had different teachers and lived in different quarters. The Theravādin account of the First Council says the Dhamma was spoken by Venerable Ānanda and the Vinaya by Venerable Upāli. While not all of the details of the First Council can be accepted as historical, surely this fundamental division must date back to well before the Buddha's passing away. And of course, the content of the two collections is almost totally different. All this suggests that the few doctrinal teachings that are found in the Vinaya have a special significance. They would have been known, not just to the doctrinal specialists, but to all the monks and nuns, dating back to the earliest days of the Buddha's mission, before the collections of teachings grew so bulky that specialization became necessary. Of course, it is not the case that all teachings shared between the suttas and Vinaya must be early; discourses may have been shifted or duplicated between the collections at a later date, and we know in some cases this did happen. So we must look for those discourses that are not merely found across the Vinayas, but are also fundamental to the structure of the text itself, things that do not seem as if they could be lightly grafted on.

15 So what are these teachings? There are several versions of the early Vinaya available—about half a dozen different schools are found in the Chinese canon, the Mūlasarvāstivāda Vinaya is available in Tibetan and partially in Sanskrit, the Theravāda is in the Pali canon; some other material is also available in hybrid Sanskrit and various Indian and even Iranian dialects. Some of these collections contain doctrinal material; however most of this material has not been translated, and such studies as have been done are mostly in Japanese. For now, we shall have to concentrate mainly on the material in the Theravāda Vinaya, with the hypothesis that similar material is available in the other Vinayas. This is confirmed in some important cases, and will be a fascinating arena for future research.

16 The outstanding doctrinal teachings in the Vinaya occur in the first chapter of the Mahāvagga. There are three main sermons: the Dhammacakkappavattana Sutta, the Anattalakkhaṇa Sutta, and the Ādittapariyāya Sutta. Alongside these are some verses, notably the Request of Brahmā for the Buddha to teach, and the Buddha's reply:

17 'Wide open are the doors to the Deathless!
Let those with ears to hear make sure their faith.'[1]

18 There are other important teachings in the Theravāda Vinaya—notably the dependent origination and the 37 wings to awakening—which reinforce my argument considerably; however these passages are not as central to the structure of the Vinaya and so until their authenticity has been confirmed through comparative study of the other Vinayas we should avoid relying on them.

19 The Dhammacakkappavattana Sutta is available in at least five Vinayas, as well as in the Nikāyas and Āgamas. It is, in fact, by far the most widespread of all the discourses, with no less than 17 existing versions, and is one of only a few discourses that survives in the four main Buddhist languages of Pali, Sanskrit, Chinese, and Tibetan.[2] Inevitably, there are many variations in details, but the basic content is substantially similar—the four noble truths. The Dhammacakkappavattana Sutta presents these teachings within a framework that clearly relates to the Buddha's own spiritual development, his self indulgence in the palace and self torture as an ascetic, and his own realization of enlightenment as the escape from these two. Thus the internal contents of the text itself suggest that it was the first discourse. The Anattalakkhaṇa Sutta also occurs in several versions, as do the Ādittapariyāya Sutta and the Request of Brahmā, although I haven't studied the full details. All these texts, however, are available in both the Nikāyas and the Āgamas.

---

[1] MN 26.21/MA 204/T № 765.4/Pali Vinaya 1.7. Taking *tesaṁ* as supplying the implied 'their' of the second line (cp. DN 18.27/DA 4/T № 9) and *pamuñcantu* as a poetic variant of *adhimuñcantu* (cp. Sn 1146, 1149, AN 1.14/EA 4.1–10). However, one Sanskrit version has *pramodanur*, and would translate as 'May those who wish to hear rejoice in faith'. Another has *praṇudantu kakṣāḥ*, 'dispel opinions'.

[2] See SMITH. There is an '18th' version at Paṭisambhidāmagga 2.6.1. Although this is now in the Khuddaka Nikāya, it is a quasi-Abhidhamma text, so we could say that the Dhammacakkappavattana Sutta occurs in all three Piṭakas.

20 These discourses form the doctrinal core of the oldest biography of the Buddha, telling the story from after the Buddha's enlightenment leading up to the formation of the Sangha. This is the root legend that forms a unifying narrative for all Buddhists. The story is told in many of the old texts, sometimes in the Vinaya, sometimes as a Sutta; in later embellished form it became a lengthy book in itself. But beneath the profuse elaborations there is a remarkable consistency in both the basic narrative and the doctrinal teachings. Even a late text like the Mahāvastu preserves teachings such as the Dhammacakkappavattana Sutta in nearly identical form.[3] They are universally regarded as the Buddha's first teachings, and so we have complete agreement between the concordance of the texts and the testimony of the tradition. Of course, it is impossible to ever establish that these texts were literally the first teachings. Nor can we deny that there are some minor differences between the versions. But these texts are fundamental to the extant collections of Buddhist scriptures, and there is no good reason why this should not simply reflect the historical position.

21 There is a substantial problem with this neat theory, however. The passage we have been considering, the first chapter of the Vinaya Mahāvagga, is also found in the Sarvāstivādin tradition. However, this is not in the Vinaya, but in the Dīrgha Āgama under the title Catuṣpariṣat Sūtra ('Four Assemblies Sūtra').[4] This discourse exists in several versions, attesting to its popularity. It is very close to the Pali version, though lacking the specifically Vinaya elements. Several scholars have suggested that this text was originally part of the Vinaya, and was later moved to the Āgamas. If this is the case, there is no problem. However, it is possible that the movement was the other way around: the text was originally a discourse that was later incorporated into the Vinaya. This would suggest that these doctrinal passages were not, in fact part of the original Vinaya. But I think it is better to consider the Catuṣpariṣat Sūtra as fundamental to both Dhamma and Vinaya. In leading up to the first sermon it supplies the background narrative for the Dhamma; and then Añña Koṇḍañña's subsequent going forth is the perfect starting point to unfold the Vinaya.

---

[3] Rāhula, pg. 8.

[4] Kloppenborg.

22 We are trying to discern a glimpse of the earliest phase of Buddhism. In the early years, there would have been relatively few teachings. All the monks would have known by heart the few texts and discourses that were regarded as central. In addition, they would have all been familiar with the simple non-legalistic codes of behaviour expected of them as Buddhist mendicants. Thus they would all have known both Dhamma and Vinaya. It would have taken a number of years for the bulk of the material to grow to the extent that specialization became necessary. From this point, certain monks and nuns would specialize in Dhamma, while others specialized in Vinaya. But this specialization has only ever been a matter of emphasis, not of exclusion. All the Vinaya specialists would have known some Dhamma, while all the Dhamma experts would know some Vinaya. It is entirely reasonable to suppose that the doctrinal teachings within the existing Vinayas are remnants, either directly or indirectly, of such a shared doctrinal body. It is also entirely reasonable to suggest that the monks and nuns would have all been familiar with the story of the Buddha's enlightenment, and that this legend would be given concrete literary form, although incorporating late details, largely to lend authority to this doctrinal core. That is to say, the Catuṣpariṣat Sūtra in its developed form may have been included in the Vinaya precisely because the Vinaya experts were already familiar with the main doctrinal teachings of that discourse, and they would then be supplied with a historical context linking the doctrine with the establishment of the Sangha and the laying down of Vinaya. So I think that the presence of the relevant doctrinal passages within the existing Vinayas remains as supporting evidence for the primacy of these teachings.

2.3 The Gāthā Theory

23 The GIST makes a strong case that the traditions, in this case, have got it right. A major scholarly challenge to this conclusion comes from what we can call the '*gāthā* theory'. This theory, which includes several eminent scholars among its adherents, claims that the earliest recorded teachings that we possess today are to be found primarily among certain of the

verse collections, notably the Aṭṭhaka and Pārāyana of the Sutta Nipāta.[5] However, while I agree that some of the verse is early, I do not think that the reasons given suffice to establish that these verses are generally earlier than the prose. To briefly state the case for and against the *gāthā* theory.

24 1) The language found in such texts harks back in some respects to the Vedas, and therefore is archaic.

25 Verse usually tends to be archaic; this could be supported in any number of cases by comparison of verse and prose passages by the same author even in modern times. This may partially be a matter of style, a preference for an archaic flavour, as in English verse one might affect 'thee' and 'thou'. Another factor is that, due to the constraints of metre, it is more difficult to translate verse as compared with prose from one Indian dialect into another; thus even in the later hybrid Sanskrit literature, the verse tends to retain more archaic Prakrit features, while the accompanying prose tends towards more formal Sanskrit. This tells us something about the translation process, but nothing about the relative ages of the different parts of the original text.

26 2) Several of these verses are referred to in the prose Nikāyas, and therefore must be earlier than those prose discourses.

27 This confirms only the chronological relationship in these few cases. In many other cases, verses are tacked on to the end of prose discourses, such as in the Aṅguttara, and there it is likely that the verses were added later. Anyway, there are also prose passages that are quoted or referred to in other prose passages, notably the Dhammacakkappavattana Sutta, which is explicitly or implicitly referred to in several important discourses. The references to the *gāthās*, moreover, while significant, never declare such passages to be the central message of the Dhamma. The key teachings, extolled over and again in the early texts, are such things as the four noble truths, the 37 wings to awakening, the dependent origination, or the 'aggregates, sense media, and elements'. None of these topics are prominent in the *gāthās*. It would be natural to assume that the earliest scriptural body consisted of teachings on just such core topics. Such references may even

5 See e.g. NAKAMURA , chapters 2.3 & 2.4.

refer to specific texts where these doctrines are elucidated. The primary source for all these topics is the Saṁyutta.

28 > 3) The Aṭṭhaka and Pārāyana have their own canonical commentary within the Khuddaka Nikāya, the Niddesa.

29 This argument has recently been repeated by Gregory Schopen, who says that these are the 'only' texts that have received commentaries by the time of the earliest known redaction.[6] This seems like a strong point, until we realize that the Niddesa really just applies Abhidhamma technique to poetry, listing synonyms in mechanical style for each word in the verses. It is very similar to the Abhidhamma Vibhaṅga, etc., and must stem from a similar period as a minor spin-off from the Abhidhamma project. The Vibhaṅga is clearly the more important work, and that consists largely of quotations and commentary of central prose passages of the Saṁyutta and Majjhima. In fact there is much 'commentarial' material even in the four Nikāyas: the Saccavibhaṅga Sutta, which we will examine further below, is an explicit commentary on the Dhammacakkappavattana Sutta. Much of the Vinaya, too, is a commentary on the Pāṭimokkha.

30 > 4) Technical terms and formulaic doctrines appear less often.

31 Again, this is simply part of the normal character of verse. Poetry is for inspiration, not information.

32 > 5) The monks lived as hermits in the forest rather than in settled monasteries, whereas in the prose this phase of Buddhism is largely absent, the discourses being normally set in monasteries.

33 This shift, from the forest life to established monasteries, is depicted in the texts themselves as having already begun within the Buddha's lifetime, and there is every reason to believe that this was so. It is difficult to live in the forest, and the Sangha must have, before very long, started taking in recruits who were elderly, or infirm, or weak, and who would have required decent accommodation. This plain common sense is confirmed in many stories in the early texts. Here we may point out the parallel with the Franciscan order, which was accused by St Francis himself of backsliding from the rigorous standards he had set. In any case, the prose does in fact constantly refer to monks living in the forest. The mistake stems in part

---

6 SCHOPEN 1997, pg. 24.

from the failure to distinguish between the teachings themselves and the narrative cladding in which the teachings appear, which must obviously be later. The outstanding example here is the teaching on the gradual training, the main paradigm for the monastic way of life, found in tens of discourses. Although the texts as they are today are set in monasteries, the body of the teaching itself refers simply to the monk, 'gone to the forest, to the root of a tree, or to an empty hut...' to meditate, with no mention of monasteries. This is a good piece of negative evidence: we know that later Buddhism was largely based in large monasteries, hence the fact that so many of the teachings extol the forest life strongly suggests these teachings must have appeared before the development of settled monasticism.

34 So in this instance the traditional belief can be maintained in the face of modern criticism. I am not saying that the discourses as found today must be word for word identical with the first teachings, but that these teachings, in largely the same words and phrases, have been treated since earliest times as the most fundamental doctrines, and the traditions give us a plausible reason why this should be so. The massive preponderance of the Dhammacakkappavattana Sutta demands an explanation. The idea, influential for a time in Buddhist studies, that these teachings hail from a 'monkish' revision of the Dhamma after the Buddha's passing away has all the romance of a conspiracy theory, and all of its plausibility.

2.4 The Earliest Collection

35 Having given grounds to establish the earliest discourses, we now ask: 'What is the earliest collection of discourses?' Here again we invoke our twin criteria: concordance of the texts and the testimony of the traditions. First we should seek for the collections that show the highest degree of congruence. Of the major collections, the following are available. The symbol ꟴ means a collection of which only a part exists. The Sanskrit Dīrgha is an exciting new finding coming out of Afghanistan and has not yet been fully edited.

Table 2.1: The Nikāyas and the Āgamas

Theravāda Nikāyas	Sarvāstivāda Āgamas	Other Āgamas (in Chinese)
Dīgha (Pali)	Dīrgha[q] (Sanskrit)	Dīrgha (Dharmaguptaka)
Majjhima (Pali)	Madhyama (Chinese)	
Saṁyutta (Pali)	Saṁyukta (Chinese)	Two 'other' Saṁyuktas[q] (unknown schools)
Aṅguttara (Pali)		Ekottara (Mahāsaṅghika?), Aṅguttara[q] (unknown school)

36 To understand this, we need to know a little about these schools. The early chronology of Buddhism is still obscure. Even the most important date, the passing away of the Buddha, is specified very differently in different traditions, and it is far from obvious which, if any, is more reliable. Following Gombrich and others we might take the dates 484–404 BCE for the Buddha as being no more unreliable than other estimates. The schisms are undateable in an absolute sense, and even the relative chronology of the schisms is disputed. This probably reflects the real historical situation, since separative tendencies may have proceeded at different rates in different areas, and there may well have been no universal agreement even at the time at to the exact dates of the schisms. It is even unsure whether the Sangha at the time would have been conscious that it was creating lasting divisions into schools in the sense that we understand it today. The full implications of the breaches may only have become apparent many years later.

37 My *Sects & Sectarianism* looks at these questions in more detail. Here I will summarize my findings. The schools arose primarily because of the geographical spread of Buddhism during the time of King Aśoka. Far-flung communities gradually developed their own doctrines, and competition for the increasing wealth available to the Sangha intensified the tensions. The first separative movement, between the ancestral Theravāda and the Mahāsaṅghika, was driven by a dispute relating to the status of the arahant. The Mahāsaṅghika proposed '5 points' of weakness that applied to some or all arahants. The Theravāda took a stricter stance on these questions, and a split resulted. The Mahāsaṅghika proceeded to splinter into

several sub-schools. The existing Ekottara Āgama, which includes some Mahāyanist interpolations, is often said to come from one of these sub-schools, but the evidence is as yet inconclusive. We will, however, follow the majority of modern scholars in treating the Ekottara as stemming from one of the Mahāsaṅghika group of schools. The results of our study of the Satipaṭṭhāna Sutta tend to support this theory; at least, the Ekottara version of this discourse is relatively more divergent than the other versions, which is what we would expect of a Mahāsaṅghika text, even though the divergences are not explicitly sectarian.

38 The ancestral Theravāda, too, underwent many further schisms. The earliest of significance for our story was the Sarvāstivāda schism, which was some time after the death of Aśoka in 232 BCE. Here the fundamental issue was the conception of time, the special Sarvāstivādin doctrine being that all dhammas past, present, and future, exist. The Sarvāstivāda schism produced, as well as the Sarvāstivāda, another school sometimes called the Vibhajjavāda, the 'Analytical School'. This label is used widely and inconsistently, but it is convenient to use it here as a term for the school ancestral to the Theravāda and the Dharmaguptaka. These schools are very similar in doctrine, the main difference apparently being a greater emphasis on devotion in the Dharmaguptaka, as evidenced by certain Vinaya rules regarding stupa worship, the comparison of the structure of the Dīghas, and the fact that they placed greater emphasis on the merit of making offerings to the Buddha rather than to the Sangha. This is all marginal stuff, and may be due to the Dharmaguptaka texts being settled somewhat later rather than a genuine sectarian divergence, for the Theravādins also embraced stupa worship very strongly, but did not insert it into their Vinaya. The only clearly sectarian difference from the Theravāda is the relative value of offerings to the Buddha and the Sangha. The divergence between these schools arose mainly due to geography, the Dharmaguptaka being a branch of the Vibhajjavāda that stayed in Northern India while the Theravāda moved to Sri Lanka. The Dharmaguptaka became well established in Central Asia and initially enjoyed success in China; Chinese bhikkhus and bhikkhunīs today still follow the Dharmaguptaka Vinaya.

39 Bearing this general information about the early schools in mind, we may return to our question as to which is the earliest collection. The

traditions typically say that all four collections were created simultaneously. Although the idea that they were put together in one session is obviously incorrect, we can still admit that the period of accumulation of texts largely overlaps. It is not implausible to even suppose that the four Nikāyas/Āgamas were started at the same time, and then finalized at the same time. This would be reinforced by the theory that each of the collections is focussed slightly differently, and was formed to cater to the needs of different sectors of the Buddhist community. Nevertheless, we may still distinguish in terms of a tendency to be earlier or later, even within this framework.

40 This question can, and should, be approached from a variety of angles—philological, doctrinal, cultural, and so on. All of these involve complex and large scale investigations, and the results of none of these inquiries are yet beyond doubt. One problem with all of these approaches is that they can tell us, at best, about relative dates of certain phrases, ideas, or passages, but not about the collection as a whole. Bearing in mind the presence of intratextuality—the persistence of earlier text in later redactions—in the Nikāyas/Āgamas, and the vast quantity of material to be dealt with, only a very large scale statistical analysis of linguistic, doctrinal, or other features could give us firm answers. I do not know of any studies that even come close to this ideal.

41 Shrouded by this mass of darkness, I would suggest that the structural analysis of the Nikāyas/Āgamas offers us, at our present state of knowledge, the closest we have to a shining light. The structural principles of the collections tell us how the redactors of the collections worked, rather than how the compilers of the individual discourses worked. With the emergence of the Sarvāstivāda Dīrgha, we now have the full structural details of three Āgamas of one, very important, school to compare with the Theravāda. This means we can directly evaluate the degree of congruence between the corresponding pairs of collections, without being overly concerned that sectarian issues might distort the picture.

42 We still lack a Sarvāstivādin collection corresponding to the Aṅguttara. Meaningful comparative studies for the Aṅguttara are limited in scope, as the Theravāda Aṅguttara and Mahāsaṅghika Ekottara are very different, calling into question whether they are in fact recensions of a single work,

or whether the existing similarities are merely due to the fact that they both use the same organizing principle. (There is another partial Aṅguttara in Chinese that is closer to the Theravādin version.) So for now, if we do not wish to delve into the complex question of whether the content of the Aṅguttaras is earlier or later, all we can do is to put them to one side. I think that the Aṅguttaras house the shorter discourses that were 'left over' from the main doctrinal topics in the Saṁyutta, so perhaps their omission from consideration is not so critical.

43 What is needed here is a comparison of the comparisons. We must ask, which collections appear to have the closest structural relationship, the three Dīghas, or the two Majjhimas, or the two Saṁyuttas? I will discuss each of these collections in further detail below, so I just present a quick overview here. In fact, the answer to this question is really obvious as soon as it is asked. The three Dīghas share many discourses in common, but the sequence and organization of the discourses are widely divergent. This is particularly the case when the Sarvāstivāda Dīrgha is compared with the two Vibhajjavāda Dīghas. Similarly, the two Majjhimas share much content but little structure in common. Almost all the chapter titles and divisions are completely different, with a few exceptions discussed further below. (Anticipating the argument, the occasional structural congruencies between the two Majjhimas and the three Dīghas may be derived from the Saṁyutta and are therefore not necessarily evidence of pre-sectarian structures in the Majjhimas and Dīghas). When we come to the two Saṁyuttas, however, the picture is radically different. They share all the same major divisions into subjects, etc., with some variations in the minor chapters and some reshuffling.[7] So we can say with some certainty that not only the content but also the structure of the Saṁyuttas were largely settled in the pre-sectarian period, whereas the structures of the Majjhimas and the Dīghas are largely sectarian. Thus, relying primarily on this very clear structural picture, we conclude that the concordance of the texts suggests that the Saṁyutta is earlier than the Majjhima and the Dīgha.

44 Some might object at this point that our reasoning proves nothing, since it is the Saṁyutta alone of the four Nikāyas/Āgamas that has a meaningful overall structure, so as soon as we choose to look at structure we will be

[7] Details in CHOONG, pp. 19–22.

drawn to it. In other words, our conclusion simply follows from our choice of methodology. This objection is perfectly true, yet I feel the argument still has force. We need some criterion, and structure is one possible means at our disposal. It is quite possible it will tell us nothing, yet we must at least ask the question and follow the answer through. The Saṁyutta does evidence a large scale structural pattern that is lacking in the other collections, and one rational explanation for this is that the Saṁyutta was settled earlier. In addition, in the case of the Majjhimas, even when there is a common structural grouping, the content of that group is usually different. Each of the Majjhimas, for example, has a vagga called the 'Chapter on Kings'. In the Pali, this has ten discourses, in the Chinese, fourteen. But only two discourses are shared in the two vaggas.[8] Most of the other discourses are found in both the Pali and Chinese sources, but not in this chapter. Thus both of the traditions had the idea of collecting some middle-length discourses together on the theme of Kings, but the selection of discourses was independent. But in the Saṁyutta, we find almost invariably, when a group of discourses has been formed around a certain theme or principle, there is a very large percentage of the actual discourses that overlap. This is consistent with the thesis that the structures of the Saṁyutta are pre-sectarian, while the occasional structural similarities in the Majjhima may have arisen through parallel development.

45 So what of the testimony of the traditions? This brings us to the important findings of Yin Shun. The Chinese and Tibetan canons contain a monumental treatise called the Yogacārabhūmiśāstra, written by Asaṅga around 400 CE. This was a fundamental and authoritative work for the Yogacāra school of Mahāyāna. A section of this work called the Vastusaṅgrāhinī is devoted to an extensive commentary on the Saṁyukta Āgama. This shows how the classical Mahāyāna heavily relied on the early discourses, something that is too often overlooked.[9] Yin Shun has shown that the Saṁyukta Āgama discussed in the Yogacārabhūmiśāstra is very close to the Saṁyukta now preserved in the Chinese canon, and has used the

---

8 MN 81/MA 63 Ghaṭikāra and MN 83/MA 67 Makhādeva.

9 The other great school of early Mahāyāna, the Mādhyamaka, takes as its textual basis Nāgārjuna's Mūlamādhyamakakārikā, which is based on the Kaccāyana Sutta of the Saṁyutta. Thus the two main schools of the Mahāyāna share the Saṁyutta as a fundamental scripture.

Yogacārabhūmiśāstra to reconstruct the earlier sequence of the Saṁyukta Āgama, which had become disordered over time. His reconstruction is considered so authoritative that it has been adopted in the Foguang edition of the Āgamas published in 1983. The Yogacārabhūmiśāstra suggests that the Saṁyukta Āgama was the foundation for the four Āgamas. Yin Shun believes that this statement can be taken literally as affirming the historical priority of the Saṁyutta among the Āgamas. There does not seem to be any direct statement to this effect in the Theravāda tradition; however there are, we shall see, a few hints. The Sarvāstivādin tradition, however, regularly lists the Saṁyutta as the first of the Āgamas. Thus as to the first collection of discourses we have satisfied our two criteria, congruence of the texts and testimony of at least one tradition.

2.5 The First Abhidhamma

46 What, then, of the first Abhidhamma? Here we rely primarily on the work of Frauwallner. He has demonstrated that three early Abhidhamma texts share much the same content and must have been derived from a common ancestor, which we call the '*Vibhaṅga Mūla'.[10] These are the Vibhaṅga of the Theravāda,[11] the Dharmaskandha of the Sarvāstivāda, and the Śāriputrābhidharma of the Dharmaguptaka. The details of these works are too complex to go into here; for now we can take this congruence as established.

47 Both the Pali and Sanskrit traditions contain evidence that these texts were considered fundamental to the Abhidhamma. The epilogue to the Chinese translation of the Dharmaskandha says that it was the basic text of the Abhidhamma and the primary source for the Sarvāstivādin school. The Vinaya of the Dharmaguptaka school outlines their Abhidhamma system, which is precisely the table of contents of the Śāriputrābhidharma. And the Aṭṭhasālinī, the main commentary on the Pali Abhidhamma, in its first chapter includes two prominent passages where the main topics of the Abhidhamma are listed; in the first passage, these are identical with the

[10] In this book postulated texts and terms are marked with an asterisk.
[11] Translated to English as *The Book of Analysis* by Ashin THIṬṬILA, Pali Text Society, 1969.

contents of the Vibhaṅga, and in the second passage very similar.[12] So here too the two criteria of the GIST are clearly satisfied.

48 To review our findings: we have demonstrated that according to both the concordance of the texts and the testimony of the traditions the following constitute the earliest strata of Buddhist texts.

49 **Earliest Discourses:** Dhammacakkappavattana, Anattalakkhaṇa, and Ādittapariyāya Suttas, and the Request of Brahmā.

50 **Earliest Collection:** Congruent sections of Saṁyutta Nikāya/Saṁyukta Āgama.

51 **Earliest Abhidhamma:** Congruent sections of Vibhaṅga/Dharmaskandha/Śāriputrābhidharma.

2.6 Some Problems

52 There is a possible objection that I would like to address here. Some might argue that our two independent criteria are not independent at all. The traditions might have decided which teachings were earliest and then invented myths expressing this, reinforcing their claim by multiplying the occurrence of these teachings in the various collections. We can see this at work even today. The Dhammacakkappavattana Sutta has been reproduced in dozens of Dhamma books, precisely because it is regarded by the traditions as the earliest teaching.

53 We must admit that this criticism has some force, especially in the case of the earliest discourses. But for the earliest collection and the earliest Abhidhamma this objection is weak, since the traditions, though preserving a dim memory of the priority of these texts, were generally not conscious of this, and did not make a display of it. Rather the opposite: the party line was that all the texts stem from the Buddha himself, so they were anxious to de-emphasize or outright deny any question of historical priority. Even in the case of the earliest discourses, though the objection carries some weight, it does not account for the massive agreement among the schools. Given the popularity of the Dhammacakkappavattana Sutta, and the universal agreement that it was the first discourse, the most plausible explanation is simply that the traditions are right. How else would it have

[12] TIN, pg. 4, 38.

gained the approval of all Buddhists in the pre-sectarian period? Who, if not the Buddha, could have imbued it with such authority?

54 Another problem is the possibility of later borrowing. There is no doubt that borrowing did take place between the traditions in all periods. For example, the sub-commentary to the Brahmajala Sutta gives an exposition of the practice of the Bodhisattva that is partly adapted from Asaṅga's Yogacārabhūmiśāstra. Later borrowing must be borne in mind as an alternative to the thesis of a shared heritage. Generally, our response to this criticism is simply to pursue the thesis of shared heritage, follow through the implications, and see whether that leads to useful results. Working with the material in detail and in depth, it becomes more and more obvious that later borrowing is unlikely to affect more than a few details. This whole book can be read as a demonstration of the fruitfulness and reasonableness of this approach. This is not, it should be remembered, an arbitrary or unusual method. Scholars working in other areas, whether Bible studies or biology, regularly make use of similar hypotheses.

55 However, it will be be useful to demonstrate a case where the thesis of later borrowing is very implausible. Let us consider the well known Bhāra Sutta from the Khandha-saṁyutta.[13] This discourse is found in versions belonging to the Theravāda, Sarvāstivāda, and (possibly) Mahāsaṅghika schools. It states that the five aggregates are the burden, and the 'person' (*puggala*) is the 'bearer of the burden'. In light of the teachings on not-self, this is an unusual statement. While most of the schools took the line that the 'person' here was just a conventional way of speaking, one important group of schools, the Puggalavāda, declared that this referred to a real entity that existed outside the five aggregates. Their Abhidhamma treatise, existing in Chinese translation, refers to this same discourse.[14] Now, the Puggalavāda schism was very early, soon after the first (Mahāsaṅghika) schism. So we have a very good spread of this discourse across all the earliest schools.

56 One of the important forces leading to schism was discussions and disagreements on the relevant doctrines. These discussions would have pre-

---

[13] SN 22.22/SA 73/EA 25.4.

[14] Sāmmitīyanikāyaśāstra (San-mi-ti pu lun), T № 1649, p. 463b11, 465b10, 463b 9–12. See Thiện CHÂU, pp. 23–24.

ceded the actual schism by a considerable time. As the split hardened, the schools began to formulate their position in accepted texts, developing sophisticated arguments to defend their interpretation. This would have been essential training material for the energetic doctrinal debates that were ongoing. There are two main records of these discussions of the early period: Moggaliputtatissa's Kathāvatthu in the Pali canon of the Theravādin school, and Devasarman's Vijñānakāya, a canonical text of the Sarvāstivāda Abhidharma preserved in Chinese. The Kathāvatthu is traditionally ascribed to the period of Aśoka; although much of the work is later, there is no reason to doubt that its origins, with some of the core arguments, stem from that period. Norman has in fact shown that the Kathāvatthu, especially the discussion of the 'person', includes an unusual number of Magadhan grammatical forms, suggestive of an Aśokan connection.[15] The edicts show Aśoka's great concern to prevent schism in the Sangha, suggesting that the schismatic tendency was evident in his time. The Puggalavāda schism was among the earliest.

57 The first and longest section of both of these works is a lengthy attack on the 'person' thesis. This was a core issue, perhaps the initial motivation for writing these works. This schism hurt. It was still fresh in their minds, felt as a direct assault on the cherished doctrine of not-self.

58 We might then ask: how can this situation best be explained? Let us assume that the Puggalavāda wrote the Bhāra Sutta to justify their special doctrine. This must have happened in the early schismatic period, while they were freshly arguing with their brothers and sisters in the other schools. The other schools were so persuaded by the authenticity of this discourse, apparently, that they borrowed it for inclusion in their central doctrinal collections, even as they were at the same time furiously arguing against the 'person' thesis as the worst of heresies. The Puggalavādins were so successful with their forged discourse that it became accepted without a murmur of protest by the schools for all time.

59 Or let us suppose that another school invented this discourse, say the Theravādins. They had been arguing with rivals, who they regarded as apostates, over the doctrine of the 'person'. Somehow, they produced a discourse that seems to justify their opponent's arguments and put it in

[15] NORMAN, 1979, pp. 279–287.

their canon, being too dim-witted to see the implications. This discourse became rapidly 'seeded' across a variety of schools over the breadth of India; one can only assume that they were very enthusiastic about their new creation and wished to spread it far and wide. When it became known to the Theravādins' arch-rivals the Puggalavādins, they leapt on it with glee to justify their main thesis, although it is not recorded that they thanked the authors for the gift.

60 If these options do not appeal, we can always fall back on the drab and hackneyed idea of shared heritage. There was an discourse called the Bhāra Sutta. This was spoken by the Buddha; or at least it was accepted as such by the first generations of Buddhists in the pre-sectarian period. As it dealt with the important doctrine of the five aggregates, it was assembled, along with many related discourses, in a collection that came to be called the 'Khandha-saṁyutta'. Thus its canonicity was assured. As discussions into the meanings of the discourses went on, some began to see a special significance in the mention of the 'person' here, to notice other places where the word 'person' seemed also suggestive, and to develop the 'personalist' thesis. Although some attempted to dissuade them, they persisted in their views, and eventually schism resulted. Each school inherited a version of the problematic discourse, which was already so deeply embedded in the received canon that its status was unimpeachable, and developed their own interpretation in accord with their views. These interpretations were included in the Abhidhamma works of the schools.

61 I trust that the reader, like myself, finds the final option the most plausible. Of course, not every discourse can be established so easily. But if even one discourse can be shown to be pre-sectarian, this makes it all the more likely that other similar discourses, and the collections in which these are found, also include pre-sectarian material.

Chapter 3

THE GIST 2—THE AGREEMENT OF THE THREE STRATA

AND SO TO OUR SECOND MAJOR QUESTION: what is the relationship of these strata to each other? The first outstanding feature is that all of the texts identified as earliest discourses are found in the Saṁyutta, the earliest collection. This is a compelling reason to consider these discourses as the root texts of all Buddhism, not in any vague or rhetorical sense, but as the literal historical seed around which the Saṁyutta and then the other collections crystallized.

3.1 The Seeds of the Saṁyutta

2 It may well be the case that the Dhammacakkappavattana Sutta was originally the first discourse in the Saṁyutta. At present it is number eleven in the Theravāda Sacca-saṁyutta; but in the Chinese it is the first in this chapter. (The position in the Pali can be explained by the later insertion of a *vagga* of ten discourses in front.) So if the Saṁyutta was the first collection and the Dhammacakkappavattana Sutta was the first discourse in its chapter, it is not such a great leap to suggest that the Saccasaṁyutta may have originally been the first topic in the Saṁyutta Nikāya. This would, of course, be logical, for the four noble truths is the

most general, all encompassing teaching, of which the other doctrinal categories are more specialized explanations.

3 There is an echo of this original structure preserved in the title given this discourse in the Pali. In most manuscripts the name 'Dhammacakkappavattana Sutta' does not occur; it is called *tathāgatena vutta* ('Spoken by the Tathāgata'). This is a bit odd, for most of the discourses are, of course, attributed to the Buddha. However the terms 'Spoken by the Buddha' and 'Spoken by the Disciples' occur in the Chinese recension, not as titles of discourses, but as titles of sections. Perhaps the label '*tathāgatena vutta*' referred originally, not to the Dhammacakkappavattana Sutta specifically, but to a section within a collection of discourses that consisted purely of teachings given directly by the Buddha himself.[1]

4 So the Dhammacakkappavattana Sutta was not the eleventh discourse in the fifty-sixth book of the third collection, but the first discourse in the first book of the first collection. The internal structure of the extant collections does not suggest that the Anattalakkhaṇa Sutta and the Ādittapariyāya Sutta ever enjoyed similar primacy within their respective collections.[2]

5 The primacy of the Dhammacakkappavattana Sutta as the cornerstone of the canonical collections is supported in some of the accounts of the First Council, preserved in the Vinayas of the schools. As one might expect, each school preserves a version of the events at this Council that serves to authorize its own canon. For example, the Theravāda states that the Brahmajāla Sutta was recited first; and in the existing Pali Tipitaka we do indeed find that the Brahmajāla Sutta is the first discourse in the first collection, the Dīgha Nikāya. This fact tends to discount the value of the sectarian accounts of the Councils as records of history. But, while not all the accounts can be accepted, there is no reason why at least one should not be substantially correct. It's not unlikely that some memory of the

---

[1] This line of reasoning suggested itself independently to both Bucknell and myself.

[2] There is some suggestion that the Request of Brahmā may have been the first discourse in the Sagāthāvagga, based on Bucknell's reconstruction, following the Yogacārabhūmiśāstra, of the Sagāthāvagga along the lines of the Eight Assemblies; however the argument is too complex to go into here. The Request of Brahmā is, surprisingly, missing from the Sarvāstivāda Saṁyukta, although it is found in the Ekottara and (Sanskrit) Dīrgha Āgamas, and probably elsewhere, appearing immediately before the Dhammacakkappavattana Sutta, just as in the Vinaya.

procedures of the main business would be preserved somewhere in the traditions. Only if the school later re-organized their scriptures would they feel the need to revise their account. Thus even if the existence of a corroborating account is not felt to strongly verify a theory of what happened at the First Council, the absence of a corroborating account would tend to falsify such a theory.

6 We should therefore consider whether any of the schools included an account of the First Council that is in line with the GIST. We do not have to look far, for the most influential of the Indian schools, the Sarvāstivādins, say the Dhammacakkappavattana Sutta was the first discourse recited at the Council. The Mūlasarvāstivāda Vinaya makes the same claim.[3] In this narrative, the holding of the First Council is presaged by the Buddha's exhortation, shortly before he passes away, for the Sangha to preserve the Dhamma by reciting the twelve aṅgas. Then, after the Buddha's passing away, having convened the Council, Venerable Mahā Kassapa requested that Venerable Ānanda recite the Suttas.[4] He first spoke the Dhammacakkappavattana Sutta. As we shall see below in the excerpt from the Catuṣpariṣat Sūtra, the Sarvastivada tradition does not include the detailed description of each of the truths (as is found in the Pali) in the first discourse. The detailed description (birth is suffering...) is here said to be the second discourse. The discourse on not-self, 'also spoken at Benares for the sake of the five monks', is therefore said to be the third discourse. When these discourses were given, all without flaw or criticism, all the arahants accepted them as the Buddha's true teaching.

> 7 Thus Ānanda now explained every teaching. Every arahant unanimously participated in the Council. And so the five-aggregate-saṁyutta

---

[3] The following account is based on the Chinese (T № 1451) and Rockhill's paraphrase of the Tibetan.

[4] Before Ānanda begins his recitation, there is a slightly odd episode where Mahā Kassapa said to all the monks: 'There will be monks who are weak in faculties and of scattered mind. They will not be able to learn and memorize the sutta-vinaya-abhidhamma. Therefore it will be fitting for us in the morning to compile the 'Brief Verses Saṁyutta', (略伽他事相應 (= *saṅkhitta-gāthā-saṁyutta*?), T24, № 1451, p. 406a22–23), in the afternoon it will be fitting to compile the sutta-vinaya-abhidhamma.' It is not clear what this is referring to; the Sagāthāvagga is referred to just below, in its proper place in the Saṁyutta, so it seems unlikely this is what is meant. Perhaps it refers to some of the verse collections of the Khuddaka.

> was compiled and placed in the Khandha Vagga. Also the six-sense-media-and-eighteen-elements-saṁyutta was compiled and placed in the Āyatana-dhātu Vagga. Also the dependent-origination-and-noble-truths-saṁyutta was compiled and placed with the name Paṭicca-samuppāda.[5] All those teachings that were spoken by disciples were placed in the Śrāvaka Vagga. All those teachings that were spoken by the Buddha were placed in the Buddha Vagga. All those dealing with satipaṭṭhāna, right efforts, bases of psychic power, spiritual faculties, spiritual powers, awakening [-factors], and the path were compiled and placed in the Magga Vagga. Also the sūtras in the 'with-verses-saṁyutta'. These are now called the Saṁyukta Āgama. All the discourses that were long teachings were named the Dīrgha Āgama. All the discourses that were middle-length teachings were named the Madhyama Āgama. All those discourses with one topic, two topics, up to ten topics, these were now named the Ekottara Āgama.[6]

8 Notice that after referring to the Anattalakkhaṇa Sutta, the passage goes on to speak of compiling a saṁyutta of texts on the aggregates. Now, the Anattalakkhaṇa Sutta is the fundamental text on the aggregates, and this is in fact found in the main group of texts on the aggregates, namely the Khandha-saṁyutta. Next the text speaks of a collection dealing with the sense media. Here the Ādittapariyaya Sutta is the basic text, and while it is not mentioned in the above account, in the Theravāda tradition this is regarded as the third discourse. It is found in the Saḷāyatana-saṁyutta. The categories 'spoken by disciples' and 'spoken by the Buddha' are in the existing Saṁyukta Āgama. The next passage clearly lists the 37 wings to awakening. These topics are the backbone of the Magga Vagga (or in the Theravāda, the Mahā Vagga) of the Saṁyutta. Finally the Sagāthāvagga is mentioned. Clearly, then, this passage authorises the Saṁyutta as the central body of the fundamental teachings, collected around the seeds of the first discourses. Then follows the other three Nikāyas/Āgamas compiled after the Saṁyutta. While it may be a sheer coincidence, it is worth noting that the title of this section of the Mūlasarvāstivāda Vinaya is 'Saṁyukta Vastu', which could be rendered 'The Story of the Saṁyutta'.

---

5 Text omits 'Vagga'; note that 緣起 can stand for either *paṭicca-samuppāda* or *nidāna*.

6 T24, № 1451, p. 407b20–c2.

9 So the Mūlasarvāstivāda Vinaya account suggests a close relationship between what we have identified as the earliest discourses and the earliest collection. It then goes on to say that Venerable Mahā Kassapa presented the mātikā, the list of contents of the Abhidhamma. This is not mentioned in the Theravāda account, and is clearly a later interpolation. But it is of interest in that it shows what was presumably regarded as the basic topics of the Mūlasarvāstivāda Abhidharma. This Abhidharma has not survived, and the given topics do not exactly match with any of the existing Abhidharma works, not even the Sarvāstivāda. Nevertheless, there are strong lines of continuity with what we shall identify as the root Abhidhamma treatise common to the schools.

> 10 The mātikā is that which makes perfectly lucid and explicit the distinguishing points of that which ought to be known. Thus it comprises the four satipaṭṭhānas, the four right efforts, the four bases of psychic powers, the five spiritual faculties, the five spiritual powers, the seven awakening-factors, the noble eightfold path, the four kinds of intrepidity (*vesārajja*), the four discriminations (*paṭisambhidhā*), the four fruits of asceticism (*sāmaññaphala*),[7] the four words of the Dhamma (*dhammapāda*),[8] non-conflict (*araṇadhamma*?), remote samādhi (*pantasamādhi*?), empty, signless, and undirected samādhi, development of samādhi, right penetration (*abhisamaya*), conventional knowledge (*sammutiñāṇa*?), samatha and vipassanā, Dhammasaṅgaṇī, Dharmaskandha—this is in what consists the mātikā...[9]

11 Here appear, yet again, the 37 wings to awakening. The standard wisdom topics—aggregates, etc.—do not appear. Most of the items are dhamma topics, but the final two are titles of books in the existing Theravāda and Sarvāstivāda Abhidhamma Piṭakas respectively. These were probably extensive Abhidhamma books, possibly sharing a common basis with their existing namesakes, and would have dealt with the wisdom topics according to the Mūlasarvāstivāda system.

---

7 SN 45.35/SA 796–797/SA 799.

8 Explained at AN 4.29 as freedom from covetousness and ill-will, right mindfulness, and right samādhi. Also found at T № 1536.7.

9 T24, № 1451, p. 408b6–11. Translation from Rockhill pg. 160. The details given by Rockhill have been corrected following Watanabe pg. 44, and from the Chinese. A few of the Chinese terms, especially in the latter part of the passage, are unclear.

12 It is a puzzling detail, highlighted at the Buddha's passing away, that the Buddha is said to have encouraged the Sangha to recite the aṅgas; but the recorded traditions of the First Council say nothing of the aṅgas. What is the missing link here? Is there some hidden connection between the aṅgas and the existing scriptures?

3.2 The Two Saṁyuttas

13 We know that the existing Saṁyuttas are substantially disordered, if only because they vary between the Pali and Chinese. Since it is obvious that they are closely related, we are bound to inquire as to why they differ. Perhaps one is right and the other is wrong, or more likely, each has diverged in its own way. Any structural similarities between the two suggest a common inheritance.

14 Before looking more closely at the contents of the Saṁyutta, we must briefly remark on a few confusing terminological ambiguities. The word 'saṁyutta', which means 'connected', in this context primarily refers to a collection of discourses on a certain Dhamma theme. Thus we have the 'Khandha-saṁyutta', the collection of discourses on the five aggregates; the 'Saḷāyatana-saṁyutta', the collection of discourses on the six senses, and so on. Sometimes the 'connection' is not a Dhamma theme, but some other criterion, such as literary style (Sagāthāvagga, Opamma-saṁyutta), or a person (Anuruddha-saṁyutta, etc.). These saṁyuttas are then gathered together in a large collection called the 'Saṁyutta Nikāya' or 'Saṁyukta Āgama', which is the 'Collection of saṁyuttas'. Thus the word 'saṁyutta' can be used to refer either to this large overall body (in which case we conventionally capitalize it as 'the Saṁyutta') or to the individual topics (which we write in lower case as 'saṁyuttas'). There is a similar ambiguity in the word 'vagga'. This is used in the sense of 'book' as a term for each of the five great divisions into which the Saṁyutta as a whole is divided. Each of these 'Vaggas' (capitalized) includes a number of saṁyuttas, and is usually named after its largest saṁyutta, which is usually also its first saṁyutta. But the more important sense of 'vagga' is the small scale (and hence lower case) use within the saṁyuttas, where it refers to

a group of usually ten discourses. The overall 'vertical' structure of the Saṁyuttas is therefore layered like this.

15 *Saṁyutta* ***Nikāya/Āgama*** ('**Group/tradition** of saṁyuttas')

Khandha ***Vagga*** ('**Book** [whose first and major section is] on the aggregates'), Saḷāyatana Vagga, etc.

*Khandha-**saṁyutta*** ('**Collection** [of discourses] on the aggregates'), Rādha-saṁyutta, etc.

*Nakulapitu-**vagga*** ('**Chapter** [starting with a discourse to] Nakulapita'), etc.

*Nakulapitu-**sutta*** ('**Discourse** to Nakulapita'), etc.

16 Here is the comparison between the reconstructed Chinese and the existing Pali Saṁyutta.

Table 3.1: The Sarvāstivāda and Theravāda Saṁyuttas

Sarvāstivāda Saṁyukta Āgama	Theravāda Saṁyutta Nikāya
	1. Sagāthāvagga
	2. Nidāna Vagga
1. Khandha Vagga	3. Khandha Vagga
2. Saḷāyatana Vagga	4. Saḷāyatana Vagga
3. Nidāna Vagga	
4. Sāvakabhāsita Vagga	
5. Magga Vagga	5. Mahā Vagga (= Magga Vagga)
6. Buddhabhāsita Vagga	
7. Sagāthāvagga	

17 The discrepancies are not as great as they seem. Most of the material found in the Sāvakabhāsita ('spoken by disciples') and Buddhabhāsita ('spoken by the Buddha') Vaggas is distributed in the minor chapters addended in the second through fifth Vaggas in the Theravāda. The Khandha, Saḷāyatana, and Magga Vaggas are in the same sequence in both collections. Only the Nidāna and Sagāthāvaggas have moved. There is internal evidence of reshuffling of these books within the Theravāda canon. The Sagāthāvagga consists of discourses with verses, and is thus clearly distinguished

from the remaining prose collections. But there is one other saṁyutta with verses; this is the Bhikkhu-saṁyutta, which in the Theravāda is at the end of the Nidāna Vagga. This suggests that it originally belonged to the Sagāthāvagga, and the Bhikkhu-saṁyutta is indeed found in the Chinese Sagāthāvagga.[10]

18 Bucknell has further shown that the Pali commentary hints of a time when the Nidāna Vagga, not the Sagāthāvagga, was the first book of the Saṁyutta Nikāya.[11] There is a passage found in the commentaries to all four Nikāyas that describes the various reasons why the Buddha teaches—in response to a question, from his own inspiration, etc. In the Dīgha, Majjhima, and Aṅguttara commentaries this appears in the commentary to the first discourse of the collection; but in the Saṁyutta it appears in the commentary to the first discourse in the Nidāna-saṁyutta. Since the Bhikkhu-saṁyutta is at the end of the Theravāda Nidāna Vagga but at the beginning of the Sarvāstivāda Sagāthāvagga, the rearrangement may have come about simply by misshelving: there were some pages left blank at the end of the Nidāna Vagga, so the scribe began the Sagāthāvagga by writing the Bhikkhu-saṁyutta on the same manuscript, but later an unmindful monk took the Nidāna Vagga out as the first book and replaced it as the second book (or took the Sagāthāvagga out as the second and replaced it as the first.) Thus the Bhikkhu-saṁyutta became separated from its natural pair, the Bhikkhunī-saṁyutta. It must be admitted that in this respect the Chinese maintains a more rational and probably more authentic tradition than the Pali. These kinds of disarrangements have contributed to the divergence from a common ancestral Saṁyutta.

19 The overall structure of the Saṁyutta Nikāya/Āgama corresponds roughly with the four noble truths. Bhikkhu Bodhi notes that this correspondence is more apparent in the Chinese than the Pali.[12] The five aggregates and six sense media pertain to the first noble truth; dependent origination (Nidāna-saṁyutta) to the second and third; and the path is the fourth. We may refer to these fundamental topics in a general sense as the 'saṁyutta-mātikā'. We mentioned above that the backbone of this Magga Vagga is the

---

[10] CDB, pg. 532.
[11] BUCKNELL, unpublished essay.
[12] CDB, pg. 27.

37 wings to awakening; in the Chinese these are preserved in an order that more closely follows the standard Sutta sequence.[13] We therefore have a number of indications that the Chinese is more structurally reliable than the Pali: the position of the Bhikkhu-saṁyutta; the overall correspondence with the four noble truths; and the sequence of the wings to awakening.

20 We have become so used to considering the 37 wings to awakening as a standard doctrinal set that we automatically think that the Magga Vagga was assembled by taking the list and collecting appropriate discourses under each topic. But perhaps the situation is the reverse: the list of 37 wings to awakening has been abstracted from the Magga Vagga topics. The discourses came first; they were collected according to topic; the collections were given titles; the titles became used as a shorthand way of referring to the collection; and then the titles became established as an independent list, repeated and elaborated in countless later works, with their origins in the Saṁyutta largely forgotten.

21 This helps explain some puzzling features of the list. For example, the five spiritual faculties and five spiritual powers consist of exactly the same dhammas, and there is no obvious reason why this set is repeated. They are traditionally explained as being the same qualities at different degrees; but this is not how the Saṁyutta sees them.[14] The situation is even stranger in the Theravāda Saṁyutta, for the Bala-saṁyutta is virtually redundant, being just a repetition series on the spiritual powers. But the Sarvāstivāda Bala-saṁyukta has a substantial collection of texts, gathering together many of the discourses on different sets of 'powers' that in the Theravāda are scattered about the canon, including the five spiritual powers. This is surely more likely to represent the original collection. The Indriya-saṁyutta, likewise, has discourses dealing with various sets of faculties in addition to the five spiritual faculties—sense faculties, feeling faculties, etc. In the Abhidhamma Vibhaṅga these became fixed into the classic set of 22 faculties. If, then, we compare the two saṁyuttas, one on various faculties, the other on various powers, they contain quite different teachings, with the five spiritual faculties and five spiritual powers being the only overlapping sets. So there is no problem understanding why there

[13] CDB, pg. 30.
[14] SN 48.43.

should be two collections, one on the faculties, one on the powers. It is only when the titles become abstracted and applied exclusively to the five faculties and the five powers that they appear redundant.

22 Seen in this way the entire Saṁyutta is a massive exposition of the four noble truths. This is the traditional assumption of the schools; books on exegetical method such as the Netti and the Peṭakopadesa teach that the correct understanding of any discourse requires that it be examined in the light of the four noble truths. But now we can give this traditional interpretation a more concrete literary form. We have seen that at least some traditions treat the Dhammacakkappavattana Sutta as the first discourse in this collection, and the seed around which the collection crystallized. This suggests that the Sacca-saṁyutta, which contains the Dhammacakkappavattana Sutta, was the first collection. This is not so now: it is in the Nidāna Vagga of the Sarvāstivāda and the end of the Mahā Vagga of the Theravāda. This type of ambiguity in position occurs whenever we try to systematize the relationship between the truths and the other doctrinal categories. Ultimately, this is because you can't impose linear textual structure on the organic structure of the Dhamma itself. The truths, though starting off as the overarching framework within which the other teachings are encompassed, come to be treated as just one more doctrinal item in the list. But they have no specific position within the list and can occur in almost any position. The correlation with the truths was uppermost in the minds of those who originally assembled the collections, but for later generations this memory became dimmed.

3.3 The Root Abhidhamma Topics

23 Let's now consider the third and last of our strata of texts, the Abhidhammas. The topics elucidated in the Saṁyutta remain very close to the fundamental doctrines set forth in the earliest discourses. Many of the discourses in the Saṁyutta are, in fact, mere variations spun out of those basic texts. The same situation obtains in the case of the earliest Abhidhammas. Below are the mātikās of the Abhidhamma texts of three schools, identified by Frauwallner as harking back to a common, presectarian ancestor.

24 He gives considerable detail; however he overlooks a couple of relevant points. The Dharmaskandha fragments from Gilgit have the dependent origination leading straight on to the 5 precepts. This suggests that the sequence in the Chinese has been disrupted, perhaps by an accidental reshuffling of manuscripts. If we moved the wisdom teachings—from the faculties to the dependent origination—to the start, this would restore the connection between the dependent origination and the 5 precepts, and would also make the structure of the Dharmaskandha broadly similar to the Vibhaṅga and Śāriputrābhidharma (and the Saṁyutta). We cannot be sure the change was accidental, though, for the existing structure is certainly rational, corresponding with the classic threesome of ethics, samādhi, and understanding. In this aspect the Dharmaskandha is similar to the later Theravāda treatise, the Visuddhimagga.

25 Another curious feature of the Dharmaskandha is that it omits the eightfold path. This would have been in the original treatise; its loss must be accidental. Perhaps it simply fell off the manuscript, or was misplaced.

26 In the following table the factors common to all three texts are bold. Even the factors not shared by all three of these texts, however, almost all have cognates elsewhere in Sutta or Abhidhamma.

Table 3.2: Three Versions of the Basic Abhidhamma Mātikā

Theravāda Vibhaṅga	Sarvāstivāda Dharmaskandha	Dharmagupta Śāriputrābhidharma
5 aggregates	**5 precepts**	**12 sense media**
12 sense media	4 stream-entry factors	**18 elements**
36 elements	4 confirmed faiths	**5 aggregates**
4 noble truths	4 fruits of asceticism	**4 noble truths**
22 faculties	4 ways of practice	**22 faculties**
Dependent origination	4 noble lineages	**7 awakening-factors**
4 satipaṭṭhānas	**4 right efforts**	3 unskilful roots
4 right efforts	**4 bases of power**	3 skilful roots
4 bases of power	**4 satipaṭṭhānas**	4 great elements
7 awakening-factors	**4 noble truths**	**5 precepts**
8-fold path	**4 jhānas**	**Elements**
4 jhānas	4 divine abidings	Kamma
4 divine abidings	4 formless	Persons[1]
5 precepts	4 samādhis	Knowledge[2]
4 discriminations	**7 awakening-factors**	**Dependent origination**
Khuddakavatthu[3]	Khuddakavatthu	**4 satipaṭṭhānas**
Ñāṇavibhaṅga[4]	**22 faculties**	**4 right efforts**
Dhammahadaya[5]	**12 sense media**	**4 bases of power**
	5 aggregates	**4 jhānas**
	62 elements	**8-fold path**
	Dependent origination	Unskilful dhammas[6]
		Saṅgraha[7]
		Sampayoga
		Prasthāna

[1] Cp. Puggala Paññatti.
[2] Cp. Ñāṇavibhaṅga.
[3] A list of defilements; the name 'Khuddakavatthu' is taken from the Dharmaskandha.
[4] A list of knowledges, comparable to the Paṭisambhidāmagga.
[5] An independent Abhidhamma work with its own mātikā: aggregates, senses, 18 elements, truths, 22 faculties, 9 causes (*hetu*), 4 nutriments, and 7 contacts, feelings, perceptions, volitions, and minds.
[6] = Khuddakavatthu?
[7] *Saṅgaha* and *sampayoga* are technical terms in the Theravāda Dhātukathā. *Paṭṭhāna* is the title of the Theravāda Abhidhamma treatise on causality.

3.4 The Three Strata Compared

27 Now that we have some idea of the content of each of the three strata, we can consider the relationship between them. Here is a comparative list of the main teachings in these strata, omitting secondary matter. In Abhidhamma sections I have identified the precise texts from which the Theravāda Vibhaṅga has sourced its material.[15] Variant or dubious texts are marked with an asterisk.

28 First a note on the efforts and bases for psychic powers. These chapters are found elsewhere in the Chinese, but together with part of the chapter on the faculties they have been lost from the existing Chinese Saṁyutta due to a failure in the transmission of the texts. Probably the manuscript was simply misfiled and later lost. Bizarrely, a passage from the 'Life of King Aśoka' (Aśokarājavadāna), which has nothing to do with the Saṁyutta, has ended up in its place—a reminder of the human fallibility of the generations of copyists who faithfully transmitted this absurdity.[16]

29 The agreement is startling, bearing in mind that we established these three strata independently, without referring to the doctrinal similarities between the strata. These topics are the backbone of the Dhamma, repeated countless times in countless variations in all schools in all the history of Buddhism. I have, with no great labour, counted over a dozen Abhidhamma and commentarial works of various schools that are based on these topics. Usually the framework of the four noble truths can still be discerned underlying the complex surface structures. It should hardy need saying that this congruence in the content of the doctrinal lists does not prove that the schools understood the doctrines in the same way. Each of the schools evolved its own interpretation, which differed both in detail and in principle.

---

[15] More details are listed in an appendix to the PTS Pali edition of the Vibhaṅga, pg. 437.

[16] Lamotte was evidently unaware of this problem when he remarked: 'As they [the Āgamas] were closed much later [than the Nikāyas], they make room for works of comparatively recent date; hence the Saṁyutta contains long extracts from the Aśokarājavadāna.' (LAMOTTE (1976), pg. 155.) More detailed examination gives no reason to conclude that the Āgamas were, generally speaking, closed earlier or later than the Nikāyas; each case needs to be treated individually.

Table 3.3: The Three Earliest Strata

Discourses	Collection	Abhidhamma
Truths	Truths	Truths (MN 141/MA 31/EA 27.1)
Aggregates	Aggregates	Aggregates (SN 22.59/SA 34)
Sense media	Sense media	Sense media[1]
	Elements[2]	Elements (MN 115/MA 181; MN 141/MA 162)
	Feelings	
Origin	Dependent origination	Dependent origination (SN 12.2/SA 298)
Defilements	Defilements[3]	Defilements[4]
	Kamma[5]	Kamma
Cessation	Dependent origination	Dependent origination (SN 12.1, 2/SA 298)
	Nibbana[6]	Nibbana
8-fold path	8-fold path	8-fold path (SN 45.8/SA 783*)
	Satipaṭṭhāna	Satipaṭṭhāna (MN 10/MA 98/EA 12.1)
	Right efforts	Right efforts (SN 49)
	Bases of psychic power	Bases of psychic power (SN 51.13)
	Spiritual faculties	22 faculties[7]
	Spiritual powers	(Spiritual powers)[8] (AN 5.14–15/SA 675)
	Awakening-factors	Awakening-factors (SN 46.3/SA 736, 740, 724*; SN 46.5/SA 733, etc.)
	Training (*sikkhā*)[9]	Training (Jhānavibhaṅga = gradual training; Sikkhāpadavibhaṅga = 5 precepts)

1 This is based on the standard list of the sense media so cannot be traced to one source.
2 The elements (*dhātu*) came to be treated with the aggregates and sense media as here, but the treatment in the Saṁyutta is more closely related to dependent origination.
3 E.g. SN 24/SA 4 Diṭṭhi.
4 Khuddakavatthu.
5 SA 41, omitted in SN but likely to be original.
6 E.g. SN 43/SA 890 Asaṅkhata, SN 55/SA 30 Sotāpatti.
7 Another hybrid group found in different positions due to the predominance of either the five spiritual faculties or the six sense faculties.
8 Omitted, no doubt being felt redundant, in the existing Vibhaṅga/Dharmaskandha/Śāriputrābhidharma, but found elsewhere in the Abhidhammas, e.g. the Pali Dhātukathā, whose mātikā is in some ways more archaic than the Vibhaṅga, since it stays closer to the original order of the wings to awakening. The Chinese Bala Saṁyutta is much more extensive than the Pali. The reference is to the relevant Vibhaṅga sutta.
9 SA 29, omitted in SN but likely to be original.

3.5 The Saṁyutta-Mātikā in the Mahāyāna

30 The persistence of the saṁyutta-mātikā in the Abhidharma is not surprising. It is more striking how important it remained for the Mahāyāna as well. The saṁyutta-mātikā is fundamental to the structure of the Heart Sūtra, and thus to the Prajñāpāramitā and Mahāyāna in general. The Heart Sūtra, which is usually dated to the 2nd century CE, starts with Avalokiteśvara seeing that the five aggregates are empty of 'intrinsic essence' (*svabhāva*), and then applying this analysis throughout the wisdom section of the saṁyutta-mātikā. The topics listed are: the five aggregates, the sense media, the 18 elements, dependent origination, and the four noble truths. These are all equated with emptiness, which Nāgarjuna, following the Sarvāstivāda Nidāna-saṁyukta, had already identified as dependent origination. Thus the Heart Sūtra critiques an interpretation of the topics of the saṁyutta-mātikā in terms of the Abhidhamma theory of 'intrinsic essence', replacing that with dependent origination. This is no innovation.

31 The Saṁdhinirmocana Sūtra offers a more explicit (and entertaining) account of what the issues are about.[17] This text was composed in the second century CE to establish the hermeneutic of the Yogacāra school. The main thrust is that conceptual understanding of the details of things—an obvious reference to the Abhidhamma schools—is born of imagination and thought-constructs, and takes these to be reality, but only with the non-conceptual unification of samādhi is true wisdom born. This passage shows how a forest monk regards the study monks, a thought that is echoed often enough today:

32
> The Venerable Subhūti addressed the Buddha and said: 'World-honoured One, in the world of sentient beings, I know a few who state their understanding without pride, but I know innumerable, untold sentient beings who cherish their pride and state their understanding in a prideful manner. World-honoured One, once I was dwelling in a grove in a forest. A large number of monks lived nearby.

[17] T № 676. I use KEENAN, which is based on the Chinese. The Tibetan is utilized in the French translation by Étienne Lamotte, *Saṁdhinirmocana Sūtra: L'explication des Mysteres* (Paris: Adrien Maisonneuve, 1935), and the English translation by John Powers, *Wisdom of Buddha: The Saṁdhinirmocana Sūtra* (Berkely, CA, Dharma Publishing. 1995).

> I saw them assemble after sunrise to discuss various issues and to propose their understandings, each according to his insight.
>
> 33 'Some proposed their understanding of the aggregates, their characteristics, their arising, their ending, their destruction, and the realization of their destruction. Others, in a similar fashion, proposed their understanding of the sense media, dependent origination, nutriments, the truths, the elements. Others proposed their understanding of the satipaṭṭhānas, their characteristics, the states they are able to control, their cultivation, their arising from a state of being non-arisen, their non-disappearance after arising, and their increase from repeated practice. Others spoke of the true severance [18] [= right efforts], bases of psychic power, spiritual faculties, spiritual powers, awakening-factors, or of the eightfold path in a similar fashion.
>
> 34 '...all of them cherished their pride, and, because they clung to that pride, they were unable to comprehend the one universal taste of the truth of ultimate meaning.'
>
> 35 Then the World-honoured One addressed Subhūti and said: 'This is so, Subhūti, for I have been awakened to the truth of ultimate meaning which is of one universal taste, most subtle, most profound, most difficult to fathom. Having been awakened, I declare, preach, explain, and illumine it for the sake of others. What is it that I have preached, Subhūti? I have preached that the purified content of understanding in all the aggregates, [text omits sense media], dependent origination, nutriments, [text omits truths], elements, satipaṭṭhāna, true severance, bases of psychic power, awakening-factors, and path factors is the truth of ultimate meaning. This purified content of understanding is characterized as being of one taste...
>
> 36 'Furthermore, Subhūti, once those practicing monks who cultivate samādhi have understood the suchness of a single group, the selflessness of the teaching on ultimate meaning, they will not engage in analysing one after the other the aggregates, sense media, dependent origination, nutriments, truths, elements, satipaṭṭhānas [etc.].'[19]

37 The text goes on to refer to this list of dhammas as a fundamental paradigm:

> 38 'The World-honoured One in a immeasurable number of sermons has explained the aggregates... sense media... dependent origination...

[18] The Pali *padhāna* ('effort') is often misread in Sanskrit as *pahāna* ('abandoning').

[19] KEENAN, pp. 22–23.

> nutriments... truths... elements... satipaṭṭhānas... right efforts... bases of psychic power... spiritual faculties... [text omits spiritual powers]... awakening-factors... eightfold path.'[20]
>
> 39 'The World-honoured One has designed the other aspect [of his teaching, that is, other than the teaching of ultimate emptiness] that ultimate meaning is without essence in reference to the pattern of full perfection, the purified content of understanding that is the non-self of all things, that is suchness, that is the pattern of full perfection. This is how the aggregates... sense media... 12 branches of existence [= dependent origination]... four nutriments... six and eighteen elements should be explained.... [also the] satipaṭṭhānas, right efforts, bases of psychic power, spiritual faculties, spiritual powers, awakening-factors, eightfold path. All these should be explained in this manner.'[21]

40 These teachings become so familiar that the text often abbreviates, simply mentioning, for example 'aggregates, sense media, all discussed above...';[22] or else 'the five aggregates, the six internal sense media, the six external sense media, and suchlike.'[23] Now, we have referred to this general list of topics as the 'saṁyutta-mātikā'. The affinity between this list and the Saṁyutta is undeniable; but in many cases in the Abhidhamma, etc., the situation is complicated by the addition of other factors. So one might suspect that here we have merely an affinity of ideas, rather than literal branches of the same historical trunk.

41 Let us compare this list, repeated with reasonable consistency throughout the Saṁdhinirmocana Sūtra, with the Sarvāstivāda Saṁyukta. We'll use those saṁyuttas identified in the Yogacārabhūmiśāstra as the central doctrinal chapters (on which more below), leaving aside the minor saṁyuttas and those spoken by disciples. Angles (<>) indicate where saṁyuttas have been omitted. In both cases we preserve the original sequence. We also give the list of topics in the Yogacārabhūmiśāstra's definition of the *sutta* aṅga in the Śrāvakabhūmi section.

---

[20] KEENAN, pg. 35.

[21] KEENAN, pp. 46–47.

[22] KEENAN, pg. 23.

[23] KEENAN, pg. 97.

Table 3.4: Three Versions of the Saṁyukta Mātikā

Sarvāstivāda Saṁyukta	Saṁdhinirmocana Sūtra	Śrāvakabhūmi[1]
Aggregates[2]	Aggregates	Aggregates
		Elements[3]
Sense media	Sense media	Sense media
Dependent origination	Dependent origination	Dependent origination
Nutriments (four)	Nutriments (four)	Nutriments
Truths	Truths	Truths
Elements	Elements	
Feelings	(no)	(no)
< >		Śrāvaka
		Pacceka Buddha
		Tathāgata
Satipaṭṭhāna	Satipaṭṭhāna	Satipaṭṭhāna
Right efforts (lost)	Right efforts	Right efforts
Bases of power (lost)	Bases of power	Bases of power
Spiritual faculties	Spiritual faculties	Spiritual faculties
Spiritual powers	Spiritual powers	Spiritual Powers
Awakening-factors	Awakening-factors	Awakening-factors
Eightfold path	Eightfold path	(Eightfold) path
		Ugliness (of the body)
Ānāpānasati	(no)	Ānāpānasati
Training (threefold)	(no)	Training
Stream-entry	(no)	Confirmed confidence
< >		

1 Śrāvakabhūmi, pg. 226.

2 The Khandha-saṁyutta in both SA and SN is followed by the Rādha and Diṭṭhi Saṁyuttas, which are really just appendices to the Khandha-saṁyutta. This is similar to the relationship between the Satipaṭṭhāna- and the Anuruddha-saṁyuttas.

3 The text has two adjacent listings for the elements: *dhātupratisaṁyukta* and *dhātusamgaṇapratisaṁyukta* ('connected with elements' and 'connected with things associated with elements'[?]). I am not sure of the significance of the twofold division; in any case, the elements seem out of sequence here.

42 The correlation is not just close, it is virtually exact. Particularly relevant is the coincidence of the four nutriments, which is not standard (the Theravāda subsumes this topic under dependent origination), and the sequence dependent origination, nutriments, truths, and elements, which is also not standard. For the Saṁdhinirmocana Sūtra, the fundamental teachings of the Dhamma are, precisely, contained within the Saṁyukta of the Sarvāstivāda. This may well be the reason why Asaṅga, in his Yogacārabhūmiśāstra, chose to comment at length on this recension of the Saṁyukta Āgama, the foundation of the other Āgamas. The Yogacāra hermeneutic of the Saṁdhinirmocana proposes that the understanding of these teachings should be based on samādhi rather than intellect. We do not have to look far within the early texts to confirm that this, like the Mādhyamaka emphasis on emptiness as dependent origination, was no innovation.

Chapter 4

THE GIST 3—THE AṄGAS

WE CAN NOW MOVE ON to the last of the major questions of the GIST: what is the relationship between these backbone texts and the rest of the discourses? In order to approach this complex question it will be helpful to first consider some more of Yin Shun's findings based on the Yogacārabhūmiśāstra. This work treats the Saṁyukta Āgama in terms of three *aṅgas* (sections): *sutta* (basic prose texts), *geyya* (verses), and *vyākaraṇa* (explanations). To understand the significance of this we shall have to take another step back and consider the aṅga classifications.

2 The chief significance of the aṅgas is that they are the earliest recorded system for classifying the teachings. The Nikāyas/Āgamas, or the Tripitaka itself, are not referred to in the early texts, and are attested only much later. They must therefore post-date the Buddha. But they cannot be very late, for the division in four main Āgamas is shared among the schools. It therefore must have been taking shape in the pre-sectarian period; however the wide divergence in internal structure suggests that the Āgamas were not yet settled in detail. Probably each school inherited a large mass of teachings, largely but not wholly overlapping, and a general arrangement of texts into the Āgamas. I think the huge task of organizing large numbers of monks and nuns to memorize such vast quantities of scriptures must have been the primary motivation in changing from the canonically authorized system of aṅgas to the new Āgama system. We think of this process taking place in the period between the first and second Councils.

It is problematic to think in terms of an 'original canon', since there is no particular evidence that the scriptures as a whole were ever considered finalized and universally accepted in the pre-sectarian period. Nevertheless, large bodies of scripture were universally accepted before and after the schisms. Since the Āgama system was developed relatively early, then if the aṅgas constitute a still earlier organizational principle, it is likely that the aṅgas, or at least the kernel of them, existed in the Buddha's own lifetime.

4.1 The Nine and the Twelve

3 There is a list of nine aṅgas, supposed to constitute the sum of the Buddha's teachings, that is familiar in the early Pali Nikāyas: *sutta*, *geyya*, *vyākaraṇa*, *gāthā*, *udāna*, *itivuttaka*, *jātaka*, *vedalla*, and *abbhūtadhamma*. These nine are also mentioned in Mahāsaṅghika texts,[1] and therefore may predate the first schism. This list is usually increased to twelve in the Sanskrit (with the addition of *nidāna*, *avadāna*, and *upadeśa*). They are all familiar terms, but the exact meaning is controversial. In the early texts they are simply listed with no further explanation. The later texts give explanations; but these vary considerably, and involve considerable anachronisms and improbabilities. Here I will not embark on a comprehensive survey, but will examine the sources that are available to me with an eye to what gleanings appear reasonable and relevant.

4 Several of the later items (*gāthā*, *udāna*, *itivuttaka*, *jātaka*) are the titles of books included in the Pali Khuddaka Nikāya, and the Theravādin commentaries straightforwardly identify such aṅgas with the books of the same name. If the later aṅgas refer primarily to the Khuddaka Nikāya, it is plausible that the first three are connected in some way with the four main Nikāyas/Āgamas. However, most modern scholars think that the

---

1 Nine aṅgas occur in the Mahāsaṅghika Vinaya (T № 1425, p. 227b), in the Saṅgīti Sūtra (T № 12, p. 227b), in the Itivuttaka (T № 765, p. 684a and 697c), in the Dharmasaṅgīti Sūtra (T № 761, p. 612a), in the Saddharmapuṇḍarika Sūtra (T № 262, p. 7c (though this seems to be a different set)), in the Dharmasaṅgraha (T № 764, p. 661a), and in the Daśavihāravibhāsa (T № 1521, p. 19b). My thanks to Venerable Anālayo for this information.

aṅgas refer to genres of text rather than to actual collections. For example, Lamotte says:

> 5 This [aṅga] classification does not correspond to any real division of the canon, but lists the literary styles represented in the canonical writings. One and the same text can be classified in several of the styles at the same time, depending on which of its characteristics is under consideration.[2]

6 Lamotte is quite correct to say that the aṅga classification is ambiguous. This, however, does not show that it was never used as a real division of the teachings, only that any such division would be imperfect. This is the case, after all, in any system of classification. Even in the existing Āgama system there are many such ambiguities; for example the Satipaṭṭhāna Sutta is middle-length, justifying its place in the Majjhima; but it deals with satipaṭṭhāna, one of the main topics of the Saṁyutta; and it teaches by numbers ('one' way path, 'four' satipaṭṭhānas), and so one Chinese version places it in the Ekottara. We shall repeatedly see such ambiguities as constituting 'breaking points', where the aṅga system starts to fall apart, contributing to the emergence of more systematic organization.

7 The most basic reason for considering the aṅgas as mere styles rather than an actual structure would be that some of the aṅgas, particularly the first three, do not occur as titles of collections; and because, of those aṅgas that are titles of existing collections, the books bearing these titles are generally held to have been compiled later than the early discourses where the list first appears. However, it is quite possible that the earliest list may have been shorter, and that as other books were compiled their names were added to the list. This is a less radical hypothesis than the proposition that the very idea of a canonical collection in the Buddha's time was invented and inserted retrospectively. The divergence between the Pali and the Sanskrit lists confirms that some additions must have been made, at least for the extra items in the Sanskrit. Here we will briefly discuss the later aṅgas before returning to a more in depth consideration of the first three. None of these attributions are beyond dispute. However, we can establish that it is possible, even plausible, that they referred to specific groupings of texts, many of which are still available.

[2] LAMOTTE (1976), pg. 144.

8 **Gāthā:** Refers primarily to the early portions of the Thera/Therīgāthā and the Sutta Nipāta. The Thera/Therīgāthā now exists only in the Pali, but is frequently referred to in the scriptures of other schools, so they must have had versions of these uplifting verses that are now sadly lost, apart from some in Chinese (eg. Theragāthā 1018–1050 occur as MA 33), and a few Sanskrit fragments.[3] The Sutta Nipāta is not found outside the Pali tradition as a collection, but many of the individual texts are known (Khaggavisana, Ratana, Muni, Sela, etc.), and even some whole chapters (Aṭṭhaka, Pārāyana). Several of these, including the Aṭṭhaka and the Pārāyana, were said to be included in the Dharmaguptaka Khuddaka Nikāya. There is clearly a tendency to collect the gāthās in distinct collections.

9 **Udāna:** There is evident confusion in the traditions between the texts known in Pali as 'Udāna' and 'Dhammapāda'. Sometimes the contents of the two are mixed, and there are Dhammapāda-like texts in Sanskrit and Chinese that are called 'Udānavarga'. The Chinese traditions regarded the Dhammapāda and the Udāna as being the same kind of text. Probably only the verses were originally called *udānas*, and were later embedded in background material of varying authenticity. A certain stage in this process is marked by the Pali book called 'Udāna'. In the verses found in the Pali Dhammapāda this process was slower or more uncertain. The background stories never gained full canonical status but, with abundant imaginative elaboration, took shape as the Dhammapāda commentary, which provided the traditional framework within which the verses were presented. It is worth noting that, even though the commentary was finalized many centuries after the verses, at least some information is historically verifiable and stems from an authentic tradition. One of the stories found in the Pali Dhammapāda commentary is attested in the Sarvāstivādin Madhyama (MA 80 Kaṭhinadhamma Sutta). The background stories to the verses as recorded in Chinese versions of the Dhammapāda have little or no correlation with the Pali stories.

10 **Itivuttaka:** The Theravāda commentaries say that this refers to the Pali book of that name; however I am not convinced. Incidental evidence of authenticity comes from the commentarial background story, which says this collection was originally memorized by a lay-woman follower from

[3] Some references in LAMOTTE (1976), pp. 161, 162.

whom the nuns later learnt it and taught it to the monks. It is unlikely that the monks would have invented such a story implying that they forgot their lessons. On the other hand there is no particular reason why that story should be attached to this particular group of texts. The Itivuttaka is a small aṅguttara-style text, including a verse summarizing each discourse, and the title is derived from the 'tag' at the beginning and end of each discourse: 'thus it was said'. This tag is entirely 'extrinsic' to the teachings and could tag any style of text. Thus the Itivuttaka is unusual among the aṅgas in that there is no intrinsic relationship between the name of the aṅga and the style of text. The Chinese version of the Itivuttaka has a similar 'tag', so if it is not original, it is not very late. There is a class of Vedic literature called 'Itihāsa', 'thus it was', i.e. 'stories of the past, legendary histories', which is sometimes equated with the Mahābhārata and the Ramāyana. By analogy, *itivuttaka* could mean 'sayings of the past'. *Itivuttaka* might then refer to the legendary histories that are found in the Nikāyas/Āgamas, such as the Aggañña Sutta,[4] and the Cakkavattisīhanāda Sutta.[5] Notice that these two discourses are paired in both the Theravāda and Dharmaguptaka Dīghas. The Sarvāstivādins preferred to place these in their Madhyama, where, however, they are not paired. This theory finds support in some sources outside the Theravāda, which treat *itivuttakas* as stories of the past, sometimes interchangeably with *apadānas*. For example, Asaṅga in the Abhidharmasamuccaya says *itivuttaka* 'narrates the former existences of the noble disciples';[6] in the Śrāvakabhūmi of the Yogacārabhūmiśāstra he says it refers to 'whatever is connected with previous practice'.[7]

11 ***Jātaka***: It might be assumed that this originally referred to the stories of the Buddha's past lives found occasionally in the four Āgamas, rather than the well known book of the same name, which is obviously later (although there is some overlap between the two strata in the Pali; and at least one of

---

4 DN 27/DA 5/T № 10/MA 154/EA 40.1/Skt. In this and subsequent references I do not give the details of the Sanskrit texts. They may be found at the relevant tables on http://suttacentral.net/. I omit them because they are long and detailed, and only relevant to a minority of scholars, who can easily find them through SuttaCentral anyway.

5 DN 26/DA 6/MA 70.

6 BOIN-WEBB, pg. 179.

7 Śrāvakabhūmi, pg. 230.

the stories in the Pali Jātaka book is found in the Sarvāstivāda Madhyama [MA 60]). However, the terms *jātaka*, '*bodhisatta*' (either 'enlightenment-being' or 'one intent on enlightenment'), and most of the other specific features associated with the Jātaka book do not occur in the Āgama stories of past lives. For example, there is no hint that the 'Buddha-to-be' was in any sense destined for enlightenment, or was undertaking practices leading to enlightenment; quite the contrary, the Buddha takes pains to state that the practices that he did in past lives 'do not lead to enlightenment'.[8]

12 If the extended list of aṅgas was added later to the first three, it is more likely that *jātaka* here refers to the book, at least to an earlier version. The canonical Jātaka book contains just the verses that tell the kernel of the story; this work is almost never found independently. This should be compared with the Udāna/Dhammapāda as noted above. The stories themselves are contained in the commentary, although they must have been passed down together with the verses in the oral tradition, for in many cases the verses are cryptic and make no sense without the story. It is crucial to remember when considering the Jātaka literature that the verses and the 'stories of the past' belong together, and rarely have any distinctively Buddhist features, being largely a product of the folk storytelling tradition. Probably the stories were adopted by Buddhist teachers originally simply as moral fables. Later some of them became identified with the Buddha in past lives. When they came to be collected as a book it was probably felt desirable to standardize the literary format; this process not only reflects other verse collections such as the Udāna/Dhammapāda, but also the Vinaya, which similarly provides each rule with an origin story of often dubious historicity (a *nidāna*, one of the later aṅgas). The 'stories of the present', which give the present-day (i.e. the Buddha's lifetime) events that were supposed to have inspired the telling of the story, are an external cladding that were added long after the stories were originally told. It is, of course, this 'cladding' that identifies the characters in the story with the Buddha, his family, etc. in past lives. This justifies the title 'Jātaka' ('Birth Story').

13 These 'stories of the present' presuppose a stage in the development of the bodhisatta doctrine significantly in advance of the early discourses.

---

8 MN 83.21/MA 67/EA 1/EA 50.4/T № 152.87/T № 211, DN 19.61/DA 3/T № 8/Skt.

The evolution of this usage can be traced in the existing Nikāyas/Āgamas as follows. The term 'bodhisatta' commonly refers to Siddhattha in his period of striving before awakening; this is the earliest use. This would suggest that the earliest meaning of the word 'bodhisatta' was 'one intent on awakening' (*bodhiśakta*), rather than 'awakening-being' (*bodhisattva*). There are apparently references in both the Chinese and Theravāda scriptures that acknowledge this meaning. The Mahāpadāna Sutta, telling the story of Vipassī, uses the word 'bodhisatta' as far back as the descent from Tusita heaven and birth in the final life.[9] The Sanskrit version of this text, although incomplete, appears to be similar in this respect. The same is also found in the Tathāgata-acchariya Sutta of the Aṅguttara.[10] The Acchariya-abbhūta Sutta (an adaptation of Vipassī's story to 'our' Buddha) extends the scope of the term back to the previous birth in Tusita.[11] The Sarvāstivādin version of the same text takes the significant step of claiming that in the time of Kassapa, the immediately preceding Buddha, the bodhisatta made the vow to become a future Buddha, an idea not found in the early tradition.[12] From there it is no great leap to imagine the Buddha-to-be toiling through countless lives in his struggle for Buddhahood.

14 ***Vedalla***: Another problematic term. It is used as titles for two discourses in the Majjhima Nikāya.[13] The two discourses occur together in both the Theravāda and Sarvāstivāda. In the Sarvāstivāda they form the last pair in the second-last chapter; thus, bearing in mind that textual units seem to frequently move about in chapters (vaggas) of ten or so discourses, they might at one stage have been the final discourses in the Majjhima.[14] However, the title 'Vedalla' is only used in the Theravāda; the Sarvāstivādin

---

[9] DN 14.1.17/DA 1/T № 2/T № 3/T № 4/EA 48.4/Skt.

[10] AN 4.127/MA 32*/EA 25.3*.

[11] MN 123.3.

[12] MA 32.

[13] MN 43/MA 211, MN 44/MA 44; the versions differ in some questions and details, but there is no obvious sectarian divergence.

[14] Immediately preceding the two Vedallas is a group of three discourses that occur together and in the same sequence in both Majjhimas: MN 77/MA 207 Mahāsakaludāyin; MN 79/MA 208 Cūḷsakaludāyin; and MN 80/MA 209 Vekhanassa. (MN 78/MA 179 Samaṇamaṇḍikā, falling as it does between the 'Mahā' and 'Cūḷa' Sakaludāyin Suttas, is obviously a later interpolation.) This group of three and the two Vedalla Suttas were probably pre-existing groups that were brought into the Majjhima.

equivalents are named after the protagonists, Mahā Koṭṭhita and Sister Dhammadinna. The word *vedalla* does not appear in the body of the texts at all, so, like the Itivuttaka, it is quite possible that the term was simply tacked on to the discourses at a late date. In fact, they are just *vyākaraṇas*, and there is no reason to invent a separate class of literature just for them. The Theravādin commentaries also include a number of similar discourses under *vedalla*. All of these are found in the Pali canon except the 'Sankhāra-bhājanīya Sutta' (implausibly identified with the Sankhāruppatti Sutta). The term *bhājanīya* ('exposition'), from the same root as '*vibhaṅga*', is rare in the early discourses, and its most familiar appearance is in the chapter titles of the Abhidhamma Vibhaṅga, which is not too dissimilar to the existing *vedallas*. The PED is unsure about the derivation of *vedalla*, improbably suggesting *veda + ariya*. But there is a root *dala* (cognate with the English 'tear'), with the basic meaning of 'break, split'.This is used for the names of certain flowers, in the sense of the unfolding and separating of the petals and leaves. The form *vidala*, attested in Sanskrit with the meaning 'dividing, separating', is exactly parallel with vibhaṅga, and *vedalla* is just the abstract form of this. One possibility therefore would be that *vedalla* was originally the proto-abhidhamma text we call *Vibhaṅga Mūla. However, given the uncertainty of the term *vedalla*, and the tenuousness of the links with the existing texts, we are unable to draw any conclusions here, except that the two texts now called *vedalla* were probably paired up together before being brought into the Majjhimas. The Sanskrit term here varies, but is usually *vaipulya*, 'abundant', which was a standard term for the sprawling Mahāyāna Sūtras. It is likely that the later translators or editors substituted this familiar term for the problematic and obscure *vedalla*, not coincidentallylending credibility to the disputed claims for the authenticity of the Mahāyāna. In fact the Abhidharmasamuccaya (a Mahāyāna Abhidhamma authored by Asaṅga) identifies this aṅga as contained in the 'Bodhisattvapiṭaka', and says that the three variant terms refer to the same thing: *vaipulya* (it helps all beings, and is profound), *vaidalya* (= *vedalla*, 'shatters all obstacles'), *vaitulya*, ('incomparable').[15] Only the second derivation has any cogency, although as said above, the meaning is more likely to be 'splitting' in the sense of 'analysis'.

[15] BOIN-WEBB, pg. 180.

15 **Abbhūtadhamma:** Probably the most straightforward of the aṅgas to interpret, this refers to such discourses as the Acchariya-abbhūta Sutta (MN 123/MA 32), the Bakkula Sutta (MN 124/MA 34), etc., which discuss the 'marvellous qualities' of either the Buddha or various disciples. Venerable Ānanda is closely associated with this type of literature. In the Theravādin canon these two outstanding examples of the genre are found together in the Majjhima. In the Sarvāstivāda, not only do these two remain close together, but they form part of a chapter of the Sarvāstivādin Majjhima called the 'Abbhūtadhammavagga'. This chapter includes a discourse where the Buddha praises Ānanda's 'marvellous qualities' (MA 33). Buddhaghosa's description of *abbhūtadhamma* refers to what is probably a similar text, which is now found in the Theravāda Aṅguttara and Dīgha (DN 16.5.16). In fact, at AN 4.127–130 there is a group of four texts of this type. Moreover, there is a cluster of five discourses of this type found together in the Aṅguttara eights, and in the Sarvāstivāda Madhyama Abbhūtadhammavagga. Thus *abbhūtadhamma* refers to actual groups of texts. The Bakkula Sutta is an interesting case. It is late, both on internal evidence, and on the statement of the commentary that it was added at the second council. This is one of the few direct admissions of a text added after the first council. The only other similar statements known to me refer to a few *gāthās* in the Thera/Therīgāthā and the Mahā Parinibbāna Sutta, which also belong to later aṅgas. This is as close as we get to an acknowledgement by the traditions that the later aṅgas were added at the second council or later.

16 The following three aṅgas only occur in the Sanskrit lists.

17 **Upadeśa:** This means 'instructions, directions'. It occurs mainly in later texts. I do not know of any early texts in the Sanskrit traditions that use this title. However, later Chinese scholars including Hsuang Tsang say that *upadeśas* are treatises that explain the sūtras.[16] This suggests a connection with the Peṭakopadesa ('Instructions in the Piṭaka'), an early work on exegetical technique that was accepted into the Khuddaka Nikāya only in Burma. Asaṅga in the Śrāvakabhūmi describes *upadeśa* as 'all the mātikā and abhidhamma' that explain the Suttas; in the Abhidharmasamuccaya

[16] GNOLI, Pt. 1, pg. xix.

he describes it as 'the precise, profound, and subtle teaching of the characteristics of all things.'[17]

18 ***Apadāna*:** This term, spelt *avadāna* in Sanskrit, is very similar to *jātaka*, usually referring to biographical stories of the past. In Pali the *apadānas* are past lives of disciples, while *jātakas* are past lives of the Buddha; but this distinction is not maintained consistently. According to Cone, the term has the basic meaning of 'cutting, reaping, harvest', applied in a metaphorical sense of 'reaping' of the fruits of one's actions (especially in past lives), and then to a story about kamma and result. The earliest usage in this sense is the Mahāpadāna Sutta, which, however, also includes elements of *abbhūtadhamma*, *vyākaraṇa*, *udāna* (or *gāthā*), *geyya*, and even Vinaya. This detail suggests a connection between *Apadāna* and Vinaya, which we will consider further below. Perhaps the early life stories found occasionally in the Nikāyas/Āgamas, such as the Māratajjanīya Sutta, could be regarded as *apadānas*; however the term itself is not used in these contexts. The term is the title of a book found in the Pali Khuddaka Nikāya, which tells the stories of the previous lives of the arahants. Similar works are found in the Sanskrit traditions.

19 ***Nidāna*:** This refers to background or source material. Here it may refer to the Jātaka Nidāna, one of the early Buddha biographies. The Abhidharmasamuccaya says *nidāna* is 'a declaration made [by the Buddha] when he is questioned, or it is the declaration of a precept with its cause.'[18] The first of these explanations applies rather to *vyākaraṇa*. However, it may refer to such episodes as when, for example, the Buddha gave his enigmatic smile, and when asked by Venerable Ānanda for the reason for this, he responded by telling a story of the past. The second explanation, connecting *nidāna* with the Vinaya, is clearly in accord with a straightforward early usage.

20 There are, in fact, many ancient sources that connect both *nidāna* and *apadāna* with the Vinaya.[19] The *nidānas* are the origin stories for the rules, while the *apadānas* are the other tales included for edification, especially those that compare events in this life with those in past lifetimes. The Śrāvakabhūmi, while including *apadāna* in the Suttas, says that *nidāna* is

---

[17] BOIN-WEBB, pg. 180.
[18] BOIN-WEBB, pg. 179.
[19] Discussed in MATSUMURA.

the Vinaya, while *upadeśa* is the Abhidhamma. This suggests that the difference between the nine and the twelve aṅgas is not necessarily a matter of historical growth of sectarian material, but that the ninefold category includes only the Suttas, while the twelvefold includes both Vinaya and Abhidhamma as well.

21 This ambiguity of classification reflects the fascinating way the Vinayas mix the hagiographic and the prosaic. For example the *locus classicus* for the *apadāna*, the Mahāpadāna Sutta, though largely hagiographic, also includes some narrative material in common with the Vinaya, suggesting that it might be considered, along with the Mahā Parinibbāna Sutta and the Catuṣpariṣat Sūtra, as occupying an ambiguous position between Dhamma and Vinaya. These three texts form the basis for all later biographies of the Buddha, such as the famous Mahāvastu of the Mahāsaṅghika Lokuttaravāda, a text which frequently uses the word *avadāna*, includes many *avadānas*, and is sometimes suggestively referred to as the Mahāvastu-avadāna. An *apadāna* is a story that forms a parable or simile; in other words, one which points to a greater reality outside the mere events recorded, in particular, a life story that forms a spiritual paradigm for emulation. In this respect, the Buddha's own life story, the 'Great Apadāna', sets the form for all that follow. The parallels between the lives of all the Buddhas presage the theme of repeated patterns, recurring ethical choices, for good or ill, followed by the inevitable results, cycling on through the births and deaths of the ages. We have versions of this story in several recensions, each vying with the other in profusion of detail and magnification of glorious and magical embroidery. A fascinating sidelight is thrown on the interrelationship between these tales by the colophon at the end of the Abhiniśkramana Sūtra, translated under the title *The Romantic Legend of Sakya Buddha*:

> 22 'It may be asked: "By what title is this Book to be called?" to which we reply, the Mahāsaṅghikas call it "Mahāvastu"; the Sarvāstivādins call it "Mahā Lalitavistara"; the Kaśyapīyas call it "Buddha-jātaka-nidāna"; the Dharmaguptakas call it "Śakyamuni-buddhacarita"; the Mahīśāsakas call it "Vinaya-piṭaka-mūla".'[20]

23 Thus each school had its own version, which were merely variations on the same theme. The Abhiniśkramana Sūtra includes some remarks,

[20] BEAL (1985), pg. 386–7; translation corrected following LAMOTTE, pg. 177.

perhaps by the later translators, on some of these variations. For example, as to the crucial question of how far did the Bodhisatta's horse travel on the night of his escape from the palace; the text says two leagues, the Mahāsaṅghikas say twelve, but the Theravādins say a hundred.[21] The 'Great Story' of the Buddha was subject to expansion almost as limitless as the round of samsara, and yet even in the most elaborate versions, the basic teachings, such as the Dhammacakkappavattana Sutta, recur in almost identical form, like little nuggets of gold washed along in a stream; the stream is constantly changing, though keeping roughly the same course, but the nuggets remain untarnished and very slow to change. As a literary style, this may again be compared with several of the other aṅgas we have discussed above. The Pāṭimokkha rules that form the core of the Vinaya, for example, are, in the existing Vinayas, embedded in origin stories (*nidānas*). But while the rules are almost identical in all the existing Vinayas, we find considerable variation in the stories; examining the Lokuttaravāda Bhikkhunī Vinaya, I was surprised to find that most of the origin stories hardly share any common elements. We have noted a parallel situation obtaining in the case of the verses; most of the collections of verse—Dhammapāda, Jātaka, Udāna—come with their own background stories, but while the stories and verses may have originated at the same time, it is the verses that were fixed in their current form earlier, embedded in a body of prose of varying flexibility.

4.2 Sutta, Geyya, Vyākaraṇa

24 So there is no very strong reason to accept the view that the aṅgas were merely literary genres rather than organized bodies of scripture. Many of the later aṅgas can be connected in some way with titles of extant texts. Even in the case of those terms that are not titles of independent books, such as *vedalla* and *abbhūtadhamma*, the relevant texts are fairly consistently gathered together in the existing collections. They have clearly exerted structural influence on the existing canons, tending to be grouped together within the larger collections. Such recognizable bodies of texts would naturally evolve into distinct books.

---

[21] Beal (1985), pg. 140.

25 Since this was the case with the later aṅgas, the first three aṅgas also originally would have been recognizable groups of texts, distinct sections within a larger framework. Given the conservatism of religious literature in general, and Buddhism in particular, it is very unlikely that no remnant of this structure should be preserved in the existing canons.

26 There are good reasons for treating the first three aṅgas as distinct from, and earlier than, the later aṅgas. Yin Shun points out that the Mahā Suññatā Sutta, in both the Sarvāstivāda and the Theravāda versions, lists just the first three: *sutta*, *geyya*, *vyākaraṇa*.[22] He takes this to show that these three were historically the earliest. Given the consistency with which the Theravāda texts treat the aṅgas, the appearance of the three alone in the Mahā Suññatā Sutta does indeed call for explanation. The Tibetan translation here has the usual list of twelve, which, as the translator Peter Skilling notes, attests to a later stage in the development in the aṅgas.[23] Here is the relevant paragraph from the Pali.

27 > 'Ānanda, it is not worthy for a disciple to follow a Teacher for the sake of *suttas*, *geyyas*, and *vyākaraṇas*.[24] Why is that? For a long time, Ānanda, you have learned the teachings, remembered them, recited them verbally, examined them with the mind, and penetrated them well by view. But such talk as deals with effacement, as favours the freedom from hindrances of the heart, and leads to complete repul-

---

[22] MN 122.20/MA 191.

[23] Pg. 957.

[24] There are some variant readings. I do not have the various Pali editions available, so my thanks go to Venerable Anālayo for the following readings. The PTS has: *suttaṁ geyyaṁ veyyākaraṇassa hetu*; Burmese and Sinhalese have: *suttaṁ geyyaṁ veyyākaraṇaṁ tassa hetu*; the Siamese has: *suttageyyaveyyākaraṇassa sotuṁ*. The PTS version would thus seem to have only two aṅgas, whose explanation the disciple wants from the Tathāgata (cp. the translation by Horner: '…for the sake of an exposition of the discourses that are in prose and in prose and verse'). But the grammar is odd; this phrase would seem rather to have formed by contraction from the Burmese/Sinhalese reading (= *suttaṁ geyyaṁ veyyākaraṇ' assa hetu*). The Chinese version reads 正經・歌詠・記說故. This does indicate that its original read *hetuḥ*, not *sotuṁ* as proposed by the Siamese edition. *Sotuṁ* ('for the hearing of…') is more straightforward; grammatically the compound formation in the Siamese edition is also more straightforward, leading me to suspect the Thai editors have normalized a difficult reading. The Chinese does not give a hint to the grammatical problems of this passage. In any case, the Chinese and most of the Pali versions have three aṅgas, and the apparent presence of two aṅgas in the PTS seems easily explicable.

> sion, fading away, cessation, peace, direct knowledge, enlightenment, Nibbana; that is, talk on wanting little, on contentment, seclusion, aloofness from society, arousing energy, ethics, samādhi, understanding, release, knowledge & vision of release—for such talk, a disciple should follow a Teacher even if he is told to go away.'

28 Here the three aṅgas clearly refer to a formalized set of scriptures. Note the ambiguity: this is typical of references to formal learning of Dhamma in the early discourses; learning is encouraged, but not as an end in itself. Such passages, which are quite common, are likely to precede the formal redaction of the Tipitaka in Sri Lanka, for there the Sangha decided that scripture came before practice.[25] They would not have invented such passages that are critical of their own position; in fact it is remarkable that they preserved so many passages that emphatically place practice over scripture. Mention of Venerable Ānanda's close connection with the three aṅgas here is intriguing; the Dhamma learnt by him was the *sutta*, *geyya*, and *vyākaraṇa*. Given that the traditions ascribe Ānanda the central role in reciting the Dhamma at the First Council, this is an indication that the Dhamma compiled there might have consisted of these three aṅgas.

29 Further evidence comes from the Sanskrit Mahā Parinirvāṇa Sūtra, which has been published as a complete reconstructed version, and a partial fragment. The list of twelve aṅgas occurs in both the complete and the partial versions, and although readings vary slightly, in both cases the first three occur in declined form, as individual words, while the remaining aṅgas are grouped all together in a long compound: *sūtraṁ geyaṁ vyākaraṇaṁ gāthodānanidānavadānetivṛttakajātakavaipulyādbhutadharmopadeśāḥ*.[26] This looks very much as if the original list of three was supplemented later. Exactly the same feature occurs twice in a Sanskrit list of the twelve aṅgas in the Śrāvakabhūmi of Asaṅga's Yogacārabhūmiśāstra.[27] This text then several times gives just the first three, and then simply says that the list should be expanded as before.[28] The distinctness of the first three is also suggested in the way Asaṅga comments on them. In both the Śrāvakabhūmi and the

[25] See the timeline in ÑĀṆAMOLI's Introduction to *The Path of Purification*, p. xi, which refers to the Aṅguttara Commentary, i.92*f*.

[26] WALDSCHMIDT (1950, 1951) 40.62; WALDSCHMIDT (1968).

[27] Śrāvakabhūmi, pg. 154, 232.

[28] Śrāvakabhūmi, pg. 154, 184, 220, 226.

Abhidharmasamuccaya he says that *geyya* is '*suttas* that require further explanation', and *vyākaraṇa* is '*suttas* that are fully explained'.[29] This treats the two as a closely connected pair; the explanation is quite close to our interpretation of these terms.

30 Another interesting case is in the two Pali works on textual interpretation, the Netti and the Peṭakopadesa. Both of these works regard the four noble truths as the key and the core of the Buddha's dispensation, referring all other teachings back to them. The Peṭakopadesa explicitly connects the Dhammacakkappavattana Sutta and the aṅgas:

31 > Between the night of his enlightenment and the night of his Parinibbāna without grasping, whatever was spoken by the Blessed One—*sutta, geyya, vyākaraṇa, gāthā, udāna, itivuttaka, jātaka, abbhūtadhamma, vedalla*—all that is the Wheel of Dhamma (*dhammacakka*) set rolling. There is nothing in the teaching of the Buddha, the Blessed One, outside the Wheel of Dhamma. In all his sutta, the noble dhamma should be sought. In the comprehension of this there is the pentad ending with 'light'.[30]

32 These works were composed at a time when the canon was more or less organized as it is today, referring to such sections as the 'Saṁyutta Nikāya', etc., and utilizing specialist Abhidhamma terminology. The Peṭakopadesa mentions the ninefold aṅgas only twice,[31] the Netti not at all. This is a bit curious for works that explain in considerable length how to analyse the discourses.

33 The Peṭakopadesa treats *sutta* very broadly, encompassing all the teachings. One of the main purposes of the work is to describe various principles by means of which one discourse may be interpreted with teachings found in other discourses. After describing some such principle, it frequently says that *gāthās* should be assessed with *gāthās*, *vyākaraṇas* should be assessed with *vyākaraṇas*.[32] While it is not explicit, this looks like our first three aṅgas, although the word aṅga is not used; *gāthā* is a synonym for

---

[29] *Neyyattha* and *nītattha*; Śrāvakabhūmi pg. 228; Abhidharmasamuccaya pg. 179, but see DE JONG's comment, pg. 295.

[30] Peṭakopadesa 1.7. In the final sentence I accept Ñāṇamoli's suggested amendment to *ālokapañcakaṁ*, referring to the series of five terms in the Dhammacakkappavattana Sutta describing the Buddha's realization of the noble truths.

[31] Peṭakopadesa 1.7, 1.22.

[32] Peṭakopadesa 1.8, 1.9, 1.12, 4.41, 5.53, 5.54, 7.105.

geyya, and *geyya* is often explained as 'with *gāthās*'. The same grouping occurs in the Netti, though only once.[33]

34 It is not immediately clear what this Peṭakopadesa passage is getting at. Perhaps, as Nanamoli's translation implies, the passage is saying that the *sutta*, the overall teachings, may be divided into verse (*gāthā*) and prose (*vyākaraṇa*). This is supported by statements such as: 'Up to this point, however, the entire *sutta*—whether *gāthā* or *vyākaraṇa*—is not [quoted].'[34] But this does not reflect the original meaning of the aṅgas very closely. The treatment of *gāthā* and *vyākaraṇa* as sub-divisions of *sutta* is reminiscent of Asaṅga's treatment of *geyya* and *vyākaraṇa* mentioned above. It evidently dates from a time when the scope of *sutta* had been expanded from meaning one section of the teachings to meaning all of them.

35 There is at least one passage that is closer to our usage, and even involves the saṁyutta mātikā. The Peṭakopadesa describes the six 'ways of entry' (*otaraṇa*—more on these below)—aggregates, elements, sense media, faculties, truths, dependent origination—and says that 'there is no *sutta* or *gāthā* or *vyākaraṇa*in which one or other of these six dhammas is not apparent.'[35] Ñāṇamoli translates this passage differently, saying 'there is no Thread [*sutta*], whether verse [*gāthā*] or prose exposition [*vyākaraṇa*]...'[36]. This is justifiable given the more usual use of these three terms in this text as we have noted, yet my edition of the Peṭakopadesa has '*suttaṁ vā gāthā vā byākaraṇaṁ vā*.' Given the very bad corruption of the text, it is unwise to make too much out of such details. Yet these mentions suggest that the Peṭakopadesa remembers a time when the texts, which all constituted elaborations on the first sermon, consisted of *suttas*, *gāthās*, and *vyākaraṇas* dealing with the topics of the saṁyutta mātikā.

36 The sequence of first three aṅgas is almost always constant, whereas the later factors exhibit considerable variation in both content and sequence.[37] This is another hint that the first three are earlier. For example the Dharmaguptaka Vinaya lists the contents of the Kśudraka Āgama

[33] Netti 89.

[34] Peṭakopadesa 1.12.

[35] Peṭakopadesa 5.53.

[36] ÑĀṆAMOLI (1964), pg. 133.

[37] There are some variations, however. According to Lamotte, the Saddharmapuṇḍarīka Sūtra has: *sūtra, gāthā, itivuttaka, jātaka, abbhūtadhamma, nidāna, aupamya, geya, upadeśa.*

(no longer existing) as: *jātaka, itivuttaka, nidāna, vedalla, abbhūtadhamma, avadāna, upadeśa, aṭṭhakavagga, dhammapāda, pārāyana* (? doubtful, perhaps 'various problems'), *uragavagga*. This is an amalgam of the later aṅgas with the existing contents of the Theravāda Khuddaka Nikāya, including several sections currently included in the Sutta Nipāta.

37 So the first three aṅgas were the earliest, or at least were the first to be established as canonical, while the subsequent aṅgas were gradually elaborated. However, it is not at all obvious exactly what they refer to. Here a little investigation is called for.

38 As one of the three aṅgas, *sutta* means just one portion of the teachings and cannot be a general term for any discourse, as it came to mean later. The root meaning of *sutta* is 'thread', and it is prominently used in the metaphorical sense of a thread on which beads are strung. I think *sutta* as an aṅga reflects this metaphor and means 'basic doctrinal statement'. This is similar to the meaning in the Brahmanical and Jain contexts. An echo of this meaning survives in the Vinaya. The collection of rules that make up the Pāṭimokkha is called, in the Pāṭimokkha itself, the *sutta*. The detailed analysis of those rules is called the *sutta vibhaṅga* ('analysis of the *sutta*'). This *vibhaṅga* material is stylistically similar to the Abhidhamma Vibhaṅga and probably dates from a similar period.

39 The early treatise on exegetical method, the Netti, gives a curious explanation for the word *sutta* in the four great references, taught by the Buddha shortly before he passed away.[38] These great references declare that if any monk, teacher, lineage, or tradition, no matter how learned and respected, makes any statement on Dhamma, that statement must be carefully compared with the Suttas and the Vinaya to ascertain whether it can be accepted as the Buddha's teachings, or should be rejected. Now in the Netti, as a work devoted to literary and textual analysis, we would expect that *sutta* here would be explained as the Sutta Piṭaka. But no—*sutta* is explained as the four noble truths.[39] These are, of course, the main doctrinal content of the Dhammacakkappavattana Sutta, and I believe we have here a relic from an early meaning of *sutta*: basic doctrinal statements, especially the first sermon. I think the Netti is essentially right here, and

---

[38] DN 16.4.7*ff.*/DA 2/T № 5/T № 6/T № 7/T № 1451/Skt.

[39] Netti 122.

that when the Buddha told us to take the *suttas* as our authority in determining what was truly spoken by the Buddha, he meant primarily those core discourses now found in the main sections of the Saṁyutta.

40 The second aṅga, *geyya*, is less difficult to interpret. It is consistently regarded as mixed prose and verse, and both the Yogacārabhūmiśāstra and the Theravāda commentaries identify it with the Sagāthāvagga of the Saṁyutta Nikāya. However, there are *geyyas* found outside this collection, too, including a few in the doctrinal saṁyuttas.

41 The word *vyākaraṇa*[40] means 'answer' (it can also mean 'grammar' and 'prophecy', but these meanings do not apply here). It is chiefly used in the sense of an explanatory answer to a doctrinal question.[41] This meaning of *vyākaraṇa* is very prominent in the Abyākata-saṁyutta, the saṁyutta on the 'unanswered questions', what has been 'not-*vyākaraṇ*-ed'. The unanswered questions are, of course, those such as 'does the Tathāgata exist after death' and so on. What is declared (*vyākata*) by the Buddha, however, is the four noble truths.[42] This alone would suggest that we look for *vyākaraṇas* in the Saṁyutta, the collection built on the scaffold of the four noble truths. Several discourses present us with a numerical series of dhamma inquiries: one question (*pañha*), one summary (*uddesa*), one explanatory answer (*vyākaraṇa*).[43] Here the meaning of *vyākaraṇa* is particularly clear. Only occasionally do we meet with *vyākaraṇa* in a more general meaning of 'declaration', without specifically being an answer to a question; even here, however, it might in fact be an answer, only the context does not make this clear.[44] In the Aṅguttara we are told of four kinds of 'answers (*vyākaraṇa*) to questions': answering by definitive statement, by analysis (*vibhaṅga*), by asking a question in reply, and by placing aside.[45] Notice that a vibhaṅga, which is a key class of doctrinal teachings, is here described as a kind of *vyākaraṇa*.

---

[40] In Pali usually spelled *veyyākaraṇa* or *byākaraṇa*.

[41] E.g. DN 11.85/DA 24/P 5595, SN 12.12/SA 372, SN 12.32/MA 23/SA 345/Skt, SN 12.70/SA 347, SN 35.116/SA 234, SN 35.204/SA 1175, SN 41.1/SA 572, MN 32/MA 184/EA 37.3/T № 154.16, MN 44/MA 210, MN 56.6/MA 133/Skt, MN 133.21/MA 165, AN 3.21, AN 6.61/SA 1164.

[42] DN 9.29/DA 28, DN 29.32/DA 17, MN 63.9/MA 221/T № 94, SN 16.12/SA 905/SA^{2} 121.

[43] SN 41.8/SA 574, AN 10.27/EA 46.8/SA 486–489*, AN 10.28.

[44] E.g. DN 18.4/DA 4/T № 9, AN 5.93, AN 6.62/MA 112/T № 58.

[45] AN 4.42/T № 1536.8.

42 This general understanding of *vyākaraṇa* is well known, but the role of the *vyākaraṇas* as explanations of the *suttas* is rarely acknowledged. However, Dutt's assessment is similar. He suggests that 'the Suttas in which Sāriputta, Mahākaccāyana, or Buddha gave detailed exposition of the four truths or the eightfold path, or of any tenet of Buddhism or of any of the pithy sayings of Buddha, should have been included [as *vyākaraṇa*].'[46]

43 Asaṅga's Abhidharmasamuccaya has this to say:

> 44 What is a *vyākaraṇa*? It is the exposition of various present existences of the noble disciples in relation to their distant past in different locations. Or it is a *sutta* that is fully explained, since it is the open exposition of an abstruse meaning.[47]

45 The first meaning here should be *apadāna* rather than *vyākaraṇa*. The second is, however, on the right track: *vyākaraṇa* is detailed explanations of points stated briefly in the *suttas*. It is surprising that this interpretation is not more widely accepted, for this form is absolutely characteristic of the Indian literary tradition in general. The laconic, cryptic aphorisms of works like, say, the Yoga Sūtra were meant to be explicated through a teacher-student dialogue. This literary style is found in the vast majority of extant discourses. Rarely do we find an exposition of any length beyond the basic doctrinal statements phrased in a straight declarative form.

46 In particular, we rarely find a disciple teaching in this way. Disciples virtually always teach in the form of a dialogue between two monks, or between a monk and the Buddha, or the teaching, though given by one monk, is phrased in 'rhetorical' question and answer format. There are a few exceptions; but they sometimes just prove the rule. In one Majjhima discourse Venerable Sāriputta sees Venerable Rāhula sitting meditation and exhorts him: 'Develop ānāpānasati, Rāhula! When it is developed and made much of, ānāpānasati is of great fruit and benefit.' This is a straightforward *sutta*; and it is a direct quote from the Saṁyutta. This association of teachings by the disciples with *vyākaraṇas* agrees with the Yogacārabhūmiśāstra, which includes the section 'Spoken by Disciples' within the *vyākaraṇa* aṅga.

---

[46] DUTT, pg. 225.

[47] BOIN-WEBB, pg. 179 (adapted following DE JONG's note, pg. 295); the Śrāvakabhūmi pg. 228 is similar, lacking only the final phrase.

47 Here is a good example of a *vyākaraṇa*.

> 48 On one occasion, many senior monks were staying at Macchikāsaṇḍa, in the Ambataka Forest. Now on that occasion, when the senior monks had returned from their alms round, after their meal they assembled in the pavilion and were sitting together when this conversation arose: 'Friends, the "fetter" and the "things that fetter": are these things different in meaning and also different in phrasing, or are they one in meaning and different only in phrasing?'
>
> 49 Some senior monks answered (*vyākaraṇa*) thus: 'Friends, the "fetters" and the "things that fetter" are different in meaning and also different in phrasing. But some senior monks answered thus: 'Friends, the "fetters" and the "things that fetter" are the same in meaning and differ only in phrasing.'[48]

50 In this case the senior monks were upstaged by Citta the householder, who explained how they were truly different in meaning:

> 51 '...the eye is not the fetter of visible forms, nor are visible forms the fetter of the eye; but rather the desire and lust that arise there in dependence on both—that is the fetter there.'

52 Now, I think the usage of *vyākaraṇa* in such passages is exactly what the *vyākaraṇa* aṅga is all about. Evidently the Peṭakopadesa is thinking along similar lines, for it refers to this very discourse 'in the Citta-saṁyutta' as *vyākaraṇa*.[49] Notice that the reply is phrased in terms of the six sense media; Citta is adapting a specific *sutta* of the Saḷāyatana-saṁyutta (SN 35.109/SA 239) to make his *vyākaraṇa*.

53 There is some ambiguity about the exact boundaries of the *vyākaraṇa* form, due to the virtual omnipresence of the 'rhetorical question' format. If we were to strictly admit only discourses with no questions at all as *suttas*, we'd be left with hardly any; even the Dhammacakkappavattana Sutta features one or more questions in some of its versions. Therefore, we will count those discourses that are simple, with a small number of rhetorical questions, as *suttas*, and the more complex discourses, with a series of questions, as *vyākaraṇas*. This obviously leaves us with some grey areas, which is only to be expected; however, we are usually able to distinguish fairly readily between the two types.

---

[48] SN 41.1/SA 572.

[49] Peṭakopadesa 10.

4.3 The Three Aṅgas and the First Discourses

54 Let us consider again the first discourses. These fall into three divisions. The first sermon, the Dhammacakkappavattana Sutta, is the root text setting forth the most basic general statement of the doctrine. The second and third sermons are similar to each other and belong together in the second division. They are a more detailed exposition of ideas mentioned briefly in the first sermon: the first commentaries. They emphasize a new literary device. The Dhammacakkappavattana Sutta is almost entirely phrased as a direct, straightforward statement of doctrine. The second and third sermons emphasize a question and answer format. While sometimes these are purely rhetorical, in the second sermon the monks actually reply; thus for the first time we hear the voices of the disciples alongside the Buddha. The third division is the Request of Brahmā, which introduces another literary form, being in mixed prose and verse.

55 This threefold division corresponds closely with the root meanings of the three aṅgas. The Dhammacakkappavattana Sutta was the paradigm for the *sutta* classification. The main paradigm for the *vyākaraṇa* aṅga is the Anattalakkhaṇa Sutta, together with the Ādittapariyāya Sutta. The third division consists of the Request of Brahmā, which is the paradigm for the *geyya* aṅga. *Geyya* literally means 'song', and is usually said to be mixed verse and prose. The Request of Brahmā differs from the previous two divisions not only in literary form, but also in content and audience. The prose discourses state philosophical and psychological doctrines in a literal, unembellished manner, whereas the verse is metaphorical and inspirational. This agrees with Asaṅga's statement that the *geyya* aṅga is those *suttas* that require further explanation. And while the prose is addressed to the monks, the verse is addressed to a non-monastic, a deity associated with the Brahmanical tradition. This is significant in that the verse style of the Buddhists evolved directly from the Brahmanical tradition.

56 So we can sum up the main features of the three aṅgas as follows.

Table 4.1: The Three Aṅgas

	Sutta	Vyākaraṇa	Geyya
Content	Basic doctrinal statements	Detailed exposition	Inspirational/devotional
Style	Declarative prose	Interrogative prose	Mixed prose and verse
Speaker	The Buddha only	The Buddha and/or disciples	The Buddha, disciples, and others
Context	Always monastic	Usually monastic	Usually with lay people or deities, often Brahmanical
Paradigm	Dhammacakkappa-vattana	Anattalakkhaṇa	Request of Brahmā

4.4 The Aṅgas and the Vedas

57 We have now covered enough ground to see the connections between this threefold structure and the three Vedas. The Dhammacakkappavattana Sutta, like the Ṛg Veda, is the prime source text. *Geyya* and *vyākaraṇa*, like the Sāman and Yajur Vedas, are secondary and derivative. We have seen how the aṅgas multiplied in threes—3, 9, 12—just as the Vedic literature multiplied in threes—3, 6, 12. We have also seen the twelvefold aṅga occurring in the Jain scriptures. Well after the effective dissolution of the aṅga system, the number three is still basic to Buddhist scriptures as the Tripitaka, the 'Three Baskets'. This term is used in all the traditions, despite the fact that only the Pali canon is meaningfully structured into three sections. Evidently, then, the *idea* of the Tripitaka exerts a fascination on the Buddhist mind beyond that of a mere classification system.

58 Other relations between the Vedas and the Buddhist scriptures are also discernable. The Buddhist texts are classified in vaggas of usually ten texts; the Ṛg Veda is classified in vaggas of about ten lines. The title *vyākaraṇa* occurs in both the sixfold and the twelvefold Vedas, but there it means 'grammar'; however it also occurs in the Jain aṅgas where it means 'answers'. We have also encountered the term *suttaṅga* to parallel the *vedaṅga*; in addition the term *suttanta* echoes *vedanta*.

Chapter 5

AṄGAS IN THE NIKĀYAS & ĀGAMAS

WE NOW RETURN TO EXAMINE the claim of Yin Shun, based on the Yogacārabhūmiśāstra, that the Saṁyukta Āgama consists of the three aṅgas. He identifies *sutta* as the major doctrinal collections, *geyya* as the Sagāthāvagga together with the Bhikkhu-saṁyutta (which is really just a stray chapter from the Sagāthāvagga), and *vyākaraṇa* as the supplementary expositions. The identification of the Sagāthāvagga is straightforward; the Pali commentaries, too, say that *geyya* is mixed prose and verse, 'particularly the entire Sagāthāvagga of the Saṁyutta Nikāya'. However, the interpretation of *sutta* and *vyākaraṇa* is not exactly along the lines we considered above.

2 One problem with the Yogacārabhūmiśāstra's interpretation is that it does not correspond very closely to the root meanings of the terms *sutta* and *vyākaraṇa*. In fact, it is not at all clear why the term *vyākaraṇa* was chosen for this collection. Another point is that the Pali commentaries include the Abhidhamma Piṭaka under *vyākaraṇa*. While this is obviously anachronistic, it is not so far off the mark, for the earliest Abhidhamma was based on texts culled largely from the Saṁyutta; however, these were taken from the major doctrinal collections, not from the supplementary chapters. This is even clearer in the portion of the Dharmaskandha that was excavated at Gilgit, which frequently quotes from central doctrinal texts

such as the Nidāna Saṁyukta, often in almost identical phrasing as the Pali, and usually refers to such discourses as *vyākaraṇa*.[1] Another problem is that Asaṅga's opinion in the Yogacārabhūmiśāstra does not seem to agree here with his statements in the Abhidharmasamuccaya. We have seen that there he describes *vyākaraṇa* as past lives of the disciples, or 'fully explained' discourses. Neither of these fit well with the *vyākaraṇa* aṅga as implied in the Yogacārabhūmiśāstra, but at least the second interpretation fits well with the GIST.

3 A closer look reveals that in at least some cases the difference is not so great after all. For example, the Rādha- and Diṭṭhi-saṁyuttas follow after the Khandha-saṁyutta in both collections. They both consist of a series of question & answers on the aggregates. The Chinese adds another similar group, called 'Abandoning', to these. These minor saṁyuttas have been spun out of a few discourses of the Khandha-saṁyutta. These are reckoned as *vyākaraṇa* according to Yin Shun's interpretation following the Yogacārabhūmiśāstra; and they are also *vyākaraṇas* by my reckoning. The Anuruddha-saṁyutta is a similar case, being a brief appendix to the Satipaṭṭhāna-saṁyutta.

4 Notice that these minor saṁyuttas directly relate to the four noble truths: the aggregates come under the truth of suffering; the satipaṭṭhānas come under the truth of the path. Now, if we examine the Sarvāstivāda Saṁyutta according to Yin Shun's reconstruction, the *sutta* aṅga is based on the four noble truths, but the *vyākaraṇa* aṅga is not. So why do these saṁyuttas not find a home in the *sutta* aṅga? There are other saṁyuttas that also fit neatly in the four noble truths, yet according to Yin Shun's reckoning they come under the *vyākaraṇa* aṅga. For example, the Sarvāstivāda preserves a Kammavipāka-saṁyutta. This contains about fifty discourses on the ten pathways of skilful action. There is no Theravādin equivalent in the Saṁyutta, but most of the discourses are found clustered together in the Aṅguttara tens. This may plausibly be explained as a saṁyutta that has been moved from the Saṁyutta to the Aṅguttara. According to Yin Shun, this belongs to the *vyākaraṇa* aṅga. But the subject of kamma, and

[1] See DIETZ e.g. pg. 26 '*kumbhopame vyākaraṇe*' (= SN 12.51/SA 292/Skt; the Pali title is '*parivīmaṁsana*'; pg. 33 '*phalguṇavavāde vyākaraṇe*' (= SN 12.12/SA 372; the Pali title is '*moḷiyaphagguna*'); pg. 52 '*pataleyavyakarane*' (= SN 22.81/SA 57).

the three unskilful roots that are mentioned in this context, belong to the second noble truth. According to the GIST, these discourses would have been incorporated in the proto-Saṁyutta's four noble truths scheme. Likewise, the Anamatagga-saṁyutta on the unknowability of the origin of samsara, with its repeated refrain about 'beings hindered by ignorance and fettered by craving', fits under the second noble truth. Or again, jhāna obviously fits under the fourth truth, the unconditioned under the third, but these are considered as *vyākaraṇa*. It is more reasonable to regard such discourses or collections as having been originally gathered under the mainstream four noble truths collection of *suttas* and *vyākaraṇas*.

5 The evolution of the aṅgas of *suttas* and *vyākaraṇas* followed a natural process. The Buddha taught the basic doctrines very often. These became collected early on. The size of the *sutta* collection is self-limiting, for there are only so many variations possible on the basic doctrines. Inquiries into the meaning of these texts were going on constantly. A very important early stratum of explanatory texts is the *vibhaṅgas*, a special kind of *vyākaraṇa* which provide the key for understanding the doctrinal frameworks normally expressed in condensed, almost cryptic form. Many of the Saṁyuttas have a *vibhaṅga*; originally perhaps all did. Some of the *vibhaṅgas* missing from the Theravāda Saṁyutta are found in the Sarvāstivāda, for example the Bala Vibhaṅga Sutta which should be restored from the Aṅguttara to the Saṁyutta.

6 But while the *suttas* are limited in size, the *vyākaraṇas* can be expanded indefinitely. It would not take long for the original simple classification to become inadequate and for new, more elaborate, structures to be required. Two possible avenues would suggest themselves at this stage. One would be to keep on accumulating individual *vyākaraṇas*, creating new collections for them out of the material spilling over from the original three-aṅga collection. Another possibility is to try to reduce the growing bulk of the texts and consequent inconvenience by assembling all of the main explanatory texts into one comprehensive Vibhaṅga to serve as a key to all the discourses. The result of the first line of development is the Majjhima, the Dīgha, and Aṅguttara, and the outcome of the second line of development is the Abhidhamma Vibhaṅga.

7 It is normally understood that the four Nikāyas/Āgamas were compiled first and the Abhidhamma Piṭaka later. But this needs some qualification. The GIST suggests that the proto-Saṁyutta was compiled first and that work on the Nikāyas/Āgamas may have been ongoing at the same time as the earliest Abhidhamma work. The terms 'abhidhamma' and 'mātikā' occur occasionally in the early texts (a *mātikā* is a list of doctrinal terms that serves as the scaffolding for an Abhidhamma work). Although these terms here cannot refer to the existing Abhidhamma Piṭaka they might well refer to some early precursor.

8 There is little hint in the early texts themselves what this might be. One passage in the Theravāda Nikāyas mentions 'abhidhamma' and then discusses the 37 wings to awakening. These form the main framework for the meditation section of the *Vibhaṅga Mūla. This is confirmed by a hint in the Dharmaskandha, the Sarvāstivādin version of the developed *Vibhaṅga Mūla material. The Sanskrit text quotes from the Saṁyukta a passage where the Buddha speaks of the 37 wings to awakening; in the Pali these are called 'dhammas', but the Sanskrit calls them *dharmaskandha*, which is of course the very title of the book where the quote occurs, and the book does indeed feature those topics. Later Sarvāstivādin accounts of the life of Aśoka say that Venerable Mahā Kassapa, the patriarch of the Sarvāstivāda, recited the mātikā, consisting largely of the 37 wings to awakening, at the first Council.[2]

9 There is another hint in the Sarvāstivādin version of the Mahā Gosiṅgavana Sutta. This says that Venerable Mahā Kaccāyana is a monk who enjoys discussing '*abhidhamma* and *abhivinaya*'.[3] One of the other Chinese versions does not mention this in the body of the text, but at the end Mahā Kaccāyana is praised by the Buddha for his ability to expound the four noble truths.[4] In the Theravāda Aṅguttara, he is praised as the foremost in those who can 'analyse (*vibhaṅga*) in detail the meaning of a saying given in brief.'[5] The Chinese extols him for his ability to discriminate the meaning

---

2 PRZYLYSKI, pp. 45, 334; cp. ROCKHILL, pg. 160.

3 MN 32/MA 184/EA 37.3/T № 154.6. The Theravāda attributes this to Moggallāna, but all three Chinese versions more plausibly praise Moggallāna for his psychic powers.

4 T № 154.

5 AN 1.197.

and teach the path.[6] This suggests that the early meaning of 'abhidhamma' should be sought among Mahā Kaccāyana's discourses. He is regarded as a founder of the Abhidhamma, and his teachings contain just the sort of material we would expect—analytical *vyākaraṇas* dealing with the sense media, aggregates, and so on. In addition, two of Mahā Kaccāyana's discourses are included in the Vibhaṅgavagga. So the earliest Abhidhamma consisted of two aspects: wisdom teachings—truths, aggregates, sense media, dependent origination, elements—and samādhi teachings—the 37 wings to awakening.

10 If the *Vibhaṅga Mūla of the Abhidhamma was derived, not from the completed Sutta Piṭaka, but from the same source as the Majjhima and Dīgha along a divergent line of development, the *Vibhaṅga Mūla may preserve some more archaic features than the existing Majjhimas. This of course would only apply to the basic content, not the existing elaborate form, which is clearly not very early. One possible example of this is the chapter on the elements. The Theravāda Abhidhamma Vibhaṅga mentions 36 elements. These are found in the Bahudhātuka Sutta, and as some of the elements are not standard there this must have been the Vibhaṅga's source (as well as elaborations from the Dhātuvibhaṅga Sutta). But the Bahudhātuka Sutta adds, after these 36, five more elements not in the Vibhaṅga. (The Sarvāstivāda has 62 elements in both the Bahudhātuka Sutta and the Dharmaskandha.) The extra five elements were added to the Bahudhātuka Sutta after it was moved out of the proto-Saṁyutta.[7]

11 The GIST does not say that the Saṁyutta discourses are early and authentic, while other discourses are later. All the collections contain a mixture of early and late material. We are generalizing about a complex process forming collections of hundreds of discourses. Discourses outside the Saṁyutta would have come from a number of sources. Some were originally included in the proto-Saṁyutta, but were moved out. Others may have been current in the community, but were not included in the basic collection. In other cases, discourses might have been passed down in remote areas and were incorporated later. Other discourses may have been formed later

[6] EA 4.2. See ANĀLAYO (unpublished essay on M 32), MINH CHÂU, pp. 251–257.

[7] Another possible instance is the Jhāna Vibhaṅga. This gives an account of the gradual training that is briefer than the usual Sutta versions. However, in this case it seems to me that this is an abbreviation rather than an archaic version.

by combining pre-existing sections of text. Still others evolved out of the relatively informal narrative and background material associated with the teachings. And some, no doubt, are pure invention.

5.1 Saṁyutta

12 We should be able to discern traces of the aṅgas in the extant collections. The GIST suggests that the major doctrinal saṁyuttas were based on *suttas*, supplemented by *vyākaraṇa* explanations. This structure can be discerned in the existing Saṁyuttas in residual form. It is very prominent in the Theravāda Saḷāyatana-saṁyutta (SN 35), where the first 52 discourses are mainly *suttas*; the fifty-third starts with 'a certain bhikkhu' approaching the Buddha to ask questions, and thus launches a long series of *vyākaraṇas*.[8] This structure is not so evident in most sections in the Pali.

13 However, many chapters in the Sarvāstivādin Saṁyukta Āgama seem to reflect this form to some degree. Thus in the Khandha-saṁyutta the first 14 discourses are *suttas*, after which is a long series of mainly *vyākaraṇas*. The Saḷāyatana, Nidāna, Sacca, Satipaṭṭhāna, Bojjhaṅga, Ānāpānasati, and Sotāpatti saṁyuttas of this collection all reflect this pattern.

14 Let us look in detail at the Sacca-saṁyutta, the doctrinal cornerstone of the whole Saṁyutta. Here are the Theravāda and Sarvāstivāda Sacca-saṁyuttas, classified into the three aṅgas. As the tables make clear, *suttas* tend to group with with *suttas*, *vyākaraṇas* with *vyākaraṇas*, and *geyyas* are in the middle.

15 In the Sarvāstivāda the tendency for *suttas* to cluster with other *suttas*, and *vyākaraṇas* to cluster with other *vyākaraṇas*, is even more apparent. Equally striking is that the collection starts off with an uninterrupted run of 23 *suttas*. Four miscellaneous texts, including *geyyas*, then intervene, and then 11 *vyākaraṇas*. Here, as in the Theravāda, the *geyyas* occur in the middle of the collection, reminding us of the sequence *sutta*, *geyya*, *vyākaraṇa*. The latter half is slightly less coherent, but still the aṅgas are readily discernable, mainly *vyākaraṇas*. Also, it starts with the biggest group of *suttas* and ends with the biggest group of *vyākaraṇas*.

---

8 In fact texts 33–52, which are represented by one text in the Sarvāstivāda, SA 196, seem to be spin-offs from the Ādittapariyāya Sutta that were multiplied to fill out the fifty.

Table 5.1: Aṅgas in the Theravāda Sacca-saṁyutta

SN 56	Sutta	Geyya	Vyākaraṇa
1–12	✓		
13–18			✓
19–20	✓		
21–22		✓	
23–29	✓		
30–31			✓
32–33	✓		
34			✓
35–41	✓		
42–43			✓
44	✓		
45–131			✓

Table 5.2: Aṅgas in the Sarvāstivāda Satya-saṁyukta

SA	Sutta	Geyya	Vyākaraṇa	Setting
379–391	✓			Benares
392		✓		
393–402	✓			
403		✓		Magadha
404			✓	Rājagaha (journeying)
405		✓		Vesali, Monkey's Pond
406			✓	Monkey's Pond
407–418			✓	Rājagaha, Veḷuvana
419–420	✓			Rājagaha, Veḷuvana
421–426			✓	Rājagaha, Veḷuvana
427–433	✓			Rājagaha, Veḷuvana
434–442			✓	Rājagaha, Veḷuvana
443	✓			Sāvatthī, Jetavana

16 But it is the settings that offer a startling, and unexpected, confirmation of our thesis. The first text is the Dhammacakkappavattana Sutta, which is of course set in the Deer Park at Benares. All of the *suttas* that follow are also set in the Deer Park. It goes without saying that it is implausible that the Buddha taught all his basic statements on the four noble truths in the one place. The settings for the following discourses have been simply mechanically repeated from the first. Exactly the same thing has happened to the *vyākaraṇas*. Leaving aside the four intervening discourses, the first of the string of *vyākaraṇas* is set in Rājagaha at the Veḷuvana, and the subsequent discourses merely parrot this setting. This conclusion is substantially reinforced by two other considerations. The first consideration is that these two discourses are virtually the only ones in the collection to have the same setting in the Pali and the Chinese. The second consideration is that most of the discourses do not have any inherent indication as to where they were spoken. They simply give a doctrinal statement that could have happened anywhere. But the Dhammacakkappavattana Sutta is deeply embedded in its narrative context. The first of the *vyākaraṇas*, too, internally confirms its setting, for, being set in Rājagaha, it tells the story of a person in Rājagaha.

17 Now let us combine these two lists, making a list of the concordance between the two versions of the Sacca-saṁyutta, expanding the detail by listing each individual discourse that occurs in both collections. In most cases the Theravāda does not specify the setting; this is indicated by empty brackets ( ). It is safe to assume that the setting of these texts was meant to be Sāvatthī. Since the Sarvāstivāda is more structurally archaic, let us use the sequence of texts in SA.

Table 5.3: Concordance of the Two Sacca-saṁyuttas

SA	SN 56	Sutta	Geyya	Vyākaraṇa	SA Setting	SN Setting
379	11–12	✓			Deer Park	Deer Park
382	29	✓			DP	( )
390–1	5–6*	✓			DP	( )
392	22/Iti 4.4		✓		DP	Koṭigāma
393.1	3–4	✓			DP	( )
393.5	25*	✓			DP	( )
394	37*	✓			DP	( )
395	38	✓			DP	( )
397	32*	✓			DP	( )
398–9	39–40	✓			DP	( )
400	34	✓ *(SA)*		✓ *(SN)*	DP	( )
401	35	✓			DP	( )
402	23	✓			DP	Sāvatthī
403	21		✓		Magadha	Koṭigāma
404	31			✓	Rājagaha	Kośambi
405	45		✓ *(SA)*	✓ *(SN)*	Monkey Pond	Great Wood
406	47			✓	Monkey Pond	( )
407	41			✓	Veḷuvana	Veḷuvana
408	8			✓	V	( )
409–10	7			✓	V	( )
411	10			✓	V	( )
412	9			✓	V	( )
416	15			✓	V	( )
417	20, 27	✓ *(SN)*		✓ *(SA)*	V	( )
418	16			✓	V	( )
421–2	42–43			✓	V	Vulture Peak
423–6	46*			✓	V	( )
428	2	✓			V	( )
429	1	✓			V	Sāvatthī
430	33	✓			V	( )
435	32*			✓	Jetavana	( )
436–7	44*			✓	J	( )
438	36	✓ *(SN)*		✓ *(SA)*	J	( )
439	49/SN 13.1*			✓	J	( )
440.1–3	52, 53, 57			✓	V	( )
441.1–60	49*, 55*, 59*			✓	J	( )
442.1–17	61–131			✓	J	( )

18 This table well illustrates the kinds of issues facing us in these studies. We have two similar collections, yet the internal sequence of texts is very different. As well as a large number of equivalent texts, we also have various anomalies: a single text in one collection becomes two or more in another collection; sometimes the texts display significant variations; occasionally a *sutta* in one collection becomes a *vyākaraṇa* in the other, and so on. Nevertheless, it is apparent that texts are frequently grouped together as either *suttas* or *vyākaraṇas*, and this should be recognized as an important structural principle underlying the formation of the extant collections. Again the list starts with a long list of mainly *suttas*, and ends with *vyākaraṇas*. Another feature is that between the *suttas* and *vyākaraṇas* are a few *geyyas*. The position of the *geyya* SN 56.22/SA 392 is evidently anomalous, for the text is closely related to SN 56.21/SA 403. The two occur together in the Theravāda, so the position in SA is evidently just a fault in the SA transmission. If we assume that its correct position was with the other *geyyas*, we can see that at least in this saṁyutta the *geyyas* fall in between the *suttas* and *vyākaraṇas*, in accordance with the sequence of the aṅgas.

19 Another striking correspondence is that, in several cases, an identifiable group of texts is found in both collections. For example, take the texts SA 408–412. This group of *suttas* corresponds with the group SN 56.7–10. It is a pre-existing unit common to both traditions. A similar situation obtains with texts SA 394–401, which loosely correspond with SN 56.32, 34, 35, 37, 38, 39, 40. On a smaller scale, several pairs of texts occur together in both collections. These correspondences raise the possibility that not merely the content, but also the sequence of the texts in the two traditions was shared, at least in part.

20 This suggestion finds spectacular confirmation in the case of the Kassapa-saṁyutta. This is a lively collection of *vyākaraṇas* that sheds interesting light on one of the great characters of Buddhism, especially in his historical role. It is one of the few prose saṁyuttas that is preserved in entirety in the Theravāda and in two of the Chinese Saṁyuttas, the Sarvāstivāda as well as the partial 'other Saṁyutta' of unknown school, possibly Kaśyapīya. Here is the list of texts, using the sequence of the restored SA.

Table 5.4: Concordance of the Three Kassapa-saṁyuttas

Sarvāstivāda SA	'Other' SA[2]	Theravāda SN 16
1136	111	3
1137	112	4
1138	113	6
1139	114	7
1140	115	8
1141	116	5
1142	117	9
1143	118	10
1144	119	11
905	120	12
906	121	13

21 The correspondence is bordering on miraculous. The two Chinese Saṁyuttas are identical in content and sequence, if we accept Yin Shun's suggested restoration of the two final texts (SA 905, 906). The Theravāda is also very close. It has two extra texts at the beginning; these may have been later additions. And one text has been moved, SN 16.5 'Old'. This text shares in common with SN 16.8 a substantial passage on such practices as forest dwelling, alms-food eating, and so on. Thus SN 16.5 should follow SN 16.8, and the two Chinese versions have in this case preserved the correct sequence. Leaving aside the two extra texts in the Theravāda, we have eleven texts, close enough to a classic vagga of ten.

22 Unfortunately, nowhere else in the prose saṁyuttas do we encounter such a neat correspondence. Wherever we turn, we are beset with anomalies and discontinuities. Each anomaly is a potential fault-line, a fissure through which we might just be able to discern an older structure.

23 For the remainder of this chapter I will investigate some structural features of the Dīghas, Majjhimas, and Aṅguttaras, in much less detail than the Saṁyutta.

5.2 Majjhima

24 There are several hints of the influence of the Saṁyutta in the formation of the extant Majjhimas. Most obvious is that several of the chapters in the Sarvāstivāda Majjhima are called 'saṁyuttas'. There is a Kamma-saṁyutta-vagga, a Sāriputta-saṁyutta-vagga, a Samudaya-saṁyutta-vagga, and a Rāja-saṁyutta-vagga. Not only does the word 'saṁyutta' occur, but also these are all similar to titles of sections in the existing Sarvāstivāda Saṁyutta. Furthermore, chapters 6–10 of the Theravāda Majjhima have titles similar to or identical with titles in the Saṁyutta: Gahapati (= Gāmaṇisaṁyutta), Bhikkhu, Paribbājaka (not in the existing Saṁyuttas, but would come under the eight assemblies), Rāja (= Kośala), and Brāhmaṇa. With the exception of the Gahapati, these are in the same sequence predicted by Bucknell's reconstructed Sagāthāvagga. Again, the final chapter of the Theravāda Majjhima, the Saḷāyatanavagga, not only shares its title and subject matter with the Saṁyutta, but all the discourses are found in the Sarvāstivāda Saṁyutta.

25 The division into three groups of fifty discourses in the Theravāda Majjhima reflects the three aṅgas, albeit faintly. The first fifty presents the main doctrines; although formally these are mainly *vyākaraṇas*, within the Majjhima as a whole they function as basic texts, in a way similar to *suttas*. The second fifty has titles similar to the Sagāthāvagga, includes a fair number of verses, and is often addressed to lay people, thus being related to the *geyya* aṅga. The final fifty tend to be more analytical and expository, classic *vyākaraṇas*, including some proto-Abhidhamma texts, the Saḷāyatanavagga, and the historically important Vibhaṅgavagga.

26 The Vibhaṅgavagga is the only chapter that shares both the title and almost all the same content in the two Majjhimas. The exact title in the Sarvāstivāda is 'Mūlavibhaṅgavagga', the 'Root Vibhaṅga Chapter', which is very suggestive. Most of the discourses deal with familiar topics such as the aggregates and sense media. Two of the discourses, the Saccavibhaṅga Sutta and the Araṇavibhaṅga Sutta, refer directly back to the Dhammacakkappavattana Sutta. (The Saccavibhaṅga Sutta is not in the existing Sarvāstivāda Vibhaṅgavagga; however Bucknell argues persuasively that it was removed accidentally at a later date). Unsurprisingly, several of the

discourses in the Vibhaṅgavagga are shared in common with chapters in the Abhidhamma Vibhaṅga. All this shows that this chapter, with its close connection to the Saṁyutta, was an early and fundamental division within the Majjhima.

27 There is one very important framework, comprising around a third of the discourses in the Majjhimas and Dīghas, which is not found, or at least is not prominent, in the existing Theravāda Saṁyutta Nikāya. This is the 'training' (*sikkhā*). This discrepancy may be why the dependence of the Majjhima on the Saṁyutta has not been noticed. However, the Sarvāstivāda Saṁyukta Āgama rectifies this. It has a Sikkhā-saṁyutta containing the basic discourses on the threefold training, which in the Theravāda are now in the Aṅguttara Nikāya. In the Majjhima and Dīgha this simple threefold training is usually elaborated into the detailed 'gradual training', resulting in many very long discourses. If all the discourses on the training were assembled, Saṁyutta-style, into one collection it would be long and cumbersome indeed. Such a long collection would readily break down into more manageable pieces to form fundamental portions, perhaps *the* fundamental portions, of the new collections.

5.3 Dīgha

28 We are uniquely fortunate to have three Dīghas available for inquiry. The Theravāda Dīgha Nikāya in Pali is well known, and has twice been translated in its entirety into English. The Dharmaguptaka Dīrgha Āgama in Chinese is much less known, and only a few discourses and passages have been translated. The Sarvāstivāda Dīrgha Āgama is almost entirely unknown, since only in the last few years have the manuscripts emerged from Afghanistan and been made available for study (although several of the individual discourses have been edited and translated previously). The following is from Hartmann's essay detailing the structure of the collection, which he has reconstructed with the help of the information in the *uddānas* (summaries of discourse titles at the end of each section), and folio numbers.[9] Hartmann says that these results are 'close to certainty'.

9 My thanks to the author for supplying me with a copy of this essay.

29 In addition to these sources, there is some information on a version of the Dīgha mentioned in Śamathadeva's Abhidharmakośopāyikanāmaṭīkā (AKO), available in Tibetan. Hartmann says his conclusions about the Sarvāstivāda Dīrgha in his earlier work based on this source have been pleasantly confirmed by the discovery of the actual manuscript; however, others have said that there are certain differences between the Dīrgha as inferable from the AKO and the manuscript.[10] Since the AKO is a commentary on Vasubandhu's Abhidharmakośa, and that work is a Sautrāntika polemic against the Sarvāstivāda, the Dīrgha used by Śamathadeva (and Vasubandhu) probably belonged to the Sautrāntikas.

30 Here are the contents of the Sarvāstivāda Dīrgha, together with the cognates in the Theravāda (Dīgha and Majjhima) and Dharmaguptaka (Dīrgha). Most of these discourses have other cognates in Chinese, Tibetan, and Sanskrit, but since we are interested in the structural principles of the collections, rather than the content of the individual discourses, I only mention the cognates in the major collections.

31 In the following tables, ∃ means 'exists in the DA^2 manuscript'; ᑫ means 'partially exists'; ∄ means 'exists only as a title in the *uddāna*'.

Table 5.5: The Three Dīghas: First Section

Sarvāstivāda	Theravāda	Dharmaguptaka
DA^2 1 Daśottaraᑫ	DN 34 Dasuttara	DA 10, 11
DA^2 2 Arthavistaraᑫ	—	—
DA^2 3 Saṅgītiᑫ	DN 33 Saṅgīti	DA 9
DA^2 4 Catuṣpariṣat∄	—[1]	—
DA^2 5 Mahāvadana∄	DN 14 Mahāpadāna	DA 1
DA^2 6 Mahāparinirvāṇa∄	DN 16 Mahāparinibbāna	DA 2

[1] = 1st chapter of Vinaya Khandhakas.

32 This 'Six-Sūtra Group' (*ṣaṭsūtrakanipāta*) was a popular set, a kind of 'greatest hits' compilation. The Dasuttara and Saṅgīti collect a wide range of teachings from the suttas and arrange them in an Aṅguttara-style numerical format. The Arthavistara, though absent from the main Nikāyas/Āga-

[10] Stephen Hodge, private communication.

mas, is found in a couple of miscellaneous translations in Chinese.[11] These are the last two of the 72 individual discourse translations located after the complete Madhyama Āgama translation, which suggests that the compilers of the Taishō edition thought they belonged to the Madhyama rather than to the Dīrgha. They are early translations, particularly T № 98, which was by An Shigao (flourished CE 148–170), a pioneer of translation into Chinese. The two translations largely agree on contents. The Arthavistara is delivered by Venerable Sāriputta and consists of 23 or 25 lists of dhammas in the style of Dasuttara and Saṅgīti, but the lists do not occur in ascending numerical order and most have numbers over 10.

33 The Catuṣpariṣat tells of the events following the Buddha's enlightenment: the turning of the wheel of Dhamma, and the establishment of the fourfold assembly. The Theravāda and other schools preferred to include this text in their Vinayas. The Mahāpadāna contains much that parallels this, set in the mythic time of Vipassī Buddha; the Mahā Parinibbāna is the complementary narrative of the close of the Buddha's life. So this 'Six-Sūtra Group' is three lists of basic doctrines, and three key biographical narratives. This makes it seem like a basic curriculum for beginners in Buddhist studies.

34 The next section, the 'Paired Group', consisting of two vaggas, contains much unshared material. However, one shared structural feature is the two pairs of discourses DN 18/DA 4/DA^2 13 Janavasabha & DN 19/DA 3/DA^2 14 Mahā Govinda; and DN 28/DA 18/DA^2 15 Sampasādanīya & DN 29/DA 17/DA^2 16 Pāsādika. These two pairs are quite similar in style, and they are found together in all three collections. They thus seem to belong together, and have maybe stuck together through the various changes in the collections. Apart from this, however, this section does not seem to share a common structural heritage.

35 This section contains several discourses that, in the Pali, are found in the Majjhima. None of these have cognates in the existing Madhyama Āgama in Chinese. Until the discovery of the Sarvāstivāda Dīrgha, this was a puzzle: were all these discourses invented by the Theravāda? But now the puzzle is solved. The two collections, the Madhyama now found in the Chinese canon, and the Dīrgha from Afghanistan, must have been edited conjointly,

[11] T № 97, T № 98. My thanks to Rod Bucknell for this information.

and the compilers avoided duplicating discourses in both collections. This confirms that they belong to the same school, the Sarvāstivāda. So both the Theravāda and Sarvāstivāda had versions of these discourses, but the Theravāda put them in its Majjhima, while the Sarvāstivāda included them in its Dīrgha. This shows we shouldn't leap to rash conclusions based on the absence of a particular discourse from one collection or other.

Table 5.6: The Three Dīghas: Second Section

Sarvāstivāda	Theravāda	Dharmaguptaka
Yuganipāta, 1st varga		
DA^{2} 7 Apannaka∄	MN 60 Apaṇṇaka	—
DA^{2} 8 Sarveka∄	—	—
DA^{2} 9 Bhārgava∄	DN 24 Pāṭika	DA 15
DA^{2} 10 Śalya∄	MN 105 Sunakkhatta	—
DA^{2} 11 Bhayabhairava∄	MN 4 Bhayabherava	—
DA^{2} 12 Romaharṣaṇa∄	MN 12 Mahā Sīhanāda	—
DA^{2} 13 Jinayabha∄	DN 18 Janavasabha	DA 4
DA^{2} 14 Govindaᑫ	DN 19 Mahā Govinda	DA 3
DA^{2} 15 Prāsādikaḥᑫ	DN 28 Sampasādanīya	DA 18
DA^{2} 16 Prasādanīya∄	DN 29 Pāsādika	DA 17
2nd varga		
DA^{2} 17 Pañcatraya∃	MN 102 Pañcattaya	—
DA^{2} 18 Māyājālaᑫ	—	—
DA^{2} 19 Kāmaṭhikaᑫ	MN 95 Caṅkī	—
DA^{2} 20 Kāyabhāvanā∃	MN 36 Mahā Saccaka	—
DA^{2} 21 Bodha∃	MN 85 Bodhirājakumāra	—
DA^{2} 22 Śaṁkara∃	MN 100 Saṅgārava	—
DA^{2} 23 Āṭānāṭa∃	DN 32 Āṭānāṭiya	—
DA^{2} 24 Mahāsamāja∃	DN 20 Mahā Samaya	DA 19

36 These discourses sit quite comfortably in the Dīgha, since all of them deal, in one way or another, with the question of the relation between

Buddhism and the other contemporary religions, which is also an outstanding theme of many of the other key Dīgha discourses, especially the Sīlakkhandhavagga discussed below. The Sarvāstivāda Vinaya Vibhāśa (a Vinaya commentary preserved in Chinese) says that the purpose of the Dīgha (presumably the Sarvāstivāda Dīrgha) was to refute the heretics. MN 60/DA^2 7 Apaṇṇaka opens with the Brahmans of Sālā hearing of the Buddha's reputation, then deciding to visit him; this stock passage is found in discourses 3–7 of the Theravāda Dīgha. MN 95/DA^2 19 Caṅkī also has a typical Dīgha-style opening and theme.[12] MN 105/DA^2 10 Sunakkhatta and MN 12/DA^2 12 Mahāsīhanāda are episodes in the dismal spiritual career of the wanderer Sunakkhatta, who also appears in DN 24/DA 15/DA^2 9 Pāṭika; thus the Sarvāstivādins preferred to assemble these discourses together in their Dīrgha. MN 4/DA^2 11 Bhayabherava is addressed to the Brahman Jāṇussoṇi, who appears, along with a number of other respected Brahmans featured elsewhere in the Dīgha, at DN 13.2. This also deals with the Bodhisatta's practices before enlightenment, which link it up with MN 36/DA^2 20 Mahāsaccaka, MN 85/DA^2 21 Bodhirājakumāra, and MN 100/DA^2 22 Saṅgārava, which all describe the Bodhisatta's ascetic practices, in response to challenges by either the Jains or the Brahmans. MN 102/DA^2 17 Pañcattaya has been described as a 'middlelength' version of DN 1/DA 21/DA^2 47 Brahmajāla, a sophisticated rebuttal of a range of wrong views. Another Dīgha-style trait is that several of these discourses deal with the gradual training: MN 60/DA^2 7 Apaṇṇaka, MN 4/DA^2 11 Bhayabherava, MN 36/DA^2 20 Mahāsaccaka, MN 85/ DA^2 21 Bodhirājakumāra, and MN 100/DA^2 22 Saṅgārava. The other discourse that appears in the Theravāda Majjhima but the Sarvāstivāda Dīrgha is MN 55/DA^2 43 Jīvaka, which occurs in the next section of the Sarvāstivāda Dīrgha. This is a slightly odd choice, for the text is quite short, unusually so even for a Majjhima discourse. Nevertheless, it also addresses the theme of the Buddha's response to criticisms from other religions.

37 The Majjhima discourses taken together number ten. Strikingly, there are also ten discourses in the opposite situation; that is, they are found in the Theravāda Dīgha but in the Sarvāstivāda Madhyama. These are as follows: DN 15/MA 97 Mahā Nidāna, DN 17/MA 68 Mahā Sudassana,

[12] Incidentally, a fragment of a Mahāsaṅghika version of this discourse also exists.

DN 21/MA 134 Sakkapañha, DN 22/MA 98 Satipaṭṭhāna, DN 23/MA 71 Pāyāsi, DN 25/MA 104 Udumbarikasīhanāda, DN 26/MA 70 Cakkavattisīhanāda, DN 27/MA 154 Aggañña, DN 30/ MA 59 Lakkhaṇa, DN 31/MA 135 Sigalovāda. Since discourses are normally grouped in vaggas of ten, these differences result from the movement of vaggas among the collections. The question then becomes, where were they moved from? In the case of two of the discourses found in the Theravāda Dīgha and the Sarvāstivāda Madhyama, that is, the Satipaṭṭhāna and the Lakkhaṇa, the Dīgha versions have substantial quantities of extra material, and the added material on internal evidence is late. Thus these two discourses were taken from the Majjhima, padded out, and placed in the Dīgha. Given that they were moved as a group, this conclusion might also hold good for the rest of the discourses, too. So the Sarvāstivāda shifted one vagga from the Madhyama into their Dīrgha, and the Theravāda shifted a different vagga from their Majjhima into the Dīgha.

38 The next section is called the Śīlaskandhanipāta in Sanskrit, which correspond to the Pali Sīlakkhandhavagga. Several of the discourses found in the Sanskrit have no known cognate. Some of the unshared discourses seem anomalous: we have already commented on the Jīvaka Sutta; this was cut adrift from its Majjhima friends. Especially startling is the inclusion of Aṅguttara-style material. Perhaps the redactors consciously used a 'principle of diversity' in assembling the texts: they wanted to include a range of different materials in the one collection, so deliberately inserted heterogenous material. This principle may be seen elsewhere, too. For example, the Vinaya, though focussing primarily on monastic discipline, finds room to encompass a broad range of other styles, from doctrinal teaching, to historical narrative, verses, story-telling, and so on. This might have been done since the reciters of any one collection had relatively little knowledge of the content of other collections. In the Theravāda, the compilers made sure, for example, that the Dīgha reciters would be exposed to key Aṅguttara-style teachings by incorporating such matter within larger discourses. The Sarvāstivāda also did this, but they also allowed room for material that had not been adapted to fit in its context.

Table 5.7: The Three Dīghas: Third Section

Sarvāstivāda	Theravāda	Dharmaguptaka
Śīlaskandhanipāta, 1st varga		
DA^2 25 Tridaṇḍin^3	—	—
DA^2 26 Piṅgālatreya^3	—	—
DA^2 27 Lohitya 1^3	DN 12 Lohicca	DA 29
DA^2 28 Lohitya 2^3	DN 12 Lohicca	DA 29
DA^2 29 Kaivartin^3	DN 11 Kevaddha	DA 24
DA^2 30 Maṇḍīśa 1^3	DN 7 Jāliya	—
DA^2 31 Maṇḍīśa 2^3	DN 7 Jāliya	—
DA^2 32 Mahallin^3	DN 6 Mahāli	—
DA^2 33 Śroṇatāṇḍya^3	DN 4 Soṇadaṇḍa	DA 22
DA^2 34 Kūṭadāṇḍya^3	DN 5 Kūṭadanta	DA 23
2nd varga		
DA^2 35 Ambāṣṭha^3	DN 3 Ambaṭṭha	DA 20
DA^2 36 Pṛṣṭhapāla^3	DN 9 Poṭṭhapāda	DA 28
DA^2 37 Kāraṇavādin^3	—	—
DA^2 38 Pudgala^3	(Cp. AN 4.198*ff.*)	—
DA^2 39 Śruta^3	—	—
DA^2 40 Mahālla^3	—	—
DA^2 41 Anyatama^3	—	—
3rd varga		
DA^2 42 Śuka^3	DN 10 Subha	—
DA^2 43 Jīvaka^3	MN 55 Jīvaka	—
DA^2 44 Rājā^3	DN 2 Sāmaññaphala	DA 27
DA^2 45 Vāsiṣṭha^3	DN 13 Tevijja	DA 26
DA^2 46 Kāśyapa^3	DN 8 Kassapasīhanāda	DA 25
DA^2 47 Brahmajāla^3	DN 1 Brahmajāla	DA 21

39 Leaving these anomalous texts aside, virtually all the discourses in this section are found in all three collections. This is the most outstanding structural feature of the existing Dīgha. In the rest of the Dīgha, most of the discourses are held in common among the traditions, especially between the Theravāda and Dharmaguptaka, but the slight structural resemblance suggests that the sequence of discourses was settled after the Dharmaguptakas in far-western Gandhārā separated from the Sri Lankan Theravādins. But in this section the discourses are found consistently grouped together, even though the sequence of texts differs considerably. The few unshared discourses mostly repeat shared discourses, so do not substantially affect the picture.

40 Even more striking, the discourses all deal with a similar topic, offering a detailed account of monastic ethical training, justifying the chapter title 'Sīlakkhandhavagga' ('Chapter on the Aggregate of Ethics'). This treatise on ethics is usually complemented by sections on the four jhānas and then the higher knowledges culminating in the realization of the four noble truths, completing the threefold gradual training (*sikkhā*). The position of the vagga is different—in the Theravāda it is at the beginning, in the Dharmaguptaka and Sarvāstivāda at the end. In fact the Theravāda here is correct, for the Vinaya of the Dharmaguptaka states that the Brahmajāla Sutta was the first discourse recited in the First Council; this text is in the Sīlakkhandhavagga of both versions, and in the Theravāda version it is the first discourse in the vagga. The Dharmaguptaka Dīrgha, therefore, must have been re-organized after their Vinaya was completed. This reorganization displaces the monastic and meditative discourses from the beginning of the collection in favour of the biographical and hagiographic; this might even have occurred under Mahāyāna influence at the time of translation. Despite this difference in the position of the vagga, and despite the fact that the internal sequence within the vagga is different, it is clear that this vagga was a key structural element in the Dīgha current in the ancestral Theravāda school before it split into Sarvāstivāda and Vibhajjavāda. This is further confirmed in the Mūlasarvāstivāda Vinaya, which says that the

Dīgha contains the Ṣaṭsūtrakanipāta and the Śīlaskandhanipāta, although it does not list the individual discourses.[13]

41 In fact, it is possible that the original Dīgha was just the Sīlakkhandhavagga. This is supported by a statement in the introduction to the Dharmaguptaka Dīrgha Āgama, which describes the collection as dealing with 'various ways of practice', which is the main thrust of the Sīlakkhandhavagga. This section has a distinctly Saṁyutta-like character—a group of ten discourses dealing with the same topic. Thus the Sīlakkhandhavagga may well have existed at first in the proto-Saṁyutta, where it comprised its own '*Silakkhandha-saṁyutta'. More likely, though, it was the largest chapter in a '*Sikkhā-saṁyutta', which was later broken up because of its excessive length. The Sarvāstivāda retains a humble Sikkhā-saṁyutta consisting mainly of short discourses on the three-fold training, but in the Theravāda this has disappeared. The shorter discourses were moved into the Aṅguttara, the medium ones into the Majjhima, and the longest ones formed a group on its own, which attracted other long discourses and became the Dīgha. These long discourses are all in dialogue form and are therefore *vyākaraṇas*, chronicling the vibrant debates between the Buddha and his spiritual contemporaries.

42 But by the time the later discourses were being added to the Dīgha, the three-aṅga classification was breaking down completely. A good example of this is the Mahāpadāna Sutta.[14] The doctrinal core of this is a Saṁyutta-style *vyākaraṇa* on dependent origination (having much in common with SN 12.4–9/SA 366). This is closely connected with a basic *sutta* passage on the rise and fall of the five aggregates taken from the Khandha-saṁyutta (this passage is connected with dependent origination in the Theravādin text SN 12.22 but not in its counterpart SA 348). This is embedded within an *apadāna*, a form found in the Sanskrit twelvefold aṅga but not in the Pali ninefold aṅga. The discourse begins with an *abbhūtadhamma*. It also contains the Request of Brahmā, which is a paradigmatic *geyya*. Vinaya material and some *udānas* (or *gāthās*) from the Dhammapāda are thrown

[13] T24, p. 35 a3 & 57 a26–7; YIN Shun (1971), pp. 720–725. In the Chinese, the second nipāta is mistakenly called the 'Sixty-three-Nipāta'.

[14] DN 14/DA 1/EA 48.4.

in for good measure. Thus we find, in one existing discourse, no less than seven distinct literary formats.

5.4 Aṅguttara

43 So if the Majjhima and Dīgha can be regarded as outgrowths of the *vyākaraṇa* aṅga, what of the Aṅguttara? The Saṁyutta and the Aṅguttara are complementary collections of the shorter discourses. While the discourses in the Saṁyutta are collected according to topic (the 'saṁyutta principle'), the discourses in the Aṅguttara are arranged by numerical sequence (the 'aṅguttara principle'). In addition to this main application within the Sutta Piṭaka, this pair of organizing principles is echoed in the Vinaya and Abhidhamma. For example the Dharmaguptaka Vinaya has two appendices, one called the 'Saṁyuktavarga', and one called the 'Vinayaikottara'.[15] We will briefly consider the Abhidhamma below. The fact that the two principles occur across the schools and also across the Piṭakas suggests that they are both fundamental. Given this, is it then possible to decide which organizing principle came first?

44 As usual, we first consider the pre-Buddhist texts. From the Ṛg Veda onwards in much of the Brahmanical literature the verses of homage to a certain deity—say, Soma, or Agni, or the Maruts—are collected in chapters. This is the saṁyutta principle; indeed, some chapters in the Sagāthāvagga, such as the Sakka-saṁyutta or the Devaputta-saṁyutta, directly recall Vedic antecedents. Some of the existing Jain texts use the aṅguttara principle, but it is not clear if this usage pre-dated Buddhism. So the major pre-Buddhist literature consists largely of short pieces of text that were gathered together at a later date and sorted out by topic into a massive architecture. The Saṁyutta can be seen as a direct literary challenge to this Vedic supremacy, taking the same formal elements and applying them far more systematically. Just as the Vedas were regarded as an emanation of Being into sound, an expression of the innate cosmic intelligence (*veda*) as a body of inspired poetry (Vedas), the Saṁyutta by embodying the four noble truths exhibits the perfect correspondence between Dhamma as lived experience and Dhamma as formalized teaching.

15 HEIRMANN, pg. 27.

45 From the pre-Buddhist tradition, let us consider the original Buddhist traditions. These were of course the individual discourses, the teachings given by the Buddha himself. Most of these discourses consist of short statements on a specific topic, where the relevant aspects of the topic can be summed up in a small number of fundamental items; for example the threefold training, the five powers, or the six recollections. So the individual discourses, the building blocks, are internally organized by topic, that is, the saṁyutta principle. This suggests that the idea of the saṁyutta principle is logically prior to the aṅguttara principle. But while in most cases thematic affinity was the magnetic force that drew these dhammas together, the manner of presenting them in lists of distinct items gives them a numerical standing. A standard style of openings for discourses is, say, 'There are these four noble truths…'. This would invite classification under either 'four' or 'noble truths'.

46 There are some discourses that use number as an internal organizing principle. For example the Dhammacakkappavattana Sutta features the interlocking set of numbers: 2, 3, 4, 8, 12. Such discourses invoke the mysterious properties of numbers, which may be divided or multiplied, as an image seen through prisms that reveal many facets or few. But in such cases the numerical relationship, though significant, is clearly subordinate to the thematic relationship. Only occasionally do we see a discourse where the numerical principle links teachings that have no strong thematic relationship. On a small scale there are discourses such as the Mahā Pañha Sutta,[16] which gives a list of questions on miscellaneous sets of dhammas from one to ten, and on a larger scale there are of course the Saṅgīti and similar discourses.[17] But even here, while there is no strong thematic relationship between the different sets of dhammas, each set of dhammas is still internally organized by topic. Wherever we peel back the skin, the saṁyutta principle lies under the aṅguttara principle.

47 Perhaps the most influential remnant of the aṅguttara principle in later Buddhism was the 37 wings to awakening. This group illustrates the interplay between the two organizing principles. It comprises seven sets of dhammas dealing with the path, which originally comprised the Mahā

[16] AN 10.27/EA 46.8/SA 486–489*.
[17] DN 33/DA 9/T № 12/Skt.

Vagga (or 'Magga Vagga' according to the Sarvāstivādins) of the Saṁyutta Nikāya. Thus the most general overall structure is the saṁyutta principle (dhammas dealing with one theme, the way of practice), and so they form part of the Saṁyutta Nikāya/Āgama. Within this overarching grouping, the standard sequence lists the groups in ascending numerical order, that is the aṅguttara principle—four (satipaṭṭhānas, right efforts, bases of psychic power), five (faculties and powers), seven (awakening-factors), eight (factors of the noble path). There is evidence that it is in fact the aṅguttara principle at work here, not some abstruse progressive structure underlying the sets. This is the second Mahā Pañha Sutta, which gives the following dhammas in ascending sequence: (one) all beings subsist on sustenance; (two) name & form; three feelings; four satipaṭṭhānas; five spiritual faculties; six elements of escape; seven awakening-factors; eightfold noble path; nine abodes of beings; ten courses of skilful action.[18] This fits as many of the wings to awakening as possible into this numerical scheme. Some of the schools, forgetting the arbitrary nature of this sequence, tried to interpret it as implying an orderly progress of practice; that is, they interpreted a collection of teachings organized by the aṅguttara principle as having been organized by the saṁyutta principle.

48 Gethin points out that many of the mātikās of both the Theravāda and Sarvāstivāda Abhidhammas are constructed with the aṅguttara principle.[19] The most important example is the Dhammasaṅgaṇī, which is based on a mātikā of 22 dyads and 100 triads of dhammas. Many of these are shared with the early Suttas and the Sarvāstivāda Abhidhamma; hence, many of the dyads and triads must be old, although the elaborate working out of them is not. Gethin sees the key Abhidhamma works as springing from the interplay of such aṅguttara-mātikās and the saṁyutta-mātikā: the Dhammasaṅgaṇī is based on an aṅguttara-mātikā, and analyses this with the saṁyutta-mātikā; the Vibhaṅga is based on the saṁyutta-mātikā and analyses this with an aṅguttara-mātikā.[20] However, while correctly stressing the importance of the aṅguttara principle, he does not really

---

[18] AN 10.28.

[19] GETHIN, 1992.

[20] However some of the Vibhaṅga topics, such as the 37 wings to awakening, suggest the aṅguttara principle, and parts of the Dhammasaṅgaṇī mātikā suggest the saṁyutta principle.

present any persuasive evidence that the aṅguttara principle was of such primary importance as the saṁyutta principle. No doubt the Buddha did teach in numbered sets, and no doubt these began to be collected from an early date. But the story told by the early texts says that the Saṁyutta is the most fundamental collection, in terms of both time and doctrine. Furthermore, saṁyutta-principle texts tend to be relatively consistent not merely in their organizing principle but also in the actual contents (the saṁyutta-mātikā), whereas there is no standard content of aṅguttara-principle texts.

49 Bucknell discusses the structural features of the Aṅguttara in some depth. Here is a sample of his findings.

> 50 The first is titled Vaggo paṭhamo (First vagga)—or, in one manuscript, Rūpādivaggo paṭhamo (First vagga, on Visible Form etc.).[21] In this case the ten short 'suttas' comprising the vagga belong together as regards both content and form. In the first of the ten the Buddha says: 'Monks, I know of no other single visible form that so enslaves a man's mind as the visible form of a woman'; in the next four he says the same of the sound, odor, taste, and feel (tactile experience) of a woman; and in the remaining five he repeats it all but with the words 'man' and 'woman' interchanged. The wording is otherwise identical in all ten 'suttas'. What the text identifies as a vagga, a collection of ten suttas, actually has the characteristics of a single sutta in ten sections, which might have been appropriately located in the Fives, or perhaps in the Tens. Now, there is a sutta in the Fives that incorporates verbatim the first five of these ten 'suttas';[22] it differs only in adding more detail, placing the lesson in a context, and supplying introductory and closing formulas. This is, therefore, likely to be the source of the first vagga of the Ones. The central portion of the source sutta was lifted out of its context, divided into five sections, and then duplicated by switching 'man' and 'woman', to yield a set of ten pseudo-suttas, each of which dealt with just one Dhamma topic.[23]

51 Bucknell notes that the ten Theravāda discourses are represented by two texts in the Mahāsaṅghika Ekottara (EA 9.7, 9.8), thus supporting the hypothesis. Similar features dominate the Ones of the Aṅguttara, and are

---

[21] AN 1.1–10/EA 9.7–8.

[22] AN 5.55.

[23] BUCKNELL, unpublished essay.

found elsewhere in the collection, too. A possible reason for such manipulation—which occurs in both Theravāda and Mahāsaṅghika versions—is simply to provide more material for poorly-represented numbers. There are lots of sets of, say, five dhammas, but few sets of one dhamma, and this may have prompted the slicing up of some texts of fives into ones.

52 Even so, there still remains the question why certain of the fives are chosen and not others. Is this merely arbitrary, or is there some other guiding principle at work? One obvious reason is that many of these texts feature the word 'one'. But not all of them do. I believe that part of the answer also lies in the symbolic resonance of the numbers. The power and mystery of numbers exerted a fascination on many of the philosophers of the ancient world; they had not become so over-familiar with figures as to see them merely as devices for mechanical manipulation and 'number-crunching'. Number promised the key to unlock the mysteries of the stars. Particular numbers clearly have a symbolic significance in the Buddhist tradition. It would be surprising if such numerological significance had no influence on a collection organized by number. For example, the number 'one' in Buddhism often denotes samādhi or 'one-pointedness of mind'. The first fifty-five *suttas* of the Theravāda Aṅguttara deal with samādhi and its hindrances, and prominently feature the word 'mind' (*citta*), a word which frequently occurs in samādhi contexts as 'one-pointedness of mind'. The first forty texts feature the word 'one', but the remainder do not. These texts are all demonstrably artificial: most of them were constructed by slicing one longer text into fragments. It is possible that this process was encouraged by the feeling that the number 'one' was particularly appropriate for a samādhi context.

53 We have already seen how some of the important doctrinal matter in the Aṅguttara was moved from the Saṁyutta. And indeed we often find, within the large-scale disorder of the Aṅguttara, smaller groups of discourses collected together according to topic, such as the threefold training, the various groups of powers, the six recollections, the tenfold path, etc.; these form mini-saṁyuttas within the Aṅguttara, which in some cases are matched by genuine saṁyuttas in the Sarvāstivāda Saṁyutta. Sometimes these form a classic vagga, such as AN 3.81–91 on the threefold training, reminiscent of the ten (or so) discourses on the gradual train-

ing found in the Dīghas.[24] Most of these are found in the Sarvāstivāda Sikkhāsaṁyutta, concentrated within one and a half vaggas. But the material most characteristic of the Aṅguttara is simple, lay-oriented teachings on ethics and devotion, and in many of the discourses the prose is supplemented by a verse summary. This reminds us of the *geyya* aṅga. In addition there is a large number of *vyākaraṇas* dealing with familiar topics such as the sense media, dependent origination, etc. About 78 discourses, mainly *vyākaraṇas*, are found in the Theravāda Aṅguttara but the Sarvāstivāda Madhyama. Some of these appear like 'Majjhima-style' discourses, and hence may have been moved from the Majjhima into the Aṅguttara. In other cases there are substantial groups of consecutive discourses in the Sarvāstivāda Madhyama that share the same number; these may have been moved from the Aṅguttara.

54 My hypothesis is that the Theravāda Aṅguttara started life as a much smaller collection derived from the *geyya* aṅga. It included shorter discourses dealing with relatively minor topics that were not included in the Saṁyutta. Its main purpose was to provide convenient material for sermons, especially for lay devotees; this function is acknowledged by the schools. At a later date it was filled out greatly with material from the Majjhima and Saṁyutta. Most of this material belonged originally to the other collections and was moved over to the Aṅguttara in order to give it more doctrinal weight, ensure that the Aṅguttara students got a complete education, and balance out the Nikāyas into four reasonably similar-sized collections for the purposes of memorization.

[24] Different editions vary the numbering of discourses by one at this point. SuttaCentral lists AN 3.81 Samaṇa to AN 3.91 Paṅkadha as having SA counterparts at 816–21, 824, 827–32.

Chapter 6

THE EVOLUTION OF THE TRUTHS

HOW DID THE TEACHINGS EVOLVE in the texts we have been discussing? We will take as the main paradigm the four noble truths. As well as having central position in the Dhamma, this framework offers a particularly clear model for the kinds of changes we are interested in here. In particular, the texts themselves suggest an evolution in the presentation of the doctrine.

6.1 Sanskrit Dhammacakkappavattana Sutta

2 The Theravāda version of the Dhammacakkappavattana Sutta, which is by far the best known, presents the teaching material in the following manner. First come the two extremes and the eightfold path; then come the definitions of the truths; finally comes the description of the 'three rounds and the twelve modes'.

3 This presentation is not common to all the versions. Most importantly for our current concerns, several omit the definitions of the truths; we have mentioned that this is the case with the SA Dhammacakkappavattana Sutta. One version even omits the truths entirely, presenting just the extremes and the middle way. The Sarvāstivāda Catuṣpariṣat Sūtra offers an interesting perspective on how these variations may have come about. Here I offer a condensation of this important narrative. This was published

as part of Kloppenborg's translation of the Catuṣpariṣat Sūtra; but I have substantially revised Kloppenborg's translation to bring out the closeness of the Sanskrit with the Pali. The teachings begin after an extended dialogue between the Buddha and the group of five monks, similar to the account in the parallel passage in the Theravāda Vinaya Mahāvagga.[1] The five monks had been criticizing the Buddha for backsliding, reverting to a luxury, abandoning the hard task of asceticism. The Buddha responded:

> 4 11.14 'Monks, these two extremes should not be cultivated nor enjoyed nor attended by one who has gone forth: devotion to indulgence in sensual pleasures, which is low, vulgar, ordinary, practiced by ordinary persons; and devotion to self-mortification, which is painful, ignoble, and pointless.
>
> 5 11.15 'Avoiding these two extremes is the middle way, which brings vision, brings knowledge, and leads to clear knowledge, enlightenment, and Nibbana.
>
> 6 11.16 'What is this middle way? It is the noble eightfold path, that is: right view, right intention, right speech, right action, right livelihood, right effort, right mindfulness, and right samādhi as the eighth.'
>
> 7 11.17 The Lord succeeded in persuading the five monks by means of this teaching. In the morning the Lord instructed two of the five monks, while three went to the village for alms. Six of them nourished themselves on that which the three brought.
>
> 8 11.18 In the afternoon the Lord instructed three of the five monks, while two went to the village for alms. The five of them nourished themselves on that which the two brought. The Tathāgata only ate in the morning, at the proper time.
>
> 9 12.1 Then the Lord addressed the five monks:
>
> 10 12.2 '"This is the noble truth of suffering." For me, monks, when I paid causewise attention to these dhammas unheard of before, vision arose, and knowledge, realization, and awakening (*buddhi*) arose.
>
> 11 12.3 '"The is the noble truth of the origin of suffering, the cessation of suffering, and the way leading to the cessation of suffering." For me, monks, when I paid causewise attention to these dhammas unheard of before, vision arose, and knowledge, realization, and awakening arose.
>
> 12 12.4 '"The noble truth of suffering should be fully known with clear knowledge (*abhjñā*)"... awakening arose.

[1] Most of this is in the widely available *Life of the Buddha* by Bhikkhu Ñāṇamoli.

13 12.5 ' "The origin of suffering... must be abandoned with clear knowledge"...

14 12.6 ' "The cessation of suffering... must be witnessed..."...

15 12.7 ' "The way leading to the cessation of suffering... must be developed..."...

16 12.8 ' "The noble truth of suffering has been fully known with clear knowledge (*abhjñā*)"... awakening arose.

17 12.9 ' "... the origin of suffering... has been abandoned with clear knowledge"...

18 12.10 ' "... the cessation of suffering... has been witnessed..."...

19 12.11 ' "The noble truth of the way leading to the cessation of suffering has been developed with clear knowledge." For me, monks, when I paid causewise attention to these dhammas unheard of before, vision arose, and knowledge, realization, and awakening arose.

20 12.12 'As long as, monks, regarding these four noble truths with the three revolutions and the twelve modes, vision did not arise, nor did knowledge, nor did realization, nor did awakening arise, even so long, in this world with its deities, its Maras, and its Brahmas, with its ascetics and Brahmans, this generation with its princes and people I could not claim to be released, destined, disconnected, liberated... with the unexcelled perfect enlightenment.

21 12.13 'But when, monks, regarding these four noble truths with the three revolutions and the twelve modes, vision did arise, as did knowledge, as did realization, and as did awakening arise, then, in this world with its deities, its Maras, and its Brahmas, with its ascetics and Brahmans, this generation with its princes and people, I claimed to be released, destined, disconnected, liberated... with the unexcelled perfect enlightenment.'

22 13.1 When this dhamma exposition was given, Venerable Kauṇḍinya attained the stainless, immaculate vision of the Dhamma regarding dhammas, together with 80 000 deities.

23 13.2 Then the Lord addressed the Venerable Kauṇḍinya:

24 13.3 'Kauṇḍinya, did you deeply understand the Dhamma?'

25 13.4 'I deeply understood, Lord.'

26 13.5 'Kauṇḍinya, did you deeply understand the Dhamma?'

27 13.6 'I deeply understood, Sugata.'

28 13.7 The Dhamma was deeply understood by Venerable Kauṇḍinya, therefore Venerable Kauṇḍinya was called "Ājñātakauṇḍinya".'

29 13.8–12 [The various orders of deities, from the earth *yakkhas* to the Brahmā gods, take up the cry to announce the revolving of the Dhamma wheel with its three revolutions and twelve modes.]

30 13.13 Thus this Dhamma-wheel of the Dhamma with its three revolutions and its twelve modes is revolved by the Lord in the Deer Park at Isipatana. Therefore this exposition of the Dhamma is called 'The Revolving of the Wheel of the Dhamma'.

31 14.1 Then the Lord said to the five monks:

32 14.2 'There are, monks, four noble truths. What four?

33 14.3 'The noble truth of suffering, the origin of suffering, the cessation of suffering, and the way leading to the cessation of suffering.

34 14.4 'What is the noble truth of suffering?

35 14.5 'Birth is suffering, aging is suffering, sickness is suffering, death is suffering, separation from the liked is suffering, association with the disliked is suffering, seeking but not getting what one wishes is suffering. In brief, the five aggregates associated with grasping are suffering. In order to fully know this, the noble eightfold path must be developed.

36 14.6 'What is the noble truth of the origin of suffering?

37 14.7 'The craving which pertains to rebirth, associated with relishing and lust, which delights here and there. In order to abandon this, the noble eightfold path must be developed.

38 14.8 'What is the noble truth of the cessation of suffering?

39 14.9 'It is the complete abandoning of that very craving which pertains to rebirth, associated with relishing and lust, which delights here and there; the relinquishing, destruction, evaporation, fading away, cessation, appeasement, and ending of it. In order to witness this, the noble eightfold path must be developed.

40 14.10 'What is the noble truth of the way leading to the cessation of suffering?

41 14.11 'It is the noble eightfold path, that is: right view... right samādhi. This must be developed.'

42 14.12 When this Dhamma exposition was given, Ājñātakauṇḍinya's mind was released from defilements without grasping, and for the rest of the five monks the stainless, immaculate vision of the Dhamma regarding dhammas arose. At that time there was one arahant in the world; the Lord was the second.

43 15.1 Then the Lord addressed the rest of the five monks:

44 15.2 'Monks, physical form is not self....'

45 15.3–18 [The Buddha teaches the Discourse on Not-self, almost identical to the Pali.]

46 15.19 When this Dhamma exposition was given, the minds of the rest of the four monks were released from defilements, without attachments. At that time there were five arahants in the world; the Lord was the sixth.

47 There are too many interesting points in this narrative to mention them all; the reader is invited to compare carefully with the Theravādin version. Obviously, the teaching sections are virtually identical. The only noteworthy differences in the content is the omission of 'sorrow, lamentation, pain, grief, and despair are suffering', a phrase that is standard in the Theravāda, but omitted elsewhere in the Sarvāstivāda, such as the Saccavibhaṅga Sutta. Also the phrases 'sickness is suffering' and 'association with the disliked, separation from the liked' are sometimes omitted in the Theravāda. None of these differences are sectarian. The most striking difference is in the structure of the narrative. The Theravāda combines the teachings into one session—the two extremes, the definitions of the truths, the three revolutions and twelve modes—at the end of which Venerable Kauṇḍinya attains the Dhamma-vision. Then, over the next few days, the Buddha gives further teachings. These are not specified, but first Venerables Vappa and Bhaddiya, and then Venerables Mahānāma and Assaji, attain stream-entry. Each, immediately on seeing the Dhamma, requests ordination under the Buddha, and this forms the thematic link to the Vinaya, serving as introduction to the development of ordination procedure. Such specifically Vinaya elements are absent from the Catuṣpariṣat Sūtra. Next, during the Discourse on Not-self, all five monks realize arahantship. So the presentation of events in the Sarvāstivāda makes good sense of the Theravāda account, too: first the basic teachings on the path and the truths were given, followed by more detailed explanation. Later the Theravāda combined the teachings into one longer discourse.

48 Some elements in the Sarvāstivāda are obviously late, such as the insertion of the '80 000 deities'; but it must be admitted that the work in general hangs together extremely well as a narrative. The two extremes and the middle way are presented more directly and explicitly in response to the critique of backsliding. Then the fundamental teachings on the three rev-

olutions and the twelve modes are given. These, here emphasized more than in the Theravāda, become a recurring theme. They are included in the proclamation of the gods, and again referred to in the later definitions of the truths, in the phrases 'In order to fully know this... [etc.]'; neither of these contexts are in the Theravāda account. It appears that in this tradition, the very meaning of the title of the discourse, 'The Revolving of the Wheel of the Dhamma', refers to these three revolutions (see section 13.13 above). Only after the presentation of the three revolutions and twelve modes is the detailed definition of the truths given. This is phrased in a rhetorical question format, whereas in the Theravāda these questions are absent. Thus in the Sarvāstivāda version the initial statement of the basic doctrine in declarative form is followed, at a later time, by the detailed exposition in question & answer form. This corresponds exactly with the *sutta/vyākaraṇa* model. Notice the structure here:

49 **1. Statement (*sutta*):** There is suffering... origin... cessation... path...
2. Question: What is suffering?
3. Explanation (*vyākaraṇa*): Birth is suffering... the five aggregates associated with grasping are suffering.

50 Now the Discourse on Not-self picks up from here, by explaining how the five aggregates are suffering. It is as if another question had been asked:

51 **1. Statement (*sutta*):** There is suffering...origin...cessation...path...
2. Question: What is suffering?
3. Explanation (*vyākaraṇa*): Birth is suffering...the five aggregates associated with grasping are suffering.
[**4. Question:** How are the five aggregates suffering?]
5. Explanation: Physical form is not self. If physical form were self, it would not lead to affliction...

52 So the explanation on one level becomes the basic text for a deeper explanation. This explanation then introduces a new field of doctrine, the five aggregates, demanding further explanation; according to the GIST, this is the source of the Khandha-saṁyutta. Thus the concept of *vyākaraṇa* is a relative one, depending on what level of text one is explaining. This

suggests that the category of *vyākaraṇa* will be flexible, and will evolve as the explanations become ever more abstracted from the original text.

6.2 Spirals of Elaboration

53 The same explanatory process is explicit elsewhere in the Suttas, too, most characteristically in the teaching of Venerable Sāriputta. Here is the beginning of the Mahā Hatthipadopama Sutta:

> 54 'Friends, just as the footprint of any living being that walks can be placed within an elephant's footprint...so too all skilful principles can be included in the four noble truths. What four? The noble truth of suffering... origin... cessation... path.
>
> 55 'And what is the noble truth of suffering? Birth is suffering... the five aggregates associated with grasping are suffering.
>
> 56 'And what are the five aggregates associated with grasping? They are: the aggregate of physical form associated with grasping, the aggregate of feeling... perception... activities...cognition associated with grasping.
>
> 57 'And what is the aggregate of physical form associated with grasping? It is the four great physical properties and the physical form derived from them.
>
> 58 'And what are the four great physical properties? They are: the property of earth... water... fire... air.
>
> 59 'And what is the physical property of earth? The physical property of earth may be either internal or external.
>
> 60 'And what is the internal physical property of earth? Whatever internally, belonging to oneself, is solid, solidified, and grasped; that is, head hairs, body hairs, nails, teeth, skin...' [2]

61 Here the recurrent rounds of text/explanation are carried out to an elaborate degree, focussing ever finer, from the truths to the aggregates to the physical properties, showing how all these 'skilful dhammas' are contained within the four noble truths. Given the pervasive ambiguity of the term 'dhamma', it is possible to read the term here as referring both to 'qualities, principles', meaning that all contemplative practice takes place in the broader framework of understanding the four noble truths, and

---

[2] MN 28.2–6/MA 30.

also 'teachings', meaning that all the teachings can be classified within the four noble truths (= proto-Saṁyutta). For the early Buddhists, this would have been, not an abstruse theory, but a reflection of how the teachings embody at a profound level the structure of reality.

62 The Saccavibhaṅga Sutta exemplifies this elaborative process even more explicitly.[3] It is set in the Deer Park at Benares, and the Buddha recalls his own teaching of the Dhammacakkappavattana Sutta there. He praises Venerable Sāriputta for his ability to teach the four noble truths in detail, and then retires to his dwelling. Venerable Sāriputta gets the hint, and proceeds to analyse the truths. Whereas in the Mahā Hatthipadopama Sutta he concentrated minutely on the four physical properties, here he offers explanations for all aspects of the truths. The teaching has the following structure:

63 **1) Statement (*sutta*):** The Buddha taught the four noble truths.
2) Question: What four?
3) Explanation (*vyākaraṇa*): Suffering... origin... cessation... path...
4) Question: What is suffering?
5) Explanation: Birth is suffering... the five aggregates associated with grasping are suffering.
6) Question: What is birth?
7) Explanation: The birth of beings of different kinds...

64 In these central texts the traditions directly correlate their historical origin with the stage of elaboration. First is the statement of the truths; then the explanation of the truths; then the explanation of the terms used in the explanation. Notice that this final level of explanation is credited to a disciple, not the Buddha himself. And these detailed explanations show considerable divergence. For example, the Sarvāstivāda offers a detailed explanation of the phrase 'sickness is suffering', which is not found in this context in the Pali (the Theravāda tradition is quite ambiguous as to the inclusion of 'sickness' in the noble truths). Much other material, too, is expanded in the Sarvāstivāda version. In particular, there is one of the most explicit statements found within the Āgamas on the Sarvāstivāda

[3] MN 141/MA 31/T № 32/EA 27.1/T № 1435.60.

doctrine of time: 'This noble truth of suffering has existed in the past, is existing in the present, and will exist in the future...'. It is easy to see how statements such as this, affirming that the Dhamma is a timeless principle, could have slipped into a doctrine that 'dhammas' (phenomena) always exist in the past, future, and present.

65 The evolution of the teachings on the four noble truths was not to stop here. The Mahā Satipaṭṭhāna Sutta incorporates the doctrinal body of the Saccavibhaṅga Sutta, adding even more material. We will examine this further in the treatment of the Satipaṭṭhāna Sutta. The main addition is a long expansion of the second and third noble truths. The truth of suffering is also expanded in more subtle ways, with the addition of 'sickness' and 'association with the disliked, separation from the liked' to both the summary and detailed explanation. There is considerable inconsistency in the way the traditions treat these phrases. Both of them are found in the Sarvāstivādin, but not the Theravādin, Saccavibhaṅga Sutta. Thus the Mahā Satipaṭṭhāna Sutta presentation of the truths clearly suggests a further historical elaboration of doctrine, although in this case the historical context is not confirmed in the text itself.

66 The Theravāda Mahā Satipaṭṭhāna Sutta presentation of the truths was taken up by the Abhidhamma Vibhaṅga in its exposition of the truths. Here we witness further additions. Instead of referring to one afflicted by 'some kind of misfortune', the Vibhaṅga specifies misfortune due to failure in family, wealth, sickness, ethics, or views. Also, 'the cutting off of the life faculty' (*jīvitindriyassupaccheda*) was added to the definition of death. Generally, however, the Sutta Exposition remains remarkably faithful to the Suttas. The Abhidhamma exposition employs the developed form of abhidhamma concepts to analyse the truths. Strangely, the first and second truths are in reverse order. As usual, the exposition trails off in an increasingly meaningless and pedantic series of questions. The only interest to the final 'questions' section, standard in the Vibhaṅga, is that it once again reflects the statement/question form we have seen evolving throughout the evolution of the texts. Here even the developed Abhidhamma Exposition becomes the basic text, subject to further questioning. In fact, the Abhidhamma is sometimes said to be characterised by this 'question method', which seems odd when we know how prevalent ques-

tions are in the Suttas, too, but becomes explicable when we realize that the Abhidhamma is largely derived from the *vyākaraṇa* aṅga.

67 The analysis of the truths evolved like this: Saccavibhaṅga Sutta → Mahā Satipaṭṭhāna Sutta → Vibhaṅga. At each stage more material was added. Some of the material added in the final Vibhaṅga version found its way back into the Burmese (VRI) Mahā Satipaṭṭhāna Sutta. This includes 'association with the disliked, separation from the liked', and the 'the cutting off of the life faculty'. This material then filtered down to the Burmese Satipaṭṭhāna Sutta, and 'the cutting off of the life faculty' even made it back into the Saccavibhaṅga Sutta, 'devolving' like this: Vibhaṅga → Mahā Satipaṭṭhāna Sutta → Satipaṭṭhāna Sutta/Saccavibhaṅga Sutta.

68 The treatment of the four noble truths is exactly as predicted by the GIST. The fundamental teachings are found in the Saṁyutta and the Vinaya. The simpler presentations of the teaching occurred first, and the more complex presentations later. The basic statement is in declarative form, spoken by the Buddha. The more complex elaborations are in question & answer form, and become attributed to disciples. These evolve from the Saṁyutta to the Majjhima to the Dīgha to the Abhidhamma.

Chapter 7

WHAT HAPPENED IN THE SATTAPAṆṆI CAVE?

BEFORE HE PASSED AWAY, the Buddha exhorted the monks:

2 > 'Therefore, Cunda, all you to whom I have taught these dhammas, having witnessed them with my own clear knowledge, should come together and recite them, setting meaning beside meaning and expression beside expression, without dissension, in order that this holy life may continue to be established for a long time, for the benefit and happiness of the many, out of compassion for the world, for the benefit and happiness of gods and humans. And what are the dhammas that you should recite together? The four satipaṭṭhānas, the four right efforts, the four bases of psychic power, the five spiritual faculties, the five spiritual powers, the seven awakening-factors, the noble eightfold path.'[1]

3 This is the Theravāda version. In the Dharmaguptaka, the 37 wings to awakening are replaced by the twelve aṅgas.[2] There is a problem here. The 37 wings to awakening and the twelve aṅgas are, on the face of it, very different things: the wings to awakening are doctrinal topics, while the aṅgas are literary styles. But if the wings to awakening are, as I suggest, primarily a table of contents of the meditation section (Magga Vagga) of

---

[1] DN 29.17/DA 17.

[2] According to BUCKNELL, unpublished essay.

the proto-Saṁyutta, and if the three aṅgas are broadly identified with the proto-Saṁyutta as a whole, then the problem dissolves.

4 There is a similar exhortation in the Mahā Parinibbāna Sutta. The Buddha, after relinquishing his will to live on, assembles the monks in the Gabled Hall in the Great Forest in Vesālī. In the Pali, the Buddha encourages the monks to learn and practice the 37 wings to awakening, in terms similar to above, but not specifically mentioning reciting them together.[3] The Sarvāstivāda has a similar passage, but the setting is the Cāpala Shrine. Just as the Pali, this mentions the 37 wings to awakening, but adds that these dhammas should be 'borne in mind, well understood, and recited'.[4]

5 Another Sanskrit version, of which we only possess this fragment, describes the same episode as taking place at the Gandhamādāna Shrine. This mentions the aṅgas as well as the wings to awakening. It is a little curious that the wings to awakening, which are teachings on practice, are to be recited, while the aṅgas, which are literary texts, are to be practiced; this dissolves any division between theory and practice, and tends to further imply the integration of these two groups. We note in passing that some of the phrases in the following passage ('with mutual rejoicing, without disputing, in unity, with unified recital...' etc.) are reminiscent of Vinaya material.

> 6 'Therefore, monks, those dhammas that I have declared, having witnessed and entered upon with my own direct knowledge—that is: the four satipaṭṭhānas, the four right efforts, the four bases of psychic power, the five spiritual faculties, the five spiritual powers, the seven awakening-factors, the noble eightfold path—therein you should all, in togetherness and harmony, with mutual rejoicing, without disputing, in unity, with unified recital, one like milk and water... (?)... should dwell in comfort.
>
> 7 'Therefore, monks, those dhammas that were taught by me—that is, *sutta, geyya, vyākaraṇa, gāthā-udāna-nidāna-avadāna-itivuttaka-jātaka-vepulla-abbhūtadhamma-upadeśa*—those dhammas should be well and thoroughly learnt; having been learnt they should be borne in mind; having been borne in mind they should be investigated; having been

[3] DN 16.3.50.

[4] Waldschmidt (1950–1951), 19.7–10.

investigated they should be understood; having been understood, in just that way they should be practiced.'[5]

8 A little after this episode, in both the Pali and Sanskrit versions, comes the famous teaching of the great references, which we have met before: when anyone makes a statement about the Buddha's teachings, no matter how learned or prestigious they may be, their statement must be compared with the Suttas and Vinaya,[6] and only if it agrees with them may it be accepted as the word of the Buddha. The Sanskrit states the essential principle more explicitly than the Pali: 'The monks must rely on the Suttas, not on individuals'.[7] In the narrative flow, this harks back to the earlier statements, implying that the '*suttas*' here are related to the wings to awakening and/or the aṅgas; i.e., the proto-Saṁyutta.

9 The Sanskrit version records an additional, similar statement. This is given great prominence by being included in the famous deathbed teachings of the Buddha. In terms identical to the previous context, the Buddha says that those skilful dhammas are to be learnt, remembered, and recited, but instead of mentioning the wings to awakening it mentions the twelve aṅgas.[8] In both of these cases, the same dhammas are found in the same contexts in the Mūlasarvāstivāda Vinaya.[9]

10 These passages support our thesis, whether or not they are authentic sayings of the Buddha. If they are not authentic, they must have been invented by the Sangha, presumably to authorize after the fact the First Council at Rājagaha. They could not be very late interpolations, for then they would surely mention the Nikāyas, as does the account in the Vinaya Cūḷavagga. The fact that they refer, seemingly without distinction, to the 37 wings to awakening and to the aṅgas, suggest that if they were an interpolation they hark back to a time when these were seen as the key teachings recited at the First Council.

---

5 WALDSCHMIDT (1968).

6 The Sanskrit traditions, including the Mahāyāna and the Sarvāstivāda, usually add *dhammatā* (the 'way of things') to *sutta* and *vinaya*, although there is one Chinese Sutta that just has the two. Remarkably, the Theravādin Netti also has *dhammatā*. See LAMOTTE, 1983–4, pg.4.

7 WALDSCHMIDT (1950–1951), 24.2.

8 WALDSCHMIDT (1950–1951), 40.62.

9 ROCKHILL, pg. 132, 140.

11 And if they are authentic, it seems incredible that the Sangha should have ignored or disregarded such an important instruction. There is no good reason to doubt that the Buddha did, shortly before he passed away, encourage the Sangha to preserve his teachings by coming together to recite them. And I believe that they did exactly as the Buddha encouraged. After he passed away, the Sangha came together in the Sattapaṇṇi Cave, in the craggy hills overlooking Rājagaha, and recited, out of compassion for the world, the core teachings of the Dhamma: the *suttas*, *geyyas*, and *vyākaraṇas* that we find today in the Saṁyutta Nikāya.

12 These inferences from the Mahā Parinibbāna Sutta dovetail rather nicely with the Theravāda exegetical tradition of the Peṭakopadesa and the Netti. The passage on the great references says a statement should checked to see if it 'fits in' with the Suttas. The word we render as 'fit in' is the Pali *otaraṇa*, literally 'descending, entering'. L.S. Cousins comments:

13
> This is an unusual expression; it is best interpreted in the light of the Peṭakopadesa tradition where *otaraṇa* is one of the sixteen *hāras* ['modes of conveying an interpretation']. It may be taken as a particular mode of exegesis which links a given discourse into the teaching as a whole by means of one of the general categories of the teaching. The Peṭakopadesa in fact specifies six possibilities: aggregates, elements, spheres, faculties, truths, dependant origination. Any of these can be used to analyse the content of a discourse and their use will automatically place it in the context of the teaching as a whole. Something on these lines, if perhaps a little less defined, is surely intended in the *mahāpadesa* ['great reference'] passages. What is envisaged for *sutta* is not then a set body of literature, but rather a traditional pattern of teaching.[10]

14 In the list of the six topics under *otaraṇa* in the Peṭakopadesa we have, of course, yet another example of the saṁyutta-mātikā. We have already noticed how the Netti treats *sutta* in the great references as pertaining to the four noble truths, which points us straight to the Dhammacakkappavattana Sutta and the major collection that it is found in. This dissolves the dichotomy set up by Cousins in his last sentence: *sutta* is a body of literature that has been patterned after the central teachings.

---

[10] COUSINS (1983), pg. 3.

15 There is a passage in the Samantapāsādika, the Theravada Vinaya commentary, that reveals the historical picture here. The passage deals with the question of how the 500 monks were chosen for participation in the First Council.

> 16 Leaving aside many hundreds and thousands of monks who had memorized the entire nine aṅga textual dispensation of the Teacher, the ordinary persons, stream-enterers, once-returners, non-returners, and dry-vipassanā arahants, the Elder [Mahā Kassapa] gathered 499 monks who had memorized the Tipiṭaka with all its textual divisions, attained to the discriminations, of great might, mostly those included in the foremost disciples, gainers of the three realizations, etc., all being arahants.[11]

17 Obviously the first group are being unfavourably compared with the latter; thus it is implied that the nine aṅga scripture is somehow inferior to the Tipiṭaka. This is implicit in the traditions anyway: since they moved from the aṅgas towards the Tipiṭaka, they must have been dissatisfied with the old system. This passage suggests that the First Council was the pivot point for this change, the time when the Tipiṭaka system started to come into its ascendancy. Although the Abhidhamma was not part of the recitation, we can agree with the suggested dynamic. Again this harmonises quite nicely with the account of the First Council in the Mūlasarvāstivāda Vinaya, for there the business of compiling the Saṁyutta Āgama (the GIST's first three aṅgas) was given pride of place, and led on to the compilation of the other Āgamas.

18 We are now poised to draw together some of the strands in the above chapters, and to paint a more coherent overall picture of the structure of the Dhamma & Vinaya. The two discourses, the Catuṣpariṣat Sūtra and the Mahā Parinibbāna Sutta, are a complementary pair. This is evident from many parallels and similarities in their details and structure. It is unnecessary to examine this in detail here; suffice to exemplify a few features. Both start out in or near Rājagaha; both involve the King of Rājagaha; both tell of the Buddha journeying; both intersperse the journey with important teachings; the Catuṣpariṣat tells of the first convert (Aññā Koṇḍañña), while the Mahā Parinibbāna tells of the final convert (Subhadda); both

---

[11] Samantapāsādika, Verañjakaṇḍavaṇṇanā, Paṭhamasaṅgītikathā.

mention the Buddha's superiority to the sage Āḷāra Kālāma; both feature divine intervention from Sakka, Brahmā, and Māra, as well as other deities; both feature displays of psychic powers, including 'walking on water'; both speak of the earthquakes and other celestial portents accompanying the chief events in the career of the Tathāgata; both integrate a large number of materials that are found elsewhere as individual Suttas; both, however, fail to fully integrate all the relevant material found elsewhere; both occupy a position intermediate to Dhamma & Vinaya; and so on. While these features imply a connection between the texts, explicit connections, too, are not lacking. The Catuṣpariṣat Sutta has the Buddha saying that he will not pass away until the four assemblies (monks, nuns, lay men, and lay women) have been fully established (on which see more below). The Mahā Parinibbāna Suttas explicitly refer to the rolling forth of the wheel of Dhamma as one of the eight causes of earthquakes; the Sanskrit even mentions the 'twelve modes' and 'three rounds', thus clarifying that it is in fact the Dhammacakkappavattana Sutta that is being referred to.[12]

19 The Catuṣpariṣat Sūtra tells the story of the beginning of the Buddha's career, while the Mahā Parinibbāna tells of the end. We have noticed above that several genres of Buddhist literature are formally structured by taking a pre-existing teaching, and furnishing this with opening and closing passages that provide a setting for the teachings. This kind of form is, of course, absolutely characteristic of the normal format for discourses: first the setting is stated, in brief or in detail; then the doctrinal teachings are given; finally the monks rejoice in what was said. Later literature such as the Jātakas, for example, provide the central story with a setting (the 'Story of the Present') in a similar way. The Pāṭimokkha rules, likewise, are preceded by origin stories (*nidānas*) and followed by case studies and analysis. What if we were to consider the Catuṣpariṣat and the Mahā Parinibbāna as constituting, in a parallel fashion, the narrative opening and closing settings for the whole of the Dhamma-Vinaya?

20 The Catuṣpariṣat gives a narrative background for the Dhammacakkappavattana Sutta and the other essential early teachings that today are found in the Saṁyutta. In this way it sows the seeds of the three aṅgas (= proto-Saṁyutta), and forms the foundation for the entire edifice of the

[12] DN 16.3.18/Skt MPS 17.17.

Dhamma. We can almost see the teachings integrated in this story starting to branch off and separate: the *geyya* verses, starting with the Request of Brahmā, are quite distinctive, and tend to occur in groups; the centrality of the *sutta* teachings of the Buddha himself, such as the Dhammacakkappavattana Sutta, is given special emphasis; and the *vyākaraṇa* dialogues with the disciples, such as the Anattalakkhaṇa Sutta, expand on the fundamental teachings.

21 Following the establishing of the Dhamma, the ordination of Aññā Koṇḍañña forms the starting-point for the Vinaya. This narrative, in the Theravāda Vinaya, merges into the formal description of ordination procedure and thus the beginning of the Khandhakas, which is the half of the Vinaya that primarily deals with the prescriptive aspects of the monastic life, the duties and so on that are to be performed. The other half of the Vinaya, the Bhikkhu and Bhikkhunī Vibhaṅga, which treats the Pāṭimokkha rules and their analysis, is primarily concerned with the proscriptive aspects of the monastic life, the various kinds of misconduct that are to be refrained from. This section begins with the story of Sudinna, the monk who had sex with his former wife to grant his parent's wishes for an heir. This episode consciously forms a negative counter-narrative to the Catuṣpariṣat material. While the Catuṣpariṣat memorably features the deities taking up the cry of rejoicing over the proclamation of the Dhammacakkappavattana Sutta, the story of Sudinna has the deities, in exactly parallel fashion, taking up the cry of the corruption that has now entered the Sangha. Thus the Catuṣpariṣat, having branched into Dhamma and Vinaya, goes on to imply the main sub-divisions within each of these areas.

22 Once the course and structure of the Dhamma & Vinaya had been set up in this manner, each of the suggested main threads proceeded to diversify and sub-divide further, resulting in the fascinating yet frustrating mass of unity and diversity of the scriptures as we have them. The Mahā Parinibbāna Sutta, as the closing narrative, attempts to pull the strands back together again. It contains much Vinaya-style material—the various sets of Dhammas leading to non-decline; the allowance to abolish the 'lesser and minor rules'; the imposition of the 'highest punishment' on the recalcitrant Channa; the ordination of Subhadda; and so on. In this sense it is a summary and reflection on some of the key principles of Vinaya. In the

same way, it reviews and emphasizes some of the key Dhamma teachings, notably the 37 wings to awakening, the four noble truths, and the threefold training of ethics, samādhi, and understanding; in other words, the key topics of the Saṁyutta.

23 We have noted that contrasting sections of the teaching may be framed within mythic settings that are consciously articulated to contrast with each other, such as the cries of the deities in response to the Dhammacakkappavattana Sutta and to the downfall of Sudinna. Likewise, the Request of Brahmā that the Buddha teach, found in the Catuṣpariṣat Sutta, contrasts with the Request of Māra that the Buddha pass away, found in the Mahā Parinibbāna Sutta. The Sanskrit makes the parallels between the Catuṣpariṣat and the Mahā Parinibbāna much more explicit and complex—far too complex to treat here.[13] This statement is not found until the recapitulation at DN 16.3.34, following the eight causes of earthquakes, whereas the Sanskrit has the full passage once only. The Pali, in between the two mentions of the Request of Māra, drags in several irrelevant sets of eight dhammas (eight assemblies, eight stages of mastery, eight liberations), an arbitrary application of the aṅguttara principle. It is, in fact, probably the inclusion of these extra sets of dhammas that necessitated the Pali recapitulating the Request of Māra; this is a classic sign of textual manipulation, technically known as 'resumptive recapitulation'. The Mahā Parinibbāna Suttas tell how Māra approaches the Buddha, bows with his head at the Buddha's feet (! in the Sanskrit only), and reminds him that, while the Buddha was staying at Uruvelā on the banks of the river Nerañjarā soon after he was enlightened, Māra had come to him and requested that the Buddha pass away. This episode is in fact found in the Sanskrit Catuṣpariṣat Sūtra, but is absent from the Pali equivalent in the Vinaya Mahāvagga. At that time, both versions of the Mahā Parinibbāna Sutta go on to say, the Buddha rejoined that he would not pass away until the fourfold assembly of monks, nuns, lay men, and lay women followers were well established and well practiced in the Dhamma, able to teach and maintain the Dhamma. (This passage, incidentally, is one of many showing that the establishing of the Bhikkhunī Sangha was not imposed on a reluctant Buddha, as appears in

[13] Skt MPS 16.1–12. The Pali has the Māra episode (DN 16.3.7), but without mentioning that Māra first requested the Buddha pass away when he was newly enlightened at Uruvelā.

the Vinaya narrative, but was an intrinsic part of his mission from the beginning.) But now, says Māra, these conditions are fulfilled: the fourfold assembly has indeed been well established, so it is time for the Buddha to pass away. The Buddha tells Māra not to worry, that he will indeed pass away in three months time. The Sanskrit adds the interesting remark that, after receiving confirmation of the Buddha's imminent Parinibbāna, Māra, full of happiness and joy, disappeared right there.[14] This stands in contrast to Māra's reaction in every other encounter with the Buddha, where he vanishes 'sad and disappointed', which is in fact what happens in the Request of Māra in the Catuṣpariṣat Sūtra.[15] These detailed correlations suggest that the two Sanskrit texts were edited conjointly, and therefore belong to the same school. This is probably the Sarvāstivāda, although it is noteworthy that in both texts, especially the Mahā Parinirvāṇa, whose main theme is impermanence, the Sanskrit refrains from any of the quasi-eternalist statements to which the Sarvāstivāda is normally prone.

24 Another example of the extra connections in the Sanskrit is that, just before the Request of Māra, the Buddha takes the alms-offering from the merchants Tapussa and Bhallika, which was the first meal after his enlightenment. Unfortunately, the food, consisting of many 'honey-lumps', was too rich for the Buddha after his austere diet, for the Sanskrit, though not the Pali, says he contracted a severe 'wind-ailment'. This immediately reminds us of the Buddha's famous illness after eating his last meal; the relation is explicitly invoked, for in the Mahā Parinibbāna Suttas the Buddha says that these two meals, the first and last, are of unparalleled merit.[16] In the Catuṣpariṣat Sūtra, the Buddha's illness is followed by the Request of Māra; then, after Māra has disappeared, Sakka the King of Gods appears before the Buddha to offer him medicine to cure his illness. This narrative structure makes it seem as if the Request of Māra has been inserted in the illness narrative.

---

[14] Skt MPS 16.12.

[15] Skt CPS 4.7.

[16] DN 16.4.42/Skt MPS 29.5–12. The Skt does not include the controversial reference to 'pig's delight', nor does it mention the illness. Instead it inserts an odd section on an 'evil monk' who carried off the 'metal pot' under his armpit, only to be revealed by the power of the Buddha.

25 The whole series of episodes offers a complex, resonant mythic fabric that is not easily unwoven into its separate strands. It is the closing of the circle. Given this profound interdependence of these two texts, it is inevitable that their conception of the scriptural Dhamma should also be interwoven. The Catuṣpariṣat Sūtra provides an authoritative narrative framework for the Dhammacakkappavattana Sutta and other central teachings; and in the same way, the Mahā Parinibbāna Suttas provide an authoritative narrative framework for the Buddha's instruction that, after he is gone, his followers should rely on the Dhamma & Vinaya. As we have seen, the Dhamma is chiefly formulated here as either the 37 wings to awakening or the aṅgas. We have identified both of these with the proto-Saṁyutta, whose existing descendants contain the essential teaching passages of the Catuṣpariṣat Sūtra.

7.1 Conclusion

26 I have tried to make as strong a case as possible for the GIST in a brief space. Doubtless I have omitted many possible counterexamples, and doubtless the real picture was more complex than any brief description. For example, I have identified the Dhammacakkappavattana Sutta as the prime paradigm of *sutta* aṅga in contrast with the *vyākaraṇa* aṅga. Yet immediately following the main discourse, the text says: 'When this *vyākaraṇa* was being spoken…' (although the Sanskrit has *dhammapariyāya*, 'exposition of Dhamma'.) To rub salt into the wound, the text ends with an *udāna*. Obviously, seeking for absolute consistency is hopeless. Still, if we reject, as we must, the traditional accounts of the origin of the Tripitaka as sectarian myths, we are bound to seek for a more plausible alternative.

27 The continuity, even identity, between the three identified strata of texts is undeniable. It reflects an intense effort to stabilize the Buddha's teachings, to preserve them against the ravages of impermanence, of which all Buddhists have been so keenly aware. Taking a leaf from Richard Dawkins' theory of memes, we can think of this textual stability in terms of the evolution of ideas. The texts themselves are not primary. They are not ends in themselves. It is the ideas, the memes, that are the driving force. The memes generate texts in order to ensure their own survival and trans-

mission through time. The surface structures of the texts are determined by expedient and contingent matters such as local technology, literary styles, and so on, and must change in time. But the memes survive. This is the only meaningful criterion by which to judge the success of this extraordinary literary endeavour: has it preserved the essential ideas through time? In the early strata we have been considering, this reproduction was maintained using the very same words and phrases repeated in the various strata. In fact we could speak, not of the creation of new strata of texts, but of different stages of evolution of one and the same text. The only genetic peculiarity is that the earlier layers are preserved alongside the later. Our task must be to peel back the layers, the delicate art of textual archaeology.

28 By doing so, though the task may seem laborious, we uncover a priceless treasure: a common Dhamma that underlies all Buddhist schools and traditions. Using our historical methods, we shed an exciting new light on a forgotten world of Buddhism.

29 For us, the lost manuscripts are not like the Dead Sea scrolls lost in the desert. The finds of ancient manuscripts from the deserts and caves of Afghanistan and Central Asia date from well after the Buddha's time and mainly substantiate, rather than undermine, the authenticity of the canons. The lost manuscripts are instead buried in an even deeper, more inaccessible place—the shrine rooms of Buddhist temples. There they remain, buried beneath the sands of interpretation, objects of worship not of study, inspiring devotion but not practice. The Buddha's urgent, repeated call was for these teachings not to remain mere words, but to inform and nourish the liberation of the heart.

PART TWO

A History of Mindfulness

This is the path of convergence
for the purification of beings,
for overcoming sorrow and lamentation,
for ending pain and depression,
for achieving the true way,
that is, the four establishments of mindfulness.

—The Buddha, SN 47.18 Brahma Sutta

Chapter 8

INTRODUCTION TO MINDFULNESS

'MINDFULNESS IS USEFUL EVERYWHERE'—so said the Buddha.[1] And in harmony with this motif, the theme of mindfulness appears in each of the teachings that make up the path to freedom. At its most fundamental, mindfulness is essential for the sense of conscience on which ethical conduct is founded; hence alcohol and drugs, by destroying mindfulness, destroy the basis for a moral life. Mindfulness, in its older sense of 'memory', remembers and recollects the teachings, forming the basis for the intellectual comprehension of the Dhamma, and bears them in mind, ready to apply right at the crucial moment. Mindfulness guards the senses, endowing the meditator with circumspection, dignity, and collectedness, not allowing the senses to play with the tantalizing toys and baubles of the world. Mindfulness re-collects awareness into the present, re-membering oneself so that one's actions are purposeful and appropriate, grounded in time and place. Mindfulness is prominent in all kinds of meditation, and in refined form it distinguishes the exalted levels of higher consciousness called samādhi. On the plane of wisdom, mindfulness extends the continuity of awareness from ordinary consciousness to samādhi and beyond, staying with the mind in all of its permutations and transformations and thus supplying the fuel for understanding impermanence and causality. And

---

[1] SN 46.53

finally on the plane of liberation, perfected mindfulness is an inalienable quality of the realized sage, who lives 'ever mindful'.

2 Given this ubiquity of mindfulness, as omnipresent as salt in the ocean, it might seem a hopeless task to isolate certain areas of the Dhamma as bearing a special affinity with mindfulness. Indeed, we might even go further and allege that any such attempt conceals a program to co-opt the unique prestige of mindfulness in the cause of one's own partisan perspective. Nevertheless, it has become a commonplace in 20th century Theravāda meditation circles that mindfulness, and in particular its chief manifestation as satipaṭṭhāna, is close or identical in meaning with vipassanā, or insight. The chief support for this idea is the Theravāda Satipaṭṭhāna Sutta, which is the only well-known early text on satipaṭṭhāna. The success of this doctrine, repeated in virtually every 20th century Theravāda text on meditation, reflects the unrivalled prestige of the Satipaṭṭhāna Sutta. Here are just a few representative quotes.

3 > [The Mahā Satipaṭṭhāna Sutta] is generally regarded as the most important sutta in the entire Pali canon.
>
> MAURICE WALSHE
> *The Long Discourses of the Buddha*, pg. 588.

4 > The most important discourse ever given by the Buddha on mental development (meditation) is called the Satipaṭṭhāna Sutta.
>
> WALPOLA RĀHULA
> *What the Buddha Taught*, pg. 69.

5 > [The Satipaṭṭhāna Sutta] is by all Buddhists rightly considered the most important part of the whole Sutta-Piṭaka and the quintessence of the whole meditation practice.
>
> BHIKKHU NYANATILOKA
> *Path to Deliverance*, pg. 123.

6 > No other discourse of the Buddha, not even his first one, the famous 'Sermon of Benares', enjoys in those Buddhist countries of the East which adhere to the unadulterated tradition of the original teachings, such popularity and veneration as the Satipaṭṭhāna Sutta.
>
> BHIKKHU NYANAPONIKA
> *The Heart of Buddhist Meditation*, pg. 11.

7 The worship, as opposed to practice, of the Satipaṭṭhāna Sutta is a remarkable feature of modern Theravāda. Here is Venerable Nyanaponika in his classic *The Heart of Buddhist Meditation*:

8 In Lanka for instance, the isle of Ceylon, when on fullmoon days lay devotees observe eight of the ten principal precepts of novice monks, staying for the day and the night in the monastery, they frequently choose this Sutta to read, recite, listen to, and contemplate. Still, in many a home, the satipaṭṭhāna book is reverently wrapped in a clean cloth, and from time to time, in the evening, it is read to members of the family. Often this discourse is recited at the bedside of a dying Buddhist, so that in the last hour of his life, his heart may be set on, consoled, and gladdened by the Master's great message of liberation. Though ours is an age of print, it is still customary in Ceylon to have new palm-leaf manuscripts of the Sutta written by scribes, and to offer them to the library of a monastery. A collection of nearly two hundred such manuscripts of the Satipaṭṭhāna Sutta, some with costly covers, was seen by the writer in an old monastery of Ceylon.[2]

9 In this atmosphere of reverential awe the question of practicing the instructions in the Satipaṭṭhāna Sutta does not arise. Hundreds of copies of manuscripts on meditation are accumulated in a monastery; but was anyone actually meditating? The Satipaṭṭhāna Sutta has been transformed into a magical totem. This eulogy of the Satipaṭṭhāna Sutta as totem appears at the beginning of the single most influential and widely read book on contemporary Theravāda vipassanā meditation. It is explicitly invoked to magnify the aura of sanctity surrounding the Satipaṭṭhāna Sutta as a key aspect of the vipassanāvāda agenda.

10 Much as we have benefited from the modern emphasis on mindfulness in daily practice, it is past time for the pendulum to swing back. This study shows without question that Buddha did not speak the Satipaṭṭhāna Sutta in its current form. It is a late and, in part, poorly organized compilation; and it is specifically the vipassanā aspects that are least authentic. In the early teachings satipaṭṭhāna was primarily associated not with vipassanā but with samatha. Since for the Suttas, samatha and vipassanā cannot be divided, a few passages show how this samatha practice evolves into vipassanā. In later literature the vipassanā element grew to predominate, almost entirely usurping the place of samatha in satipaṭṭhāna. Subtle differences in emphasis between the schools can be discerned in their treatment of satipaṭṭhāna, differences that can be seen to relate to the basic metaphysi-

2 NYANAPONIKA, pg. 11.

cal controversies underlying the schisms. Thus the Satipaṭṭhāna Sutta is interesting not because it represents the 'unadulterated tradition of the original teachings', but because it provides suggestive evidence for how sectarian adulterations crept even into the early discourses.

11 In making such claims, claims that will be seen as an attack on the authority of the most respected 20th century meditation schools, I cannot say emphatically enough that what I am criticizing here is not the teachers of vipassanā, or the meditation techniques that have been marketed as 'vipassanā', but the textual sources of the *vipassanāvāda*, the doctrine that vipassanā is the central meditation taught by the Buddha.

12 The *vipassanāvāda* must be understood in its historical context, for it is this, rather than the textual sources, that shapes its essential features. The *vipassanāvāda* grew up as part of the movement of 'modernist Buddhism', which started in the colonial era as the schools of Buddhism responded to the challenges of the modern age. This movement swept over the whole of the Buddhist world in a number of guises. In all its varieties, however, the key aspect of modernist Buddhism was rationalism. Meditation, especially samatha, was suspect, since in traditional Buddhist cultures it had often degenerated into a quasi-magical mysticism. Samatha is emotional rather than intelligential. It cultivates the non-rational aspects of consciousness, and so when it degrades it shades off into psychic tricks, fortune-telling, magic, and so on, all of which are rampant in Buddhist cultures. Some forms of Buddhist modernism did away with meditation altogether; this parallels the Protestant movement in Europe, which similarly opposed the contemplative aspect of religion. Contemplation is a threat to religious orthodoxy, since there is always the uncomfortable possibility that the truth a meditator sees may not agree with the truth that the books say they're supposed to see. However in Buddhism, unlike Christianity, the contemplative life lies at the very heart of the Founder's message. So other modernist Buddhism movements, perceiving that Buddhist meditation was based on rational psychology, developed contemplative systems on that basis. These schools, originating in Burma, marginalized or disparaged samatha and developed the *vipassanāvāda* as theoretical basis for their 'vipassanā-only' approach. The strength of these schools is that they have championed an energetic and rational approach to meditation. But with

our advancing knowledge of the Buddhist texts the scriptural authority for their special doctrines lies in tatters.

13 My claims fly in the face of virtually every modern interpreter of satipaṭṭhāna. Such an accumulated weight of authority cannot be discarded frivolously, so I must proceed with care. I will therefore make my coverage as comprehensive as reasonably possible, casting an eye at every available important early text on satipaṭṭhāna, as well as a range of later passages. I am not trying to hide my agenda. Everyone, no matter how 'objective', has their own agenda, and it is more honest to be open with one's perspectives than to pretend—to others or to oneself—that one has no bias.

8.1 Samatha & vipassanā

14 The key to the approach used in this work is to analyse the various strata of texts on satipaṭṭhāna in terms of samatha and vipassanā. It is therefore necessary to start by explaining what I mean by these. There are two key aspects of how the Suttas speak of samatha & vipassanā: their nature, and their function. Their specific nature is clearly distinguished in these passages.

> 15 'A person who has samatha of the heart within himself but no vipassanā into principles pertaining to higher understanding should approach one who has vipassanā and inquire: "How should activities be seen? How should they be explored? How should they be discerned with vipassanā?" And later he can gain vipassanā...
>
> 16 'A person who has vipassanā into principles pertaining to higher understanding but no samatha of the heart within himself should approach one who has samatha and inquire: "How should the mind be steadied? How should it be settled? How should it be unified? How should it be concentrated in samādhi?" And later he can gain samatha...
>
> 17 'One who has neither should inquire about both [and "should put forth extreme enthusiasm, effort, endeavor, exertion, unflagging mindfulness, and clear comprehension to acquire them, just as if one's turban or hair were ablaze, one would put forth extreme effort to quench the flames."[3]]

[3] Inserted passage from AN 10.54.

> 18 ‘One who has both, established in these beneficial qualities should make further effort for the evaporation of defilements.’[4]
>
> 19 ‘Just as if, Nandaka, there was a four-legged animal with one leg stunted and short, it would thus be unfulfilled in that factor; so too, a monk who is faithful and virtuous but does not gain samatha of the heart within himself is unfulfilled in that factor. That factor should be fulfilled by him... A monk who has these three but no vipassanā into principles pertaining to higher understanding is unfulfilled in that factor. That factor should be fulfilled by him.’[5]

20 The description of vipassanā mentions the seeing, exploring and discerning of activities (*saṅkhārā*). The mention of ‘activities’ here implies the three characteristics—impermanence, suffering, not-self—of phenomena, conditioned according to dependent origination. The meditative discernment of the nature of conditioned reality is the core meaning of vipassanā. While this definition may be too narrow for some contexts, still vipassanā is commonly used in this sense in the Suttas and in the present day.

21 Samatha is the steadying, settling, and unifying of the mind.

> 22 ‘How does he steady his mind within himself, settle it, unify it, and concentrate it in samādhi? Here, Ānanda, he enters and abides in the first jhāna... second jhāna... third jhāna... fourth jhāna.’[6]

23 Here, as in virtually all central doctrinal contexts in the early texts, samatha or samādhi is the four jhānas. We must therefore conclude that the four jhānas are an essential, intrinsic part of the path. Establishing these points formed the burden of the argument of *A Swift Pair of Messengers*, so I won’t repeat the reasons here. It is necessary to mention this, however, for anyone who persists in the very common practice of interpreting early texts on samādhi in terms of the commentarial ideas of ‘access samādhi’ and ‘momentary samādhi’ will certainly misinterpret the present work, and, I believe, will also misinterpret the Suttas.

24 The second mode of treating samatha and vipassanā is in terms of their function, that is, the results of the practice.

> 25 ‘Monks, these two principles share in realization. What two? Samatha and vipassanā.

---

[4] AN 4.94.

[5] AN 9.4.

[6] MN 122.7–8; cp. MN 19.8–10, MN 4.22–26, SN 40.1.

> 26 'When samatha is developed, what purpose is achieved? The mind is developed. When the mind is developed, what purpose is achieved? Lust is abandoned.
>
> 27 'When vipassanā is developed, what purpose is achieved? Understanding is developed. When understanding is developed, what purpose is achieved? Ignorance is abandoned.
>
> 28 'Monks, the mind tainted by lust is not released; understanding tainted by ignorance is not developed. Thus the release of heart is due to the fading away of lust; the release by understanding is due to the fading away of ignorance.'[7]

29 Thus the purpose of samatha is to alleviate lust, which here stands for all emotional defilements, whereas vipassanā eliminates ignorance, that is, intelligential defilements. Both of these key Sutta passages strongly emphasize the complementary, integrative nature of these two aspects of meditation. While there is a clear conceptual distinction, they are not divided up into two separate baskets (still less into two separate meditation centres!). The early texts never classify the various meditation themes into either samatha or vipassanā. They are not two different kinds of meditation; rather, they are qualities of the mind that should be developed. Broadly speaking, samatha refers to the emotional aspects of our minds, the heart qualities such as peace, compassion, love, bliss. Vipassanā refers to the wisdom qualities such as understanding, discrimination, discernment. Samatha soothes the emotional defilements such as greed and anger, while vipassanā pierces with understanding the darkness of delusion. It is apparent that all meditation requires both of these qualities, so as we disentangle them we remain in the twilight zone of emphasis and perspective, avoiding the easy clarity of black-&-white absolutes.

[7] AN 2:3.10.

Chapter 9

PREVIOUS STUDIES

MANY SCHOLARS HAVE STUDIED and commented on the various versions of the Satipaṭṭhāna Sutta. I have learned something from each of these, and any virtue in my work is solely because I stand on such broad and strong shoulders. I try to avoid repeating topics that have already been well-treated, except where re-evaluation is necessary in light of the special methods and materials of the current work. A survey of the general writings on satipaṭṭhāna would be a pleasant but over-long task, but we may briefly survey those who have undertaken comparative and historical studies.

9.1 Von Hinüber

2 Oskar von Hinüber hinted at some of the issues involved:

> 3 More complicated is the relation of the Satipaṭṭhāna Saṁyutta, SN V141–192 to the Satipaṭṭhānasuttantas found in DN № 22 Mahāsatipaṭṭhānasuttanta and MN № 10 Satipaṭṭhānasuttanta, which deserves a detailed study, because it seems that sometimes SN has preserved smaller parts from which larger units were built, or pieces of texts, which for some reason or other were not incorporated into the larger suttantas.[1]

[1] VON HINÜBER, pg 37.

9.2 Anālayo

4 Venerable Anālayo has published a full-scale study of satipaṭṭhāna, titled *Satipaṭṭhāna: The Direct Path to Realization*. This is a valuable work, which ably discusses most of the practical and theoretical issues in the study of satipaṭṭhāna. The author draws from a vast spectrum of sources, showing a warm appreciation for the perspectives opened up by different scholars and meditators. Anālayo is influenced by the vipassanā interpretation of satipaṭṭhāna, but his presentation is refreshingly moderate. He does no more than hint at the possible implications of a historical analysis of the subject:

> 5 But the detailed instructions found in the Mahā Satipaṭṭhāna Sutta and the Satipaṭṭhāna Sutta apparently belong to a later period, when the Buddha's teaching had spread from the Ganges valley to the distant Kammāsadhamma in the Kuru country, where both discourses were spoken.[2]

6 It is indeed strange that such an important teaching should have been given only in such an obscure, far-away town. (The Kuru country is near present-day Delhi, and marks the extreme western limit of the Buddha's wanderings). Stranger still that the discourse would have been given twice, with only the expansion of one section differentiating them. In fact, it is not merely strange but incredible that the Buddha should have taught only the basic pericope in all his years at Sāvatthī, etc., and in one of his rare visits to the border countries he gave such a vastly elaborated teaching, not once but twice. Were the students in the main centres to be left high and dry for all those years, deprived of the key for fully understanding satipaṭṭhāna? This reinforces our contention that the shorter, mainstream teachings on satipaṭṭhāna found especially in the Saṁyutta should be more closely examined, and that the longer discourses should be seen in this light.

7 Although Anālayo is aware of the different versions of the satipaṭṭhāna material, his focus remains firmly on the Theravāda Satipaṭṭhāna Sutta.[3] For example, the comparison of the contents of the body contemplation

[2] ANĀLAYO, pg. 16.

[3] Since completing the study of satipaṭṭhāna, Venerable Anālayo has undertaken a systematic comparative study of all the suttas in the Majjhima Nikāya with their Chinese

shows, as we shall see later, that certain exercises, particularly the investigation of the parts of the body, are common to all traditions, while other exercises are particular to certain traditions. Anālayo remarks:

> 8 The reasons for the omissions are open to conjecture, but what remains of the unanimously accepted core of the contemplation of the body in all the different versions is a thorough investigation of its anatomical constitution.[4]

9 The very fact that the investigation of the body parts is unanimously accepted suggests that the other meditative exercises are more likely to be additions than omissions. If the traditions inherited a common list of meditation practices, and some subsequently were lost, there is no reason why some exercises would be left out rather than others, and therefore no reason why there should be a certain practice preserved with complete consistency. Or again if there was no common core, and all the detailed lists were invented independently by the traditions, there would seem no reason for such consistent features. Another problem is that some of the exercises, especially in the Sarvāstivāda Smṛtyupasthāna Sūtra, are clearly anomalous and best understood as additions. While undoubtedly conjectural, the most reasonable way of explaining both the similarities and the differences is that there was a simpler, common root text, elaborated in somewhat divergent manner by the schools.

9.3 Thích Nhất Hạnh

10 Thích Nhất Hạnh has published full translations of all three major versions of the Satipaṭṭhāna Sutta in his *Transformation and Healing*. The translations, by him and Annabel Laity, offer an invaluable and almost unique opportunity to compare in English a major Sutta in recensions from three different schools. However the translations sometimes bend too far to accommodate the translators' ideas. Some comments on the texts are included, but the main orientation of the book is practical, so he does not

---

and other cognates. He has been kind enough to share with me some of his draft studies. This includes a comparative study on the Satipaṭṭhāna Sutta, covering much the same material as this work from a somewhat different angle.

4 ANĀLAYO, pg. 121.

pursue textual questions in great depth. The most relevant passage in our current context is this.

> 11 Other differences in the second version [Sarvāstivāda] are teachings on the kind of concentration which gives birth to joy and happiness, which is equivalent to the first jhāna, and a concentration which abandons joy but maintains happiness, which is equivalent to the second jhāna, as well as meditations on purity, clear light, and signs. All this is evidence that the practice of the four jhānas had already begun to infiltrate the *Sūtra Piṭaka*, although discretely. By the time of the third version [Mahāsaṅghika], the practice of the jhānas is mentioned quite openly, by name. The meditation which observes the pure light can be seen as announcing the first steps in the formation of Pure Land Buddhism, and the meditation on the sign will be developed in the use of the kasiṇa, a symbolic image visualized as a point of concentration.

12 Apparently Thích Nhất Hạnh believes that the jhānas were a later infiltration into Buddhism; this would entail that all of the hundreds of discourses mentioning jhānas in the canons were composed later than the current text. He offers no evidence for this extraordinary view. His comments here almost all miss the point, simply because he assumes that the current text, the Sarvāstivāda Smṛtyupasthāna Sūtra, is the original source of these various practices. However they are all found elsewhere in the canons and the current text is probably a somewhat later compilation. His association of the perception of light with Pure Land is far-fetched; the perception of light is the standard remedy for sloth & torpor, and surely the origins of Pure Land should be sought rather among the devotional passages in the early discourses, particularly the practice of the 'recollection of the Buddha' (*buddhānussati*). Again, his comment regarding the 'meditation on the sign' misses the point, for he apparently has been misled by the translation into thinking that the practice described is visualization, whereas comparison with the Pali version shows that it in fact refers to reviewing of jhāna.[5] Thus, however beneficial Thích Nhất Hạnh's practical advice may be, his textual analysis is not very useful for a historical inquiry.

---

[5] AN 5.28.

9.4 Ṭhānissaro

13 Ṭhānissaro Bhikkhu discusses the issues briefly in *The Wings to Awakening*. He renders 'dhammas' in satipaṭṭhāna as 'mental qualities' rather than 'phenomena', since he believes that the various groups of dhammas are chiefly variations on the abandoning of the hindrances and the development of the awakening-factors. He mentions the Vibhaṅga and the Sarvāstivāda version as historical support for this argument. However he retains a typically reserved attitude towards the possibility of reconstructing a projected original text. While it is certainly true that the main factors in the fourth satipaṭṭhāna are mental qualities, other aspects of satipaṭṭhāna are also mental qualities, such as feelings, so this does not serve to adequately distinguish the meaning here. Below we will see that the most significant difference between the fourth satipaṭṭhāna and the rest is that it treats of causality, so if I were to translate dhammas here I would use 'principles'.

9.5 Thích Minh Châu

14 Thích Minh Châu furnishes some details of the Sarvāstivāda Smṛtyupasthāna Sūtra in his invaluable work *The Chinese Madhyama Āgama and the Pali Majjhima Nikāya* He points out that satipaṭṭhāna is the only group of the 37 wings to awakening to exhibit any noteworthy variation between the Sarvāstivāda and Theravāda. But he overlooks the importance of the differences when he remarks: 'Both versions offer almost the same materials, as the basic approach to the contemplations is identical.' It is therefore necessary to modify his conclusion that: 'both versions were derived from the same source but the selection of details was left to the compilers more or less freely.' As Thích Minh Châu has himself demonstrated in several other contexts, the differences in arrangement are not 'free', but reflect the emerging doctrinal stances of the two schools.

9.6 Gethin

15 R.M.L. Gethin in his *The Buddhist Path to Awakening*, notes some of the divergences between the various versions of the Satipaṭṭhāna Sutta, and says that:

> 16 This has led some scholars, such as Schmithausen and Bronkhorst, to speculate on the nature of the 'original' specification of the first and fourth satipaṭṭhānas: the former suggests that watching the body originally consisted only of watching the postures of the body, and the latter (following the [Abhidhamma] Vibhaṅga) suggests that it consisted only of watching the different parts of the body. Much of their discussion is at best highly speculative, and at worst misconceived.
>
> 17 Schmithausen, for example, suggests that the redactors of the Pali canon have put the watching of breath first because in some canonical texts, such as the Ānāpānasati Sutta, it is presented as the preliminary stage of the four satipaṭṭhānas. This is a misunderstanding. As we have seen, in the Ānāpānasati Sutta watching the breathing is not a preliminary of the satipaṭṭhānas, it actually is the satipaṭṭhānas.[6]

18 In defence of speculation, bold hypotheses are essential for the advancement of knowledge; but they must be tempered by a cautious evaluation of evidence. Gethin's observation that ānāpānasati *is* satipaṭṭhāna is correct; but Schmithausen's error is understandable, for he may have been influenced by Sarvāstivādin texts such as the Abhidharmakośa, which, as we shall see, do indeed treat ānāpānasati as a preliminary to satipaṭṭhāna. Schmithausen's article is in German, of which I know none, but I have kindly been supplied with a summary by Roderick Bucknell. I rely on this for the remarks below, and hope that I do not misrepresent the author.

9.7 Schmithausen

19 Schmithausen considers the three extant versions of the Satipaṭṭhāna Sutta. He does not take the Abhidhamma texts into account; if he had done so, he may have reached different conclusions. He notes, correctly, that the section in the Satipaṭṭhāna Suttas dealing with the feelings and the

[6] GETHIN, pg. 59. Gethin cites SCHMITHAUSEN (1976) pp. 241–66 and BRONKHORST (1985) pp. 309–12.

mind are similar in all versions (as indeed they are in the Abhidhamma, too). He then notes that they share a similar phrasing, for example: 'When feeling a pleasant feeling, one understands: "I feel a pleasant feeling".' He assumes that the other sections in the original version would have had a similar structure. Certain of the sections in the Pali text do share a similar format. In the contemplation of postures, for example, it says: 'When going, one understands "I am going"; when standing one understands "I am standing"...' and so on. But other passages, especially some of the exercises in body contemplation, are phrased in a different manner; for example, unlike the sections on feelings and the mind, they are illustrated with similes. Schmithausen believes that these were unlikely to have been authentic.

20 However, the fact that the exercises do not consistently have similes would, at the most, suggest that the similes were added; in addition, one could argue that similes are appropriate for these meditations, which have an aspect of visualization. Another point is that the sections on the parts of the body and the elements, though not formally identical with the contemplation of feelings and mind, do correlate well with the basic satipaṭṭhāna formula. One is advised to 'review this very body...' (*imam'eva kāyaṁ... paccavekkhati*). The emphatic *imam'eva kāyaṁ* ('this very body') is reminiscent of the repetitive *kāye kāya-...* ('a body in the body...'); and the ocular *paccavekkhati* ('reviews') is similar to *-anupassī* ('contemplates'). Elsewhere the contemplation of the parts of the body is summed up like this: 'Thus one dwells contemplating ugliness in this body' (*iti imasmiṁ kāye asubhānupassī viharati*).[7] This is similar to the standard satipaṭṭhāna formula, 'one dwells contemplating a body in the body...' (*kāye kāyānupassī viharati*). These close parallels in the manner of phrasing of the practices clearly indicate that these passages are describing similar kinds of things. These considerations do not, in and of themselves, prove that the contemplation of the parts of the body was originally part of the Satipaṭṭhāna Sutta, but they are sufficient to establish that such practices at least fit in with the general manner of presenting satipaṭṭhāna.

21 In any case, Schmithausen concludes that the original text consisted of the passages that are formally congruent with the contemplations of

---

[7] AN 10.60/Tibetan (Peking edition, Otani reprint, Tokyo 1956) 754.

the feelings and the mind; namely, the awareness of the four postures in body contemplation, and the sections on the hindrances, sense media, and awakening-factors in contemplation of dhammas. He also concludes, I think rightly, that the 'vipassanā refrain' (contemplation of principles of origination and dissolution) of the Theravāda Satipaṭṭhāna Sutta was not original. He adduces various other supports for his conclusions, primarily the agreement between the different recensions. This does indeed offer support for some of his conclusions, especially as regards the contemplation of dhammas; but he rejects the section on the parts of the body even though it occurs in all three of his texts (and the Abhidhammas). Thus Schmithausen is prepared to stick by his formal analysis against the universal testimony of the texts. This is going too far. I would say that the fact that the texts do not correspond with the analysis suggests there is something wrong, or at least incomplete, with the analysis.

22 Schmithausen believes that the original text would have been phrased in a consistent style. However, the Abhidhamma texts employ a more consistent, rigorous style than the Suttas, so the congruent sections could be dismissed as evidence of later scholastic formalism. So I think his criterion of stylistic consistency is merely suggestive, and cannot carry enough weight to support any solid conclusions.

23 There is, however, an analysis of the meaning of the texts that Schmithausen employs parallel to his purely formal analysis; and it is here, I believe, that his deeper agenda is revealed. He says that the sections on feelings and mind, which are established as authentic by textual agreement, describe a practice of non-judgmental awareness, simply knowing the situation as it is, without evaluating it or attempting to change it. He also says that this is how the essence of mindfulness practice is portrayed in the opening paragraph of the Satipaṭṭhāna Sutta. This claim is in agreement with almost every modern exposition of satipaṭṭhāna—and I think it is wrong. A monk once remarked to me in this connection that we are more influenced by Krishnamurti than by the Buddha; perhaps a greater influence than both of these has been *Zen and the Art of Motorcycle Maintenance*. It is important to be clear on this point, for otherwise the significance of much the discussion to follow will be misconstrued. Here are a few objections to this view.

24 1) The most obvious, and probably most important, objection to the idea that satipaṭṭhāna is essentially a system of choiceless awareness is simply the fact that there are four satipaṭṭhānas. One is obviously supposed, in some sense or another, to choose one of these four as a framework for meditation. One has to judge, discriminate, and direct the mind, at least to some extent, even just to stay within the domain of one's meditation. Nowhere do the early texts imply that the four frameworks may be neglected or promiscuously mixed, and nowhere is satipaṭṭhāna described as just 'being aware of whatever arises in the present moment'. We shall see that as this idea gained hold during the historical evolution of satipaṭṭhāna the importance of the division into four sections becomes marginalized. In fact, the practice of 'being aware of whatever arises' is in the Suttas called 'clear comprehension' (*sampajañña*), not satipaṭṭhāna.

25 2) Schmithausen concludes that the sections dealing with body contemplation were later interpolations, because they involve a more directed kind of meditation. However this fact corresponds with a well-known principle of meditation. In the beginning stages the hindrances are likely to be strong and mindfulness weak, so the wise meditator will direct and hold awareness with some strength onto a chosen object. As the hindrances weaken and mindfulness grows strong, one can gradually let go more and more until finally one relinquishes all control and enters samādhi. The pattern of the Satipaṭṭhāna Sutta precisely mirrors this principle. It is thus plausible to interpret the variations in the style of the various exercises, not as evidence of textual corruption, but as indicating different approaches suitable for different progressive stages of meditation.

26 3) Several Suttas clearly suggest the use of choice and judgment within the context of satipaṭṭhāna. In fact, there is even a discourse in the Saṁyutta that explicitly describes how to develop satipaṭṭhāna in both 'directed' and 'undirected' modes.[8] As suggested above, the undirected mode of satipaṭṭhāna is relevant for one who has already dispelled the hindrances through the attainment of samādhi.

27 4) I do not know on what grounds Schmithausen believes that the opening paragraph of the Satipaṭṭhāna Sutta, which is of course the stock description of satipaṭṭhāna, portrays a practice of direct nonjudgmental

[8] SN 47.10.

observation. The most likely reason would be the use of the term *anupassanā*. I will show later that a close investigation of the meaning of this term does not justify this conclusion. Suffice to note here that, although Schmithausen believes that such choiceless awareness is incompatible with such practices as the meditation on ugliness (*asubha*), in fact the phrase *asubhānupassī* occurs several times in the canon.[9]

28 Schmithausen was a pioneer, and while I disagree with some of his arguments, he must be given credit for bringing these textual variations to light. In fact, although each of the scholars mentioned above might disagree on details, all of them agree on a number of important points. Firstly, that the texts as we have them are the outcome of a historical process. Secondly, that there is no *a priori* reason to assume that the Pali tradition, or any other tradition, is the authentic one. Thirdly, that the variations in the Satipaṭṭhāna Sutta are significant enough to warrant investigation.

9.8 Bronkhorst

29 The conclusions reached by Bronkhorst are a considerable advance. He makes good use of the Theravāda Abhidhamma Vibhaṅga and the Sarvāstivādin Dharmaskandha, although he still omits the Dharmaguptaka Śāriputrābhidharma and the Prajñāpāramitā. I agree with most of what he says specifically dealing with satipaṭṭhāna; in several cases I arrived at the same conclusions independently. It is worth quoting at length his main points. I have added a few expansions in square brackets for clarity.

> 30 The Vibhaṅga itself must—as pointed out by Frauwallner[10]—have developed out of an earlier work which also underlay the Dharmaskandha of the Sarvāstivādins...
>
> 31 Our question is: did the 'Original Vibhaṅga' make use of the Sūtras in their finished form, or did it rather use pieces of tradition which were still more or less free-floating and would only later be taken into the Sūtras known to us? In the former case the agreement between the descendants of the "Original Vibhaṅga" and the Sūtras would

[9] E.g. AN 10.60, Iti 80, 81, Dhp 7, 8.

[10] Frauwallner (1995), pg 43*ff*.

have to be great; in the latter, we might hope to find in the Vibhaṅga and Dharmaskandha traces of a time prior to the compilation of the Sūtras.

32 Whether such traces have survived is not certain. There is, however, one passage in the Pali Vibhaṅga which may retain some ancient features. It occurs in the explanation of the 4 satipaṭṭhānas[11] ...

33 The 'Original Vibhaṅga' must have contained this same description of the 4 satipaṭṭhānas, because it is also found in the Dharmaskandha, with the difference that the Dharmaskandha adds items after those given in the Vibhaṅga...The items added are also found in the same or similar form in the Sūtras which deal with the 4 satipaṭṭhānas, and we may assume that the Dharmaskandha was influenced by them...

34 It is possible, but unfortunately far from certain, that the specification preserved in the Vibhaṅga is older than most of those found in the Sūtras... [Here Bronkhorst summarizes Schmithausen's arguments and raises some objections to them]...

35 Apart from these in themselves not very decisive considerations, there is one argument which lends some plausibility to the view that the 'observation of the positions of the body' was not originally the first of the 4 satipaṭṭhānas [as maintained by Schmithausen]. Briefly stated it is that in Buddhism mindfulness is of two kinds (or better perhaps: degrees); "observations of the positions of the body" is of one kind, the 4 satipaṭṭhānas of the other.

36 In order to recognize the two kinds of mindfulness we turn to the stereotype description of the road to liberation which often recurs in the Sūtras [i.e. the 'gradual training']. It distinguishes between preparatory exercises on the one hand, and "meditation" proper on the other, the two being divided by the moment when the monk went to a lonely place and sat down in the prescribed manner. Mindfulness plays a role both before and after this moment, but in different ways. Before this moment the monk 'When going out and returning acts with clear comprehension; when looking forward and to the side... when bending and stretching his limbs... when bearing his robes and bowl... when eating and drinking... when defecating and urinating... when going, standing, sitting, sleeping, waking, speaking, and keeping silent acts with clear comprehension';[12] in short, the monk practices the 'observation of the positions of the body'. After this moment

[11] I omit Bronkhorst's lists of the specifications of the satipaṭṭhānas in the Vibhaṅga and Dharmaskandha, which contain some errors of detail.

[12] DN 2.65, etc. Here I substitute my translation for Bronkhorst's for consistency.

> the situation changes. The monk no longer makes any movement. Yet his first act in this motionless position is 'calling up [establishing] mindfulness' (*parimukhaṁ satiṁ upaṭṭhapetvā*). As the expression indicates, it is here that the satipaṭṭhānas ['establishings of mindfulness'] would seem to come in. If this is correct, there is no place for 'observation of the positions of the body' in the 4 satipaṭṭhānas.
>
> 37 What then constitutes satipaṭṭhāna on the body in this motionless position? Obviously only this: the monk directs his mindfulness to the different parts of the body... We may... consider the possibility that 'observation of the constituents of the body' was originally the satipaṭṭhāna on the body. And this would confirm the view that the 'Original Vibhaṅga' was composed before the 4 satipaṭṭhānas were given the explanations we now find in the Sūtras.

38 The remainder of that portion of Bronkhorst's article which deals with satipaṭṭhāna mainly concerns the Mahāsaṅghika Ekāyana Sūtra. He develops some arguments to the effect that this text may contain some archaic features—which is possible, although the text as a whole is late—and suggests that the original specification of contemplation of dhammas may therefore have been the awakening-factors only. I discuss this below.

39 A key point in Bronkhorst's argument is that there are two different degrees of mindfulness in the gradual training, and that it is the second of these, 'meditation proper', that can be identified with satipaṭṭhāna. I agree with this; but it is, for some, such a radical claim that it requires more detailed reasoning. I would adduce the following arguments in support of this theory.

40 1) The standard description of 'observations of the positions of the body' does not include the word 'mindfulness' in the description of the practice itself. The act is described, as above, by saying the monk 'acts with clear comprehension' (*sampajānakārī hoti*). Accordingly the overall practice is called simply 'clear comprehension' in the Saṁyutta.[13] In the early Pali idiom it is normal to describe the practice of being aware throughout one's daily activities without even using the word 'mindfulness'. Only in the developed version of the gradual training, however, is the practice described as 'mindfulness & clear comprehension'. On the other hand, the use of the word 'mindfulness' in the case of the monk who sits down cross

[13] SN 47.2, SN 36.7, 8.

legged in the forest to meditate is absolutely standard, consistent, and intrinsic to the description of the practice.

41 2) The word 'establishment' (*upaṭṭhāna*) does not occur in the standard description of awareness of activities. To be sure, it does occur occasionally elsewhere in similar contexts, chiefly sense restraint, but it is not standard in the gradual training. On the other hand, the term 'establishment' is intrinsic to the passage on the monk who sits down in the forest to 'establish mindfulness'.

42 3) The various versions of the gradual training, so far as I know, never specifically mention the four satipaṭṭhānas at the stage of awareness of daily activities. But, while it is not standard, there are at least some contexts that mention the four satipaṭṭhānas at the stage of sitting down to meditate. In a Sarvāstivāda version of the Gaṇakamoggallāna Sutta, after the section on clear comprehension the four satipaṭṭhānas are brought in, leading as usual to jhāna and then various psychic abilities, culminating in enlightenment.[14] The Dantabhūmi Sutta is similar, although there the four satipaṭṭhānas are placed a little later, after the abandoning of the hindrances in the place normally taken by the first jhāna.[15] The Dharmaguptaka version of the Sāmaññaphala Sutta, however, differs from all these in placing the four satipaṭṭhānas *before* awareness of activities.[16]

43 4) The practice of ānāpānasati is invariably described after the monk has gone to a forest to sit meditation. This obviously pertains to the same stage in the gradual training. Since ānāpānasati is a major, or *the* major, paradigm for satipaṭṭhāna meditation, this clearly implies that satipaṭṭhāna starts when the monk sits down to meditate in the forest.

44 5) Several texts available in Theravāda and Sarvāstivāda versions list sequences of qualities, closely connected with the gradual training, that place mindfulness & clear comprehension early on as a basic practice. One such text explicitly differentiates between 'mindfulness & clear comprehension' and the four satipaṭṭhānas: associating with true persons → hearing the true Dhamma → faith → causewise attention → mindfulness & clear comprehension → sense restraint → three ways of good behaviour (by

---

[14] MA 144 = MN 107 Gaṇakamoggallāna Sutta.
[15] MN 125/MA 198.
[16] MEISIG , pg. 273.

body, speech, and mind) → four satipaṭṭhānas → seven awakening-factors → realization & release.[17]

45 6) The following passage speaks of exactly the same actions as the formula for clear comprehension: 'Then, after he has gone forth thus, his companions in the holy life advise and instruct him thus: "You should move to & fro thus; you should look ahead and to the side thus; you should flex and extend the limbs thus; you should wear the outer robe, bowl, and robes thus"...'[18] This is instruction in the basics of monastic protocol, especially regarding the morning alms round, when a monk or nun leaves the leafy seclusion of the monastery to venture into the distractions of the village. This shows that the passage on clear comprehension pertains more to preliminary ethical conduct than to the practice of meditation.

46 Thus Bronkhorst's brief observation finds considerable support. This suggests that an idiomatic rendering of satipaṭṭhāna would be simply 'meditation'. Establishing mindfulness, abandoning the hindrances, and entering jhāna are the key meditative stages in the gradual training.

[17] AN 10.62/MA 51–53.

[18] MN 67.16.

Chapter 10

MEDITATION BEFORE THE BUDDHA

MEDITATION WAS NOT INVENTED BY THE BUDDHA. The Buddhist texts always assume that meditation was a widespread and well-known practice. Given this, it is perhaps surprising to find that the extant pre-Buddhist sources do not have all that much to say about meditation.

10.1 Early Brahmanical Sources

The earliest evidence for meditative culture anywhere in the world is from the Indus valley civilization. This was a vast, sophisticated, and well-organized society which, at its peak in 2500–3000 BCE, stretched from what is now Pakistan to the Ganges valley. The evolution of this civilization can be traced as far back as 7000 BCE in Afghanistan, with a series of villages that became towns, and then towns that became cities. It was therefore an indigenous Indian culture. There is a strong continuity with later Indian culture, although we are not quite sure who these people were. The iconography suggests that they were the 'noseless' and 'black' peoples (Dravidians?) whose destruction at the hands of the Aryans is still dimly remembered in the Ṛg Veda. Perhaps the most intriguing remnants of their brilliant world are the thousands of exquisitely carved seals, little clay tablets that were probably worn by the citizens as a religious/family/occupational icon, and, of course, as a magic totem. These seals contain some of the world's oldest writings, which are as yet undeciphered.

2 The most interesting for our current purpose are a few seals that depict a god as a yogi sitting in meditation. These are astonishingly similar to the amulets that are still widely popular in Buddhist countries today. The yogi is usually identified on the basis of iconography as a 'proto-Śiva'. He sits, not in the 'lotus posture' of the Buddha, but in either *siddhāsana* (with legs crossed at the ankles) or *mūlabandhāsana* (with soles of the feet pressed together). Both of these postures are associated with psychic powers. One of the images depicts snakes rising beside him, a startling image familiar from Eden to the Pali canon. The image of the Buddha with a serpent rising over him is still popular today, taken from the Mucalinda Sutta of the Udāna. It is, of course, most famous as the symbol of the 'kundalini' of the Hindus. But whereas the serpent rises over the Buddha, signifying transcendence, in the proto-Śiva image the serpent rises only to the forehead. In later theory this place, the *jñāṇacakra*, was associated with lights, subtle forms, and psychic powers, and would therefore seem to be equivalent to the Buddhist form jhānas. These possibilities are too tenuous to make much of. However, it is certain that here is an ascetic who has, as the Buddhist texts say, 'gone to the forest, to the root of a tree, or to an empty hut, sat down cross-legged, and set his body erect…'. Has he taken the next step in this meditative training: 'establishing mindfulness'?

3 *Sati* in Buddhism is functionally described in terms of either *sara* 'memory', or *anupassanā* 'observation'. The relation between these two ideas is, to our mind, strange, and is best explained as a historical, linguistic development. *Sara* is from the same root as *sati*, and is the historical meaning. *Sati* came to mean, in the Brahmanical tradition generally, 'received tradition, memorized texts.' This meaning is attested in the early Suttas, where it is treated identically in Buddhist and Brahmanical contexts: one 'remembers what was said and done long ago'.

4 *Sati* is apparently used since the Ṛg Veda (perhaps a thousand years before the Buddha) in two senses: to 'remember' or 'recollect', and to 'bear in mind'. The significance of this should not be overlooked. *Sati* is not just a word one uses to refer to some texts one remembers; it is probable that the development of the culture of memorizing texts lead to the discov-

ery, investigation, and development of what 'memory' is. That is to say, those who memorized the Vedic mantras were engaged in an early form of mental culture, a mental culture where 'memory' was a vital quality. This mental culture was one of the strands that became woven into what we know today as 'meditation'.

5 In the Chāndogya Upaniṣad a father asks his son to fast for 15 days, then tests him on his memory of the Vedic texts. He fails dismally; but after eating again he can remember easily. His father explains:

> 6 'If, from a great blazing fire, there is only one coal left glowing, it can easily be made to blaze up again by putting grass on it. Even so, my dear son, there was [due to fasting] but one part in sixteen left to you and that, lighted up with food, blazed up and by it you remember now the Vedas.' After that he understood what his father meant when he said: 'Mind, my dear son, comes from food, breath from water, speech from fire.'[1]

7 The Buddha was once asked by a Brahman why the (Vedic) mantras are sometimes easy to remember and sometimes not.[2] Typically, he answers that when the five hindrances are present the mantras are not clear; when the five hindrances are absent the mantras are clear. This is a straightforward example of how the science of memorizing texts would lead naturally to investigation of the mental qualities necessary for success in such an ambitious venture. We still use the 4000 year old word 'mantra', which originally referred to the Vedic texts, as a term for a meditation word, a sound or phrase traditionally taken from the ancient texts that one repeats over and again as a support for meditation. The relation between recollection and meditation is strong even today in Buddhism. For example, most Buddhists are familiar with the basic passages for 'recollection' (*anussati*) of the Triple Gem. These form the basis for both the regular chanting at Buddhist ceremonies, and also the meditation on the Triple Gem.

8 In a similar fashion, the verses of the Vedas had a highly numinous, mystical significance for the ancient Brahman priests, and it would have been natural for the more contemplative among them to induce exalted states of consciousness through the ecstatic recollection of the sacred words. In

---

[1] CU 6.8.5–6.

[2] AN 5.193, SN 46.55.

order to memorize long texts it is, of course, necessary to repeat passages over and over again. If one does this mechanically, without interest, the memorizing will not succeed. One must bring inspiration, joy, attention, and understanding to the task. One must learn to 'stay with' the present moment—and here we are crossing over to the familiar Buddhist idea of 'mindfulness'.

9 This psychology also emerges in the usage of the word *dhī*, familiar as the root of the Buddhist term 'jhāna'. *Dhī* is used early on in the sense of 'thought', and has a special connection with the 'visioning' of the Vedic poetry: *dhī* is the intuitive awareness as the poet/priest 'sees' the verses. This 'thought' (*dhī*) or 'mind' (*manas*) is disciplined (*yoga*) by the reciters.

> 10 'The priests of him the divine Savitr well-skilled in hymns
> Harness their mind, yea, harness their *holy thoughts.*'[3]

11 But jhāna did not develop its meaning of 'deep absorption' until the Buddha. In the Bṛhadāraṇyaka, jhāna is contrasted with the stillness of the True Self.

> 12 'Which is the Self?
> 13 'That person here made of cognition among the senses [breaths], the light within the heart. He, remaining the same, wanders about the two worlds as if thinking (*dhyāyati*), as if playing (*lelāyati*).'[4]

14 The Upaniṣads constantly remind us to preserve the correct mental attitude; to perform the rituals with one's whole being, contemplating the significance of each aspect as one carries it out. Even the earlier Brahmanas allow that if a ritual cannot be carried out physically it may be performed by 'faith', i.e. as a purely mental act.[5] In this immersion of awareness in one's actions we can discern a precursor to the Buddhist emphasis on mindfulness through all one's activities.

15 It is a curious thing that when we look at the sources most likely to be contemporary with the Buddha—namely the Bṛhadāraṇyaka and the Chāndogya—we find that these well-known meditative terms are used less frequently, and a word apparently foreign to Buddhist meditation is found far more often. This word is *upāsana*. Edward Crangle, following Velkar,

---

3 Rv 5.81.1

4 BU 4.3.7.

5 Aitareya Brahmaṇa 5.5.27.

has studied this term in detail, and lists the frequency of occurrence. In the Bṛhadāraṇyaka, *upāsana* occurs 63 times, *jhāna* thrice, and *yoga* twice. In the Chāndogya, *upāsana* occurs 115 times, *jhāna* twelve times, and *yoga* again twice.[6] *Upāsana* is a key term in considering the emergence of meditative psychology in Indian tradition. It is translated sometimes as 'worship' and sometimes as 'meditation', and embodies the shift from an external worship and ritual towards inner contemplation. Crangle says *upāsana* is 'a contemplative process wherein the object of worship is an object of concentration.'[7] The following conveys the mystical tone of *upāsana*:

> 16 'Next, of this breath, water is the body. Its light-form is that moon. As far as the breath extends so far extends water and that moon. These are all alike, all endless. Verily, he who meditates/worships (*upāsana*) them as finite wins a finite world. But he who meditates/worships them as infinite wins an infinite world.'[8]

17 *Upāsana* encompasses a wide spectrum of spiritual consciousness. Velkar says it is meditative, emblematic (involving elaborate symbolism), and analytic (in making philosophical distinctions). It takes a large variety of objects, concrete and abstract: God, 'om', sun, moon, lightning, wind, space, fire, water, breath, 'That as Great', 'That as Mind', etc.

18 Crangle makes the intriguing suggestion that *upāsana* is related to the Buddhist term satipaṭṭhāna, especially the last element of this compound, *upaṭṭhāna*.[9] This is supported on a number of grounds. The sound of the words is almost identical, especially in Sanskrit (*upasthāna* and *upāsana*). Though they are from different roots, the construction and basic meanings are similar: *upa + ās* means to 'sit near'; *upa + sthā* means to 'stand near'. From there they both developed the sense of 'wait upon, serve, attend', and then to 'pray, worship'. In a specifically meditative context they are both used in the sense of the initial grounding on the meditation object, rather than the resulting state of absorption. Some of the meditation objects for *upāsana* are also found in satipaṭṭhāna: the breath, water, fire, space, bliss, mind, etc. So Crangle's suggestion can be accepted. The major contemplative practice of the pre-Buddhist period is *upāsana*, and this practice finds

---

6 CRANGLE, pg. 71.
7 CRANGLE, pg. 74.
8 BU 1.5.14.
9 CRANGLE, pg. 198.

its closest Buddhist connection, surprisingly enough, not with jhāna or samādhi, but with satipaṭṭhāna.

19 Investigation of pre-Buddhist meditation terminology is hampered by the fact that the Vedas have little or nothing on meditation and the early Upaniṣads have nothing clear. The earliest clear descriptions of meditation outside of Buddhism are in later texts of the Upaniṣads and the Jains. These are later than the Suttas, however, there is no reason why even late texts should not preserve old traditions.

20 In recent years some scholars have doubted the accepted wisdom that the early Upaniṣads were pre-Buddhist. The Suttas do not mention the Upaniṣads in their standard list of Brahmanical texts. But one passage in the Tevijja Sutta, discussing contemporary controversies among the Brahmans, refers to Brahmanical schools teaching different paths.[10] These have been equated by Jayatilleke with several of the Brahmanas (which include the Upaniṣads) as follows.

Table 10.1: Brahmanical texts in the Tevijja Sutta

Schools in the Tevijja Sutta	Brahmanical schools	Brahmanical Text
Addhariyā	Yajur Veda Addhariya	Śatapatha Brahmaṇa[1]
Tittiriyā	Yajur Veda Tittirya	Taittirīya Brahmaṇa
Chandokā	Sāman Veda Chandoga	Chāndogya Brahmaṇa
Bavharijā	Ṛg Veda Bavharija	Bahvrvas Brahmaṇa

[1] Including the Bṛhadāraṇyaka.

21 This suggests that the Upaniṣadic schools were in existence, but their tenets were still in ferment. Perhaps the Upaniṣads that we have today derive from the later settled tenets of each of these strands of Brahmanical thought.[11] But whether or not the Upaniṣads in their current form existed at the Buddha's time, there is no doubt that ideas we can call 'Upaniṣadic' were prominent. In the sphere of metaphysics we can cite the Buddha's critique of such ideas as that the self is infinite (*anantavā attā*), or that the self is identical with the world (*so attā so loko*), or that 'I am He'

[10] DN 13.10. The cognate DA 26 mentions three paths: 自在欲道・自作道・梵天道 (T1, № 1, p. 105, b13). It is not clear to me how closely these might match with the Pali.

[11] See 'A Pali Reference to Brahmaṇa-Caraṇas', included in WIJESEKERA.

(*eso'hamasmi*); or indeed the Buddha's condemnation of the suggestion by a certain Brahman cosmologist that 'All is oneness' (*sabbaṁ ekattaṁ*). It is only natural to connect such metaphysics with samādhi attainments, as implied by the Brahmajāla Sutta.

22 The early Upaniṣads, especially the Bṛhadāraṇyaka, usually regarded as the earliest and most important, are a very mixed bag. The Bṛhadāraṇyaka has passages of lyrical beauty, sophisticated philosophy, exalted metaphysics, and witty dialogue. It is closely concerned with ideas like the mind, the breath, and oneness, which are suggestive of a meditative culture. It distinguishes between mere perception (*saññā*) and liberating understanding (*paññā*), and emphasizes awareness (*viññāṇa*) in contrast with the more dynamic conceptual and emotive aspects of mind (*mano*). Therefore it insists on personal experience rather than mere book learning. It frequently upsets preconceptions—women have strong supporting roles, and sometimes Brahmans are depicted as having to learn about Brahmā from the Kṣatriyas.

23 But the Bṛhadāraṇyaka also retains much that is banal and even brutal. It endorses the sacrifice. It is unabashedly materialistic. It is full of thaumaturgy and hocus-pocus. It contains black magic—a curse to place on one's rival in love. It includes crude sex magic. If one's woman is reluctant to participate she should first be bribed with presents; 'and if she still does not grant him his desire, he should beat her with a stick or his hand and overcome her'.[12] Such abuse is quite incompatible with any genuine mind culture. The text is a testament to the diversity of ideas that the ancient Brahmans could regard as 'spiritual', and to the elasticity of the compilers of the text we have today.

24 Let us look at some of the passages most suggestive of meditation. From the Bṛhadāraṇyaka:

> 25 'Let a man perform one observance only, let him breath up and let him breath down, that the evil death might not reach him.'[13]

> 26 'The unseen seer, the unheard hearer, the unthought thinker, the uncognized cognizer... There is no other seer but he, no other hearer,

[12] BAU 6.4.9.
[13] BAU 1.5.17.

> no other thinker, no other cognizer. This is thy self, the inner controller, the immortal...' [14]

> 27 'Therefore, knowing this, being calm, tamed, quiet, enduring, concentrated, one sees the soul in oneself.' [15]

28 By themselves such passages are too vague for any clear conclusion regarding meditative practices. And even the last passage, which is the most suggestive, has 'faithful' as a variant reading for 'concentrated'. The Chāndogya has a slightly more explicit passage.

> 29 'As a bird when tied by a string flies in every direction and, finding no rest anywhere, settles down at last on the very place where it is fastened; exactly so, my son, that mind, after flying around in every direction and finding no rest anywhere, settles down on breath; for indeed, my son, mind is fastened to breath.'[16]

30 For clear teachings on meditation we must go to the (probably post-Buddhist) Śvetāśvatara Upaniṣad.

> 31 'By making his body the under-wood and the syllable "Om" the upper-wood, man, after repeating the drill of meditation, will perceive the bright god, like the spark hidden in the wood.'[17]

> 32 'If the wise man holds his body with the three upright parts even, and turns his senses with his mind towards the heart, he will then in the boat of Brahman cross over all the fearful streams.'[18]

> 33 'Compressing his breath, let him, who has subdued all motions, breath forth through the nose with gentle breath. Let the wise one, being heedful, keep hold of his mind, that chariot yoked with wild horses.'[19]

> 34 'When yoga is being performed, the forms that come first, producing apparitions in Brahman, are those of misty smoke, sun, fire, wind, fire-flies, lightnings, and a crystal moon.'[20]

---

[14] BAU 3.7.23.
[15] BAU 4.4.23.
[16] CU 6.8.2.
[17] SU 1.14.
[18] SU 2.8. Cp. Sn 1034*f.*
[19] SU 2.9.
[20] SU 2.11.

35 These are fairly straightforward references to meditation, and they will not sound unfamiliar to anyone versed in Buddhist meditation. The simile of meditation like two fire-sticks is well known in the Buddhist texts.[21] Notice the close connection in SU 2.9 between 'heedfulness' (*appamāda*) and 'keeping hold' (*dhāraṇa*), a term semantically equivalent to *sati*. The earliest Brahmanical meditation subjects were the breath and the contemplation of the mystical syllable 'Om'. Of course, the 'breath' and the 'word' are closely related and are mystically identified in the Upaniṣads; the yogis may have recited 'Om' together with the breath. The Upaniṣads are full of passages that assert the supremacy of the breath over the sense faculties and mind ('mind' here meaning thoughts and emotions). These can be understood as an allegorical description of the evolution of awareness from the diversity of externals towards a unity with the breath.

36 The breath is a prime exercise in satipaṭṭhāna body contemplation, and other aspects suggestive of satipaṭṭhāna can also be discerned in the Upaniṣadic tradition. Just as in the Satipaṭṭhāna Saṁyutta, the dependence of the breath (body) on food is stressed.[22] The elements appear commonly in the ancient world, and were worshipped as deities. For example Agni (Fire) was a major deity in the Vedas, and undoubtedly inspired ecstatic contemplation. Vāyu (air) was also worshipped in the Vedas. The Earth (Mother), whose symbols pervade the iconography of Buddhism, was also widely revered, and was associated with the Indus Valley religion. The parts of the body are worshipped in the Chāndogya Upaniṣad: hair, skin, flesh, bone, marrow.[23] All of these appear in the Satipaṭṭhāna Sutta list of body parts, and in the same order. Charnel grounds have long been a favourite haunting ground of a certain type of ascetic. The later Maitrī Upaniṣad opens with body contemplations for inducing dispassion (*virāga*), but this is probably under Buddhist influence.[24]

37 The other satipaṭṭhānas—feelings, mind, and dhammas—might even be compared with the famous Brahmanical threesome: mind, being, bliss (*cit*, *sat*, *ānanda*). Mind and bliss are obvious enough. As for being, this is a fundamental philosophical term for the Upaniṣads, just as dhamma

[21] E.g. MN 36.17*ff.*
[22] E.g. BAU 5.12.
[23] CU 1.19.
[24] Maitrī 1.3, 3.4.

is the fundamental term for Buddhism. The dhamma theory was clearly developed to provide an explanation for phenomenal reality opposed to the Brahmanical conception of an absolute underlying ground of being. And indeed the contemplation of dhammas prominently features the same term for being, *sat*, that was so important for the Brahmans; yet here it is treated, as always, in a thoroughly empirical, anti-metaphysical way: the 'presence' or 'absence' of good or bad mental factors according to conditions. Another list also reminds us of the satipaṭṭhānas: food, breath (= body), mind (or thought, *manas*), cognition (*vijñāna* = mind, *citta*), bliss (= feelings).[25] Whether or not there is any real historical link between these specific sets, both traditions used simple lists of physical and mental phenomena as a guide to spiritual practice.

38 Towards the end of this study we'll see that some of the later Buddhist theorists posited a relationship between the evolution of the stages of understanding in meditation and the stages of understanding in the philosophical outlook of the various schools. It is not so far-fetched to see a similar progress here; the Upaniṣads themselves seem to be aware on some level of this evolution. We can analyse the stages of Indian religion in terms of the four satipaṭṭhānas. The earliest stages were wholly physical—rituals, chants, the breath, sacrifices—pursued with the goal of fertility and prosperity. This developed into the practice of self-torment, which while still physical was predicated on the ability to endure painful feelings. The next stage was the emphasis on refined states of consciousness identified as the cosmic self. Finally, the Buddhist critique of metaphysical absolutism, the analysis of dhammas as conditioned and not-self.

39 Thus some of the facets of satipaṭṭhāna have their precedents in the Brahmanical traditions. The difference is in what is left out (hocus-pocus, rituals, deity worship, metaphysics, etc.), and in the manner of treatment. The practice is cool, rational, and sensible. The terminology has been subsumed into the Buddhist system. The presentation is purely in terms of discernable empirical phenomena without any metaphysical overtones. It is not trying to persuade you of a theory but to point you towards your own experience.

---

[25] Taittirīya Upaniṣad 3.2–6.

10.2 The Buddhist Sources

40 Given the paucity of references to meditation in pre-Buddhist texts we are thrown back on the Buddhist texts as our earliest source. There are a number of problems with this. The compilers of the Suttas may not have had much knowledge of non-Buddhist practices, and may have succumbed to the temptation to put their opposition in a bad light. In addition, they quite likely described the practices of other schools in terminology they were familiar with, but which was not authentic to the other schools. Nevertheless, both the Buddhist and the non-Buddhist sources agree in broad terms in their description of pre-Buddhist meditation. There are two such streams, represented by the two styles of practice undertaken by the Bodhisatta before his enlightenment. These are the samādhi practitioners of the Upaniṣads and the self-tormenters of the Jains.

41 The best-known passage referring to such 'Upaniṣadic' yogis is the tale of the Bodhisatta's apprenticeship.[26] I wish to first note why I consider the significance of this passage to be seriously overrated. According to the GIST, the Buddha's main teachings are found in the basic doctrinal statements (*suttas*) together with the interrogative discussions of these statements (*vyākaraṇa*). This material does not include much biography, beyond stating that it was through understanding the four noble truths, etc., or through practicing the eightfold path, etc., that the Buddha realized enlightenment. Biography as such is one of the later aṅgas, *avadāna*. However, after the Buddha's passing away the community found that the Buddha's life story gave the teachings that 'personal touch' so essential for the development of Buddhism into a popular mass religion. From that time until the present day the Buddha's life, rather than being occasionally used to illustrate a doctrinal point, became the main focus of attention. The events that are included in the Buddha's life story are known to all Buddhists, and as a result sometimes minor incidents have been blown up out of all proportion to their original significance. One obvious example of this is the Buddha's last meal, an obscure incident of dubious interpretation, absent in some versions, which has become the main battle ground in the controversy regarding the Buddhist position on vegetarianism, with

[26] MN 26/MA 204.

the result that the several straightforward discourses directly addressing the issue, as well as the frequent mention of meat-eating in the Vinaya, are virtually ignored. Another case is the touching story of the difficult attempts by the Buddha's foster-mother Mahā Pajāpati to secure women's ordination. This story is known to all and is regularly invoked to deny women the opportunity for full participation in the renunciate life, while ignoring the frequent mention of the 'fourfold assembly' (including nuns) that the Buddha regarded as the sign of a complete, successful, and long-lasting religion. Taking note of this principle does not in and of itself mean that these passages are inauthentic, nor that they should not be taken account of, nor does it suggest taking any specific stand on such controversies; but it does suggest that we should be more careful in how we weigh and evaluate the evidence in the early texts.

42 Nevertheless, even though the story of the Bodhisatta's apprenticeship already suffers from too many discussions, here's one more. Virtually all discussions have ignored the obvious point that the Ariyapariyesana Sutta mentions three stages of this apprenticeship. Firstly, learning and lip-reciting of the texts.[27] This is a hint that these are ascetics in the mainstream Vedic tradition; the nature of the texts is not specified here, but elsewhere the Buddha recalls that Uddaka Rāmaputta claimed to be a *vedagū*, a master of the Vedas.[28] Anyway, as we noted above, the Vedas are the only texts that are known to the early Suttas.[29] Secondly the path, here described as faith, energy, mindfulness, samādhi, and wisdom.[30] Thirdly, the goal—formless attainments. These three stages correspond with the classic three aspects of Buddhism—study, practice, and realization. The five factors of the path are the Buddhist five spiritual faculties—a fact that is comveniently overlooked by those who wish to interpret this passage as implying the 'non-Buddhist' nature of samādhi in general, or of formless attainments in particular. We cannot know how these qualities were

[27] The Sanghabhedavastu of the Mūlasarvāstivāda Vinaya omits the mention of lip recital.

[28] SN 35.103.

[29] It is sometimes said that these teachers belong to the Sāṁkhya school, but this claim is based on the much later Buddhacarita of Aśvaghoṣa, and is anachronistic.

[30] The Sarvāstivādin version (MA 204) mentions only faith, energy, and wisdom here, but includes mindfulness just below. The Sanghabhedavastu (GNOLI pg. 97) and the Lalitavistara (239.2) mention all five spiritual faculties.

understood in detail in this context; but terms such as *prajñā*, etc., occur commonly in the Upaniṣads. If it is true that the five spiritual faculties were genuinely associated with the Vedic/Upaniṣadic tradition, it may be no coincidence that it is in the spiritual faculties that we most frequently meet *sati* treated as 'memory'.[31]

43 The Bodhisatta did not reject the formless attainments in & of themselves. It is not the case that he practiced samādhi meditation but not mindfulness meditation. Rather, he practiced mindfulness meditation to get into samādhi. Samādhi is emphasized in this account because it was the highest, the most exalted quality acknowledged in those systems, and because of its sublime peacefulness it was mistakenly taken to be the final end of the spiritual path. The Bodhisatta became disillusioned with 'that Dhamma', i.e. with the teaching taken as a whole, because it led only to rebirth in the formless realm, and was therefore 'insufficient' to reach the 'excellent state of peace', the ending of birth, aging, and death.

44 This is in perfect accord with the main stream of the Suttas. Elsewhere it is said that ordinary people attain samādhi (here the four jhānas[32] and the four divine abidings[33]), are reborn in the Brahmā realms, and after a long period of bliss fall back into lower realms. But noble disciples, after reaching the Brahmā realms, attain Nibbana from there. The difference is not in the states of samādhi as such—these are just the mind at peace. The difference is in the views and interpretations, the conceptual wrapping that the experience in bundled up in. The path must be taken as a whole. If one starts out with wrong view, one's meditation experiences will simply reinforce one's preconceptions. If one practices samādhi with the view that one's soul will become immersed in some exalted state of being, well, one will get what one wishes for.

45 This is the most important feature distinguishing this episode from the later occasion (quoted below) when the Bodhisatta recollected his former experience of first jhāna. This occurred as a child, seated in the cool shade of a rose-apple tree. When the Bodhisatta remembered this experience he realized that: 'That indeed is the path to enlightenment'.

---

[31] E.g. SN 48.9.

[32] AN 4.123.

[33] AN 4.125.

As a child, his mind was uncluttered with views; he had no metaphysical agenda. The peace of the mind was just the peace of the mind; and so he realized that although such states were not the final goal he had been yearning for, they were indeed the path to that goal. This account is found in the Mahā Saccaka Sutta (MN 36), the Mahāvastu (of the Mahāsaṅghika Vinaya), the Saṅghabhedavastu (from the Mūlasarvāstivāda Vinaya), and the Dharmaguptaka Vinaya. Accounts in the Ekottara (EA 31.8) and the Lalitavistara attribute all four jhānas to the Bodhisatta as child; while the Mūlasarvāstivāda Vinaya and an individual Chinese translation (T № 757) place the attainment of jhāna soon after the going forth. Thus this is clearly regarded by all the schools as a crucial event in the Bodhisatta's path towards awakening.

46 One of the most interesting sources for understanding the meditation practices of Brahman ascetics is the Pārāyana Vagga of the Sutta Nipāta. This text, one of the earliest texts in the Pali canon, consists of a series of questions and answers between the Buddha and a group of sixteen Brahman meditators. There are several connections between this text and the Upaniṣad-style traditions we have been considering; in fact the closeness of some parallel phrases suggests direct literary influence of one sort or another,[34] although there are also direct connections between some of these verses and Jain texts. The list of Brahmanical texts given is substantially shorter than that in the Bṛhadāraṇyaka, suggesting that it is earlier. It has a satirical reference to an evil Brahman who threatens to 'split heads'; the same threat occurs several times in the Bṛhadāraṇyaka, the difference being that there someone's head actually does get split![35] The Buddha of course dismisses the efficacy of Vedic knowledge, ritual, sacrifice, and metaphysical conceptions of 'Self'. We meet again the phrase 'seen, heard,

[34] Compare the following verses. Muṇḍaka Upaniṣad 3.2.8: *Yathā nadyas syandamānās samudre/Astam gacchanti nāmarūpe vihāya* (Just as rivers flowing into the ocean/Go to their end, having dropped name & form); *Tathā vidvān nāmarūpād vimuktaḥ/Parāt-param puruṣam upaiti divyam.* (Thus the realized [sage], freed from name & form/Beyond the beyond is that Man he enters, divine). Sutta Nipāta 1080: *Acci yathā vātavegena khittaṁ/Atthaṁ paleti na upeti saṅkhaṁ.* (Just as a flame tossed by a strong wind/Goes to the end, and does not enter reckoning); *Evaṁ muni nāmakāyā vimutto/Atthaṁ paleti na upeti saṅkhaṁ.* (Thus the sage, freed from the name-group [i.e. mental factors]/Goes to the end, and does not enter reckoning).

[35] BU 3.9.26

thought, cognised' that we have encountered in the Bṛhadāraṇyaka, and also frequent reference to the pairing of cognition with name & form, another Upaniṣadic idea.

47 The faith and devotion of these yogis is very moving, and stands in decided contrast with the sometimes strained relationship between the Buddha and the scholastic and ritualistic Brahmans. In this friendly atmosphere the Buddha would have, wherever possible, kept his normal policy of encouraging his disciples to continue developing whatever spiritual practices were most inspiring and useful. The introductory verses, which are somewhat later, refer indirectly to the five spiritual faculties,[36] and say the sixteen Brahmans are practitioners of jhāna.[37] The teachings are brief and non-technical, but there is recognizable reference to the fourth jhāna[38] and to the sphere of nothingness.[39] And time and time again, the Buddha exhorts these yogis to be 'ever mindful'. This confirms the association of mindfulness with Brahmanic culture; the Buddha would hardly have used the term if he did not expect his audience to understand it.

48 Three discourses in the Bojjhaṅga-saṁyutta present the claims of non-Buddhist wanderers to develop Buddhist-style meditation. They say they exhort their disciples to abandon the five hindrances and to develop, in two cases, the seven awakening-factors,[40] and in a third case the four divine abidings.[41] Elsewhere too the divine abidings are attributed to great sages of the past, notably the Buddha in past lives.[42] However, although these are found in the later Brahmanical tradition, they are not attested in any pre-Buddhist texts. The awakening-factors include mindfulness and investigation of dhammas, which is equivalent to vipassanā, as well as samādhi. The wanderers ask, then, what is the difference between their

---

[36] Sn 1026.

[37] Sn 1009.

[38] Sn 1107.

[39] Sn 1070, Sn 1113*ff.* The sphere of nothingness is described in Sn 1070 as a 'support' (*ārammaṇa*) for crossing over. This may be compared with the Mahābhārata passage quoted above that describes the unconcentrated mind as 'without support'. The Jhāna Saṁyutta also speaks of developing 'skill in the support'.

[40] SN 46.52, SN 46.53.

[41] SN 46.54.

[42] E.g. MN 83/MA 67/EA 1/EA 50.4/T № 152.87/T № 211 Makhādeva; DN 19 Mahāgovinda also has the divine abidings, but not DA 3, T № 8, pp. 207c–210b, and Mv 3.197–224.

teaching and the Buddha's? The Buddha responds, not by referring to, say, the four noble truths, not-self, or dependent origination, but by claiming that the wanderers do not fully understand samādhi practice in all details. This is what the Buddha was referring to when he claimed to have 'awakened to jhāna' (*jhānaṁ abujjhi*);[43] not that he was the first to practice jhāna, but that he was the first to fully comprehend both the benefits and the limitations of such experiences.

49 The Brahmajāla Sutta is a classic source for non-Buddhist meditation. It presents a bewildering array of 62 doctrinal views, many of which were derived from or reinforced by misinterpretation of samādhi experiences, including both form jhāna and formless attainments. Yogis include both the mainstream Vedic/Upaniṣadic 'Brahmans' as well as the radical nonconformist 'samanas'. Five terms describe the path to samādhi: ardency (*ātappa*), striving (*padhāna*), commitment (*anuyoga*), heedfulness (*appamāda*), and right attention (*sammā manasikāra*). All of these terms are commonly found in Buddhist contexts; *ātappa* occurs in the satipaṭṭhāna formula. 'Heedfulness', which we encountered above in the Śvetāśvatara Upaniṣad, lies close in meaning to 'mindfulness'. 'Attention' is the basis for wisdom, and is closely associated with insight. So here wisdom appears as a forerunner for samādhi.

50 But the Suttas typically present the contemporary Brahmans as having fallen away from their glorious past. This is important: the Suttas do not see the fact that pre-Buddhists practiced jhāna as a reason for denigrating samādhi. Rather, they praise for the sages of old, who are a role model for emulation and inspiration. Here is an example, spoken by Venerable Mahā Kaccāna to some rude and abusive Brahman youths.

51 'Those men of old who excelled in virtue,
    Those Brahmans who recalled the ancient rules;
Their sense doors guarded, well protected
    Dwelt having vanquished wrath within.
They took delight in Dhamma and jhāna—
    Those Brahmans who recalled the ancient rules.

---

[43] SN Sagāthāvagga verse 269, AN (4)449–51. This phrase was somewhat misleadingly rendered by Bhikkhu BODHI in CDB as 'discovered jhāna'. Perhaps the accusative here could be read as instrumental ('awakened by means of jhāna').

52 'But these having fallen, claiming "We recite!"
Puffed up by clan, faring unrighteously,
Overcome by anger, armed with diverse weapons,
They molest both frail and firm.

53 'For one with sense doors unguarded
All the vows he undertakes are in vain,
Just like the wealth a man gains in a dream.

54 'Fasting and sleeping on the ground,
Bathing at dawn, [study of] the three Vedas,
Rough hides, matted locks, and dirt,
Hymns, rules and vows, austerities,
Hypocrisy, bent staffs, ablutions:
These emblems of the Brahmans
Are used to increase their worldly gains.

55 'A mind that is well concentrated,
Clear and free from blemish,
Tender towards all living beings—
This is the path for attaining Brahmā.'[44]

56 Understandably, the Brahman youths were not too pleased with this. So they went to their teacher, the Brahman Lohicca, and told him. He too was displeased, but he reflected that he should not condemn on mere hearsay, so he visited Venerable Mahā Kaccāna to discuss the matter. He asked what the meaning of 'sense doors guarded' was.

57 'Here, Brahman, having seen a visible form with the eye, one is not attracted to a pleasing visible form and not repelled by a displeasing visible form. One abides having established mindfulness of the body, with a measureless mind, and understands as it has become that heart-release, understanding-release, where those evil unskilful qualities cease without remainder....'

58 Here again we see the connection between pre-Buddhist meditation and mindfulness. The sequence—sense restraint, mindfulness, samādhi, understanding, release—allows Mahā Kaccāna to present the Buddhist ideal as the natural fulfilment of the practices of the Brahmans of old, so he can skilfully lead Lohicca on in a non-confrontational manner.

---

[44] SN 35.132.

10.3 Later Brahmanical Sources

59 Since there are no contemporary records to illuminate these ideas further, we take the risky path of comparing them with later texts. The Mahābhārata post-dates the Nikāyas/Āgamas, and shows Buddhist influence. However, the events are set in a semi-mythical time before the Buddha, and it has undoubtably preserved some genuine old traditions. It mentions the 'fourfold *jhānayoga*', but only the first jhāna is described in detail.

60 'The mind that is wandering,
With no support,
With five gates, wobbling,
The steadfast one should concentrate in the first jhāna.'[45]

61 'When the sage enters samādhi
Of the first jhāna in the beginning,
Sustained application (*vicāra*) and initial application (*vitakka*)
And seclusion (*viveka*) arise in him...'[46]

62 'Conjoined with that bliss,
He will delight in the practice of jhāna.
Thus the yogis go to Nirvana that is free of disease...'[47]

63 The Yoga Sūtra of Patañjali (300–500 CE?) is an early presentation of a fairly systematic path of practice from a non-Buddhist school. The Yoga school, regarded as the practical wing of the Sāṁkhya philosophy, became one of the six schools of classical Hinduism, which were orthodox in regarding the Vedic tradition as authoritative, although they differed in interpretation. The Yoga Sūtra is a fairly short work in four chapters, comprising a series of brief aphorisms, or sūtras, a style which, incidentally, well illustrates the meaning of *sutta* as discussed in the GIST. The sūtras are often cryptic and as good as incomprehensible without a commentary; the work as a whole may well be a collection of sayings that was assembled in the current form by the commentator.

---

[45] MBh 12.188.9.

[46] MBh 12.188.15. BRONKHORST (2000) pg. 71 notes that here, as well as in the Yoga Sūtra and in some Buddhist works, *vitakka* and *vicāra* 'are apparently looked upon as special faculties in the first jhāna, not as mere thought remaining from ordinary consciousness'.

[47] MBh 12.188.22.

64 Here we merely wish to investigate the meditation terminology in relation to Buddhist meditation, so we can afford to ignore many of the knotty questions raised by the text and focus mainly on those passages closest to Buddhism. This methodology will lead to a biased view of the work as a whole, and it should be remembered that the Yoga Sūtra stays faithful to its own distinctive philosophy; it is not just a Buddhist rip-off. Doctrinally, it mentions ideas familiar to the Sāṁkhya/Yoga—the three 'qualities' (*guṇas*) of stimulation (*rajas*, literally 'desire'), depression (*tamas*, 'darkness'), and vitality (*sattvas*, 'being') that make up our worldly state, the fundamental ground of nature (*prakṛti*) from which these evolved, and the individual soul (*puruṣa*), whose purity and clear discernment lead to the state of consummation (*kaivalya*). The main emphasis is on the practical means, especially meditation, for reaching this state. Occasionally it critiques Buddhist philosophy. Sūtras 4.16–18, for example, assert that it is impossible for a changing object to be known by one mind-moment (as the ābhidhammikas claimed); the fluctuations of the mind are known due to the changelessness of the *puruṣa*, the One Who Knows. Sometimes the text bears on the controversies among the Buddhists, such as when it asserts that 'the past and the future exist in their own form',[48] which is reminiscent of the Sarvāstivādin doctrine of time: 'all exists'.

65 The first chapter of the Yoga Sūtra deals with samādhi. It starts with a famous definition: yoga is the cessation of the fluctuations of the mind. The fluctuations, which are caused by ignorance, are listed as valid knowledge (*pramāṇa*, defined in a way similar to the Buddhist epistemologists: direct experience, inference, and scripture), error, fantasy, sleep, and recollection (mindfulness, *sati*). This list is odd; it is difficult to see how, say, direct experience (*pratyakṣa*) could be an obstacle to samādhi. The treatment of mindfulness in a negative sense is obviously different from the Buddhist approach. For the Brahmanical schools, the word *sati* had the sense of 'memorised textual traditions', so in meditation contexts the meaning of 'memory' was more prominent than 'awareness', hence the negative slant. This situation suggests two consequences: first, that when *sati* is used in a positive sense in the Yoga we should suspect a Buddhist influence; and second, that the Yoga would need to develop an alternative terminology to

---

48 YS 3.12.

speak about mindfulness within their own system. We shall find that the Yoga Sūtra supports both of these theses. However, despite this difference, the Yoga Sūtra defines *sati* the same way as the Buddhist schools: the non-forgetting of an experienced object.

66 After emphasising the necessity for sincere practice and dispassion, the text goes on to speak of a form of samādhi (the word 'samādhi' is not used, but is plausibly supplied by the commentary) called *samprajñāta*, which it describes as: 'accompanied by initial application, sustained application, bliss (*ānanda*), [the concept] "I am", and form.'[49] This is virtually identical with the first of the four Buddhist 'form jhānas'. The idea 'I am' clearly refers to a deluded perception that takes what is not the True Self, the *puruṣa*, to be the True Self. The phrase is foreign to the standard jhāna formula, but is similar to one of the deluded forms of 'Nibbana here & now' described in the Brahmajāla Sutta:

67 > 'When, sir, this self, quite secluded from sensual pleasures, secluded from unskilful qualities, enters and abides in the first jhāna, which has initial & sustained application, and the rapture & happiness born of seclusion, at that point the self attains Nibbana here & now....' [50]

68 Both contexts are criticising the assumption of self in this state of samādhi; for the Buddhists, of course, there is no True Self, while in yoga the True Self is discerned only with more subtle development of consciousness. The Yoga Sūtra goes on to speak of another (higher) form of samādhi, which is called *asamprajñāta* (although again the term is not supplied in the extremely laconic text itself). Sūtra 18 describes this as 'preceded by practice in renunciation, and having just a residue of activities (*saṁskāraśeṣa*)'.[51] Sūtra 19 is obscure: 'For the bodiless, absorbed in fundamental Nature, [such an] existence is conditioned (*bhavapratyayo videhaprakṛtilāyanam*)'. This seems to mean either that this state of consciousness generates a bodiless (*videha* = formless, *arūpa*?) rebirth, or that for one without a body, such a state of consciousness is a natural condition, not something that must be attained through spiritual practice. Sūtra 20 says that 'for others' (presumably this means not the 'bodiless' ones referred to in sūtra 19),

---

[49] YS 1.17. The word 'form', *rūpa*, does not occur in all texts.

[50] DN 1/DA 19.

[51] YS 1.18.

asamprajñāta samādhi comes after 'faith, energy, mindfulness, samādhi, and wisdom'.[52] Here once more we meet the Buddhist five spiritual faculties, which are presumably what is meant by the 'practice in renunciation' mentioned in sūtra 18. Note that *sati* here is in positive sense, as usual in Buddhism, and not in negative sense, as earlier in the Yoga Sūtra; this supports the argument of Bronkhorst that this chapter was composed from two sources, one 'orthodox' and one Buddhist.[53] The samādhi in this group of five, which precedes *asamprajñāta* samādhi, is presumably the *samprajñāta* samādhi, i.e. form jhāna. The *asamprajñāta* samādhi may therefore be plausibly identified with the Buddhist formless attainments, which are also preceded by form jhāna, are the outcome of a 'gradual cessation of activities', generate a bodiless rebirth, and the highest of which is called 'an attainment with a residue of activities'.[54] It is very striking that the way of attaining this *asamprajñāta* samādhi—the five spiritual faculties—is identical with the way of practice taught by Āḷāra Kālāma and Uddaka Rāmaputta for attaining formless samādhi, and is also mentioned in the Pārāyana Vagga.

69 The text goes on to speak of various obstacles to samādhi, similar to the hindrances, etc., including the term 'scattered mind' familiar from the Satipaṭṭhāna Sutta. These result in bodily and mental discomfort and unsteadiness of breath, and should be countered by one-pointedness. Several meditations are recommended that lead to clarity of mind: these include the Buddhist divine abidings of loving-kindness, compassion, appreciation, and equanimity. Some of the other meditations, such as breath meditation and the mind free of lust, again remind us of the Satipaṭṭhāna Sutta. Next the text speaks of attainments both with initial application (*vitakka*) and without; the latter is associated with purity of mindfulness, as in the Buddhist fourth jhāna. Attainments with and without sustained application (*vicāra*), which are said to be subtle conditions, are also mentioned; like the Buddhist second jhāna, absence of sustained application comes with 'inner clarity' (*adhyātma prasāda*). The wisdom of this brings truth. All these

---

[52] YS 1.20.

[53] Bronkhorst (2000), pp. 72*ff.*

[54] SN 14.11.

states are 'samādhi with seed'; but when even these cease all ceases, and this is 'samādhi without seed'.

70 While the first chapter of the Yoga Sūtra recalls the Buddhist treatment of samādhi, the second chapter contains some Buddhist-style instructions on vipassanā:

> 71 'Ignorance, "I-am-ness", desire, aversion, and insistence (*abhiniveśa*) [are to be eliminated by practice]. Ignorance is the cause of the rest, whether they are dormant, weak, suppressed, or aggravated. Ignorance thinks of the permanent as impermanent, of the pure as impure, of the painful as pleasurable, of the not-self as self...'[55]

72 The definition of 'I-am-ness' is obscure ('taking the two powers of seer and seen as a single self'); evidently it is the error of seeking a unified self in the diversity of experience. Desire and aversion are defined just as in Buddhism: the inherent compulsions (*anusaya*) regarding pleasure and pain. All these 'fluctuations' are to be overcome with jhāna. The result of action (*karma*) rooted in defilement (*kleśamūla*) is experienced in pleasant or painful rebirth, according to whether the causes are good or evil. But for the discerning, all this is suffering.

73 Halfway through the chapter is introduced the famous 'eight-factored yoga', which is obviously modelled after the Buddhist eightfold path. A similar sixfold yoga is found in the Buddhist-influenced Maitrī Upaniṣad: breath control, sense control (*pratyāhāra*), jhāna, remembering (*dhāraṇa*), reason (*tarka*), samādhi.[56] This leaves out the preliminary three practices of the eightfold yoga and adds 'reason'. The eightfold scheme of the Yoga Sūtra, however, was to become standard. The first factor, *yama*, is basic ethics similar to the five precepts; the second factor, *niyama*, concerns purity, austerity, contentment, chanting, and devotion to God. To counter thoughts of harming, etc., that are rooted in greed, hatred, and delusion, it is recommended that one develops the opposite thoughts as antidotes. This is identical with the Buddhist path-factor of right intention. The same principle of opposites is applied not just to wrong thoughts but to wrong actions as well: 'When one is firm in not stealing, all treasures appear'. The third factor, posture (*āsana*), is dealt with swiftly, involving merely

---

55 YS 2.3–6.

56 Maitrī 6.18.

steadiness, comfort, and relaxation; no mention is made of the special postures for physical exercise that we identify with the word ‘yoga’. Next follow breath control and sense control, completing the external practices.

74 The next chapter introduces the ‘internal’ practices. First is *dhāraṇa*, defined as ‘fixing the mind on one place’.[57] *Dhāraṇa*, like *sati*, means ‘remembering, bearing in mind’, and the Abhidhamma lists *dhāraṇa* as a synonym of *sati*. Above we noted the close relation of *dhāraṇa* with *appamāda*, mirroring the close connection in the suttas between *sati* and *appamāda*. The change in terminology from *sati* to *dhāraṇa* is because of the different connotations of the term *sati* in the two traditions, not because of a difference in the meaning. *Dhāraṇa* is followed by *dhyāna* (jhāna), which is defined very obscurely and, for me, untranslatably. It seems to mean a realm of mental unification brought about by the practice of *dhāraṇa*. So both the Yoga and the Buddhist tradition place ‘remembering/bearing in mind/mindfulness’ as the practice on which jhāna is based.[58]

75 One difference between the two systems is that, while for the Suttas, jhāna and samādhi are usually synonymous, the Yoga Sūtra places samādhi as the final step of the path, following jhāna. However, *dhāraṇa*, jhāna, and samādhi are together said to make up ‘restraint’ (*saṁyama*), so they are not thought of as totally separate. The description of samādhi is even more obscure than jhāna: ‘The shining forth of just that mere object as if empty of its own form is samādhi’. Much of the rest of the Yoga Sūtra deals with Yoga/Sāṁkhya philosophy and practice, the attainment of various psychic powers, realization of the True Self, and of the disentanglement of the Self from the world and its constituent qualities; the Upaniṣadic non-dual metaphysic is not evident.

76 The above considerations lead me to conclude the following. There is a thread of Indian meditative tradition referred to in the Nikāyas/Āgamas, which stems from the pre-Buddhist period, finds philosophical expression in the Upaniṣads, and in the later Yoga texts is developed into a practical method using the sophisticated psychological terminology developed by the Buddhists. This tradition, through its commitment to memorizing

[57] YS 3.1.

[58] CRANGLE pp. 117–119 discusses the similarity between Buddhist *sati* and yogic *dhāraṇa*, and their role as support for jhāna.

ancient texts (*sati* = *sara*), gradually evolved an appreciation of the benefits of mindful awareness (*sati* = *anupassanā*). In metaphysics these yogis emphasized the Self, sometimes mystically identified with the cosmos. This metaphysic was pre-eminently realized in the practice of samādhi, especially formless attainments. The chief way to develop these formless attainments was to develop the five faculties, especially mindfulness and form jhāna. The Buddha adopted the relevant practical aspects of this tradition into his teaching, his chief innovation being to not interpret samādhi experience in terms of a metaphysical 'self'.

10.4 The Jains

77 We turn now to the second thread of pre-Buddhist meditation. The classic description here is the account of the Bodhisatta's austerities. His striving was most terrible: 'crushing mind with mind', doing the 'breathless jhāna' until he felt as if his head was being pierced with a sword or crushed with a leather strap. But he could not make any progress. Why?

> 78 'My energy was roused up and unflagging, my mindfulness was established and unconfused, but my body was afflicted and not tranquil because I was exhausted by the painful striving. But such painful feeling as arose in me did not invade my mind and remain.'[59]

79 The Mūlasarvāstivāda account available in Sanskrit confirms that the Bodhisatta practiced mindfulness during his period of striving.[60] Here, 'mindfulness' is obviously used in the sense of 'present moment awareness' rather than 'memory'. This is confirmed in the following passage:

> 80 'Such was my scrupulousness, Sāriputta, that I was always mindful in stepping forwards and stepping backwards. I was full of pity even for [the beings in] a drop of water, thinking: "Let me not hurt the tiny creatures in the crevices of the ground." '[61]

81 The Buddha explained why he struggled on with such grim self-torture.

---

[59] MN 36.20, etc.
[60] Gnoli, pg. 103.
[61] MN 12.47.

> 82 'Prince, before my enlightenment, while I was still an unenlightened Bodhisatta, I too thought thus: "Pleasure is not to be gained through pleasure; pleasure is to be gained through pain." '[62]

83 This is wrong view, being one of the chief tenets of the Jains.[63] Having tortured himself near death because of that view, he reflected thus:

> 84 ' "Whatever ascetics or Brahmans, past...future...and present experience painful, racking, piercing feelings due to exertion, this is the utmost, there is nothing beyond this. But by these racking austerities I have not attained any truly noble distinction of knowledge & vision beyond human principles. Could there be another path to enlightenment?"
>
> 85 'I considered: "I recall that when my father the Śakyan was working, while I was sitting in the cool shade of a rose-apple tree, quite secluded from sensual pleasures, secluded from unskilful qualities, I entered and abode in the first jhāna, with initial & sustained application [of mind], and the rapture & happiness born of seclusion. Could that be the path to enlightenment?" Then, following on that memory came the awareness: "That indeed is the path to enlightenment."
>
> 86 'I thought: "Why am I afraid of that pleasure that has nothing to do with sensual pleasures and unskilful qualities?" I thought: "I am not afraid of that pleasure, for it has nothing to do with sensual pleasures and unskilful qualities." '[64]

87 Here the friendly, relaxed, reasonable feel stands in refreshing contrast with the steely force of his earlier efforts. He then decided that he could not attain jhāna while so emaciated and must therefore take some food; we have already seen that the dependence of the mind on food, and hence the deleterious effects of fasting on one's mind-state, is an Upaniṣadic idea.[65] Although the Bodhisatta never identifies himself in this period as following any teacher, his practices and views are identical with the Jains. And when the group of five ascetics abandoned him they went to stay in the 'Rishi's Park' in Benares, where even today there is a Jain temple.

88 Such ideas were not exclusive to the Jains; they were common in the Indian yogic tradition, and are met with frequently in the early Brahman-

---

62 MN 85.10/DA2 21/T № 1421.10.

63 MN 14.20.

64 MN 36.30–2, MN 85, MN 100.

65 CU 6.7.

ical scriptures as well, as Mahā Kaccāna's verses above indicate. In fact the Jains were reformists, in that they rejected forms of asceticism that might harm living beings, and they also laid stress on the proper mental attitude. Earlier, more primitive, 'professors of self-torture' had believed in the efficacy of the physical torture itself, irrespective of any mental development. Also, their goal was typically psychic powers, whereas the Jains aimed at liberation of the soul. Thus the Bodhisatta's austerities are closer to the Jains than any other group we know of; the Jains themselves preserve a tradition that the Buddha spent time as a Jain ascetic.

89 The implication of this episode is that the Jain system emphasized effort and mindfulness, but not until the Bodhisatta developed the tranquillity and bliss of samādhi was he able to see the truth. Elsewhere in the Suttas, Mahāvīra (the leader and reformer of the Jains, known in Pali as Nigaṇṭha Nātaputta) is depicted as asserting the impossibility of stopping initial & sustained application of mind.[66] Thus he would not admit any higher than the first jhāna at most. To me, the Jain teachings and practice have a roughness that does not fit well with samādhi attainments. The Jain sources don't help much. The earliest Jain sūtras emphasize ethical practices, lifestyle, and basic principles, and don't mention meditation in any recognizable form. Slightly later we find the following:

90 > 'Then having preserved his life, the remainder of his life being but a short period, he stops activities and enters dry jhāna,[67] in which only subtle activity remains and from which one does not fall back. He first stops the activity of mind, then of speech and of body, then he puts an end to breathing…'[68]

91 In Buddhist context this passage would imply the fourth jhāna; but we have no guarantee that the terminology is being used in the same sense. The context is different; here we have not just a meditator, but someone who is culminating a spiritual path by fasting to death. Later texts refer to familiar ideas such as samādhi, one-pointedness, discriminating insight, reflection on impermanence (*anicca*), change (*vipariṇāma*), and ugliness (*asubha*).[69] Dayal says that the Jains attached great importance to funeral

[66] SN 41.8.
[67] *Sukkajjhāna*. Compare the commentarial notion of *sukkavipassanā*.
[68] Uttarajjhāyana 29.72/1174.
[69] E.g. Ṭhānaṅga Sutta. See BRONKHORST (2000), pg. 38*ff*.

contemplations.[70] There are apparently references to mindfulness as part of the Jain path, but I don't know what period they belong to. The later schools developed a list of twelve 'contemplations'. The term used here, *anuprekṣā*, is semantically identical with the term *anupassanā* that is so prominent in the Buddhist practice of satipaṭṭhāna. The list is as follows.

92 1) Impermanence
2) No-refuge
3) Coursing on (in rebirth, *saṁsāra*)
4) Solitariness (*ekatvā*)
5) Difference (between the soul and the body)
6) Uncleanness (of the body)
7) Influx (of pollutions, *āsava*)
8) Restraint (of kamma)
9) Wearing away (of kamma)
10) The world (as suffering)
11) The difficulty of attaining enlightenment
12) The well-expoundedness of the Dhamma

93 Some of these are similar to Buddhist contemplations (1, 2, 3, 4, 6, 10, 11, 12), while some are specifically Jainist in nature (5, 7, 8, 9). They appear to involve reflecting on or thinking over a theme rather than awareness meditations; and so most of them lie closer to vipassanā than samatha. The Jain sources also speak of several varieties of 'jhāna'.

94 1) Depressive brooding jhāna
2) Ferocious jhāna
3) Dhamma jhāna (contemplation of scriptures; removing afflictions of oneself and others; kamma and result; samsara and the pure soul)
4) Pure jhāna

95 Only this last might correspond with the Buddhist jhānas, although some of the other meanings, such as 'brooding', are connected with jhāna or related terms in non-technical passages. According to Prasad, 'pure jhāna' has four kinds:

[70] DAYAL, pg. 95.

96 [Manifold, with initial & sustained application]: Absorption in meditation of the Self, unconsciously allowing its different attributes to replace one another.

97 [Unified, with initial but without sustained application]: Absorption in one aspect of the Self, with changing the particular aspect concentrated upon.

98 The very fine vibratory movements in the Soul, even when it is deeply absorbed in itself, in a Kevali [consummate one].

99 Total absorption of the self in itself, steady and undisturbedly fixed without any motion or vibration whatsoever.[71]

100 This is clearly describing states of deep concentration. Whether they are equivalent to the Buddhist jhānas is impossible to say. What we can say with some certainty, though, is that meditation, in the Buddhist sense of reflective contemplation, never played as major a role in Jainism as it did in Buddhism. The ascetic practices were central, and the Jain emphasis on the *physicality* of karma downplays the significance of purely mental development. Moreover, any contemplative culture that might have existed had waned by medieval times, so that the mention of meditation states in ancient texts came to be a matter of merely scholastic interest.

10.5 Conclusion

101 Satipaṭṭhāna is depicted in the early texts as a distinctively Buddhist practice. While we have gone to some lengths to unearth elements in common with non-Buddhist systems, in the final end this re-emphasizes how much was new, in both the expression and the meaning. The rational, progressive approach, the empirical and psychological description, the details of the four satipaṭṭhānas—none of these can be found in a straightforward way in any pre-Buddhist texts. Even the post-Buddhist texts, while showing Buddhist influence in the meditation terminology, did not adopt the satipaṭṭhānas as they did the jhānas or the divine abidings.

102 The early Buddhists were extraordinarily generous in their assessment of the spiritual attainments of outsiders. They were quite happy to attribute to them such central elements of the Buddhist meditation system

[71] PRASAD, pp. 167–168.

as mindfulness, jhānas, spiritual faculties, awakening-factors, divine abidings, and formless attainments. In this complex weave, we can discern threads of both samatha and vipassanā. Although it is impossible to fully untangle these threads, it is possible to discern different emphases in the meditative approaches of the different schools that correlates with their philosophical positions.

103 The Upaniṣadic tradition espouses a non-dual pantheism. Brahman is the ultimate reality, which creates the world, underlies the illusion of diversity, and is immanent in all existence. Thus existence is inherently good; we already partake of the divine essence, and our spiritual practices empower us to realize this identity fully. This tradition emphasizes meditation practices leading to blissful identification with the One; as later traditions summed it up: 'mind, being, bliss.'

104 The Jains, on the other hand, have a naturalistic and non-theistic view of existence. The world is not an illusion; it really exists 'out there', and the ultimate reality is not a pan-theistic non-dual 'ground of being', but is the countless irreducible atomic monads or 'souls'. Later Jain theory developed this pluralistic approach into a vastly complex scheme for classifying the various elemental phenomena, an Aristotelian project like those favoured by the Abhidhamma schools of Buddhism. Enlightenment consists, not in the mystic identification of the self with the universe, but in the disentanglement of the individual soul from the polluting effects of kamma. They therefore emphasize, as part of their overall strategy of forcibly stopping all activity, contemplation of the impermanence of the world, and the ability to mindfully endure painful feelings in order to get free from the defiling influences.

105 The Brahmanical tradition leaned to the side of samatha, while the Jain tradition leaned to the side of vipassanā, each shaping its presentation and emphasis in accord with its metaphysical predilections. The evidence of the non-Buddhists themselves, as far as it goes, tends to confirm that the picture painted by the early Suttas of the non-Buddhist traditions is generally accurate. In the absence of any evidence to the contrary, we can conclude that the earliest Buddhist traditions accept that both the Brahmanical and the Jain contemplative traditions included the practice of mindfulness.

Chapter 11

BUILDING BLOCKS

LET'S NOW CONSIDER MINDFULNESS in the Buddhist context. In accordance with the GIST we should start with the earliest statement on mindfulness in the Dhammacakkappavattana Sutta.

11.1 The Function of Satipaṭṭhāna

2 This is addressed to the group of five ascetics, and thus locates the Buddha's message within the existing spiritual context. It starts by dismissing the wrong practices of sensuality and self-mortification, then expounds the right way, the noble eightfold path. This consists of: right view, right motivation, right speech, right action, right livelihood, right effort, right mindfulness, and right samādhi. This formulation of the Buddha's earliest teaching is preserved in texts of the Theravāda, Mahīśasaka, Dharmaguptaka, (Mūla) Sarvāstivāda, and Mahāsaṅghika schools. The factors of the path are not further defined here, apart from right view, which is implied in the discussion of the four noble truths. The text therefore suggests that the audience was already familiar with the remaining seven factors.

3 By listing the factors thus, even without further definition, the text does two important things. Firstly it specifies which factors are really essential for the goal; and second, it places them in a sequence implying a conditional relationship between the factors. Elsewhere this relationship is made explicit. The very first discourse of the Magga-saṁyutta stresses the

causal relationship between the factors of the path including mindfulness and samādhi: 'For one of right mindfulness, right samādhi comes to be'. An important definition of 'noble right samādhi', found in all four Nikāyas, also emphasizes that the path factors, culminating in right mindfulness, function to support samādhi.

4 > 'What, monks, is noble right samādhi with its vital conditions, and with its prerequisites? There are: right view, right intention, right speech, right action, right livelihood, right effort, right mindfulness. One-pointedness of mind equipped with these seven factors is called noble right samādhi "with its vital conditions" and also "with its prerequisites".'[1]

5 The same principle appears in Bhikkhunī Dhammadinnā's analysis of samādhi.

6 > 'One-pointedness of mind, friend Visākha, is samādhi. The four satipaṭṭhānas are the basis for samādhi. The four right strivings are the prerequisite of samādhi. The cultivation, development, and making much of these same principles is the development of samādhi therein.'[2]

7 Or again, in the context of the five spiritual faculties:

8 > 'It is indeed to be expected, bhante, for a faithful noble disciple whose energy is roused and whose mindfulness is established that, having made relinquishment the support, he will gain samādhi, he will gain one-pointedness of mind.'[3]

9 Elsewhere the path is analysed into three—ethics, samādhi, and understanding. If satipaṭṭhāna was primarily a vipassanā practice, it would of course be included in the understanding section. But both the Theravāda and the Sarvāstivāda Suttas include satipaṭṭhāna in the section on samādhi, never the section on understanding.[4] All of the basic statements on the

---

1 DN 18.27, MN 117.3, SN 45.28, AN 7.42. The term *parikkhāra* more familiarly refers to a monk's four requisites—bowl, robes, dwelling, and medicine. Here it means the factors that are 'pre-requisite' for attaining jhāna. Later it is replaced in this sense by its etymological twin *parikamma*, usually rendered something like 'preparatory work'.

2 MN 44.12.

3 SN 48.50.

4 MN 44.11/MA 210.

function of satipaṭṭhāna in the path confirm that its prime role is to support samādhi, that is, jhāna.

10 This can be made clearer by presenting a structural analysis of the truths and the path. This is parallel to Venerable Sāriputta's analysis of the four noble truths in the Mahā Hatthipadopama Sutta. This analysis of the path is found in the Saccavibhaṅga Sutta and the Mahā Satipaṭṭhāna Sutta, so it is clearly relevant to satipaṭṭhāna. The basic definitions are derived from the Magga Saṁyutta.

11
> 1) The noble truth of suffering... origin... cessation... path.
> 2) And what is the noble truth of the path? Right view... right mindfulness, right samādhi.
> 3) And what is right mindfulness? One contemplates a body in the body... feelings... mind... dhammas. What is right samādhi? Quite secluded... one enters the first jhāna... second jhāna... third jhāna... fourth jhāna.

12 The Satipaṭṭhāna Sutta picks up from here:

13
> How does one contemplate a body in the body? Here a monk, gone to the forest... establishes mindfulness. Ever mindful he breaths in, ever mindful he breathes out...

14 Thus the explanations of the various satipaṭṭhānas follow on from the basic definitions of the path. They are a more elaborated stage of the teaching. Those who learned the Satipaṭṭhāna Sutta would have been familiar with this basic context. In other words, the students would already know that satipaṭṭhāna is the seventh of the eight factors of the path, and that its function there is to support jhāna.

15 There is, however, one important context where mindfulness appears immediately before a wisdom factor rather than samādhi. This is the seven awakening-factors: mindfulness, investigation of dhammas, energy, rapture, tranquillity, samādhi, equanimity. First we may notice the obvious fact that, although mindfulness comes before investigation of dhammas, both of these ultimately support the range of samatha qualities, which form such a prominent portion of the awakening-factors. We may still wonder why the wisdom factor appears near the beginning, instead of its normal position towards the end.

16 The answer lies in the ambiguous usage of both mindfulness and investigation of dhammas in this context. The awakening-factors are presented sometimes in a teaching context, sometimes in meditation context. Mindfulness and investigation of dhammas are the only factors whose definitions differ in the two contexts. In a teaching context, we hear of the monk who hears the teachings, then recollects and remembers that teaching with mindfulness, and then investigates the meaning of the teaching.[5] More meditative contexts speak, in the Theravāda, simply of mindfulness, but the Sarvāstivāda supplies the expected identification with the four satipaṭṭhānas.[6] Investigation of dhammas, in both versions, is the inquiry into skilful and unskilful dhammas. While the meditation contexts occur far more frequently in the Theravāda, the one teaching-context text in the Theravāda is represented by three in the Sarvāstivāda, and the same passage forms the basis for the relevant section of the Abhidhamma Vibhaṅga. It must therefore be regarded as of considerable importance. In the Bojjhaṅga-saṁyutta, it is in this teaching context alone, never in the meditative context, that the seven awakening-factors are said to arise in a progressive sequence, each dependent on the previous. So when considering the significance of the *sequence* of the awakening-factors, the primary meanings of the terms mindfulness and investigation of dhammas should be 'recollection' and 'investigation' into the teachings. This then inspires the development of samādhi. This explains why mindfulness in the awakening-factors appears directly before the wisdom factor, rather than the samādhi factors.

17 As usual, however, matters are not quite so cut-&-dried. In the context of ānāpānasati, the sequential arising of the enlightenment factors is also spoken of.[7] This context, being a synthesis of several established doctrinal frameworks, is not as fundamental as the usage in the Bojjhaṅga-saṁyutta. The main point of the section is not really to analyse the sequential origin of the awakening-factors, but to stress their integration with ānāpānasati and satipaṭṭhāna. Of course, in ānāpānasati we are in samatha home turf, and vipassanā is normally said to emerge in the final tetrad, that is, coming

5 SN 46.3/SA 736/SA 740/SA 724*.

6 SN 46.51/SA 715.

7 E.g. SN 54.13/SA 810.

well after the establishment of mindfulness and the attaining of samādhi. Thus the sequential arising of the awakening-factors is a little odd in this context, and is probably no more than an application of the standard sequence in a derived context, without special significance.

18 The function of satipaṭṭhāna as support for jhāna is suggested in a very common Sutta idiom, whose significance tends to be obscured in translation. The term *satipaṭṭhāna* (establishing of mindfulness) resolves into *sati* and *upaṭṭhāna*. The alternative resolution into *sati* and *paṭṭhāna*, though favoured by the commentaries, is spurious. The difference between the two is that while *upaṭṭhāna* expresses the subjective act of establishing or setting up mindfulness, *paṭṭhāna* would refer to the 'foundations' of mindfulness, the objective domains on which mindfulness is established. The basic meaning of *upaṭṭhāna* is to 'stand near', and it is commonly used to mean 'serve', 'approach', even 'worship'. Taranatha Tarkavacaspati's Sanskrit dictionary gives the meaning of 'causing to remember' (especially past lives), which would be identical with *sati*, but as this does not seem to be attested in any early text it is probably under Buddhist influence. We have already remarked that the closest parallel in the Upaniṣads is the term *upāsana*.

19 *Upaṭṭhāna* occasionally occurs in vipassanā contexts, though not, so far as I know, in any central collection in the Saṁyutta. In the Aṅguttara sixes, one is encouraged to 'establish perception of impermanence [suffering, not-self]' regarding all conditioned activities.[8] Here, although it is not in the context of satipaṭṭhāna, we see a similar subjective role for *upaṭṭhāna*, with the object in locative case, as in satipaṭṭhāna and elsewhere. In the context of satipaṭṭhāna, *upaṭṭhāna* suggests that one is to make mindfulness stand close by, to be present, to serve the meditation. *Sati* and *upaṭṭhapeti* stand in the same organic relation as do *saddhā* with *adhimuccati*, or *viriya* with *ārabbhati*. These terms, all commonly used in conjunction, indicate a reiterative emphasis. Just as one 'decides faith' or one 'rouses up energy', so too one 'establishes mindfulness'. In fact, we could render this phrase 'one does satipaṭṭhāna', the difference being merely verbal. Because the verb *upaṭṭhapeti* has such an organic relationship with the noun *sati* they are found together in a variety of settings, just as *sati* is found everywhere.

[8] AN 6.102–4.

But by far the most important, common, and characteristic use is in the gradual training, where the phrase refers to taking a seated posture for meditation before the abandoning of the hindrances and entering jhāna.

20 In the gradual training, *sati* and *upaṭṭhāna* occur in the idiom *parimukhaṁ satiṁ upaṭṭhapeti*. The term *parimukha* is one of those simple words that is so hard to interpret. It literally means 'around the mouth', but the Vibhaṅga says 'at the nose tip', while modern renderings usually use something vague like 'in front'. However the phrase occurs outside of ānāpānasati, making the interpretation 'at the nose-tip', or any literal spatial interpretation, unlikely. The Sanskrit has a different reading, *pratimukha*.[9] This has many meanings, among which are 'reflection' and 'presence'. Both of these are appropriate in a meditative context. But the word usually, as here, occurs with *upaṭṭhāna*, which also means 'presence'. I think here we have an example of that common feature of Pali or Sanskrit, a conjunction of synonyms for emphasis: literally, 'one makes present a presence of presence of mind', or more happily, 'one establishes presence of mindfulness'.

21 The gradual training is the main paradigm for the way of practice in pre-sectarian Buddhism. In the GIST we have seen how this teaching is fundamental to all the early collections, especially the Dīghas. Here is a table with the gradual training in relation to a number of other key teaching frameworks. I use the ten-fold path rather than the eightfold, since this correlates more neatly with the gradual training.

22 Our main concern is the middle factors, from contentment to abandoning hindrances. These are part of the training in samādhi.[10] However I have not specified their exact relationship with the relevant path-factors. They are a loose grouping of affiliated practices that form a bridge between ethics and samādhi. Since they involve behaviour, they pertain to ethics. Several—contentment, sense restraint, moderation in eating, clear comprehension—relate to a monk's relation with his alms-food, and so relate to right livelihood. They are included within samādhi because they emphasize the mental attitude in various contexts, and thus form a special training-ground for the serious meditator.

---

[9] E.g. Skt MPS 27.16; Skt CPS 6.1; Skt SPS 63.

[10] DN 10.2.1–18/DA^2 42. WALSHE's translation is faulty. He has: 'This comes to him through concentration'. It should read: 'This is, for him, what pertains to concentration'.

Table 11.1: The Truths, the Path, and the Training

4 Noble Truths	3-fold Training	10-fold Path	Gradual Training
Suffering		Right view	Hearing the teaching
Origin			Gaining faith
Cessation			
Path		Right intention	Going forth
	Ethics	Right Speech	Rules of discipline
		Right action	
		Right livelihood	Purifying livelihood
	Samādhi	Right effort	Contentment
			Sense restraint
			Moderate eating
			Wakefulness
		Right mindfulness	Clear comprehension
			Seclusion
			Establishing mindfulness
			Abandoning hindrances
		Right samādhi	Four jhānas
	Understanding	Right knowledge	Knowledge & vision
			Mind-made body
			Psychic powers
			Divine ear
			Reading minds
			Past lives
			Divine eye
			Noble truths
		Right release	Liberation

23 I have correlated the practices from contentment to abandoning the hindrances with right effort and right mindfulness in a general fashion, without trying to tie them down too precisely. Even right effort and right mindfulness cannot be fully disentangled from each other: one practicing satipaṭṭhāna is said to be 'ardent' (with right effort); while one abandoning the hindrance of sloth & torpor is said to be 'mindful & clearly comprehending'. There are other ambiguities in this section. For example, sense restraint is said to counteract 'evil, unskilful qualities', a phrase that recurs in the formula for the four right efforts. These bad qualities are further described as 'covetousness & aversion', the same words that appear in the satipaṭṭhāna auxiliary formula. The Sanskrit here adds the word 'for the world', thus increasing the parallel with satipaṭṭhāna. It also adds the phrases 'controlled in mindfulness, guarded in mindfulness' (*nipakasmṛti, guptasmṛti*); similar phrases are found elsewhere in the Pali. This simply says that the path is practiced as a whole, and any division is provisional, useful for ease of exposition and understanding. Thus I place right effort next to 'wakefulness', and right mindfulness next to 'establishing mindfulness' to indicate their most direct correlation, but without separating them from the other factors.

24 This ambiguity provides a ready explanation for how clear comprehension came to be included within satipaṭṭhāna. We have already seen several considerations in support of Bronkhorst's view that we must distinguish between two levels of mindfulness in the account of the gradual training: the preliminary stage of 'mindfulness in daily life', usually called 'clear comprehension', and, when the yogi sits down in the forest to meditate, the undertaking of satipaṭṭhāna proper. Clear comprehension, like other practices such as sense restraint, wakefulness, etc., involves mindfulness in its role of preparing for meditation. But because, in the gradual training, clear comprehension comes close before the 'establishing of mindfulness' in meditation, it would quite naturally become subsumed under satipaṭṭhāna as that practice grew in scope and importance.

25 So there is a progressive, causal sequence in the factors of the path as presented in the Dhammacakkappavattana Sutta. One's understanding of the Dhamma impels one to renounce in search of peace; one undertakes the rules of conduct and livelihood; applies oneself to restraint and

mindfulness in all activities and postures; resorts to a secluded dwelling; establishes mindfulness in satipaṭṭhāna meditation; and develops the four jhānas leading to liberating insight. This understanding of the path is deeply embedded in the Buddha's conception of the way spiritual practice unfolds. The more detailed, explicit teachings emerge and spread out from the concise scheme of the Dhammacakkappavattana Sutta, like light passing through a pinhole and radiating out.

11.2 Mindfulness Itself

26 We now examine mindfulness itself under a closer focus, examining the phrases and sayings regarding satipaṭṭhāna that are found widely distributed among the various collections. In the Theravāda canon, mindfulness is described in two stock formulas. The simpler one emphasizes the older, Brahmanical, meaning of 'memory'.

27 > 'Here, monks, a noble disciple is mindful, endowed with highest mindfulness and self-control, able to remember, to keep in memory what was said and done long ago.'[11]

28 This formula does not explicitly treat mindfulness as meditation. It is less closely associated with satipaṭṭhāna as such rather than ordinary mindfulness. As I have shown elsewhere, the term *nepakka*, 'self-control', here implies sense restraint, not wisdom (as the commentaries have it.[12])

29 The Sarvāstivāda offers a different description of mindfulness.

30 > 'When there is mindfulness for, mindfulness against, or having no mindfulness towards (anything) he is mindful, widely mindful, keeping in mind, not forgetful. This is called right mindfulness.'[13]

31 It's not at all clear what this means. Perhaps the mysterious first three terms refer to the practice, which we will meet later, of perceiving the beautiful in the ugly, the ugly in the beautiful, and avoiding both through equanimity.

32 We've become so used to the equation of mindfulness = vipassanā that it comes as a shock to find that the word 'mindfulness' hardly occurs in

---

[11] SN 48.9, etc.

[12] *A Swift Pair of Messengers*, Appendix A.10.

[13] MA 189, etc.

the central vipassanā collections. In fact, it never occurs in the Khandha-, Saḷāyatana-, or Nidāna-saṁyuttas in the direct sense of contemplating impermanence, etc. On the few occasions it appears, it does so in secondary contexts, typically in the Saḷāyatana-saṁyutta in its role to assist sense restraint. The primary function of sense restraint is to reduce sensual lust, so this must be understood as falling on the side of samatha. On the other hand, 'mindfulness' appears regularly in such straightforward samatha contexts as the jhāna formula, descriptions of the divine abidings and six recollections, ānāpānasati, the 'establishing of mindfulness' for abandoning hindrances, and so on.

11.3 The Fourfold Establishing of Mindfulness

33 The next layer of complexity describes satipaṭṭhāna as fourfold. In keeping with the pragmatic and relativist perspective of the Suttas, this is not a definition of mindfulness but a prescription of how to practice. The standard formulas have both an objective aspect—what to meditate on—and a subjective aspect—how to approach the practice. I will discuss the objective aspect first. All traditions agree in listing four basic objects of satipaṭṭhāna meditation: body, feelings, mind, and dhammas. Curiously, these are rarely described in any detail. Only in the various versions of the Satipaṭṭhāna Sutta are the meanings specified. Presumably the Satipaṭṭhāna Sutta acted then, as it does today, as a key with which the brief texts could be interpreted.

34 A crucial point here is that the fourfold formula introduces certain specific objects of meditation, moving towards treating satipaṭṭhāna as such in a narrower way than mindfulness in general. Satipaṭṭhāna is the only context in the main formulations of the path—the wings to awakening, the gradual training, the dependent liberation—to specify the object of meditation. Generally there tends to be a somewhat curious distance in the Suttas between the subjective and objective sides of meditation. For example, the Suttas describe jhāna in terms of the subjective mental qualities, and elsewhere describe various meditation objects that are intended to develop jhāna, yet they virtually never speak of, say, 'ānāpānasati jhāna' (but there is 'ānāpānasati samādhi'), or '*kasiṇa* jhāna' (though there is a

slightly dubious reference to 'compassion jhāna'.) This distance is not systematically bridged until the Dhammasaṅgaṇī. So satipaṭṭhāna, being thus more 'grounded' and specific, fulfils an important practical function in the path. The implication is that the particular meditation objects here are an intrinsic and hence non-optional part of the path. All meditators must develop at least some of the satipaṭṭhāna practices.Meditation subjects outside of the satipaṭṭhāna scheme are very frequently taught in the Suttas, notably the divine abidings and the six recollections, but they are not so essential; however, the feelings, mind states, and dhammas associated with them fit under satipaṭṭhāna. This crossover 'objective' aspect of satipaṭṭhāna makes it an odd man out in the 37 wings to awakening, and we shall repeatedly see ambiguities and incongruities emerging in the later attempts to thoroughly systemize these groups.

35 Why these four? Later texts of several schools suggest that the four oppose the four perversions. Contemplation of the body opposes the perversion of seeing beauty in ugliness; contemplation of feelings opposes the perversion of seeing suffering as pleasure; contemplation of the mind opposes the perversion of seeing the impermanent as permanent; and contemplation of dhammas opposes the perversion of seeing self in what is not-self. Certainly they can work in that way; there is no doubt that, say, the contemplation of the body is oriented towards dispelling sensual lust and that the meditation of ugliness is an important part of this strategy. And it is indeed in the survival of the mind, *citta*, that many seek the solace of eternal bliss. Overall, however, this explanation is *post facto* and artificial. Since this teaching is not found in the early Suttas, nor is it intuitively obvious, it is probably a case of later borrowing between the sects.

36 A more pertinent consideration in the formulation of satipaṭṭhāna in terms of these specific four subjects is that they progress from coarse to subtle. The body is mainly treated as the basic object for developing meditation. Feelings are the most obvious of the mental qualities. The mind, the inner sense of cognition, the 'knowing' rather than the 'known', is more subtle, and is properly approached through the first two. As we shall see, both the treatment of the terms themselves, and the correlation with ānāpānasati, suggest that a key facet of this progressive refinement of contemplation so far is the undertaking, development, and mastery of

jhāna. This much is straightforward, and the traditions are more-or-less in agreement, although they tend to de-emphasize this progressive structure. This is because they treat the next factor, dhammas, as meaning various phenomena, many of which are not more subtle than the first three, and thus disturbing the sequence. This is a mistake. Dhammas in satipaṭṭhāna are not a miscellaneous grab-bag of left-overs from the first three, but a distinctive and more profound aspect of meditation: the understanding of the causal principles underlying the development of samādhi.

11.4 How the Practice is Described

37 While the list of the four objects of satipaṭṭhānas is common to all traditions, the description of the subjective aspect differs substantially, even within the basic pericope; however this is a mere matter of editing preferences rather than sectarian divergence.

11.4.1 Simple and Complex Formulas

38 The Sarvāstivāda, in both the Saṁyutta and Majjhima, is the simplest: one develops 'the establishing of mindfulness of contemplating a body in the body...' etc. The Sanskrit versions of the Dasuttara and Saṅgīti Suttas, which are also Sarvāstivādin, feature a similar formula. The Mahāsaṅghika Ekāyana Sūtra is elaborated from a similarly simple formula; it refers to meditating on the body to remove unwholesome thoughts and anxiety, and meditating on the other three to gain peace and joy.

39 The main Theravāda Nikāyas do not contain such a simple version. However the later Pali texts do include similar formulations. The Niddesa, an algebraic abhidhamma-style commentary on the oldest parts of the Sutta Nipāta (Aṭṭhaka Vagga, Pārāyana Vagga, Khaggavisāna Sutta) that is one of the most obscure and little-read corners of the Pali scriptures (and that's saying something!), includes such a phrase in its standard gloss on 'mindful'.[14] Similar phrases also occur in the Paṭisambhidāmagga, which is of a similar or later time.[15] By the time of the commentaries it becomes fairly

[14] E.g. Mahā Niddesa 1.1.3.
[15] Paṭisambhidāmagga 169.

frequent. The fact that this simple version becomes more frequent in later Pali works suggests that it is not original. In this case, the shorter formula is a later summary rather than an early form.

40 This conclusion is supported by SA 612 of the Sarvāstivāda Satipaṭṭhāna Saṁyutta. After the standard ending this adds an editorial gloss:

> 41 All sūtras on the four satipaṭṭhānas are to end with the following phrase, that is: 'Therefore a monk developing and practicing the four satipaṭṭhānas, giving rise to exalted aspirations, with refined striving and skilful means, with right mindfulness and right knowledge, should train.'

42 Thus the short formula in the Sarvāstivāda is merely a function of the abbreviation of the texts, and the tradition itself states that the abbreviated version should be expanded in every case. This expanded formula is similar to the standard Theravādin version. They both differ from the abbreviated form in leaving out the term 'satipaṭṭhāna' from the formula itself, and in adding a series of terms qualifying the practice. In the Theravāda version, one contemplates 'ardent, clearly comprehending, mindful, having removed covetousness & aversion for the world'. This phrase is found across the schools, and we'll refer to it as the 'auxiliary formula'. The Sarvāstivāda version omits the phrase 'having removed covetousness & aversion for the world'. This is found elsewhere in the Saṁyutta,[16] however, so its omission here might be accidental. In speaking of 'exalted aspirations, refined striving, and skilful means', it expands the simple 'ardent' of the Theravāda versions. 'Skilful means' is reminiscent of the Mahāyāna; but before that, it was a characteristic of Venerable Upagupta, an early patriarch of the Sarvāstivāda, so the difference between the Sarvāstivāda and Theravāda here might be sectarian. The phrase 'right mindfulness, right knowledge' is commonly found in the Chinese texts, and is equivalent to the Theravāda's 'mindful, clearly comprehending'.

43 One attempt to interpret these terms is found in the Netti, which says, in agreement with the schools, that these qualities correspond with four of the five spiritual faculties: ardent = energy; clearly comprehending = understanding; mindful = mindfulness; having removed covetousness & aver-

[16] SA 610/SN 47.39.

sion for the world = samādhi.[17] However, the correlation with the spiritual faculties is not really very close. For example, the spiritual faculty of understanding (*paññā*) is defined as 'the understanding of rise and fall that is noble and penetrative, leading to the full ending of suffering'.[18] Clear comprehension (*sampajañña*), although etymologically parallel to 'understanding' is never used in this exalted sense, but is usually restricted to the more mundane sense of 'awareness of activities in daily life', or else it expresses the wisdom dimension of jhāna.

44 A better way of seeing these terms is suggested by the Sanskrit Mahā Parinirvāṇa Sutta. There is a famous episode when the gorgeous courtesan Ambapālī comes to visit. In the Pali, the Buddha urges the monks to be 'mindful and clearly comprehending'. The Sanskrit expands this: 'Monks, dwell ardent, clearly comprehending, and mindful. Ambapālī the courtesan comes here!'[19] The texts goes on to define 'ardent' as the four right efforts, 'clearly comprehending' as awareness in daily activities, and 'mindful' as the four satipaṭṭhānas. This corresponds exactly to the usage in the satipaṭṭhāna formula itself. Now, these practices are all a standard part of the gradual training.

11.4.2 Covetousness & Aversion

45 This suggests a connection between the final phrase, 'having removed covetousness and aversion for the world' with the preparatory phase of the gradual training, especially sense restraint. The standard passage on sense restraint, which in the Theravāda account of the gradual training usually occurs just before 'clear comprehension', includes the same words 'covetousness & aversion' (*abhijjhā-domanassa*) that occur in the satipaṭṭhāna formula.[20] In the Sanskrit the parallel with satipaṭṭhāna is even clearer, for there the phrase is 'covetousness & aversion for the world' (*abhidhyā-daurmanasye loke*).[21] Also, the Sanskrit, for example the

[17] Netti 4.23.

[18] SN 48.9/SA 647.

[19] Waldschmidt (1950, 1951) 10.8.

[20] DN 2.64/DA 27/T № 22/EA 42.7/SA 154–163*, etc.

[21] Meisig, pg. 268.

Śrāmaṇyaphala Sūtra and the Śrāvakabhūmi, uses the word 'mindfulness' more frequently here.

46 Let us examine more closely how the key words *abhijjhā* and *domanassa* are used. *Abhijjhā* is used in two clearly defined senses. As one of the ten 'pathways of unskilful actions' it means covetousness: 'Oh! What belongs to him should be mine!'[22] As an alternative to *kāmacchanda* ('sensual desire') as the first of the five hindrances, it is much more subtle, encompassing any desire or interest in sensual experience. In the gradual training, both the Pali and the Sanskrit describe the overcoming of this hindrance as 'abandoning covetousness for the world', which again is very similar to the satipaṭṭhāna formula. The term *domanassa*, which I render here as 'aversion', usually means 'mental suffering', but in at least one context it stands for the hindrance of ill-will,[23] and this must be the meaning in satipaṭṭhāna, too. While the use of exactly the same phrase *abhijjhā-domanassa* underscores the closeness of the phrase in satipaṭṭhāna with sense restraint, I do not see any major significance in the exact choice of terms for 'ill-will'; the Pali uses a number of terms more-or-less synonymously. While as a hindrance ill-will can be very subtle, in the ten pathways of unskilful actions, it is defined in very strong terms: 'May these beings be destroyed, killed, and wiped out!' So these two terms, 'covetousness' and 'aversion', encompass various levels of intensity. The coarse forms are abandoned through the preliminary practices, especially sense restraint, while the subtle forms are abandoned on entering jhāna.

11.4.3 Satipaṭṭhāna Compared with Loving-kindness

47 The satipaṭṭhāna auxiliary formula sounds much more like samatha than vipassanā. Similar descriptions of the meditative state of mind are not found in direct vipassanā contexts. But let us compare it with this description of the practice of loving-kindness.

48 **Satipaṭṭhāna Auxiliary formula**

... ātāpī, sampajāno, satimā, vineyya loke abhijjhādomanassaṁ.

Ardent, clearly comprehending, mindful, having removed covetousness and aversion for the world.

---

[22] AN 10.176.

[23] Sn 1112.

49 **Loving-kindness**[24]
... vigatābhijjho, vigatābyapado, asammuḷho, sampajāno, patissato mettā-sahagatena cetasā...
Free of covetousness, free of ill will, unconfused, clearly comprehending, mindful, with a heart full of loving-kindness...

50 This is simply a slight variation in expression describing a similar subjective process of meditation. The passage on loving-kindness is obviously referring to jhāna, and the similarity of the two passages suggests that jhāna, rather than being a pre-requisite, is part of the complete fulfilment of satipaṭṭhāna.The main point of the auxilliary phrase is to emphasize that mindfulness is not developed alone, sufficient unto itself, but in the context of the path as a whole; and in this all the traditions are in full agreement.

11.4.4 Variants on the Basic Formula

51 As well as the standard formula, the texts, mainly of the Saṁyutta, offer a number of interesting variants. Below I list some of the main variations in the Pali tradition. Several of these variations in their original contexts follow on after the standard Pali formula; these are marked with an arrow.

52 1) *Kāye kāyānupassana-satipaṭṭhānaṁ...* (Sanskrit, Niddesa, etc.)
The establishing of mindfulness of contemplating a body in the body...

53 2) *Kāye kāyānupassī viharati; ātāpī, sampajāno, satimā, vineyya loke abhijjhādomanassaṁ...* (standard auxilliary formula)
One abides contemplating a body in the body; ardent, clearly comprehending, mindful, having removed covetousness & aversion for the world...

54 3) → *Kāye kāyānupassī viharato yo kayasmiṁ chando so pahīyati; chandassa pahānāya amataṁ sacchikataṁ hoti...* (SN 47.37)
For one abiding contemplating a body in the body, desire for the body is abandoned; with abandoning of desire the deathless is witnessed...

55 4) → *Kāye kāyānupassī viharato kāyo pariññāto hoti...* (SN 47.38)
For one abiding contemplating a body in the body, the body is fully known...

[24] SN 42.8/SA 916/SA2 131, AN 10.219.

56 5) → *Kāye kāyānupassī viharanto pi upahanet'eva pāpake akusale dhamme...* (SN 54.10/SA 813/Skt)
When one abides contemplating a body in the body, one crushes evil unskilful qualities...

57 6) → *Kāye kāyānupassī viharato cittaṁ virajjati vimuccati anupādāya āsavehi...* (SN 47.11/SA 614)
For one abiding contemplating a body in the body, the mind fades away and releases from the defilements without grasping...

58 7) *Kāye kāyānupassī viharatha; ātāpīno, sampajānā, ekodibhūtā, vippasannacittā, samāhitā, ekaggacittā...* (SN 47.4/SA 621)
Abide contemplating a body in the body; ardent, clearly comprehending, unified, with clear mind, in samādhi, with one-pointed mind...

59 8) → *Kāye kāyānupassī viharami; ātāpī, sampajāno, satimā, 'sukhasmī' ti pajānāti...* (SN 47.10/SA 615)
I abide contemplating a body in the body; ardent, clearly comprehending, mindful, I understand: 'I am blissful'...

60 9) → *Kāye kāyānupassī viharato cittaṁ samādhiyati upakkilesā pahīyanti...* (SN 47.8/SA 616)
For one abiding contemplating a body in the body, the mind enters samādhi, the taints are abandoned...

61 10) → *Kāye kāyānupassī viharanto tattha sammā samādhiyati sammā vippasīdati...* (DN 18.26/DA 4)
When one abides contemplating a body in the body, there one gains right samādhi, right clarity...

62 11) → *Kāye kāyānupassī viharahi, mā ca kāyūpasaṁhitaṁ vitakkaṁ vitakkesi...* (MN 125.24/MA 198)
You should abide contemplating a body in the body, but do not think thoughts connected with the body...[25]

63 These variants fall naturally into three groups. The first pair (1 & 2) give the most basic statement or summary of the practice. Second are the variants that describe the result of the practice in general terms similar to the

[25] Bhikkhu Bodhi has changed his rendering here from 'connected with the body' to 'connected with sensual desire'. According to his note 1177 in the revised 2001 edition of MLDB, the PTS edition has *kāyūpasaṁhitaṁ* (connected with the body), abbreviates the next two, then has *dhammūpasaṁhitaṁ*. The Burmese editions, supported by a 1937 Sinhalese edition, have *kāmūpasaṁhitaṁ*. He also cites the Chinese translation in support. The Sanskrit version quoted just below, however, supports *kāyūpasaṁhitaṁ*.

description of many other modes of practice (3–6). The remainder (7–11) describe the actual meditation itself and are more specific to satipaṭṭhāna. It is striking that these variants deal explicitly with samādhi. Three (7, 9, 10) mention the word samādhi. One of these (7) reinforces samādhi with the synonyms 'unified, one-pointed mind'. This variant, in common with one other (10), also has the term *vippasāda*, which is similar to the *sampasāda* of the second jhāna. The mention of 'bliss' (8) also suggests jhāna; the context confirms this. The remaining variant in this group (11) encourages the stilling of *vitakka*, which refers to the second jhāna; and again this is confirmed in the context. Later texts of the schools furnish us with even more variants on the basic formula. I will just list a few for the sake of comparison. The first is virtually identical to the standard Pali version; the second and third offer minor elaborations.

64 12) *Adhyātmam kāye kāyānupaśyī viharaty ātāpī samprajanaḥ smṛtiman viniyabhidhyā loke daurmanasyam...* (Sarv Mahā Parinirvāṇa Sūtra)
Internally one abides contemplating a body in the body; ardent, clearly comprehending, mindful, having removed covetousness for the world, and aversion...

65 13) *Kāye kāyānupaśyino viharataḥ kāyālambanānusmṛti tiṣṭhati saṁtiṣṭhati...* (Abhidharmakośa 342)
For one abiding contemplating a body in the body, recollection supported by the body is set up, well set up...

66 14) *Kāye kāyānupaśyino viharataḥ upaṣṭhita smṛti bhavaty asammuḍheti...* (Abhidharmakośa 342)
For one abiding contemplating a body in the body, unconfused mindfulness is established...

67 15) *Kāye kāyānudarṣī viharati, na ca kāyasahagatan vitarkan vitarkayati...* (Pratyutpannabuddhasammukhāvaṣṭhitasamādhi Sūtra 15J, 18B)[26]
One observes a body in the body, but one does not think thoughts associated with the body... (cp. Version 11 above.)

68 Thus we find that within the existing variations on the basic satipaṭṭhāna formula, several refer quite explicitly to samatha, while none mention the contemplation of impermanence and causality that is the hallmark of vipassanā.

[26] HARRISON. The Sanskrit has been tentatively reconstructed by the translator.

69 The outstanding feature of all the formulas, the definitive statement of what satipaṭṭhāna involves, is that one 'abides contemplating a body in the body… (feeling, mind, dhammas)'. Here, there are two features that demand explanation. One is the repetitive idiom, which I render 'a body in the body'; the second is the word *anupassanā*, 'contemplation', which expresses the mode of awareness characteristic to satipaṭṭhāna.

11.4.5 'A Body in the Body'

70 The reflective idiom 'a body in the body' has been often commented on. Some hold that it is merely idiomatic, with no particular significance; but surely such repetition must at the very least signify emphasis. The normative explanation in recent times, based on the Theravādin tradition, is that the repetition delineates and defines the object, excluding taking the body (etc.) to be something that it is not, i.e. a self. This explanation makes sense in a context that takes it for granted that satipaṭṭhāna is primarily vipassanā. However, it might be reinterpreted to suit a samatha context as well—not straying outside the bounds of the given meditation. But none of these interpretations enjoy direct support from the Suttas. To find this, we must turn to a somewhat cryptic passage found in the Ānāpānasati Sutta, and in slightly different form in the Saṁyutta. This gives a unique set of phrases qualifying each of the four objects of satipaṭṭhāna in the context of breath meditation. They are as follows:

> 71 (Body) 'I call this a certain body [among the bodies], Ānanda, that is, breathing & breathing out…
>
> 72 (Feelings) 'I call this a certain feeling [among the feelings], Ānanda, that is, close attention to breathing in & breathing out…
>
> 73 (Mind) 'I say, Ānanda, that there is no development of samādhi by breathing in & breathing out by one who is muddled and who lacks clear comprehension…
>
> 74 (Dhammas) 'Having seen with understanding the abandoning of covetousness & aversion, he watches over closely with equanimity…'[27]

75 All these raise interpretive issues. It is not good to rely on such unclear passages, but in the absence of other relevant passages we have no choice. The sections on feelings and mind are obscure, and I will not discuss them

[27] SN 54.10/SA 813, SN 54.13/SA 810, MN 118.23*ff*.

here. The dhammas section is interesting, but I will defer a discussion until we consider ānāpānasati in general.

76 The first saying, dealing with the body, is straightforward. Evidently, the 'breath' is considered as a kind of 'body', or we might say in English, a kind of physical phenomenon, an aspect of the body. The bracketed portions appear in the Majjhima version only, not the Saṁyutta. However, they do not substantially alter the meaning. The meditator is to select this sphere within the entire field of physical experience as the focus of awareness. This is entirely in keeping with the thesis that satipaṭṭhāna is first of all a samatha practice. This interpretation is also in clear accord with the Satipaṭṭhāna Suttas. The descriptions of all the practices in all versions speak of a series of contemplations of discrete aspects of the given topic. For example, one contemplates pleasant feeling, then painful feeling, then neutral feeling, and so on. So we are on the right track: the repetitive idiom in the satipaṭṭhāna formula narrows the focus of attention within each of the four objects of satipaṭṭhāna.

11.4.6 'Contemplation'

77 The second crucial part of the satipaṭṭhāna formula, then, is the term *anupassanā*. In the Abhidhamma this is glossed with the standard register of terms for understanding, which is not very helpful, as it ignores the subtleties of context. This is one reason why later writers have equated *anupassanā* with vipassanā. However this explanation does not do either term justice. Let's start with a verse from the Ṛg Veda.

78 'He **contemplates** with loving favor the mortal who,
Like a rich man, pours for him the Soma.
Māghavan [i.e. Indra, King of Gods] in his bended arm supports him.
He slays, unasked, the men who hate devotion.'[28]

79 Here *anupassanā* is a strongly one-sided regard, the very opposite of 'non-judgemental'. The same usage is found in the early Buddhist texts. Here are two examples, the first from the Sutta Nipāta, the second from the Dhammapāda.

[28] Ṛg Veda 10.160.4.

80 'He is no friend who is ever diligently[29]
Suspecting dissension, **contemplating** only flaws;
But on whom one rests, like a child at the breast,
He is a true friend, who is not alienated by others.'[30]

81 'For one who **contemplates** the faults of another,
Whose thoughts are always critical;
His defilements increase—
He is far from the ending of defilements.'[31]

82 'Contemplation' (*anupassanā*) here is seeing only (*eva*) one side of a situation. Moreover, it means seeing that one side not occasionally but constantly (*sadā, niccaṁ*).

83 The Īśa Upaniṣad shows a friendlier face of *anupassanā*.

84 'He who **contemplates** all beings just as the self,
And the self as all beings—
He is not revulsed because of that.'

85 'When all beings are just the self for the discerning one,
Then what delusion, what sorrow,
For one who **contemplates** oneness?'[32]

86 In Buddhist context this would imply the practice of universal lovingkindness. In Upaniṣadic context the more pregnant metaphysical sense of 'Self' is intended. Here *anupassanā* refers to a mode of contemplation that sees two sides of things—all beings as the self, the self as all beings—and resolves this surface duality into a deeper unity. The word 'oneness' (*ekatvā*) here relates to the classic description of satipaṭṭhāna as the 'path going to one' (*ekāyana magga*). The 'two-into-one' movement finds its Buddhist counterpart in the Dvāyatānupassanā Sutta of the Sutta Nipāta. This presents a series of 'contemplations' arranged in pairs, many of which correspond with factors of dependent origination. Here is an example.

87 ' "This is suffering, this is the origin of suffering"—this is one **contemplation**. "This is the cessation of suffering, this is the way of practice leading to the end of suffering"—this is a second **contemplation**.

[29] The use of 'diligence' (*appamāda*) in a negative sense is very unusual; normally, of course, diligence is closely connected with mindfulness.

[30] Sn 255.

[31] Dhp 253.

[32] Īśa 6–7.

> Monks, for a monk, rightly **contemplating** this pair, abiding diligent, ardent, and resolute, one of two fruits may be expected: profound knowledge in this very life, or, if there is a remnant, non-return.'[33]

88 Here, just as in the Īśa, two contrasting contemplations are given. But the contrast is really a complement, so the full realization of these two contemplations leads to one goal.

89 The Śvetāśvatara's use of *anupassanā* is explicitly metaphysical.

90 'The one controller of the many, inactive,
Who makes the one seed manifold,
Standing in the self—the wise who **contemplate** him,
To them belongs eternal bliss, not to others.'[34]

91 Here, too, there is a connection between *anupassanā* and the 'one'. The wise are to contemplate the one, inactive source, not the multiplicity of appearance; only this leads to happiness. The Bṛhadāraṇyaka also uses *anupassanā* as a contemplation, a beholding, of the divine.

92 'If one clearly **contemplates** him as the self, as God,
As the Lord of what has become and what will be,
One does not shrink away from him.'[35]

93 The following verses from the Dhammapāda fall between the colloquial early usage of *anupassanā* and the more specialized sense in satipaṭṭhāna.

94 'One who abides **contemplating** beauty,
Unrestrained in his sense faculties,
Immoderate in eating,
Lazy, with deficient energy;
Truly Māra overthrows him
As the wind, a weak tree.

95 'One who abides **contemplating** ugliness,
Restrained in his sense faculties,
Moderate in eating,
Faithful, with roused-up energy;
Truly Māra does not overthrow him
As the wind, a rocky mountain.'[36]

---

33 Sn 3.12.

34 Śvetāśvatara 12.

35 BU 4.4.15.

36 Dhp 7, 8.

96 Here one contemplates either beauty or ugliness (*subha, asubha*); again, one is focusing on just one aspect of things, ignoring the other side.

97 *Anupassanā* in these verses is aimed at eliminating sensual lust, and hence falls on the side of samatha. *Anupassanā* does, however, occur in vipassanā contexts, too. For example, there are a few discourses in the Khandha-saṁyutta that speak of 'contemplation' of impermanence, suffering, and not-self.[37] Elsewhere we read of 'contemplation of impermanence', etc. regarding feelings.[38] The proper place of 'contemplation of impermanence' in satipaṭṭhāna is in the fourth satipaṭṭhāna, as is clear from ānāpānasati.

98 So *anupassanā* is used in both samatha and vipassanā contexts, and cannot be exclusively categorized as either. Although related to the word 'vipassanā', *anupassanā* is not used when standing alone, as vipassanā is, to mean the meditative enquiry into impermanence and causality. The prefix *anu-* suggests 'following, conforming, after', and lacks the analytical sense of *vi-*. It is a mode of contemplation that 'conforms' to the relevant context; thus *anupassanā* is normally the second member of a compound where the first member defines the specific subject of meditation: 'contemplation of…'. In psychological contexts *anu-* implies 'continuing'. Thus *vitakketi* means 'to think'; *anuvitakketi* means 'to keep on thinking'. The same usage occurs in the definition of *sati* as 'memory' that we have encountered above. There two terms are used: *sara* and *anussara*, which mean 'remembers, keeps in memory.' There is a similar nuance in two of the terms in the Abhidhamma gloss for the jhāna factor *vicāra—anusandhanatā* and *anupekkhanatā*—which mean 'sustained application, sustained observation'. *Anupassanā* is semantically parallel with *anupekkhanatā*, and so also means 'sustained observation'. This sustained, continuous aspect of *anupassanā* is emphasized in the verses we saw above. The Visuddhimagga's commentary makes this sense explicit: 'he keeps re-seeing (*anu anu passati*) with jhāna knowledge and insight knowledge'.[39]

---

37 SN 22.39–42/SA 27, SN 22.147/SA 48.

38 SN 36.7/SA 1028, SN 36.8/SA 1029, MN 37/SA 505/EA 19.3.

39 See Vsm trans. (ÑĀṆAMOLI), pg. 168 note 47.

11.4.7 Clear Comprehension

99 The term *sampajañña*, found in some of the satipaṭṭhāna formulas and elsewhere together with mindfulness, is also glossed by the Abhidhamma with the standard register of synonyms for wisdom, and has been equated by some writers with vipassanā. But although *sampajañña* is etymologically equivalent to *paññā* 'understanding', it is not explicitly equated with vipassanā. It is indeed used occasionally in the sense of vipassanā; we will examine this in the Satipaṭṭhāna-saṁyutta below. But *sampajañña* is most characteristically used in the context of 'daily life awareness' as a preparation for jhāna. In the Subha Sutta, it is listed under the 'aggregate of samādhi'; and in the Abhidhamma it finds its place in the Jhāna Vibhaṅga. Nowhere in the Suttas or Abhidhamma is the awareness of bodily activities treated as vipassanā.

100 The other common usage of *sampajañña* is in the formula for the third jhāna, where it expresses the wisdom dimension of samādhi. Most of the exercises of the Satipaṭṭhāna Sutta use the verb form of *paññā* in a similar sense, for example: 'One understands "I am breathing in a long breath"... One understands "I am standing"... One understands "I am experiencing a pleasant feeling"...' and so on. So there is this understanding in the sense of clear awareness through the meditation. Jhānas too can be qualified by such terms; sometimes jhāna is classified under wisdom, or one in jhāna is said to 'know & see', and so on. The use of such terms cannot mean that this is a vipassanā practice as distinguished from a samatha practice. Reality is more subtle: all meditation must include both peace and wisdom. The question is: what is the context, how are these qualities being applied here? Every context we have seen shows that the primary purpose of satipaṭṭhāna is to develop samādhi, and there is nothing here to change that conclusion. All we can rightly conclude is that the development of jhāna involves a dimension of wisdom.

11.5 Internal/External

101 In satipaṭṭhāna we are encouraged to practice internally, externally, and internally-externally. These internal/external modes of satipaṭṭhāna are

attested in all the Nikāyas, Āgamas, and Abhidhammas. We shall meet them time and time again in the later texts. There is a slight difference between the Theravāda and Sarvāstivāda Satipaṭṭhāna Suttas and most other presentations. These Suttas present the basic formula first, then add the internal/external contemplation as part of the refrain following the detailed explanation. But usually the internal/external contemplation is integrated into the formula from the start: 'One contemplates a body in the body internally…'. We call this the 'integrated internal/external formula'. This is found in the Pali sources apart from the Satipaṭṭhāna Sutta itself, such as the Saṁyutta, the Dīgha, and the Vibhaṅga; also in the Sarvāstivāda Saṁyukta,[40] Ekāyana Sūtra, Dharmaskandha, and Śāriputrābhidharma; also fairly consistently in later sources such as the Avataṁsaka Sūtra, Abhidharmasamuccaya, and Arthaviniścaya Sūtra. Obviously there is no real difference in the meaning, but such details are useful in tracing textual affiliations and editorial fiddling.

102 There is an interpretive problem here, for we normally understand that meditation is the 'inward path', and yet the texts agree that satipaṭṭhāna should be practiced externally also. In informal mentions of mindfulness, such as in verse, we are frequently encouraged to direct mindfulness inwards, and there is no doubt that this is the prime focus for mindfulness meditation. For example, one passage reminds us that: 'For one well established in internal presence of ānāpānasati, there are no disturbing thoughts drifting outside.'[41] Yet the external aspect remains—how are we to understand this?

103 In general Sutta usage, the terminology of internal and external is found both in the context of both samatha and vipassanā. As a samatha example, take the eight liberations or the eight bases of transcendence: 'Perceiving form internally, one sees forms externally, limited, fair and ugly; by transcending them one perceives thus: "I know, I see". This is the first base of transcendence.'[42] While the phrasing is a little obscure, such passages refer to the development of visualization as an object of samādhi, such as is known in the later works as a '*nimitta*'. 'Perceiving form internally'

---

[40] SA 610, but not its cognate SN 47.2.
[41] Iti 3.36. This includes the unusual phrase '*ajjhattaṁ parimukhaṁ*'.
[42] MN 77.23.

refers to imagining a part of the body as the initial stage in developing a true samādhi *nimitta*. This would fall within the sphere of satipaṭṭhāna. As a vipassanā example, we need look no further than the second sermon, the Discourse on Not-Self, where the Buddha speaks of each of the five aggregates as 'internal or external'. This passage is one of the fundamental vipassanā pericopes.

104 There is a passage that explicitly shows what 'internal' and external' mean in satipaṭṭhāna. Through 'internal' contemplation one enters samādhi, then gives rise to knowledge & vision (i.e. psychic vision) of the body, etc., of others externally.[43] Within the Satipaṭṭhāna Sutta, internal and external contemplation emerges most naturally in the charnel ground contemplations, which are depicted as imaginative exercises: 'As if one would see a corpse discarded in a charnel ground, one, two, or three days dead, bloated, livid, and oozing matter, a monk compares this very body with it thus: "This body too is of that same nature, it will be like that, it is not exempt from that fate." '[44]

105 Mention should also be made of the Vijaya Sutta of the Sutta Nipāta. This little poem compresses most of the Suttas' body contemplations into a few verses. Although it does not mention satipaṭṭhāna, it is the main teaching on body contemplation in the Sutta Nipāta, and might have been composed for that very reason. After describing some charnel ground meditations, it says:

106 'As this is, so is that;
As that is, so is this—
Internally and externally, one should dispel desire for the body.'[45]

107 The internal/external contemplation of the elements is treated in detail in the Mahā Hatthipadopama Sutta. For example, the internal water element is defined as the watery parts of one's own body, such as sweat and blood, etc., and the external water element is the waters in floods, the ocean, etc. Both internal and external water element are merely water element, and should be seen rightly as not-self and impermanent. This passage shows that the third stage, where internal and external are com-

---

[43] DN 18.26.
[44] MN 10.14.
[45] Sn 205.

bined, is a synthesis where the difference between the inner and outer is surmounted.

108 Interestingly, the treatment of impermanence of the external water element, as too the other elements, speaks of the destruction of the earth at the end of the universe, which is most emphatically not a 'momentary' conception of impermanence. This extends the application of 'external' not just to the 'there' but also to the 'then', outside in both space and time. Similar notions are preserved in the Sarvāstivādin Abhidharma; the Sarvāstivāda Dharmaskandha refers to past and future lives. This might ultimately derive from the Saṁyukta. We have seen above that one of the Sarvāstivāda Saṁyukta discourses adds an editorial gloss after the usual ending. This happens elsewhere, too. One such example is in a discourse called 'Development'.[46] In the Sarvāstivādin version, 'development' refers to the practice of satipaṭṭhāna internally and externally. Tacked on after the end of this discourse is the sentence:

> 109 The development of the four satipaṭṭhānas in the past and future are also taught in this way.

110 This must be one of the most obvious sectarian interpolations in the Āgamas. It establishes a clear connection between 'internal/external' and 'past/future'.

111 Here we find with an inescapable aspect of Buddhist, or more generally Indian, thought, the correlation between the personal and the cosmic. In the Upaniṣads this is most famously expressed in the identity of Ātman and Brahman, the individual soul and the world-spirit being in essence the same. Parallel ideas are found in Buddhism, for example, in the correlation between different stage of jhāna and the different realms of rebirth that they produce. One of the clearest explanations of this is by Venerable Anuruddha:

> 112 'Suppose an oil-lamp is burning with an impure wick; because of the impurity of the oil and the wick it burns dimly. So too, when a monk resolved upon and pervading a defiled radiance his bodily disturbance has not fully subsided, his sloth & torpor have not been fully eliminated, his restlessness & remorse have not been fully removed. Because of this he practices jhāna, as it were, dimly. With the break-

[46] SN 47.39/SA 610.

> up of the body, after death, he reappears in the company of the Gods of Defiled Radiance.'[47]

113 Peter Masefield has discussed this in Buddhist and Upaniṣadic texts, and says that the usage of 'internal' (*ajjhattaṁ*) is identical in both contexts, while the Buddhist usage of 'external' (*bahiddhā*) embraces both the 'cosmic' (*adhidaivataṁ*) and the 'objective' (*adhibhūtaṁ*) of the Upaniṣads.[48]

114 Another interesting indication for the meaning of internal/external is in the phrasing of the contemplation of mind in the Satipaṭṭhāna Sutta: 'One understands mind with lust as "Mind with lust"...' etc. The phrasing is identical with the psychic power of reading minds; this also correlates with the claim by Venerable Anuruddha that his own development of such powers was due to satipaṭṭhāna. The passage on the psychic powers appears often in the gradual training, whereas the passage on knowing the mind in satipaṭṭhāna appears just once. Surprisingly, then the passage on psychic powers should be regarded as the basic source context.

11.6 'The Path of Convergence'

115 Finally we come to that most definitive of satipaṭṭhāna slogans: *ekāyana magga*. The etymology is simple: *eka* means 'one'; *ayana* means 'going'; and *magga* means 'path'.[49] But further interpretation is difficult for: the word *eka* is used in many different senses; the exact grammatical relationship between *eka* and *ayana* is not clear; and idiomatic uses of the phrase are few and/or obscure. The commentators offer many different interpretations, which I will not repeat here, since they have been treated often enough before.[50] The commentators are concerned to expand the meaning, which

---

[47] MN 127.16.

[48] MASEFIELD. My thanks to the author for supplying me with a copy of this article.

[49] The Saṁyutta commentary says: '"*Ekāyañvayan"ti ekāyano ayaṁ.*' This is simply a resolution of the compound; but the interesting thing is that the reading *ekāyañvayaṁ* differs from the Majjhima and other versions, which have *ekāyano ayam*. The sub-commentary remarks that this is a tradition of the Saṁyutta reciters. The reading *ekāyano ayaṁ*, has made its way back into the Saṁyutta in the Burmese Tipiṭaka that I am using—making the commentarial gloss nonsensical—but *ekāyañvayaṁ* is preserved in some other editions.

[50] E.g. MLDB, pg. 1188, note 135; GETHIN (2001), pg. 60.

is fine—especially when used, as often appears to be the intention, as raw material for oral instructions—but it is not very useful to pin down the original denotation as precisely as possible. An unfortunate result of such vagueness is that terms can be usurped for polemic purposes. Renderings of *ekāyana* as 'the one and only way' tell us more about the biases of the translators than about the meaning of the Pali.

116 The Chinese renderings merely confirm that the Chinese translators were likewise uncertain: the Sarvāstivāda Smṛtyupasthāna Sūtra has 'there is one path' (有一道); SA has 'one vehicle path' (一乘道 = *eka* + *yāna*; evidently the translator used this more familiar Mahāyāna term); SA² 102 has 'there is only one path' (唯有一道); while the Mahāsaṅghika Ekāyana Sūtra has 'there is one entrance path' (有一入道 = *eka* + *āyatana*). The uncertainty of the traditional interpretations suggests that the term stems from a context that the later writers were unfamiliar with. In the Theravāda tradition, it is not unusual to find the commentators struggling to explain terms and ideas that are strongly embedded in the Indian cultural background.

117 Gethin includes an interesting discussion.[51] He cautions against any attempt to settle on a single concrete definition for such a term, which early on seemed to carry spiritual/mystical connotations, and is used in a variety of senses in the Brahmanical scriptures. The Chāndogya Upaniṣad lists the 'Ekāyana' as an ancient Brahmanical text, which according to the commentator dealt with *nītiśāstra*, 'social ethics' or 'politics'; perhaps the idea here is that social policy leads to a unified society. Gethin notes that the non-Buddhist contexts for *ekāyana* suggest two groups of meanings: the 'lonely' or 'solo' way; and a way that leads to one, a convergence point. 'Solo way' is accepted by the commentators, but one could ask whether this was a suitable interpretation, in the light of several texts in the Saṁyutta that encourage one to develop satipaṭṭhāna also for the benefit of others. Further, this meaning always occurs in literal contexts, not with a derived significance appropriate for meditation. Moreover, only the second meaning, which also claims commentarial support, is explicitly found elsewhere in the early Nikāyas.

---

[51] Gethin (2001), pp. 59–66.

118 This context, found in the Majjhima Nikāya, suggests a meaning of 'leads to one place only'.[52] Since Ñāṇamoli, translators such as Bhikkhu Bodhi have relied on this as the only straightforward contextual meaning available in Pali, and have rendered the term the 'direct way' or the 'oneway path'. While this interpretation is a marked improvement over the polemic 'one and only way', it does not fully capture the term. It derives from a literal context that has nothing to do with meditation, and needs evaluation in light of the philosophical/meditative usages, which are more relevant in satipaṭṭhāna. Since the Brahmanical usages of this term encompass a wide spectrum of meaning, there is no reason to assume the Pali means the same thing in different contexts. So it is essential to examine the Brahmanical references more closely. We start by asking: just how relevant are the Brahmanical contexts here?

119 Before we can answer this question clearly, we need to straighten out the occurrences of the phrase in the existing Saṁyuttas. Luckily, relevant texts are present not only in the two complete Saṁyuttas, but also the two partial Saṁyuttas. All the existing versions follow the *ekāyana* phrase by saying this is 'for the purification of beings...' and so on. Most of the extant versions place the statement in the period immediately after the Buddha's enlightenment, when the Buddha reflected on satipaṭṭhāna as the *ekāyana magga*.[53] There are three versions of this passage in the various versions of the Saṁyukta Āgama in Chinese.[54] All of these are located in the Sagāthāvagga due to the presence of the verses.

120 These versions are, allowing for translation issues, very close, except SA^3 has less verses. They all follow the *ekāyana* passage by saying that one without the four satipaṭṭhānas is without the noble Dhamma, one without the noble Dhamma is without the noble path, and one without the noble path is without the deathless; but if one is with the four satipaṭṭhānas, then all the reverse is true. Then Brahmā, understanding the thought in the Buddha's mind, vanishes from the Brahmā realm and reappears before the Buddha. He applauds the Buddha's thought, repeats it, and adds verses in praise of the *ekāyana* path. The Chinese versions have some beautiful

[52] MN 12.37/T № 757/SA 612*/SA 684*/SA 701*/EA 27.6*/EA 31.8*/EA 46.4*/EA 50.6*/T № 780*/T № 781*/T № 802*/Skt*.

[53] SN 47.18/SA 607/SA 1189/SA^2 102/SA^3 4.

[54] SA 1189/SA^2 102/SA^3 4.

images, with two of them saying the path is like 'a river flowing down to the ocean of sweet dew' ('sweet dew' being the standard Chinese rendering of 'deathless').[55] So we have three main textual components: the *ekāyana* passage; the 'without' passage; and the verses. '*Ekāyana*' and 'without' originate with the Buddha and echoed by Brahmā, while the verses belong to Brahmā alone.

121 Two of the Pali versions are quite similar, the main differences being that they lack the 'without' passage, and the verses are shorter.[56] These feature a unique variation in the satipaṭṭhāna pericope; instead of the normal 'a monk abides contemplating a body in the body' (*bhikkhu kāye kāyānupassī viharati...*) we have 'should a monk abide contemplating a body in the body' (*kāye vā bhikkhu kāyānupassī vihareyya...*). In other words, the mood shifts to optative, presumably because at the time these words were spoken there were no monks yet. Even though these are *geyyas*, they are in the Theravāda Satipaṭṭhāna-saṁyutta; the fact that all the Chinese versions are in the Sagāthāvagga makes us suspect the Pali tradition shifted them at a later date.

122 The Chinese has similar passage, but it is in the Anuruddha-saṁyutta. Here Venerable Anuruddha takes the part of the Buddha, reflecting in seclusion about the four satipaṭṭhānas as the *ekāyana* path—one without these is without the noble Dhamma, and so on, all as the Sagāthāvagga versions. Venerable Mahā Moggallāna takes the part of Brahmā, reading Anuruddha's mind, vanishing and 'swift as a strong man might bend his arm' reappearing in front of Anuruddha, applauding and repeating his thought. In place of the verses, Moggallāna asks Anuruddha how one delights in the four satipaṭṭhānas. Anuruddha replies with the normal pericope, but adds 'with stilling & quietude, cultivating oneness of mind'.[57] This restates in psychological terms what the Sagāthāvagga versions state in mythic terms, since Brahmā attained his exalted status and special powers through the practice of jhāna.

123 The text listed as cognate by Akanuma here, SN 52.1, shares none of the special features of this text except for the setting. Instead, it mentions the

---

[55] SA 1189, SA² 102.

[56] SN 47.18, SN 47.43.

[57] The Chinese partly overlaps SN 47.8/SA 616.

internal/external refrain, the rising and falling refrain, and perceiving the repulsive in the unrepulsive (etc.). Thus it replaces the samādhi emphasis of the Sarvāstivāda version with vipassanā.

124 There is, then, a strong unity in the presentation of the *ekāyana* passage that we have seen so far. The two main doctrinal units ('*ekāyana*' and 'without') occur together in all the Chinese versions, and always in a context that suggests psychic powers and samādhi. The doctrinal passages also occur in the Sarvāstivāda Smṛtyupasthāna-saṁyukta. SA 607 presents the *ekāyana* passage as a simple *sutta* at Sāvatthī, while the next *sutta*, SA 608, presents the 'without' passage. Thus the original Sagāthāvagga discourse was taken up, shorn of the special setting and split into two discourses for inclusion in the Smṛtyupasthāna-saṁyukta.

125 The Pali has gone one step further. Now, the *ekāyana* passage occurs in the first discourse of the collection. The beginning of a collection is always particularly susceptible to editorial funny business, as it is so easy to slip in a new discourse. Perhaps the word 'one' suggested placing this discourse here. The setting is given at Ambapālī's Mango Grove. This is implausible, as this setting is related to the relevant passage in the Mahā Parinibbāna Sutta, and there is no sign in the versions of this that the *ekāyana* passage belongs here. Rather, they have the Buddha encouraging the monks to be mindful since Ambapālī is coming. This passage is the second text of the Theravāda Satipaṭṭhāna-saṁyutta, immediately after the *ekāyana* discourse. Thus the *ekāyana* discourse has mistakenly copied the setting from the following discourse.

126 This reinforces the idea that the *ekāyana* discourse was a subsequent insertion at the beginning of the collection. If it had been situated later in the collection, as it is in the Sarvāstivāda, once the original setting was lost it would have been assumed that the setting was at Sāvatthī. But this, as so often, may have been left implicit and not literally spelled out. Thus when the discourse was cut-&-pasted into the beginning of the collection, it lacked a meaningful setting, and was simply inserted after the setting of the previous first discourse, which became number two.

127 The 'without' passage is similarly problematic. There is no real corresponding passage in the Theravāda, but perhaps SN 47.33 'Neglected' is a cognate. However, this just says one who has neglected satipaṭṭhāna has

neglected the path to the end of suffering (and the reverse), lacking the progressive series of Dhammas found in all five Chinese versions. If it does come from the same source, then, it has suffered decay.

128 To sum up: the *ekāyana* passage normally occurs in Brahmanical context. This is attested in all existing versions of the Saṁyutta. These feature Brahmā in a setting similar to the 'Request of Brahmā', which the GIST identifies as the root text of the *geyya* aṅga. The other versions appear to be derived from this usage. The further the texts drift from the standard version, the greater the number of editing/textual problems occur. The conclusion of all this is very simple: the term *ekāyana* was associated primarily, if not exclusively, with the Brahmanical context.

129 Let's look at the matter from the reverse perspective: do the contexts in which the term *ekāyana* appear in the Brahmanical scriptures suggest a connection with Buddhism? The key passage is in the Bṛhadāraṇyaka Upaniṣad. We have already remarked that the Bṛhadāraṇyaka is the oldest and most important of the Upaniṣads. This passage in particular is justly famous, perhaps the most significant dialogue in the whole Upaniṣadic tradition. Gethin has already referred to this source, but his summary treatment does not bring out the full significance.[58] The relevant passage occurs twice in the Upaniṣad. Occasionally the readings differ; generally I follow the first occurrence.[59]

> 130 1. 'Maitreyī', said Yājñavalkya, 'I am about to go forth from this state (of householder). Look, let me make a final settlement between you and [my other wife] Kātyāyanī.'
>
> 131 2. Then Maitreyī said: 'If, indeed, Venerable Sir, this whole earth filled with wealth were mine, would that make me immortal?' 'No,' said Yājñavalkya, 'Your life would be then like that of the rich. But there is no hope of immortality through wealth.'
>
> 132 3. Then Maitreyī said: 'What should I do with that by which I do not become immortal? Tell me, Sir, what you know.'
>
> 133 4. Then Yājñavalkya said: 'Ah, dear, you have been dear, and now you speak dear words. Come, sit, I will explain to you. Reflect on what I say.'

---

[58] GETHIN (2001), pg. 61.

[59] The second occurrence adds material, especially emphasizing the immortality of the Self, and includes the famous description of the Self as: 'Not this! Not this!'

134 5. Then he said: 'Truly, not for the sake of the husband is the husband dear, but for the sake of the Self. Not for the sake of the wife... sons... wealth... Brahmanhood... Kṣatriya-hood... worlds... gods... beings... not for the sake of all is the all dear, but all is dear for the sake of the Self. Truly, Maitreyī, it is the Self that should be seen, heard, considered, and reflected on. By the seeing, hearing, considering, and cognizance of the Self, all this is known.

135 6. 'The Brahman ignores one who knows him as different from the Self. The Kṣatriya... worlds... gods... beings... all ignores one who knows it as different from the Self. This Brahman, this Kṣatriya, these worlds, these gods, these beings, and this all are this Self.

136 7, 8, 9. 'As when a drum is beaten... a conch is blown... a lute is played, one is not able to grasp the external sounds, but by grasping the lute or the lute-player the sound is grasped.

137 10. 'As from a lighted fire laid with damp fuel various smokes issue forth, even so, my dear, the Ṛg Veda, the Sāman Veda, the Yajur Veda, the Ātharva, Aṅgirasa, histories, legends, sciences, Upaniṣads, verses, sūtras, explanations, and commentaries are all breathed forth from this.

138 11. 'As the ocean is the convergence (*ekāyana*) of all waters, as the skin is the convergence of all touches, as the nose is the convergence of all smells, as the tongue is the convergence of all tastes, as the eye is the convergence of all forms, as the ear is the convergence of all sounds, as the mind is the convergence of all thoughts (*samkalpa*), as the heart is the convergence of all realizations (*vidya*), as the hands are the convergence of all actions, as the genitals are the convergence of all pleasure, as the anus is the convergence of all excretion, as the feet are the convergence of all movements, as speech is the convergence of all Vedas.

139 12. 'Just as a lump of salt thrown in water becomes dissolved in the water and there would not be any to be seized by the hand, but wherever you might take it up it is salty; so too this great being, infinite, with nothing beyond it, is a sheer mass of cognition (*vijñāna-ghana eva*). Having arisen out of these elements, one perishes back into them. When departed, there is no more perception (*saṁjñā*). This is what I say, my dear.' So said Yājñavalkya.

140 13. Then said Maitreyī: 'In this, indeed, you have confused me, Venerable Sir, by saying that "when departed, there is no more perception".' Then Yājñavalkya said: 'Certainly I am not saying anything confusing. This is enough for cognizance.'

141 14. 'For where there is duality, as it were, there one smells another, one sees another, one hears another, one addresses another, one thinks of another, one cognizes another. But where All has become identical with Self, then by what and whom should one smell… see… hear… speak… think… by what and whom should one cognize? That by which all this is cognized, by what is that to be cognized? By what, my dear, should one cognize the cognizer?'[60]

142 The time of the great sage Yājñavalkya was not long before the Buddha. The Brahmanical grammarian Kātyāyana, commenting on Pāṇini, says that the Yājñavalkya scriptures are 'of too recent origin; that is to say, they are almost contemporaneous with ourselves'.[61] Pāṇini lived no earlier than the 4th century BCE, and Kātyāyana later still; in other words, they are later than the Buddha, but 'almost contemporaneous' with Yājñavalkya. So Yājñavalkya was maybe a generation or two before the Buddha. In fact, Yājñavalkya's favorite interlocuter is King Janaka, a historical character mentioned in the Jātakas, whose city is still called 'Janakpur' today. He was a king in the Mithila region a few generations before the Buddha. So Yājñavalkya's teachings were part of the immediate religious context of the Buddha.

143 Furthermore, virtually every aspect of this classic dialogue has close connections with the Suttas, with the obvious exception of the metaphysical 'Self' doctrine. Yājñavalkya's aspiration to go forth (1) betrays influence from the samana traditions such as Buddhism. The sentiment of the futility of wealth in the face of death (2, 3) is classic Buddhism, but alien to the older Vedic tradition. The statement that the husband, etc., is dear for the sake of the Self (5) is similar to a passage in the Sagāthāvagga.[62] The list of seen, heard, thought, and cognized (5) is presented in the same way in the Suttas.[63] The list of various principles culminating in the 'all' (5, 6) is reminiscent of the Mūlapariyāya Sutta, a text which the commentarial

---

60 BU 2.4, 4.5.

61 WIJESEKERA, pg. 282.

62 SN 3.1.8, as pointed out by Bhikkhu BODHI. Curiously, this has no cognates.

63 The commentaries say that *muta* here means cognized by the nose, tongue, or body; that is, they correlate this list with the six senses; thus some contemporary translators render it as 'sensed'. But *muta* is just a past participle of the normal word 'to think', and never means 'sensed'. The Upaniṣadic context makes it plain that the meaning here is what has been 'thought' or 'conceived'.

tradition associates with Brahmanism.[64] The similes of the drum, conch, and lute (7, 8, 9) all appear in the Suttas. The similes of the conch[65] and the lute,[66] in particular, are treated in a strikingly similar way: the sound manifests from the coming together of the parts and the appropriate effort and cannot be grasped of itself. The image of the rivers flowing into the sea (11) occurs in the Kāyagatāsati Sutta, and even more strikingly, occur in the verses accompanying the *ekāyana* passage in two of the Chinese versions. The simile of salt (12) is like the Buddha's saying the great ocean has just one taste, the taste of salt, just as the Dhamma-Vinaya has the taste of liberation.[67] The description of cognition as infinite (12) occurs in the standard formula on the formless attainments. The bewilderment of one trying to grapple with the subtle state of the realized sage after death (13) also recurs in the Suttas, in similar terms.[68]

144 The second version of this dialogue phrases the culminating revelation of the Self slightly differently: 'without internal or external, just an entire mass of understanding' (*anantaro'bāhyaḥ, kṛtsnaḥ prajñānaghana eva*[69]). The internal/external reminds us of satipaṭṭhāna. *Kṛtsnaḥ* is the Pali *kasiṇa*, a well known meditation term which for the Suttas meant not 'external device for meditation' (as it came to mean in the later traditions), but 'totality' [of consciousness in samādhi], just as here. Even though the Pali-English Dictionary says the derivation of *kasiṇa* is unknown, this derivation and meaning have been adopted in Cone's recent *A Dictionary of Pali*, and also conforms to the Chinese rendering. The standard Sutta description of *kasiṇa* is 'above, below, across, non-dual, measureless', which once again reminds us of the Upaniṣadic passage. This version substitutes *prajñāna* ('understanding') for the first version's *vijñāna* (cognition); while these are usually distinguished in Buddhism, they are often synonyms in the Upaniṣads, and remnants of this remain in the Suttas, too.

---

[64] MN 1/MA 106/T № 56.

[65] DN 23.19/DA 7/MA 71/ T № 45.

[66] SN 35.246/SA 1169.

[67] AN 8.157.

[68] MN 72.17/SA 962/SA^{2} 196.

[69] BU 4.5.14.

145 Just as the central usage of *ekāyana* in the Suttas looks to the Brahmanical context, the central usage of *ekāyana* in the Upaniṣads looks to the Buddhist context.

146 Yājñavalkya's message is the return to the One. All diversity is undercut and relativized. The repeated, emphatic use of *ekāyana* drives home the centrality of this doctrine of Oneness. An *ekāyana* is both the source from which the things of the world spring, and the place of convergence, where the diversity of external phenomena come together in a profound unification. It is the inner subject that makes the external objects possible. And it is precisely the term *ekāyana* that is singled out as the most exact expression of this insight. This verse occurs immediately before the dramatic revelation that 'this great being', the cosmic self that is the All, is but a 'sheer mass of cognition'. In this infinite consciousness the limiting, diversifying conceptions and perceptions (*saṁjñā*) disappear.

147 Philosophical uses of *ekāyana* elsewhere support this reading.

> 148 'The mind (*citta*) is the convergence (*ekāyana*) of all these, mind is the self (*ātman*), mind is the foundation (*pratiṣṭha*).' (CU 7.5.2)

> 149 'He who would be devoted to convergence (*ekāyana*), in silence, not thinking about anything, having previously renounced, would be one who has crossed over and is free from obstacles.' (MBh 14.19.1)

150 The first passage suggests that 'convergence' includes states of unification in samādhi. The terminology is suggestively Buddhist; no less than three words in this short verse (*citta, ekāyana, pratiṣṭha*) are used in the context of satipaṭṭhāna. The second passage has puzzled commentators,[70] but surely a samādhi context is also implied.

151 The spiritual significance of *ekāyana* for the Brahmanical tradition is the convergence of the mind in samādhi. This accords with the etymology. The suffix *-ayana* means literally 'going', and when used in a compound it means the 'going' to whatever the first member of the compound is. For example, the Brahmā Purāṇa says that God first created the waters that are called *nara* and then he released his seed into them, therefore he is called 'Narāyana'. Closer to home, the Pārāyana Vagga says: 'This path goes to the beyond (*pāra*); therefore it is called "Pārāyana".' So *ekāyana*

[70] See GETHIN (2001), pg. 62 note 142.

means 'going to one'. This is the primary meaning that Gethin ends up with, which is the final of the commentarial readings (*ekaṁ ayati*).

152 The question then becomes, what does 'one' mean in the Buddhist context? Gethin suggests, with the support of the Pali commentary, that 'one' refers to Nibbana. He says that the term 'one' here need not carry absolutist metaphysical connotations in the Nikāyas. The sub-commentary supports this by explaining 'one' here as 'without a second' and 'supreme'. But the 'one' was a pregnant metaphysical term for the whole Brahmanical tradition ever since the Ṛg Veda spoke of the 'One Being', and so the Suttas carefully avoid using the 'one' to refer to Nibbana. However, they are quite happy to use 'one' to refer to samādhi. By far the most common and idiomatic usages of 'one' in the Suttas' meditation vocabulary are the terms 'one-pointedness' (*ekaggatā*) and 'unification' (*ekodibhāva*), which are standard synonyms of jhāna or samādhi. This is the only sense in which 'one' is used in the Satipaṭṭhāna-saṁyutta, and we have already seen a discourse where Venerable Anuruddha closely associates the *ekāyana* passage with the development of 'oneness of mind' through satipaṭṭhāna.

153 Since the purpose of satipaṭṭhāna is to lead to jhāna, the contextual meaning of *ekāyana* must be 'leading to unification (of mind)'. This is precisely the explanation offered by the Mahāsaṅghika Ekāyana Sūtra:

> 154 'Why is it called the "one entrance"? It is so-called because it is [the way to] concentration and oneness of mind.'[71]

155 The Chinese phrase I have rendered by 'oneness of mind' here is identical to that in Anuruddha's discourse on the *ekāyana* path. Although the Ekāyana Sūtra is somewhat later than the Theravāda and Sarvāstivāda Satipaṭṭhāna Suttas, this statement is the earliest clear definition of this phrase.

156 This explanation would also furnish an answer to the question why the Suttas reserve the term *ekāyana* for satipaṭṭhāna alone among the 37 wings to awakening. While all the groups are associated in one way or another with samādhi or one-pointedness, satipaṭṭhāna is singled out as playing the key role of bringing the mind to samādhi.

[71] 云何名爲一入。所謂專一心 (T02, № 125, p. 568, a4–5).

11.7 'Achieving the Way'

157 The statement on the 'path leading to unification' is followed, in the Satipaṭṭhāna Suttas, by the statement that this is: 'For the purification of beings, for surmounting sorrow and lamentation, for ending bodily and mental suffering, for achieving the way, for witnessing Nibbana'. Most of these are straightforward enough, but the phrase 'achieving the way' (*ñāyassa adhigamāya*) is vague, in Pali as well as in English. The term *ñāya* is sometimes used in the context of dependent origination, and some have seen this as the meaning here. This is not unreasonable, for there are clear connections between satipaṭṭhāna and dependent origination.[72] However there is no strong reason to think that this is the primary meaning.

158 The most common, standard occurrence of *ñāya* is in the formula for recollection of the Sangha: 'The Sangha of the Blessed One's disciples has practiced well, practiced directly, practiced according to the way (*ñāya*), practiced properly.' Here we are in the realm of practice, and this, rather than dependent origination, is where we should seek the meaning of *ñāya* in satipaṭṭhāna. The commentaries gloss *ñāya* here as 'the noble eightfold path'. There are a whole series of texts that use the word *ñāya* in the context of practice, which do not mention dependent origination, or for that matter satipaṭṭhāna, even though some of them use the very same pericope of 'for the purification of beings…'.[73] These passages deal with the overall way of training, and all include samādhi. The most detailed context is in the Sandaka Sutta of the Majjhima. First the gradual training is taught, from the appearance of the Tathāgata to the abandoning of hindrances; up to this stage the term *ñāya* is not used. Then the text continues:

> 159 'Having abandoned these five hindrances, defilements of the mind that weaken understanding, quite secluded from sensual pleasures, secluded from unskilful qualities, he enters and abides in the first jhāna, which has initial & sustained application, with rapture & bliss born of seclusion. An intelligent person would certainly live the holy life with a teacher under whom a disciple attains such an exalted

[72] The relation between satipaṭṭhāna and dependent origination is implicit in the Samudaya Sutta, which we will discuss below, and made explicit in the Śāriputrābhidharma.

[73] AN 3.75/EA 21.4, AN 4.35, AN 4.194/SA 565, AN 6.26/SA 550, AN 6.30/T № 1536.16, AN 9.37/SA 557.

> distinction, and while living it he would attain the way (*ñāya*), the Dhamma that is skilful.'[74]

160 The text goes on with the rest of the jhānas and higher knowledges culminating in arahantship, repeating the concluding sentence each time. The association of *ñāya* with *kusala*, 'skilful', is also relevant in the context of satipaṭṭhāna, for satipaṭṭhāna in the context of developing samādhi is said to be 'for achieving the skilful' (*kusalassadhigamāya*), just as it is said to be 'for achieving the way' (*ñāyassa adhigamāya*).[75] Thus *ñāya* is associated with the progressive way of practice in general, and samādhi or jhāna in particular.

11.8 The Aṅguttara

161 This is a convenient place to survey the satipaṭṭhāna material found in the existing Aṅguttara Nikāya. Here we find little material on satipaṭṭhāna.[76] This is no surprise, for the Saṁyutta and Aṅguttara are complementary collections of the shorter discourses, and the main doctrines are mostly included in the Saṁyutta. Satipaṭṭhāna appears in the Aṅguttara alongside the other groups of the 37 wings to awakening in various repetitive series appended to some of the sections. One passage mentions six things to be abandoned in order to achieve success in satipaṭṭhāna: fondness of work, speaking, sleeping, and company; lack of sense restraint; and eating too much.[77] This is similar to the gradual training, and as in the gradual training, these practices prepare one for the meditative development of satipaṭṭhāna. The contemplation here is treated as internal and external.

162 The only substantial Aṅguttara discourse on satipaṭṭhāna treats it purely as samatha.[78] This has the appearance of a discourse from the Satipaṭṭhāna

---

[74] MN 76.43/SA 973*/SA^2 207*.

[75] DN 18.28/DA 4/T № 9.

[76] None of these texts are found in the Ekottara Āgama. However this is of little significance given the generally large divergence between this collection and the other Nikāyas/Āgamas. The Ekāyana Sūtra seems to be the only substantial discourse in the Ekottara dealing with satipaṭṭhāna.

[77] AN 6.117*ff.*

[78] AN 8.63.

Saṁyutta, and the GIST suggests that it was originally included in that collection and was later moved into the Aṅguttara in order to provide the Aṅguttara students with at least one substantial teaching on such an important topic. This discourse is not found in the Sarvāstivādin Saṁyukta, nor, apparently, elsewhere in the Chinese. One is exhorted first of all to develop the four divine abidings, then to develop 'that samādhi' in the mode of all the jhānas. Next one is, in identical terms, exhorted to develop the four satipaṭṭhānas, and to develop 'that samādhi' in the mode of the jhānas.

163 There is another interesting text, which, while it does not deal with satipaṭṭhāna directly, is similar enough in its subject matter and terminology to suggest that it influenced later expositions. Venerable Ānanda lists five 'bases for recollection' (*anussatiṭṭhāna*; notice the similarity to *satipaṭṭhāna*).[79] They are: the first three jhānas; the perception of light; the 31 parts of the body; contemplation of death; and the fourth jhāna. To these the Buddha adds a sixth—mindfulness of one's bodily postures. These are obviously close to the Theravāda Satipaṭṭhāna Sutta's section on body contemplation. They are even closer to the Sarvāstivāda Smṛtyupasthāna Sūtra, which includes in its section on body contemplation the four jhānas and the perception of light. Perhaps the Sarvāstivāda was influenced by the present text. The fact that the Buddha added the awareness of postures as an extra practice suggests that this stood outside the other, more specifically meditative, practices. It is characteristic of the Buddha in such cases to focus attention on the cause.[80] Thus he emphasized awareness of postures in order to encourage the practice that would lead on to the higher stages.

164 Another short discourse focuses on the wisdom aspect of mindfulness, although again this is not within the satipaṭṭhāna framework.[81] Five meditations are recommended: one should 'clearly establish mindfulness on the rise and end of dhammas', and develop perceptions of the loathsomeness of food, the ugliness of the body, boredom with the whole world, and impermanence of activities. These are the 'bitter pill' meditations designed

[79] AN 6.29.
[80] Cp. MN 32/MA 184, MN 123/MA 78.
[81] AN 5.122.

to overcome our neurotic aversion and fear of acknowledging the negative and unpleasant side of life. In the Aṅguttara the other 'bitter pills', which include both samatha and vipassanā aspects, are taught much more frequently than the contemplation of dhammas. 'Dhammas' here does not mean 'all dhammas', for not all dhammas are impermanent; it has the same meaning as in the satipaṭṭhāna contemplation of dhammas.

165 To summarize the teachings on satipaṭṭhāna in the Aṅguttara Nikāya:

166 1) Satipaṭṭhāna is a meditative practice developed in the context of the gradual training.
2) It can be a mode of jhāna.
3) It is to be developed both internally and externally.
4) Mindfulness of the rise and fall of dhammas is one of the practices developing wisdom.

Chapter 12

THE SAṀYUTTA

THE SATIPAṬṬHĀNA-SAṀYUTTA IS A RICH COLLECTION, with parables and metaphors, glimpses into the daily life of the Sangha, inspiring lay meditators, humour and tragedy, and a strong narrative element. Several texts shine light on satipaṭṭhāna beyond the basic formula; yet there is no detailed analysis. We will analyze the structure and content of this collection, then look at some related saṁyuttas that also feature satipaṭṭhāna.

12.1 The Satipaṭṭhāna-saṁyutta

2 The Theravāda Satipaṭṭhāna-saṁyutta comprises five chapters (*vaggas*) of exactly ten discourses each, followed by the inevitable 'Ganges Repetition Series'. To start with, let's classify the texts into the aṅgas, as we did with the Sacca-saṁyutta. While there are some significant blocks of texts grouped according to the aṅgas, still the formation is less striking than in the case of the Saccasaṁyutta. There is some hint of an underlying *sutta/vyākaraṇa* structure. Seven of the first eight texts are *suttas*; and of the 22 texts between 47.9–30, 17 are *vyākaraṇas*. This possibly represents an underlying collection of one vagga of *suttas* and two of *vyākaraṇas*. The rest of the collection does not support this, as many suttas are included in the later portion, where we would expect to find vyākaranas. On the other hand, many of these texts are mere artificial repetitions, so do not represent the ancestral collection.

Table 12.1: Aṅgas in the Theravāda Satipaṭṭhāna-saṁyutta

SN 47	Sutta	Geyya	Vyākaraṇa
1–2	✓		
3			✓
4–8	✓		
9–13			✓
14	✓		
15–16			✓
17	✓		
18		✓	
19	✓		
20–23			✓
24	✓		
25–30			✓
31–39	✓		
40			✓
41	✓		
42			✓
43		✓	
44–45	✓		
46–47			✓
48–104	✓		

3 Let's see what SA has to offer us. The *sutta/vyākaraṇa* structure of this collection is obvious. Fourteen of the first eighteen texts are *suttas*, and these are followed by a sequence of nine straight *vyākaraṇas.* We even have the extra grace of three *geyyas* appearing more-or-less between the two main aṅgas, just as we saw in the Sacca-saṁyutta. The *sutta/vyākaraṇa* structure is far more obvious in the Sarvāstivāda collection.

Table 12.2: Aṅgas in the Sarvāstivāda Smṛtyupasthāna-saṁyukta

SA	Sutta	Geyya	Vyākaraṇa
605	✓		
606	✓		
607	✓		
608	✓		
609			✓
610	✓		
611	✓		
612	✓		
613	✓		
614			✓
615			✓
616	✓		
617		✓	
618	✓		
619	✓		
620	✓		
621			✓
622		✓	
623		✓	
624			✓
625			✓
626			✓
627			✓
628			✓
629			✓
630			✓
631			✓
632			✓
633	✓		
634	✓		
635	✓		
636	✓		
637	✓		
638			✓
639			✓

4 Let us now combine the two collections, and remove those discourses that are not common to both, thus approximating the pre-sectarian collection. A few texts appear as a *sutta* in one collection and a *vyākaraṇa* in the other; these are noted. I also note the discourses in the form of a parable, which I call 'tales'; these are discussed below.

Table 12.3: Concordance of the Two Satipaṭṭhāna-saṁyuttas

SA	SN 47	Sutta	Geyya	Vyākaraṇa
606	24	✓		
607	1	✓		
608	33*	✓		
609	42			✓
610	39	✓		
611	5	✓		
614	11			✓
615	10			✓
616	8	✓		
617	6	✓ *(SN) (tale)*	✓ *(SA) (tale)*	
619	19	✓ *(tale)*		
620	7	✓ *(tale)*		
621	4	✓ *(SN)*		✓ *(SA)*
622	2, 44*	✓ *(SN)*	✓ *(SA)*	
623	20		✓ *(SA) (tale)*	✓ *(SN)*
624	16			✓
625	15			✓
627	26*			✓
628	21*			✓
634	17	✓		
635	34*	✓		
638	13			✓
639	14			✓

5 The *sutta/vyākaraṇa* structure is still apparent, and in addition another feature becomes prominent. There are ten *suttas*, three *geyyas*, and ten *vyākaraṇas*. This is the classic grouping of ten discourses to a vagga. Perhaps the ancestral collection consisted of two vaggas, one of *suttas* and one of *vyākaraṇas*, and a few *geyyas*.

6 Having considered the collection's structure, let's look at the content.

12.1.1 The Tales

7 Two literary characteristics of the Satipaṭṭhāna-saṁyutta deserve further consideration: the tales and the narratives.

8 The tales leaven the collection with humour and homely action. They extol satipaṭṭhāna as a safe place, a refuge, reflecting the exhortation in the narrative passages to abide with oneself as one's refuge through practicing satipaṭṭhāna. Psychologically, they emphasize that one is 'caught' if one strays outside one's native domain, and 'freed' if one knows how to 'let go'; and that this freedom, apparently paradoxically, comes from containing one's 'attention' within the proper context—satipaṭṭhāna.

9 **SN 47.8/SA 616 The Cook:** The Pali and Chinese here are quite similar. The foolish cook doesn't know how to prepare the right kinds of food to please his master, so misses out on a bonus. Similarly, the foolish monk, not understanding the ways of his mind, practices satipaṭṭhāna, but his mind 'does not enter samādhi, he does not abandon defilements…'. But for the skilful cook and the skilful monk it is just the opposite—he enters samādhi and abandons defilements.

10 **SN 47.6/SA 617 The Hawk:** Tells of a quail who is caught by a hawk if he ventures outside his 'native habitat', but is safe when inside. The unsafe ground for a monk is the realm of sensuality, and the native habitat is satipaṭṭhāna. Here again satipaṭṭhāna, as the opposite to the five strands of sensual pleasures, plays the same role as the four jhānas. The Chinese is very close, sharing some of the exact phrases of the Pali, and also adds a verse. This repeats the story, then says that to know one's own mind is better than the power of 100 000 dragons.

11 **SN 47.19/SA 619 Sedaka:** A parable of harmony and mutual support, illustrated by the story of two acrobats, one supporting the other on top of a bamboo pole. The Pali contains an anomaly here, for it has the student saying 'you protect yourself and I'll protect myself'. The Buddha then applauds this statement, but changes it to 'protecting oneself, one protects others, protecting others one protects oneself.' The Chinese does not have this problem, for it has the student saying just that.

12 **SN 47.7/SA 620 The Monkey:** The story concerns a foolish monkey who gets his hand stuck in a tar trap. Trying to free himself, he gets his other hand stuck, too, then both his feet and even his muzzle. Stuck at five

places, the hunter does with him what he will. In the same way, the monk should stay within his native habitat, just as in 'The Hawk'. The Chinese adds a further description of the foolish monk who goes into town with senses unrestrained.

13 **SN 47.20/SA 623: The Most Beautiful Girl in the Land:** On one side is an excited crowd; on the other a dancing girl; in between you must walk carrying a bowl brimful of oil, with a man with a drawn sword following right behind you, ready to chop off your head if you spill a drop! In just the same way should you develop 'mindfulness of the body'. This text is unique in being a 'tale' that includes a *vyākaraṇa*. The Pali is anomalous in that it mentions 'mindfulness of the body', and is the only text in the Satipaṭṭhāna-saṁyutta to omit the satipaṭṭhānas. SA, on the other hand, does include the four satipaṭṭhānas. It also adds some verses, which mention the pot of oil and encourage concentration. Another difference is that the Theravāda version is set at Sedaka. This unusual location is the same as the preceding discourse and has been mechanically copied over from there, a phenomenon that we saw was very prevalent in the Sarvāstivāda Satya-saṁyukta. The Sarvāstivāda version is set in the Deer Park at Benares.

12.1.2 The Narratives

14 The narratives fall into two main groups: those that recall the Buddha's awakening, and those that recall his passing away. There is a complex relationship between these texts—some of which include narrative, and some of which merely imply a narrative context—and the long narratives (*apadānas*) of the Dīgha and Vinaya.

15 Of those that recall the Buddha's awakening, there are the 'Brahmā' suttas. As discussed above, these are found in the Sagāthāvagga in the Chinese versions, but the Satipaṭṭhāna-saṁyutta in the Theravāda. They recall the 'Request of Brahmā' that we have treated as the paradigmatic *geyya* passage.[1] Both events are set at the 'Goatherd's Banyan Tree', but I can find no trace of our current text in any of the accounts of the post-enlightenment period that are available to me. Between the two there is a

[1] SN 47.18/SA 607/SA 1189/SA^{2} 102/SA^{3} 4; SN 47.43.

crucial difference in the role played by Brahmā. In the 'Request of Brahmā', the deity plays the ancient mythic role of initiator of action, a personification of divine inspiration. Here, in keeping with the humble position of gods that is more normal in Buddhism, he merely echoes and supports the Buddha. The other memory of this period found in the Satipaṭṭhānasaṁyutta is called 'Unheard Before', which treats the satipaṭṭhānas in terms of the three revolutions and twelve modes of the Dhammacakkappavattana Sutta.[2] This implies that understanding satipaṭṭhāna was integral to the enlightenment experience. Similar claims are made of most of the familiar doctrinal categories, reflecting the holistic nature of the Dhamma. This text is not found in the Chinese, so we suspect it to be a later text; but the content is not controversial.

16 More material is found around the time of the Buddha's passing away. We have already referred to the discourse set in Ambapālī's mango grove, where the Buddha stayed shortly before the Parinibbāna, encouraging the monks to be 'mindful & clearly comprehending'. This passage appears in the Mahā Parinibbāna Sutta, in both Theravāda and Mūlasarvāstivāda versions. The appropriateness of this reminder, in anticipation of the visit by a famous courtesan, is obvious in context, and this is more explicit in the Sarvāstivāda than the Theravāda.

17 SN 47.9 'Ill' tells the moving story of the Buddha's illness shortly before his passing away.[3] It is one of the most poignant passages in the canon that frankly confronts the Buddha's frail humanity. This passage also contains the Buddha's famous declaration that he does not have the 'closed fist of a teacher'. This became a controversial issue, especially for those later schools that claimed to be descended from an esoteric transmission outside the main scriptural lineage.

18 SN 47.11–14 form a mini biography of Venerable Sāriputta. In the first text we see him discussing with the Buddha the nature of a perfected human. Next we see Venerable Sāriputta in his home town of Nāḷandā, approaching the Buddha, and exclaiming that by an 'inference according to dhamma', he understands that all Buddhas, past, future, and present,

---

2 SN 47.31.

3 This sutta does not appear as an individual sutta outside the Pali, but partial parallels are found in several texts of the Mahāparinibbāna Sutta.

become enlightened by abandoning the five hindrances, being well established in the four satipaṭṭhānas, and developing the seven awakening-factors.[4] This episode occurred during the Buddha's last journey north from Rājagaha, and records the last meeting between the Teacher and his greatest disciple. Bearing in mind that the seven awakening-factors are virtually synonymous with samādhi, this grouping parallels the meditation phase of the gradual training: one 'establishes mindfulness', abandons hindrances, and develops the jhānas. Similar sets recur frequently in the Suttas; below we will see that this 'inference according to Dhamma' is the original content of the contemplation of dhammas in satipaṭṭhāna. Nevertheless, the connection with satipaṭṭhāna is relatively tenuous—they are merely mentioned in passing—so it is not surprising to find that the Sarvāstivāda preferred to allocate this text to their Sāriputta-saṁyutta. The episode is found in the Theravāda Mahā Parinibbāna Sutta, but not in the Sarvāstivāda or the Dharmaguptaka versions of that text.[5] It also forms the kernel for the much longer dialogue in the Sampasādanīya Sutta.[6]

19 SN 47.13/ SA 638, the next text in the Theravāda collection, relates how Venerable Sāriputta became ill and passed away. This occurred at 'Nālakagāma'. The commentarial story has it that Venerable Sāriputta, aware that his time was near, returned to his home town to convert his mother, an ardent Brahman, to Buddhism. The novice Cunda—said by the commentary to be Venerable Sāriputta's younger brother—was his attendant during his illness. On his passing away, he took Venerable Sāriputta's bowl and robes and went to where the Buddha was staying. The Theravāda says he was at Sāvatthī, which is incongruous—Sāvatthī is 200 km to the northwest, and it is inconceivable that the Buddha made such an extravagant detour in his last, feeble, journey, a detour attested in no other text. The Sarvāstivāda says the Buddha was staying in Rājagaha, at the Veḷuvana. But this is little better, for the Mahā Parinibbāna Sutta says that Sāriputta visited the Buddha in Nāḷandā, after he had already taken the north road from Rājagaha. Venerable Ānanda, the first to hear the bad news, is distraught, and the Buddha asks him whether Sāriputta took with him the

4 SN 47.12.

5 DN 16.1.16–17.

6 DN 28/DA 18/T № 18.

aggregates of ethics, samādhi, understanding, release, and knowledge & vision of release; the Chinese adds to this the 37 wings to awakening. Ānanda says no, but that Sāriputta was so helpful to his fellows in the holy life. The Buddha encourages him: 'How can it happen that what is born, come to be, conditioned, of a nature to disintegrate should not disintegrate? That is impossible! Therefore, Ānanda, dwell with yourselves as your own island, your own refuge, with no other refuge. Dwell with the Dhamma as your island, your refuge, with no other refuge.' One does this through the practice of satipaṭṭhāna. This is much like the Mahā Parinibbāna Sutta, and it is surprising that this text finds no place in that narrative.

20 This text forms a pair with SN 47.14/SA 639, which follows immediately in both collections. The Theravāda recension is set in the Vajjī Republic, at Ukkacelā on the banks of the Ganges. The Chinese, however, places this episode in Madhura, by the Bhadra River. Vajjī is a plausible setting, being along the route towards the Parinibbāna. The Buddha says the Sangha seems empty to him now that Sāriputta and Moggallāna have attained final Nibbana, like the largest branches falling off the great tree of heartwood.[7] In the teachings, this text largely repeats the previous. However, it includes some extra literary features, suggestive of the later aṅgas. The Buddha says that all the Buddhas in the past and the future will have a chief pair of disciples like Sāriputta and Moggallāna; this reminds us of an *avadāna*. Next he praises their 'wonderful and marvellous' qualities, an *abbhūtadhamma*; however, this section is absent from the Chinese.

21 There are some more texts that might also be set in the time following the Parinibbāna, although the narrative context is not spelt out in the texts themselves, nor are they included in the longer developed narratives of the Dīgha and the Vinaya. These are the discourses featuring Venerable Ānanda and Venerable Bhadda at the Cock's Monastery in Pāṭaliputta.[8] The only Sarvāstivāda cognate stands at the head of a whole series of texts at the same location; in a manner similar to the Satya-saṁyukta, we infer that only the first setting is genuine, and the rest were mechanically repeated. The Theravāda texts do not mention the Buddha as being alive at the time;

---

[7] Venerable Moggallāna's death is not recorded in the canon, but the later Theravādin and Tibetan accounts agree in their general outlines.

[8] SN 47.21*/SA 628; SN 47.22; SN 47.23.

although the Sarvāstivāda version does mention the Buddha, this might just be a result of mechanical standardization. The location is unusual, a little-known monastery in Pāṭaliputta between Kusinārā, where the Buddha passed away, and Rājagaha. It was from Rājagaha that the Buddha set out on his final journey, and back to Rājagaha that the monks, including Venerable Ānanda, returned to recite the scriptures in the First Council after the Buddha's passing away. The 'Duration' discourses, in particular, express evident concern over the Buddha's passing away. It is possible that here we have a record of the discussions and debates that took place within the Sangha as, resting on the journey back from Kusinārā to Rājagaha, they contemplated the future of Buddhism without the Buddha. It is surprising that the 'Duration' discourses, which say that the long-lasting of Buddhism is due to the practice of satipaṭṭhāna, find no cognate in the Sarvāstivāda, for the long-lasting of the sasana was one of their characteristic concerns.

22 It is interesting that several of the events that took place around the time of the Buddha's enlightenment and passing away do not appear in the developed narratives of those events. The relation between these short texts and the long narratives has been debated by scholars. Some opine that the long narratives emerged first, and the shorter texts were abstracted from them. This is implausible, and the current situation supports this: if the shorter texts were abstracted from the longer, where do the short texts that are not in the long narratives come from? There were many incidents and teachings remembered around these critical times, which were retold with a more-or-less casual reference to the historical circumstances. The need for definitive accounts became stronger in the absence of the living Buddha. So the events were gradually linked up in a narrative whose outlines were very old and have changed remarkably little in the millennia of retellings, but whose specific form was elaborated over time. Not all the remembered events found a home in the story; presumably the choice was dictated by the demands of story telling.

23 These narratives enrich and inform the presentation of satipaṭṭhāna, contextualizing the abstract meditation formula within the drama of life and death. Another discourse also emphasizes satipaṭṭhāna in the context of death. This discourse, SN 47.30/SA 1038 Mānadinna, depicts Venerable Ānanda approaching the householder Mānadinna, who is gravely

ill. Ānanda encourages him, even in that final extreme, to develop satipaṭṭhāna. Mānadinna responds that he does indeed practice satipaṭṭhāna; and furthermore, he has abandoned the five lower fetters. Ānanda then praises him as one who has declared the attainment of non-returning, the penultimate stage of enlightenment.[9]

24 As always in the Suttas, death and impermanence are closely related: anxiety over death precipitates the spiritual quest; and when the suttas talk about impermanence, they often mean death. Examples from the Satipaṭṭhāna-saṁyutta include 'come to be' (*bhūta*) and 'conditioned' (*saṅkhata*). Death is the primary form of impermanence in satipaṭṭhāna. But in these narratives we only see the connection between satipaṭṭhāna and death by association. There is no hint as to how this might be integrated in the meditation, which does not mention impermanence at all.

12.1.3 Clear Comprehension

25 Further light on this is shed by SN 47.35, which presents a variation on the theme of 'mindfulness & clear comprehension'. The standard passage on clear comprehension is the description of awareness of daily activities, which usually occurs in the gradual training leading up to the four jhānas. The Sarvāstivāda includes two discourses on the gradual training that have no Theravāda counterparts. SA 636 gives the standard description of one who hears the Dhamma, then decides to go forth out of faith. He then rectifies his bodily conduct, protects the four kinds of right speech, purifies livelihood, guards the sense doors, and practices clear comprehension when going out and returning, and so on. Then he resorts to a tree or a lonely place, sits down and establishes the mind in a 'peaceful abiding'. He abandons the five hindrances that entangle the bright power of the mind, and goes on to practice the four satipaṭṭhānas. This is called the 'development of the four satipaṭṭhānas.' The next text, SA 637 is essentially similar (in fact it abbreviates, and instructs the reader to expand as the previous discourse). It adds a few extra factors of the gradual training, such as the restraint of the Pāṭimokkha and contentment with requisites, just like a

---

[9] This discourse exists in the Sarvāstivāda, but in another saṁyutta, and was therefore not in our concordance. The previous, almost identical, text in SN 47 is absent from the Sarvāstivāda.

bird is content with its wings. In both of these discourses, satipaṭṭhāna takes the place normally occupied by the four jhānas.

26 The practice of clear comprehension in one's daily activities is presented more simply in a discourse, found in both collections, that exhorts the monks to be 'mindful & clearly comprehending'. 'Mindfulness' is defined as the four satipaṭṭhānas, and 'clear comprehension' as the awareness of activities.[10]

27 SN 47.35 has no SA counterpart, so it may be a secondary formation in imitation of this. In this discourse, mindfulness is, as usual, the four satipaṭṭhānas, but clear comprehension involves remaining aware of feelings, perceptions, and thoughts as they arise, remain, and end. It is therefore 'contemplation of mind-objects', a label usually incorrectly ascribed to the fourth satipaṭṭhāna.

28 Elsewhere, this practice is the third of four kinds of 'development of samādhi'.[11] These 'developments of samādhi' are progressive, and the fact that they start out with jhāna shows they are advanced practices, the higher 'development' of samādhi. The first two are on the side of samatha: the four jhānas, which lead to a pleasant abiding here & now; and the perception of light, which leads to 'knowledge & vision' (= psychic powers). The third, our current practice, leads to 'mindfulness & clear comprehension'. The fourth is the standard practice of observing the origin and dissolution of the five aggregates, which leads to the ending of defilements. These both focus on impermanence, and so are vipassanā. What is the difference between them? Why does one lead to enlightenment, and one merely to mindfulness & clear comprehension?

29 When contemplating the rise, persistence, and ending of feelings, perceptions, and thoughts, the field of insight is not yet complete. The body is left out. The primary meaning of impermanence regarding the body is the big issue, life and death. One's own death, as such, cannot be contemplated directly, but must involve some kind of inference in time. This practice excludes this. It is solely concerned with the experience in the present moment, and has not yet deepened to an understanding of the principle underlying experience. To use terminology derived from elsewhere in the

---

[10] SN 47.2/SA 610.

[11] AN 4.41/T № 1536.7.

Suttas, it involves *dhamme ñāṇaṁ* (knowledge regarding phenomena), but not *anvaye ñāṇaṁ* (inferential knowledge).[12] The other important limitation is that this practice 'clearly comprehends' the known, not the knowing itself, which is the key to really deep insight. This is also because this practice involves only direct observation of phenomena as they occur, not inference of the causal principle describing how these events unfold over time. According to the Suttas, cognition (the knowing) arises dependent on mental objects (the known). If cognition were to directly observe itself this would entail the fallacy of something being it's own cause. So cognition can never be self-supporting; in other words, one cannot directly observe the act of cognition. Insight into cognition requires, on some level, an inferential process involving time. So our contemplation of mind objects, while valuable, will not lead to liberation until it deepens into a more full comprehension of the entire field of experience, past and future, as well as present.

30 Both this meditative development of clear comprehension and the awareness of bodily activities are clearly distinguished from satipaṭṭhāna as such; they are related, not equated. No doubt in practice they may not be isolated from one another, but the Saṁyutta nowhere subsumes these practices of clear comprehension within the four satipaṭṭhānas.

31 The meditative practice of clear comprehension, moreover, has different objects than satipaṭṭhāna. Only feelings directly correlates. While one might try to equate perceptions and thoughts with one or the other of the four satipaṭṭhānas (traditionally they would be slotted under dhammas), the actual descriptions of the practices, in all versions, do not support this. Again, the reason may be readily inferred. One of the key satipaṭṭhāna exercises is ānāpānasati. The special function of this meditation is to quell thoughts. This is reinforced in the Sarvāstivāda Smṛtyupasthāna Sūtra, which includes practices for quelling and suppressing thoughts. So the primary purpose of satipaṭṭhāna is not to be mindfully aware of thoughts as they pass through the mind; it is to eliminate thoughts so that the mind may be brought to stillness.

32 The meditative development of clear comprehension described here is clearly of secondary importance; the passage occurs once only in each

[12] SN 12.33/SA 356, SN 12.34/SA 357.

of the Saṁyutta, Majjhima, and Dīgha Nikāyas, and three times in the Aṅguttara. Many of the contexts this passage appears in do not inspire confidence as to its historical importance. In the Dīgha it occurs in the Saṅgīti Sutta (an aṅguttara-principle proto-abhidhamma compilation); in the Majjhima in the Acchariya-abbhūta Sutta (an *abbhūtadhamma*); and in the Aṅguttara in the context of the *paṭisambhidās*, a minor category. In the Theravāda Satipaṭṭhāna-saṁyutta, it occurs in the middle of the fourth vagga, a chapter that has few cognates in the Sarvāstivāda, and appears to be composed of largely artificial texts.

12.1.4 The Vibhaṅga Sutta

33 Several of the discourses identified above deal with the samādhi aspect of satipaṭṭhāna. These have withstood any test of authenticity I have been able to throw at them, and must stand as representing a central, mainstream conception of satipaṭṭhāna. Finally, however, we turn to the two remaining texts in the Satipaṭṭhāna-saṁyutta that deal directly with satipaṭṭhāna as vipassanā: SN 47.40 Vibhaṅga and SN 47.42/SA 609 Samudaya ('Origination').

34 The Vibhaṅga Sutta is not attested in the Chinese canon. This alone makes it look like a secondary development; a closer look confirms this. Like the discourse of mindfulness and clear comprehension we have just discussed, it is found at the end of the fourth vagga, which is a dubious chapter because almost all of the discourses seem to be artificial, or at least could have been produced by artificial means. The Vibhaṅga Sutta, being at the end of this vagga, precedes an unrelated discourse called 'Deathless', which is followed by Samudaya. Thus 'Deathless' is arbitrarily inserted between the closely related Vibhaṅga and Samudaya.

35 The Vibhaṅga Sutta starts out with the Buddha saying: 'I will teach you…'. This standard opening seems innocuous enough. Normally, however, 'teaching' (*desanā*) in brief is contrasted with 'analysis' (*vibhaṅga*) in detail. So the title and the text itself seem to be telling us two different things. The status of titles of discourses is often dubious, since in Pali texts the titles usually do not accompany the discourse itself, but are merely inferred from the mnemonic verses at the end of the vagga. So the statement of the text itself should be given more credence. And indeed, in accordance

with the text itself, and in contrast with the title, the discourse appears more like a teaching (in brief) than an analysis (in detail). There is no proper 'vibhaṅga' analysing the individual elements. Rather, a threefold teaching is presented: satipaṭṭhāna (the usual formula), the development of satipaṭṭhāna (contemplating the nature of origination and dissolution regarding the body, etc.), and the way leading to the development of satipaṭṭhāna (the noble eightfold path).

36 This should be compared with the Iddhipāda-saṁyutta. There, one discourse presents a fourfold 'Teaching': psychic power; the basis for psychic power (simply described as the practice leading to psychic power); the 'development' of the bases for psychic power (one 'develops' the four bases for psychic power according to the standard formula); and the way leading to the development of psychic power (the noble eightfold path).[13] The internal coherence in the usage of the terms 'teaching' and 'development' argue for the authenticity of this text. The next discourse presents an 'Analysis' of this teaching, which is in classic vibhaṅga style.[14] This shares some significant and unusual features in common with the Satipaṭṭhāna Sutta. The terms 'constricted mind' and 'scattered mind' occur in the contemplation of mind, and the 31 parts of the body occur in the contemplation of the body. Some other passages in the Sarvāstivāda Smṛtyupasthāna Sūtra are even closer to the Analysis of the Bases for Psychic Power:

> 37 'And again monks, contemplating a body in the body, a monk cultivates a glorious bright mind, well received, well grasped, well remembered: as before, so after; as after, so before; as by day, so by night; as by night, so by day; as below, so above; as above, so below. In this way he is not confused at heart, he does not have entanglement. He cultivates a glorious bright mind, a mind that is finally not obscured by darkness.'[15]

38 Perhaps the Vibhaṅga Sutta of the Satipaṭṭhāna-saṁyutta should be called 'Teaching'. It would then have been complemented by a more extensive discourse in vibhaṅga style. The only text that might fit the bill is the Satipaṭṭhāna Sutta, or more correctly the *Satipaṭṭhāna Mūla, which is very similar to the chapter on satipaṭṭhāna in the Abhidhamma Vibhaṅga,

---

[13] SN 51.19 (No SA cognate, as the Iddhipāda Saṁyutta has been lost from the Chinese.)

[14] SN 51.20.

[15] MA 98; cp. SN 51.20.

and has strong parallels with the Vibhaṅga of the Iddhipāda Saṁyutta. Several other vibhaṅgas on Saṁyutta topics are now found in the Majjhima.[16] These are distinguished from the vibhaṅgas left in the Saṁyutta by length: the shorter vibhaṅgas are in the Saṁyutta, the longer ones in the Majjhima. I suggest that the Satipaṭṭhāna Sutta was earlier a Vibhaṅga Sutta of the Saṁyutta, but with extra expansion was removed to the Majjhima.

39 Another problem with the Vibhaṅga Sutta is that here the observation of rise and fall is called 'development'. Normally, as in the discourse from the Iddhipāda-saṁyutta described above, development (*bhāvanā*) is described in terms of the 'cultivation, development, and making much of' the relevant dhammas. But there are three texts in the Pali Satipaṭṭhāna-saṁyutta which depict 'development', and each does so in their own way. There are two texts that use 'Development' for their title. Only the first of the two 'Development' discourses meaningfully refers to 'development' in the discourse itself: 'These four satipaṭṭhānas, when developed and cultivated, lead from the near to the far shore.'[17] The Sarvāstivāda contains several discourses of this type, some of which are merely listed in summary, each substituting a different stock phrase describing the benefits of developing satipaṭṭhāna; it leads to the complete ending of suffering, or to great fruit and benefit, etc. The second Development Sutta in the Theravāda is of a type elsewhere titled 'Teaching' (*desanā*).[18] It starts off with the Buddha saying: 'Monks, I will teach you the development of the four satipaṭṭhānas.' The discourse merely gives the basic satipaṭṭhāna formula and says this is the development of the four satipaṭṭhānas. The closest Sarvāstivāda cognate to this, SA 610, elaborates development as the contemplation of the satipaṭṭhānas internally and externally. This understanding of development is found in later works like Asaṅga's Abhidharmasamuccaya, which adds to the body of evidence that Asaṅga used a Saṁyukta very like the one we have in Chinese.[19]

40 So we now have four descriptions of the 'development of satipaṭṭhāna': one is to 'cultivate and develop' the basic practice; the second simply

---

[16] Saccavibhaṅga, Dhatuvibhaṅga; Saḷāyatanavibhaṅga is in MN but the Sarvāstivāda counterpart remains in SA, surely its original home.

[17] SN 47.34/SA 634.

[18] SN 47.39/SA 610.

[19] BOIN-WEBB, pg. 160.

presents the basic formula; the third, found only in the Sarvāstivāda, is to contemplate internally and externally; and the fourth, found only in the Theravāda, is to contemplate the objects of satipaṭṭhāna as impermanent. Only the first of these fits the normal use of 'development'. The internal/external practice, while not how development is presented normally, is appropriate enough, for it teaches how to broaden and extend the basic practice, in terms commonly found in the mainstream satipaṭṭhāna discourses. The contemplation in terms of impermanence is apt in a certain sense, since it depicts an advanced practice for those already grounded in the fundamentals.

41 So our final assessment of the Vibhaṅga Sutta is that it is late because of its position within the Saṁyutta, lack of Sarvāstivādin counterpart, and internal incongruencies. There might have been an earlier version, more aptly called 'Teaching', that described 'development' as the 'cultivation, development, and making much' of the four satipaṭṭhānas, or the internal/external contemplation, and later on this was replaced by the section on rise and fall.

12.1.5 The Samudaya Sutta

42 We may now go on to examine the Samudaya Sutta. The Sarvāstivādin version is significantly longer than the Pali, raising the question as to which is the original. A number of considerations taken together make it virtually certain that the Sarvāstivāda version is more original. In order to make the following discussion as clear as possible I will first present here the essential doctrinal elements in the Chinese version, adapting the Chinese translation to conform more obviously with standard renderings of the Pali.

> 43 1) I will teach you, monks, the origination and dissolution of the four satipaṭṭhānas. Listen well and pay attention; I will speak... What is the origination and dissolution of the four satipaṭṭhānas?
>
> 44 2a) Due to the origination of food there is the origination of the body; due to the cessation of food there is the dissolution of the body.
>
> 45 2b) In this way, monks, a monk contemplates the nature of origination in the body, he contemplates the nature of dissolution in the

body, he contemplates the nature of origination and dissolution in the body.

46 2c) He abides independent, not grasping at anything in the world.

47 3a) Due to the origination of contact there is the origination of feelings;[20] due to the cessation of contact there is the dissolution of feelings.

48 3b) In this way, monks, a monk contemplates the nature of origination in the feelings, he contemplates the nature of dissolution in the feelings, he contemplates the nature of origination and dissolution in the feelings.

49 3c) He abides independent, not grasping at anything in the world.

50 4a) Due to the origination of name & form there is the origination of the mind; due to the cessation of name & form there is the dissolution of the mind.

51 4b) In this way, monks, a monk contemplates the nature of origination in the mind, he contemplates the nature of dissolution in the mind, he contemplates the nature of origination and dissolution in the mind.

52 4c) He abides independent, not grasping at anything in the world.

53 5a) Due to the origination of attention there is the origination of dhammas; due to the cessation of attention there is the dissolution of the dhammas.

54 5b) In this way, monks, a monk contemplates the nature of origination in the dhammas, he contemplates the nature of dissolution in the dhammas, he contemplates the nature of origination and dissolution in the dhammas.

55 5c) He abides independent, not grasping at anything in the world.

56 The major doctrinal content is the causes for the four objects of satipaṭṭhāna, and in this both traditions are in complete agreement. However much of the remaining structure differs. The Theravāda has the introductory section 1, but instead of asking 'What is the origination and dissolution of the four satipaṭṭhānas' it asks 'What is the origination of the body?' This is clearly an editing glitch. We would expect that this question should be repeated for the other three satipaṭṭhānas, but it is not; also, the question just refers to origination, but the text refers to both origination and dissolution. These editing anomalies are not found in the Chinese. The phrasing also departs from the standard form. Normally the Buddha says: 'I will

---

[20] CDB mistakenly has the singular 'feeling'.

teach you x... Listen to that... And what is x?' But here he says 'I will teach you x... Listen to that... And what is y?' This kind of change could have happened if the text was written half on one page and half on the next; the question became detached from the introduction and was included with the section on the body (as in the PTS Pali and translations), and so later copyists assumed the question must refer to the body. The Chinese version is more rational and so more likely to be authentic.

57 Sections b and c are absent from the Theravāda Samudaya Sutta; they are however very similar to the 'vipassanā refrain' of the Theravāda Satipaṭṭhāna Sutta. Elsewhere in the Theravāda Saṁyutta, section b occurs, but not in association with section c. This suggests that the early version of the Samudaya Suttas preserved in Chinese was a decisive influence on the formation of the vipassanā refrain of the Theravāda Satipaṭṭhāna Sutta; this must have occurred before the breakup of the Samudaya Sutta.

58 Section b is now found in the Vibhaṅga Sutta, which as we have seen is likely to be a later development. When the Samudaya Sutta was broken up, sections b and c were moved into the original *Vibhaṅga Sutta, which was moved to the Majjhima and retitled the 'Satipaṭṭhāna Sutta'. Somehow, the original *Desanā Sutta that was paired with its *Vibhaṅga Sutta remained in the Saṁyutta, but took the title 'Vibhaṅga' and also section b from the Samudaya Sutta.

59 Having established that the Sarvāstivāda is more likely to represent the pre-sectarian text of the Samudaya Sutta, we should now consider whether this is likely to have been in the original collection. The phrases 'principle of origination, principle of dissolution, principle of origination and dissolution' occur in a sequence of three discourses in the Khandhasaṁyutta.[21] These discourses, together with the two following, are combined into one discourse in the Chinese. The explanations for 'origination' and 'dissolution' in satipaṭṭhāna are also reminiscent of the causes for the arising and ceasing of the five aggregates, as in the important Seven Cases Sutta, which is one of the most widely distributed of all the discourses; it functions like a *Khandhavibhaṅga Sutta in the absence of a proper text of this type).[22]

[21] SN 126–128/SA 256.

[22] SN 22.57/SA 42/EA 41.3. Also in the partial 'Other translation' of SA, and forms the basis of a long independent Seven Cases Sutta in the Chinese, which appears to be a Saṅgīti Sutta style compilation.

This says that 'due to the origination of food there is the origination of physical form [= body]... due to the origination of contact there is the origination of feeling... [and] perception... [and] conceptual activities... due to the origination of name & form there is the origination of cognition...'. Since these kinds of vipassanā teachings are prevalent throughout the Khandha-saṁyutta, it is likely that that was their original home and they were included in the Satipaṭṭhāna-saṁyutta as a secondary development. This was prompted by the partial correspondence between the four satipaṭṭhānas and the five aggregates: body = physical form; feeling = feeling; mind = cognition; dhammas = (perception and conceptual activities?). This correspondence was made explicit in the later texts of the schools, as we shall notice.

60 Despite these doubts, however, the Samudaya Sutta is an important pre-sectarian text and deserves closer consideration. It says that the origin of the body is food; the origin of feelings is contact; the origin of the mind is name & form; and the origin of dhammas is attention. These dispose of the idea that impermanence in satipaṭṭhāna means momentariness. Food sustains life; if you stop eating you'll die. Clearly here cessation or passing away just means 'death'. Contact is the origin for feelings in both the five aggregates and the dependent origination. Attention as origin for dhammas is interesting. Attention is the basis for wisdom, and is most typically treated as inquiry into causes, especially the causes of good and bad dhammas. This suggests that vipassanā is intrinsic to this satipaṭṭhāna.

61 'Name & form' is in the Samudaya Sutta said to be the origin of mind. 'Name' is elsewhere defined as 'feeling, perception, volition, contact, attention'[23] It is the group of mental factors that form concepts, literally 'naming'.[24] Normally (in the aggregates and dependent origination) 'name & form' is said to be the origin of 'cognition' (*viññāṇa*), rather than 'mind' (*citta*). Obviously here *citta* and *viññāṇa* are synonyms; but why does this terminological shift occur here? Typically, *viññāṇa* is used in vipassanā contexts, such as dependent origination, the five aggregates, and the process of sense cognition. It is therefore treated under the first noble truth,

[23] SN 12.1/SA 298/T № 124/Skt etc. The Chinese sometimes has 'the four immaterial aggregates', which is almost certainly a later corruption; however, this does not affect the current argument.

[24] DN 15.20/DA 13/T № 14/MA 97/T № 52/Skt.

and is 'to be fully known'. *Citta* is more difficult to pin down, for it is widely used in non-technical contexts to mean simply 'mind', 'thought', 'mood', 'state of mind'. However, when it is used in a technical sense it is often a term for samādhi—the 'higher mind' (*adhicitta*), 'endowment with mind' (*cittasampadā*), etc. It is therefore treated under the fourth noble truth, and is 'to be developed'. This is why *citta* is appropriate for satipaṭṭhāna—it encompasses both the ordinary mind and the mind developed in samādhi. But when the normal samatha context of satipaṭṭhāna is extended to include vipassanā, we end up with *citta* appearing out of character in a role normally played by *viññāṇa*.[25]

62 Uniquely in the Nikāyas, this text treats 'satipaṭṭhāna' in an objective sense. Normally 'satipaṭṭhāna' ('establishing of mindfulness') refers to the subjective act of setting up or focussing mindfulness on one of the four fields. But here satipaṭṭhāna refers to the objects of mindfulness, that is, the body, etc. ('things on which mindfulness is established'). This objective sense if taken literally is absurd—it would mean that the body is the 'one-way path' to Nibbana. This might come as pleasant news; for since food is the nutriment for the body, eating must be the nutriment for the path! This ambiguity results from the shift in perspective as the framework designed for samatha is extended to include vipassanā, under the influence of the five aggregates. In normal satipaṭṭhāna one is 'inside' the four fields, 'getting into' the field of meditation, whereas here one has 'pulled back' from and objectified the process for the purpose of analysis. Like the difference between reading a story, where one enters into the characters and emotions—you feel angry or sad or happy—and reading a review of the story, where one develops a critical, analytical insight into how the story works—you understand how the text made you feel angry or sad or happy. We shall see later that this ambiguity caused considerable confusion in later writings.

63 So there are several issues with the Samudaya Sutta: editing problems in the Pali; lack of close congruence between the Sarvāstivāda and Theravāda; possible influence from the Khandha-saṁyutta; unusual treatment of the subject raising serious interpretive difficulties. So while I have conceded

[25] A similar vacillation between *citta* and *viññāṇa* occurs in other contexts where samatha and vipassanā overlap, e.g. MN 138/MA 164 Uddesavibhaṅga.

it a place in the concordance, its authenticity is dubious. One feature, however, attests to the earliness, which is attention as the origin for dhammas. This fits well with the earlier content of the contemplation of dhammas section, but not with the developed content of the existing Satipaṭṭhāna Sutta. Also, this statement can't have been derived from the Khandhasaṁyutta or anywhere else. If the Samudaya Sutta is a secondary addition, then, it is not very late.

12.2 The Anuruddha-saṁyutta

64 We may now briefly consider the treatment of satipaṭṭhāna in the rest of the Saṁyutta. The Anuruddha-saṁyutta deals exclusively with satipaṭṭhāna, the thematic unity underlined by the fact that all the discourses were spoken by Venerable Anuruddha.

65 The Theravāda Anuruddha-saṁyutta starts with the most complex vipassanā analysis so far.[26] This combines the internal/external contemplation with the impermanence contemplation. One contemplates the principle of arising, of vanishing, and of arising & vanishing regarding the body internally. Then one contemplates the body externally in the same way, and so on. Each section is then addended with the standard auxiliary formula. This is the only place where the vipassanā section is embedded within the satipaṭṭhāna formula itself. Then it introduces another framework, familiar elsewhere in the suttas. One contemplates the repulsive in the unrepulsive; the unrepulsive in the repulsive; then ignores both and abides in equanimity. Remember that in the Theravāda Satipaṭṭhāna-saṁyutta Vibhaṅga Sutta one first was established on all four satipaṭṭhānas, and only then was impermanence introduced. Now, however, impermanence is introduced from the first, giving the impression, without stating so explicitly, that one may undertake vipassanā from the start of practice. Here we see the beginnings of a trend that can be traced over later expositions of satipaṭṭhāna.

66 This discourse does not have a close cognate. There is one text in the Sarvāstivāda Anuruddha-saṁyutta that mentions seeing the repulsive in

[26] SN 52.1.

the unrepulsive, and so on, which we might regard as cognate.[27] But this has quite a different setting (like the 'Brahmā' discourses that proclaim the 'way to convergence') and omits the mention of rise and fall. The pair to this discourse, as mentioned above, complements the 'way to convergence' by saying this leads to unification of mind, a saying not found in the Theravāda.[28] Given Venerable Anuruddha's reputation as an quietist, this is a more plausible saying.

67 Most of the rest of the Anuruddha-saṁyutta emphasizes this samādhi aspect of satipaṭṭhāna, as Anuruddha systematically ascribes his success in every kind of psychic power to satipaṭṭhāna. This follows naturally from the basic function of satipaṭṭhāna as support for jhāna. Many of these formulaic passages are abridged in the Sarvāstivāda-saṁyukta.

12.3 The Vedanā-saṁyutta

68 The Vedanā-saṁyutta is clearly oriented towards vipassanā, speaking frequently of understanding the impermanence of feelings. But this does not mean that the samatha dimension is ignored. Several discourses teach that one understands the cessation of feelings through the jhānas.[29] All of the jhāna discourses are included in the Sarvāstivāda, while the two mentioning satipaṭṭhāna are not. There are 31 discourses in the Theravāda Vedanā-saṁyutta; only five are missing from the Sarvāstivāda, all of which deal with vipassanā.[30]

69 Satipaṭṭhāna is invoked in two very similar discourses taught for sick bhikkhus.[31] One should develop satipaṭṭhānas, have clear comprehension, and contemplate the conditionality and impermanence of feelings. These discourses occur next to each other in the saṁyutta (although in the Sarvāstivāda they are in another saṁyutta, dealing with illness), and they are both given in the identical setting, the Hall with the Peaked Roof in the Great Wood of Vesali. This is an unusual location, and begs the question

[27] SA 536.
[28] SA 535.
[29] SN 36.11, 36.15–20.
[30] SN 36.2, 36.7–10, 36.22.
[31] SN 36.7, 36.8.

why two such almost identical discourses were given here and nowhere else. The only difference between them is that the first states that feeling is conditioned by the body, while the second says feeling is conditioned by contact. The latter is the normal position of the Suttas, repeated many times in the Vedanā-saṁyutta itself, so the statement that feelings are dependent on the body is questionable. We are probably dealing with one text, and fairly early on the word 'body' was substituted for 'contact', perhaps by mistake, to yield a pair of discourses.

70 The sequence of these texts is interesting: four satipaṭṭhānas; clear comprehension of bodily activities; contemplation of feelings. In other words they first present the basic teaching on satipaṭṭhāna, then offer explanations of the first two, body and feelings. This was pointed out to me by Rod Bucknell, who suggested that this was evidence that the original specification of body contemplation was the clear comprehension of activities, rather than the parts of the body, as I argue in this paper. However, a closer examination suggests that this conclusion is not required.

71 First up, the texts don't say that the clear comprehension of activities, or the contemplation of the impermanence of feelings, fall under the relevant satipaṭṭhānas. The discourses start off with the Buddha visiting the sick monks and encouraging them to 'wait their time' mindful and clearly comprehending, saying that 'this is our instruction to you.' Then he explains 'mindful' as the four satipaṭṭhānas, and 'clearly comprehending' as awareness of activities. This is just as in the Satipaṭṭhāna-saṁyutta, and here as there, the surface of the texts present these as two distinct practices, with no attempt at integrating them. This is not to say that they are not integrated or connected, but simply that the text does not spell this out. One practice is stated; then the next is stated; then the Buddha sums up by repeating that 'this is our instruction to you.' So the body of the teaching is just the same as the Satipaṭṭhāna-saṁyutta, and the repeated injunction closes off this section of the discourse.

72 Next is introduced the contemplation of feelings, with a distinct change in mood. Whereas previously we had a straightforward exhortation, now the text shifts to a hypothetical mood: 'If, monks, for a monk abiding thus mindful, clearly comprehending, diligent, ardent, resolute, there arises pleasant feeling…'. This shift might be caused by the conjunction of two

different textual pericopes. While this does not prove that the text as we have it is inauthentic, it does call into question its reliability as an early authority. Certain of the phrases here, such as the repeated use of 'contemplates,' reminds us of satipaṭṭhāna, but some of the details are different. Unlike satipaṭṭhāna, the investigation into causality is made explicit: 'On what [is this feeling] dependent? It is dependent on contact.' And interestingly, whereas satipaṭṭhāna famously has us contemplate 'a body in the body', 'a feeling in the feelings', etc., this passage says: 'One abides contemplating impermanence in contact and in pleasant feelings.'[32] So while satipaṭṭhāna is about focussing intently and exclusively on one aspect of experience, our current passage is depicting a more complex, many-faceted meditation, seeing different kinds of phenomena, their relationship and mutual dependence, and their nature as impermanent.

73 It is in contexts such as this that we find clear descriptions of vipassanā as investigation into causality, which are so strikingly absent from the basic meditation practices in the Satipaṭṭhāna Sutta itself. Here the development of vipassanā into feelings is stated *after* satipaṭṭhāna; and it is described as investigating their causal dependence, then contemplating their impermanence, vanishing, fading away, cessation, relinquishment. These terms are virtually identical with the fourth tetrad of ānāpānasati; in other words, the contemplation of dhammas.

74 Feelings are an intrinsic part of satipaṭṭhāna, so it is no surprise that satipaṭṭhāna is introduced in the collection of discourses dealing with feeling. However, the four satipaṭṭhānas are not mentioned at all in the Saḷāyatana-saṁyutta and hardly in the Khandha-saṁyutta, suggesting that the sense media and the aggregates were not considered as specially related to satipaṭṭhāna. The Khandha-saṁyutta mentions satipaṭṭhāna a couple of times when listing the 37 wings to awakening. In one other discourse they are mentioned, but not in connection with the aggregates:

75 > 'And where, monks, do these three unskilful thoughts cease without remainder? For one who abides with a mind well established on the four satipaṭṭhānas, or who develops the signless concentration.'[33]

---

[32] *So phasse ca sukhāya ca vedanāya aniccānupassī viharati.*

[33] SN 22.80.

76 Unskilful thoughts cease in the first jhāna;[34] ānāpānasati is the normal practice for cutting off thoughts. Controlling thoughts also features in the Sarvāstivāda Smṛtyupasthāna Sūtra. In line with the trend emerging above, this treatment of the samatha side of satipaṭṭhāna is also found in the Sarvāstivāda.

77 Even though the four satipaṭṭhānas as such are not mentioned in the Saḷāyatana-saṁyutta, yet there is a closer connection between mindfulness and the six sense media than between mindfulness and the five aggregates. This reflects a subtle difference in orientation between the two frameworks. Meditation on the aggregates is specially associated with eradicating wrong view, while that on the sense media is attuned towards transcending desire. It therefore emphasizes sense restraint, which is closely associated with mindfulness, especially mindfulness of the body. The standard passage was included above in Venerable Mahā Kaccāna's reply to the Brahman Lohicca.[35] There the order of the teaching is: sense restraint; mindfulness of the body; measureless mind (i.e. jhāna); understanding; release. Another passage says that a monk should train himself regarding the six senses so that they do not obsess his mind, his energy is tireless, his mindfulness is well established, the body becomes tranquil, and the mind enters samādhi.[36] Thus the usage of mindfulness here is much the same as we have seen above.

12.4 The Ānāpānasati-saṁyutta

78 Mindfulness of breathing was the meditation the Buddha practiced underneath the Bodhi tree, and remained his preferred meditation even after his enlightenment. Because of this it has always claimed a special prestige as the royal road to Nibbana. The chief source is the Ānāpānasati Sutta in the Theravāda Majjhima Nikāya.[37] There is no Ānāpānasati Sutta as such in the Sarvāstivāda Madhyama Āgama, but it does exist as an iso-

[34] MN 78/MA 179 Samaṇamaṇḍikā.
[35] SN 35.132, etc.
[36] SN 35.134.
[37] MN 118.

lated text in the Chinese canon.[38] The 16 steps, moreover, are found in the Sarvāstivāda Madhyama and Saṁyukta. In the Theravāda Majjhima and the Theravāda and Sarvāstivāda Saṁyuttas the 16 steps of ānāpānasati are analysed against the four satipaṭṭhānas. The correlation is as follows.

Table 12.4: Satipaṭṭhāna & Ānāpānāsati

Satipaṭṭhāna	Ānāpānāsati
1. Contemplation of the body	Breathing long Breathing short Experiencing the whole body Tranquillising the bodily activities
2. Contemplation of feelings	Experiencing rapture Experiencing bliss Experiencing mental activities Tranquillising mental activities
3. Contemplation of the mind	Experiencing the mind Gladdening the mind Centering the mind in samādhi Releasing the mind
4. Contemplation of dhammas	Contemplating impermanence Contemplating fading of lust Contemplating cessation Contemplating relinquishment

79 In the context of ānāpānasati the 'body' and the 'bodily activities' are defined as the breath, while the 'mental activities' are feeling and perception. The first tetrad evidently describes the process of gradually settling and calming the breath. Contemplation of feelings is described purely as the bliss of samatha; there is no place for contemplation of pain here, and apparently no need for it. Contemplation of the mind is even more explicitly framed in terms of samādhi experiences.

80 In accordance with the mainstream teachings on satipaṭṭhāna, not until the fourth tetrad, equivalent to contemplation of dhammas, do we

[38] Chih-ching, according to MINH CHÂU, pg. 347. These miscellaneous discourses, found addended to the major collections, consist of alternative translations and sometimes texts not found in the major Āgamas. Their doctrinal affiliations are usually unknown and they have been even less studied than the major collections.

encounter vipassanā.[39] Similar terms expressing vipassanā occur, with minor variations, throughout the Suttas. The most fundamental group, as in the Anattalakkhaṇa Sutta, etc., is: knowledge & vision, repulsion, fading of lust, release. The Sarvāstivāda has impermanence, repulsion, fading of lust, cessation; again, a minor variation describing the same process.

81 In the Ānāpānasati Sutta, as well as both the Theravāda and Sarvāstivāda Saṁyuttas, developing ānāpānasati develops the satipaṭṭhānas, developing the satipaṭṭhānas develops the seven awakening-factors, and developing the seven awakening-factors leads to liberation. This reminds us of the 'inference according to dhamma' we met above, as well as the meditative phase of the gradual training. The connection between ānāpānasati and the awakening-factors also helps us to understand the way contemplation of dhammas in ānāpānasati and satipaṭṭhāna are related. Where ānāpānasati has 'impermanence, fading away of lust, cessation, relinquishment', satipaṭṭhāna has a list of dhammas which includes the seven awakening-factors; and the standard passage on these says they are 'dependent on seclusion, dependent on fading away of lust, dependent on cessation, maturing in relinquishment'.

82 The fourth tetrad of ānāpānasati contemplates impermanence; but the impermanence of what? We should relate this to the inner structure of the meditation itself. The whole course of ānāpānasati emphasizes a gradual, progressive stilling, appeasement, ending of activities. The breath is calm and becomes very subtle and fine. The endless chatter of thinking is stilled and one experiences ever more refined bliss and tranquillity. The hindrances end and the clamour of sense impingement fades away. This successive stilling is the entire world of the meditator's experience at that time, and is the field in which they come to understand impermanence. An interesting perspective is thrown on this by the phrase, which we have already quoted above, describing this contemplation of dhammas in ānāpānasati:

83 > 'Having seen with understanding the abandoning of covetousness & aversion, he watches over closely with equanimity...'[40]

[39] The commentary tries to read the first three tetrads as pertaining to both samatha and vipassanā, but can claim no support in the text.

[40] SN 54.10/SA 813, SN 54.13/SA 810, MN 118.23*ff.*

84 'Covetousness & aversion' recalls the satipaṭṭhāna auxiliary formula. In the Satipaṭṭhāna Sutta, the contemplation of dhammas starts with the five hindrances. The first two of these are sensual desire and ill-will, which are identical with 'covetousness & aversion'. Seeing the abandoning of these 'with understanding' brings the focus on causality that is characteristic of this section; the same word 'abandoning' also occurs in the contemplation of dhammas, in reference to the abandoning of the five hindrances. The contemplation of dhammas also includes the seven awakening-factors, and these are the forces that can overcome the five hindrances. So our text finishes by saying that one should 'watch with equanimity'; for equanimity is the last of the awakening-factors. The contemplation of dhammas in ānāpānasati is fulfilled by understanding how the hindrances are abandoned through the awakening-factors, and with the fulfilment of this process one dwells in equanimity.

85 Compared with the conservative, incremental evolution the teachings on satipaṭṭhāna underwent in the Satipaṭṭhāna-saṁyutta, the Satipaṭṭhāna Sutta in the Majjhima Nikāya appears as an unpredictable quantum leap. It is instructive to compare this with the Ānāpānasati Sutta. This contains no new teachings, being merely a presentation of material from the Ānāpānasati-saṁyutta with a more elaborate setting. In other words this is a more normal teaching, taught more often. In the Satipaṭṭhāna Sutta we see, not a dainty step up in size like in ānāpānasati, but a massive blowout in several directions at once. First, each of the four satipaṭṭhānas is expanded into a detailed exercise or series of exercises, few of which occur elsewhere in the context of satipaṭṭhāna. Then each exercise is followed by a lengthy section dealing with insight. This is substantially similar to the insight section in the Samudaya Sutta of the Sarvāstivāda Saṁyukta. These extra sections did not appear all at once: the Satipaṭṭhāna Sutta as we have it is the end result of a long process of textual accretion.

Chapter 13

EARLY ABHIDHAMMA

I TAKE THE UNUSUAL STEP of considering the Abhidhamma texts before the Satipaṭṭhāna Suttas, even though this runs counter to the historical sequence. This is for two reasons. One is that the Abhidhamma material on satipaṭṭhāna preserves certain features that are more archaic than the Suttas. The second is that I want to deconstruct perceptions of what satipaṭṭhāna is all about, perceptions that are conditioned by the modern *vipassanāvāda* interpretation of the Theravāda Satipaṭṭhāna Sutta.

2 The Abhidhamma literature is a formalized, scholastic systemization of the Dhamma according to the perspectives of the schools. Whereas the Sutta and Vinaya literature is largely common to all schools, the Abhidhammas of the schools diverge widely. This is because the Suttas and Vinaya derive from the pre-sectarian period, while the Abhidhamma literature is sectarian. In our discussion of the GIST, however, we noted a significant exception to this rule. There are three Abhidhamma texts that all seem to be derived from a common source, which we call the '*Vibhaṅga Mūla'. These texts are the Vibhaṅga of the Theravāda, the Dharmaskandha of the Sarvāstivāda,[1] and the Śāriputrābhidharma of the Dharmaguptaka.[2] The common core of these works was a *mātikā*, a matrix or schedule of doctrinal categories, furnished with explanations from the Suttas and with word-

---

1 T № 1537.

2 T № 1548. FRAUWALLNER (1995) discusses the relations between these texts in detail. See pp. 15*ff.*, 43*ff.*, and 97*ff.*

definitions. Since this work was started before the schisms and the Suttas were not finalized until later, there is some overlap in the compilation of the Suttas and the Abhidhammas.

13.1 Vibhaṅga

3 The Vibhaṅga includes a discussion of satipaṭṭhāna as one of a series of chapters dealing with the 37 wings to awakening. The discussion is divided into a 'Sutta Exposition' and an 'Abhidhamma Exposition'. The Sutta Expositions in the Vibhaṅga remain close to the Suttas. The Abhidhamma Exposition is later and contains distinctively abhidhammic material. We will look at the Sutta Exposition of the Vibhaṅga here, reserving a discussion of the Abhidhamma Exposition for a later chapter.

4 The Vibhaṅga starts out with the basic satipaṭṭhāna formula, elaborated with the internal/external contemplation. The detailed structure then unfolds as follows.

5 In the Vibhaṅga the body is treated just as the 31 parts. This is more primitive than the Theravāda Satipaṭṭhāna Sutta. The elements and corpse meditations, which are found in all three Sutta versions, are also found in the Dhammasaṅgaṇī, so it is not clear why they are not here. The enumeration of 31 parts of the body is also early, being found in the four Nikāyas; but by the time the Khuddakapāṭha was compiled (in Sri Lanka?), the brain had been added to complete the now classic 32 parts. I will discuss the body contemplations below, in the context of the Śāriputrābhidharma.

6 In addition to the usual threefold analysis of feelings, the satipaṭṭhāna material introduces the distinction between 'carnal' and 'spiritual' feelings. This distinction is only explained in the Vedanā-saṁyutta.[3] Since 'carnal' and 'spiritual' are unusual terms in this context, perhaps the Vedanāsaṁyutta passage was intended to explain the Satipaṭṭhāna Sutta. This is confirmed by another unusual feature, the inclusion of 'rapture' as a kind of feeling. Rapture is not mentioned in the feeling section of the Satipaṭṭhāna Sutta, but it does fall under feelings in ānāpānasati. This suggests that the Vedanā-saṁyutta passage synthesizes and explains the feelings sections in both satipaṭṭhāna and ānāpānasati.

[3] SN 36.31/SA 483.

Table 13.1: The Structure of the Vibhaṅga

1. Body	2. Feelings	3. Mind	4. Dhammas
How to contemplate body internal?	How to contemplate feelings internal?	How to contemplate mind internal?	How to contemplate dhammas internal?
Body parts internal	3 feelings, pleasant spiritual/carnal, etc. internal	Mind with lust, etc. (16 kinds) internal	5 hindrances & 7 awakening-factors internal
Develops 'that nimitta', compares with external	Develops 'that nimitta', compares with external	Develops 'that nimitta', compares with external	Develops 'that nimitta', compares with external
How to contemplate body external?	How to contemplate feelings external?	How to contemplate mind external?	How to contemplate dhammas external?
Body parts external	3 feelings, etc. external	Mind with lust, etc. external	5 hindrances & 7 awakening-factors external
Develops 'that nimitta', compares with internal/external	Develops 'that nimitta', compares with internal/external	Develops 'that nimitta', compares with internal/external	Develops 'that nimitta', compares with internal/external
How to contemplate body internal/external?	How to contemplate feelings internal/external?	How to contemplate mind internal/external?	How to contemplate dhammas internal/external?
Body parts internal/external	3 feelings, etc. internal/external	Mind with lust, etc. internal/external	5 hindrances & 7 awakening-factors internal/external
So one contemplates body internal/external	So one contemplates feelings internal/external	So one contemplates mind internal/external	So one contemplates dhammas internal/external
Defines: contemplates, abides, ardent, clearly comprehending, mindful, world, covetousness, aversion, remove	Defines	Defines	Defines

7 The explanations that concern us here are as follows. Carnal feelings are those connected with the senses. Spiritual rapture is in the first two jhānas, spiritual pleasant feeling is in the first three jhānas, while spiritual neutral feeling is in the fourth jhāna. Spiritual painful feeling is the depression that arises as one longs for the peaceful liberations one has not yet realized (a feeling I grow more familiar with as this book grows longer!). The spiritual feelings are primarily defined in terms of jhāna, and so this non-standard classification was introduced in satipaṭṭhāna to emphasize the importance of the refined bliss of samādhi. Just as we cannot know darkness until we have seen the light, we cannot know the nature of sensual feelings until we have the perspective of contrast.

8 The contemplation of mind speaks first of understanding the mind with and without greed, anger, and delusion. Normally the abandoning of these is arahantship, but there is no need to assume that here. Sometimes this kind of phrasing is used in straightforward samatha contexts, such as this passage from the Aṅguttara.

> 9 'On an occasion, friends, when a noble disciple recollects the Buddha, on that occasion his mind is not overwhelmed with lust, his mind is not overwhelmed with anger, his mind is not overwhelmed with delusion. At that time his mind is upright—departed, released, and risen from greed. "Greed" is a term for the five kinds of sensual pleasures. That noble disciple abides with a heart totally like the sky, vast, exalted, measureless, free of hatred and ill-will. Having made this the support, some beings here are purified.'[4]

10 Notice the similarities with satipaṭṭhāna, especially contemplation of mind: the practice is a 'recollection' (*anussati*); the term 'mind' (*citta*) is without lust, hatred, and delusion; doing this, one's mind is 'released'; and the result is the 'purification of beings'. The subjective aspect of the contemplation of mind is, therefore, similar to the six recollections.

11 Returning to the contemplation of mind, the overall context, the progressive structure of the discourse, and the inclusion of the mind 'compressed' (by sloth) and 'scattered' (by restlessness) all suggest that here we are dealing with the abandoning of the hindrances by samādhi, an interpretation confirmed by the commentary. A distinctive facet of the satipaṭṭhāna

---

[4] AN 6.26/SA 550.

material is the direct experience of the 'exalted' mind, the 'unexcelled' mind, the mind 'in samādhi', the 'released' mind—all terms for jhāna.

12 The sections on feeling and mind share a common syntax. For example: 'When feeling a pleasant feeling, one understands "I feel a pleasant feeling".' Or in the contemplation of mind: 'One understands mind with lust as "mind with lust".' This reflexive structure is shared with ānāpānasati: 'When breathing in a long breath, one understands "I am breathing in a long breath".'

13 The phrasing in 'quotation marks' (representing the Pali particle *iti*) prompted some schools to equate satipaṭṭhāna meditation with mental noting. But this is a naïvely literal interpretation. Similar usages are found, for example, in the standard passage on the formless attainments. Due to the idiomaticness of the Pali, this is difficult to translate; literally it would be: ' "Space is infinite", one enters & abides in the field of infinite space.' Usually translators would say something like: 'Aware that "Space is infinite", one enters & abides in the field of infinite space.' Obviously here the meditator has passed well beyond thinking or noting anything. The use of *iti* with repetitions in such contexts mirrors the reflexive nature of meditative contemplation. One is not merely knowing the feeling, but one is conscious *that* one is knowing the feeling.

14 The Vibhaṅga contemplation of dhammas has the hindrances and awakening-factors only, a pairing that is by now becoming familiar. Unlike the Satipaṭṭhāna Sutta, here there are no introductory and concluding sentences to separate and define each section, such as: 'And how does one abide contemplating a dhamma in the dhammas regarding the five hindrances?' The hindrances and awakening-factors simply run on into each other.[5] Otherwise, however, the phrasing is identical with the Sutta.

15 The contemplation of the five hindrances and seven awakening-factors is primarily a samatha practice, and invites consideration as to how this section differs from the previous sections. For example, the first two hindrances are sensual desire and ill-will, which seem to simply repeat the contemplation of 'mind with lust' and 'mind with anger'. But if we look

[5] Such sentences are found in the Dharmaskandha, but the Sarvāstivāda Smṛtyupasthāna Sūtra has only the concluding sentences; this is perhaps the only point at which the Dharmaskandha is closer to the Theravāda Satipaṭṭhāna Sutta.

closely, some subtle differences make themselves evident. The first thing is that in the contemplation of mind, the direct object of contemplation was the mind itself; the qualities of the mind, such as lust, hatred, etc., function as adjectives qualifying the mind. This suggests that the prime focus in this contemplation is the nature of knowing itself, the cognitive power of awareness in various conditions. In the contemplation of dhammas, the direct object of contemplation is not the mind, but the associated mental qualities—sensual desire, etc.

16 A more obvious distinction is the introduction of an investigation into causality in the contemplation of dhammas. Here we compare the contemplation of mind and dhammas, keeping the translation as literal as possible.

Table 13.2: Contemplation of Mind and Dhammas

Contemplation of Mind	Contemplation of Dhammas
One understands mind with lust as 'mind with lust.'	There being internal sensual desire, one understands 'There is for me internal sensual desire.'
One understands mind without lust as 'mind without lust.'	There not being internal sensual desire, one understands 'There is not for me internal sensual desire.'
	And one understands how the unarisen sensual desire comes to arise.
	And one understands how the arisen sensual desire comes to be abandoned.
	And one understands how the abandoned sensual desire comes to not arise in the future.

17 The chief difference in the mode of contemplation is the final three sentences in the contemplation of dhammas. This is investigation into causality, into the reasons behind the rise and fall of the various good and bad qualities; an investigation, moreover, that is attuned precisely to removing the cause and abandoning forever the bad qualities. For the awakening-factors, of course, the situation is changed: one is to understand how the awakening-factors arise, and how they are developed to fulfilment. The causes for abandoning the hindrances are precisely the awakening-factors; and the causes for obstructing the awakening-factors

are precisely the hindrances. Thus these two sets of dhammas are intertwined, the light and shadow of the mind. This, then, is the distinguishing feature of the contemplation of dhammas: the investigation into causality.

18 This, of course, is vipassanā, and it is here in the contemplation of dhammas that vipassanā finds its rightful home in satipaṭṭhāna. But this is, of course, not 'dry' vipassanā, not insight separate from samatha. Quite the opposite: it is insight that emerges from understanding samādhi, why the mind is sometimes radiant and peaceful and sometimes caustic and fractured. But the mind in meditation, we learn through satipaṭṭhāna practice, is no different in nature from the mind outside of meditation: it's just the mind responding to conditions. So learning to understand the process of meditation one is learning to understand the mind. As the insight through contemplation of dhammas matures and deepens it will naturally broaden to encompass all states of mind, all that is knowable, and will ripen in the deepest insights. So the presentation of contemplation of dhammas in the Vibhaṅga is highly convincing as a natural depiction of the meditative process.

19 In the Vibhaṅga each section is integrated with the internal/external contemplation, here elaborated slightly from the standard form found in the Saṁyutta. One is to cultivate, develop, make much of, and clearly define body contemplation internally before progressing to body contemplation externally, and so on each stage step by step.

20 Then follows a word definition, a later abhidhammic addition. Most of the definitions, or rather, strings of synonyms, are standard enough. 'World' is defined thus: 'This very body [feeling, mind, dhamma] is the world; also the five aggregates associated with grasping are the world.' The mechanical nature of these definitions is shown up by the gloss on *domanassa*, which follows the normal meaning of 'sadness', failing to recognize the contextual meaning here of 'aversion'.

21 Certain sutta material is absent from the Vibhaṅga: there are no similes, which in Abhidhamma literature is expected. More significant, there is no vipassanā refrain, in striking contrast to the well-integrated internal/external refrain.

22 This absence demands an explanation. One possibility is that the compilers of the Vibhaṅga were slack; but the work as a whole is well edited

and does not give the impression that the compilers were unable to read a well-known Sutta.

23 A more plausible explanation is that the absent material is not suitable in Abhidhamma context. This is true for, say, the setting and the similes. But much of the absent material would be quite at home in the Abhidhamma: the elements, aggregates, sense media, and truths, each of which have their own chapter in the Vibhaṅga, and are found throughout the Abhidhamma.

24 Perhaps, then, the opposite is the case: the compilers deliberately removed the Abhidhamma-style material. This would be a strange procedure; repetition was never an obstacle for the Ābhidhammikas. Moreover, some of the absent material, such as the charnel ground contemplations, or the awareness of activities, is not distinctively Abhidhammic. Particularly curious is the absence of the opening questions defining the five hindrances and the awakening-factors. This kind of question is absolutely characteristic of the Abhidhamma method, so much so that it is sometimes defined as the 'with-questions' method. To remove them in order to fit in an Abhidhamma context is unthinkable.

25 Another problem is the location of the chosen practices. In the contemplation of the body, the Vibhaṅga has the fourth of fourteen practices in the Sutta; in the contemplation of dhammas, it has the first and fourth out of five. It seems bizarre that a redactor would somehow remove all the practices leaving just the fourth. If the Vibhaṅga results from the culling of the Satipaṭṭhāna Sutta, we would expect to have the first practice left over, which would imply that the rest were to be filled out.

26 The conclusion is inescapable: the absence of material in the Vibhaṅga is not dues to loss from the Satipaṭṭhāna Sutta, but because the Vibhaṅga compilers were working with a shorter source text.

13.2 Dharmaskandha

27 In most aspects the Dharmaskandha is similar to the Vibhaṅga. The correlations are very strong, even down to the details. For example, the Pali has the standard phrase 'cultivates, develops, and makes much', followed by the emphatic abhidhamma phrase 'makes defined, well defined' (*svatthitaṁ vavattheti*); the Chinese exactly follows suit. As well as including

practically all of the material in the Vibhaṅga the Dharmaskandha adds the following extra material.

28 The Dharmaskandha gives the setting at Sāvatthī, just as in the Suttas. This claim of authenticity is not found in the Pali Abhidhamma. However, unlike the Pali tradition, which later claimed that the Abhidhamma was composed by the Buddha, the Sarvāstivāda tradition ascribed their Abhidharma to disciples; the Dharmaskandha is attributed to Venerable Sāriputta.[6] Perhaps, then, the Sutta-style opening is just an indication that the opening text has been cut-&-pasted from the Suttas.

29 The basic satipaṭṭhāna formula contains the standard auxiliary formula, rather than the abbreviated Sarvāstivāda version. The internal/external contemplation is integrated from the start. Then it says that in the past, present, and future, monks will practice the same way. This is reminiscent of the start of the Sarvāstivāda Smṛtyupasthāna Sūtra, and reflects the Sarvāstivādin perspective on time.

30 The specification of each of the four satipaṭṭhānas is very similar to the Vibhaṅga. All the changes to the Vibhaṅga are additions; and virtually all those additions are the same as the Sarvāstivāda Smṛtyupasthāna Sūtra. In body contemplation, the Theravāda Satipaṭṭhāna Sutta has four elements while the Sarvāstivāda has six. This is in line with the Sarvāstivādin preference to add space and cognition to the usual four, even though cognition is obviously incongruous in body contemplation. The section on feelings is also shared with the Sarvāstivāda Smṛtyupasthāna Sūtra but not with any Pali text. The intrusion of the sense media between the hindrances and the awakening-factors weakens the unity of the Vibhaṅga's presentation. The six sense media are also presented exactly as the Sarvāstivāda (although the position is like the Theravāda). The Sarvāstivāda Smṛtyupasthāna Sūtra presents the sense media identically to the hindrances (present, absent, arising, abandoning, future non-arising) whereas the Theravāda has a specific phrasing for the sense media; one understands, for example, the eye, visual forms, and the fetter that arises dependent on them both. Here the Theravāda is more apt; the Sarvāstivāda version probably arose through a mechanical misapplication of the hindrance phrasing to the sense media.

---

6 Some of the discourses used as basic texts in the Vibhaṅga were in fact spoken by Venerable Sāriputta (Saccavibhaṅga Sutta, Mahā Hatthipadopama Sutta).

Table 13.3: The Structure of the Dharmaskandha

1. Body	2. Feelings	3. Mind	4. Dhammas
a. What is 'contemplating internal body, ardent, etc.?'	a. What is 'contemplating internal feelings, ardent, etc.?'	a. What is 'contemplating internal mind, ardent, etc.?'	a. What is 'contemplating internal dhammas, ardent, etc.?'
b. Defines internal	b. Defines internal	b. Defines internal	b. Defines internal
c. Body parts (no simile)	c. Three feelings[1]	c. Mind with/ without lust, etc. (11 pairs)	c. Sensual desire present, absent, arising, abandoning, future non-arising
d. Defines: contemplates, abides, ardent, clearly comprehending, mindful, covetousness, aversion	d. Defines (as 1.d)	d. Defines (as 1.d)	d. Defines (as 1.d)
e. Six elements (as Sarv Sūtra; no simile)			e. The rest of the five hindrances (abbreviated)
f. Defines (as 1.d; from here text abbreviates.)			f. Eye, visual forms, fetters present, absent, arising, abandoning, future non-arising (as Sarv Sūtra)
			g. Defines (as 1.d)
			h. Other sense media
			i. Awakening-factor of mindfulness present, absent, arising, developed
			j. Defines (as 1.d)
			k. Other awakening-factors (abbreviated)
g. Tribulations[2]	e. Tribulations	e. Tribulations	l. Tribulations
h. Defines	f. Defines	f. Defines	m. Defines
(repeats 1.a–h 'external')	(repeats 2.a–f 'external')	(repeats 3.a–f 'external')	(repeats 4.a–m 'external')
(repeats 1.a–h 'int/ext')	(repeats 2.a–f 'int/ext')	(repeats 3.a–f 'int/ext')	(repeats 4.a–m 'int/ext')

[1] As Sarvāstivāda Sūtra: plain, bodily/mental, carnal/spiritual, sensual/non-sensual.
[2] Vipassanā refrain; see SN 22.122/SA 259.

31 The additions to the Dharmaskandha over the Vibhaṅga are specifically Sarvāstivādin. The exception to this is in contemplation of mind, where the three extra factors added to the eight standard in the Theravāda do not correspond particularly closely with the Sarvāstivāda Smṛtyupasthāna Sūtra. Here is a table comparing these two Sarvāstivāda sources, compared with the Sanskrit text of the Śrāmaṇyaphala Sūtra, also Sarvāstivādin. I include the factors in contemplation of mind listed by Asaṅga in the Śrāvakabhūmi for comparison.

Table 13.4: Four Versions of the Contemplation of Mind

Smṛtyupasthāna Sūtra	Śrāmaṇyaphala Sūtra	Dharmaskandha	Śrāvakabhūmi
Greedy	Greedy	Greedy	Greedy
Angry	Angry	Angry	Angry
Deluded	Deluded	Deluded	Deluded
Defiled			
Contracted	Contracted	Contracted	Contracted
Slothful	Slothful	Slothful	Slothful
Small		Small	
Lower			
Developed			
	Restless	Distracted	Distracted
	Tranquil	Tranquil	Tranquil
Samādhi	Samādhi	Samādhi	Samādhi
	Developed	Developed	Developed
Released	Released	Released	Released

32 The Śrāmaṇyaphala Sūtra is much closer to the Dharmaskandha than the Smṛtyupasthāna Sūtra. The only significant difference is the omission of 'small/great', but since this is found in most versions (including the Pali), it is most likely a loss in the Śrāmaṇyaphala Sūtra, rather than an addition to the Dharmaskandha. On the other hand, the Śrāvakabhūmi, while in all other respects identical, agrees with the Śrāmaṇyaphala Sūtra in omitting this pair, suggesting that Asaṅga used a version of the contempla-

tion of mind from the same lineage as this version of the Śrāmaṇyaphala Sūtra. Leaving this pair aside, the four pairs in the Dharmaskandha from 'contracted' to 'quiet' are virtual synonyms. The Pali commentaries say contracted means 'with sloth & torpor', while scattered means 'with restlessness'. These extra terms in the Sarvāstivāda may have started life as commentarial glosses on 'contracted/scattered', which were later read into the text. This would suggest that 'small/great' (*amahaggatam/mahaggatam*) should belong after tranquil/untranquil. If we further recognize that the Sarvāstivāda's 'developed/undeveloped' is another virtual synonym of the Theravāda's 'excelled/unexcelled', then the two versions of contemplation of mind in the two schools become very close indeed. In any case, the comparison implies that here the Dharmaskandha is more authentic to the old Sarvāstivāda tradition, while the Smṛtyupasthāna Sūtra version has drifted further away. Apart from helping us to trace textual affiliations, though, the variations are all trivial.

33 Far more significant is the addition of a vipassanā refrain at the end of each section:

> 34 'Furthermore the monk, with regard to this internal body, observes and contemplates all their many tribulations, namely: this body is like a sickness, like a boil, like a dart, troublesome, impermanent, suffering, empty, not-self, changing, wearisome, a great entanglement. It is of a nature to be lost and to decay, rapidly and incessantly becoming weak, not enduring. It cannot be relied on or trusted. It is of a nature to change and decay...'

35 This is derived from passages in the Nikāyas, especially the Khandhasaṁyutta.[7] It is not found in the early texts in the context of satipaṭṭhāna, and evidences the growing tendency to treat the satipaṭṭhānas in terms of the aggregates. It is clearly a different passage than the vipassanā refrain of the Theravāda Satipaṭṭhāna Sutta and cannot have come from the same source. Notice that, while the Theravāda Satipaṭṭhāna Sutta places its vipassanā refrain at the end of each exercise, in the Dharmaskandha it occurs only at the end of each section, thus being less closely integrated within the practice as a whole. It is also less integrated than the internal/external refrain, in which respect the Dharmaskandha is consistent with the Vibhaṅga.

---

[7] SN 22.122/SA 259.

36 Thus far the Sutta material. As the table shows, the additional abhidhammic content is restricted to word definitions. The definitions of internal and external are interestingly different from the Theravāda and are clearly sectarian. For the Theravāda, as for the early Suttas, 'internal' means pertaining to oneself, especially one's own body and mind, while 'external' is the bodies and minds of others. But for the Dharmaskandha 'internal' is 'one's own body [etc.], which in the present continuum has been gained and not lost.' In other words 'internal' refers to this life. 'External' is 'one's own body [etc.], which in the present continuum has not yet been gained or is already lost, together with the bodily phenomena of others, possessing spirit'. This refers to past and future lives. The phrase 'possessing spirit' is odd; the phrase might render *saviññāṇaka*, which we could relate to the familiar idea of '[kammically] acquired' (*upadinna*), i.e. loosely 'organic' or 'sentient' matter. Anyway, this modification exhibits the Sarvāstivādin concern for time.

37 The definitions of internal and external say that 'dhammas' here is the aggregates of perception and conceptual activities. This significant redefinition was also adopted by the Theravāda commentaries, and has by today become standard. Here we see a common pattern—the various sectarian schools, despite their mutual polemics, often share more in common with each other than they do with the Suttas. There is nothing in the actual description of 'dhammas' here that requires or even suggests such a definition. How, for example, can the six sense media be explained as perception or conceptual activities?

38 This definition does not aim not to draw out the meaning of 'dhammas' here, but to integrate the four satipaṭṭhānas with the five aggregates.[8] This is a crucial assumption of the Abhidhamma project: that the various doctrinal frameworks of the Suttas each offer a different way of categorizing the same reality; and that it is therefore possible to equate the dhammas in

8 A similar shift happened to *nāma*. Although the suttas take pains to define this excluding cognition, the later scholastics explained it as all four immaterial aggregates, including cognition. This interpretation is already found in the Sarvāstivāda Nidāna Saṁyukta, from where it no doubt made its way into the Sarvāstivāda Abhidhamma. So in the case of *nāmarūpa*, as in the case of the satipaṭṭhānas, we see the tendency to integrate other doctrinal formulas with the aggregates first appear in the Sarvāstivāda, then later in the Theravāda.

one framework with those in any other. The result of this process was the complex Abhidhamma mātikās, which subsequently displaced the earlier frameworks. The core frameworks for this project are the five aggregates, the six sense media, and, less standardized, the elements. Even in the Suttas we see a tendency to treat the various faculties in a similar manner, including the five spiritual faculties, which accordingly begin to spill over from the fourth noble truth to the first three.[9] Now we see the same pattern in the satipaṭṭhānas. A group originally part of the fourth noble truth, the path, is being equated with dhammas of the first noble truth, the five aggregates. The incongruity of the results reflects the inappropriateness of the method. 'Dhammas' here is not 'phenomena' but rather 'principles'; not 'what is there' but 'how it works'. While 'phenomena' is one of many meanings of 'dhammas' in the Suttas, there was a pronounced drift in the Abhidhamma period to emphasize this meaning at the expense of others, and a corresponding misinterpretation of relevant Sutta contexts.

39 The other addition is a word definition of the basic satipaṭṭhāna formula; this is a list of synonyms in Abhidhamma style. The gloss for *anupassanā* lists terms for wisdom, including vipassanā; this is much the same as the Vibhaṅga. This word definition defines the basic formula, but it is repeated after each section throughout the text—except the basic formula. This is incongruous, an example of abhidhammic over-systemization. Sometimes the abhidhamma is uncannily like a computer error.

40 Compared with the Sutta Exposition of the Vibhaṅga the differences in the Dharmaskandha are:

41 1) All additions, no subtractions;
2) Often incongruous (setting, six elements, sense media, dhammas as perception/conceptual activities, definitions);
3) Sometimes hinting at sectarianism (past, present, future; influence of Sarvāstivāda Smṛtyupasthāna Sūtra).

42 These considerations all suggest that the Dharmaskandha here is later than the Vibhaṅga. They shared the same pre-sectarian text, the *Vibhaṅga Mūla; the Sarvāstivādins expanded that for the Dharmaskandha,

9 SN 48.2–7.

while the Theravādins, content with the simple version for the Sutta Exposition, wrote a new Abhidhamma Exposition.

43 The chief difference between the two is clear. Apart from the contemplation of dhammas, there is no vipassanā material in the Vibhaṅga. There is no rise and fall, no six elements, no sense media, and no dhammas as perception/conceptual activities. The vipassanā material must have been added later. But the most striking similarity is that both the content of the exercises and the form of the refrains are simpler than the Satipaṭṭhāna Suttas. This clearly—and startlingly—suggests that the *Vibhaṅga Mūla is earlier than the Satipaṭṭhāna Sutta.

13.3 Śāriputrābhidharma

44 This is an abhidhamma text on a larger scale than the Vibhaṅga and the Dharmaskandha. It represents the whole field of abhidhamma in the Dharmaguptaka system, containing material comparable to that found in the Theravāda Dhātukathā, Paṭṭhāna, Puggala Paññatti, and Dhammasaṅgaṇī, as well as the Vibhaṅga. The mātikās of the Vibhaṅga and the Dharmaskandha are discernable, though the form is more divergent. Thus the work as a whole is later than the Vibhaṅga and Dharmaskandha, and the treatment of satipaṭṭhāna bears this out.

45 The eccentric structure of this text becomes clearer if we recognize that the main paradigm is exemplified in the contemplations of feelings, mind, and dhammas; body is divergent, so we will leave that until later. The first question, 'what is contemplating the feelings [etc.]' is answered by defining feelings [etc.]. This doesn't really answer the question; presumably the question was originally intended to cover the whole section, and the definitions were inserted later.

46 The definition of the body is standard. The definition of feelings is also standard, although the Suttas do not treat feelings in satipaṭṭhāna as based on the six senses; this shift is also found in the Theravāda commentaries.

47 The definition of mind is similar to the treatment of contemplation of mind in ānāpānasati in the Paṭisambhidāmagga.

48 The definition of dhammas is also late, and is similar in meaning to the Dharmaskandha; but the phrasing is identical to the Paṭisambhidāmagga.

Table 13.5: The Structure of the Śāriputrābhidharma

1. Body	2. Feelings	3. Mind	4. Dhammas
a. What's contemplating body?	a. What's contemplating feelings?	a. What's contemplating mind?	a. What's contemplating dhammas?
b. Body is four elements	b. Feelings based on six senses	b. Defines mind	b. Everything but body, feeling, mind
c. What's contemplating internal body?	c. What's contemplating internal feelings?	c. What's contemplating internal mind?	c. What's contemplating internal dhammas?
d. Impermanent, etc. Dependent origin to six senses.	d. Impermanent, etc. Dependent origin to feeling.	d. Impermanent, etc. Dependent origin to cognition.	d. Impermanent, etc. Complete dependent origin.
e. Body postures			
f. Movements			
g. Ānāpānasati			
h. Parts of the body			
i. Four elements			
j. Food			
k. Space			
l. Nine orifices			
m. Defines standard formula	e. Defines 'internal'; others 'as above'	e. Defines 'internal mind'	e. Defines 'internal dhammas'
n. As 1.d 'external'	f. As 2.d 'external'	f. As 3.d 'external'	f. As 4.d 'external'.
o. Defines 'ext'; others 'as above'	g. Defines 'external'; others 'as above'	g. Defines 'external mind'	g. Defines 'external dhammas'
p. As 1.d 'int/ext'	h. As 2.d 'int/ext'	h. As 3.d 'int/ext'	h. As 4.d 'int/ext'
q. Charnel ground	i. 3 feelings, carnal/spiritual, etc.	i. Mind with/without lust, etc.	i. 5 hindrances, rise & fall.
			j. Senses, rise & fall
			k. Awakening-factors, rise & fall
			l. 4 noble truths
r. Contemplate rise & fall to know, let go body	j. Contemplate rise & fall to know, let go feelings	j. Contemplate rise & fall to know, let go mind	m. Contemplate rise & fall to know, let go dhammas
s. Repeats formula for internal, etc.	k. Repeats formula for internal, etc.	k. Repeats formula for internal, etc.	n. Repeats formula for internal, etc.

49 Internal contemplation is described in terms similar to the vipassanā refrain from the Khandha-saṁyutta, just as the Dharmaskandha. It is not clear whether the Śāriputrābhidharma copied from the Dharmaskandha or they both borrowed from the Khandha-saṁyutta. The vipassanā refrain is expanded by adding factors from dependent origination, appropriately adjusted in each case. This may have been inspired by the Satipaṭṭhāna Vibhaṅga Sutta, which as we have seen treats causality in satipaṭṭhāna in terms similar to dependent origination; however the specifics are different. The whole first half of these sections, describing 'internal, etc.' in terms of vipassanā is largely an addition; vipassanā is integrated from the start of the meditation, rather than being left until the end as the Dharmaskandha.

50 Strangely, the authentic satipaṭṭhāna material is presented after the additions. This second half of each section, featuring the meditation objects and the refrain, is very similar to the Theravāda Satipaṭṭhāna Sutta, and presumably was influenced by the (now lost) Dharmaguptaka Satipaṭṭhāna Sutta. The most significant difference from the Theravāda is the absence of the five aggregates from contemplation of dhammas.

51 The structure of the section on body contemplation diverges from the pattern of the other three. The list of meditations has been split in two, with the bulk inserted awkwardly in the 'internal' section, while the charnel ground contemplations alone follow the internal/external section. The charnel ground contemplations are described in the Suttas as comparing one's own body with a dead body, which probably suggested placing this exercise after the internal/external section. This is in line with the Suttas; but then the other exercises had to fit in somewhere. Placing them under internal contemplation implies that they may not be practiced externally, which differs from the Suttas. These exercises were likely split at the Abhidhamma stage, and may not reflect the Dharmaguptaka Satipaṭṭhāna Sutta. However, we shall see that a similar distinction is made in the Prajñāpāramitā, although there the charnel ground contemplations are said to be external, rather than internal/external.

52 The long list of body contemplations falls into three divisions. The first two exercises are very similar, basically 'awareness of movements'. In the standard passages such as the gradual training, only the passage on clear comprehension occurs. The four postures pericope is much less common.

Since the two largely overlap, the inclusion of both is redundant; however all the recensions of the satipaṭṭhāna material either include both of these pericopes or neither. The four postures passage is probably more original in this context, since it always appears before clear comprehension, and the phrasing is more similar to the other sections of satipaṭṭhāna. It has a more generalized, meditative scope, rather than specifically illustrating a lifestyle training. Perhaps this simpler, vaguer passage was felt in need of concrete illustration, so the section on clear comprehension was brought in from the gradual training.

53 The next division is ānāpānasati. This follows clear comprehension in a similar manner to the normal sequence of the gradual training. In all versions of the Satipaṭṭhāna Sutta, the normal sixteen steps have been abbreviated to four. This is the only context where this happens (apart from the related Kāyagatāsati Sutta). The full sixteen-step version is the more fundamental one. It clearly outlines a full sequence of meditative training. The first tetrad describes the establishment of mindfulness on the basic meditation object and the tranquilization of it; the second tetrad speaks of the development of bliss and rapture; the third, attaining of samādhi; and the fourth, contemplation of impermanence. The first tetrad on its own is incomplete; nowhere does the Buddha speak of meditation merely for attaining bodily tranquillity.

54 The idea that the full development of ānāpānasati must involve all sixteen steps is borne out in a Sutta where Venerable Ariṭṭha describes his practice of ānāpānasati as having dispelled sensual desire for things past and future, and having dispelled perceptions of aversion towards things internally and externally, just mindful he breathes in and out.[10] The removal of desire and aversion, and the reference to internal/external, is very like satipaṭṭhāna. Venerable Ariṭṭha's practice had not progressed beyond simple observation of the breath, without samādhi and insight. The Buddha, while acknowledging that this was indeed ānāpānasati, encouraged Venerable Ariṭṭha to fully develop ānāpānasati through the whole sixteen steps.

55 The third division consists of diverse contemplative exercises, starting with the parts of the body. Many such are taught throughout the Suttas,

[10] SN 54.6/SA 805.

and such lists as these are early attempts to collate and organize these practices. We have seen that the Vibhaṅga has just the parts of the body, while the Dharmaskandha adds the six elements as well. The Śāriputrābhidharma also has the parts of the body and the elements, and in the same order; in fact this sequence is maintained in all versions of the satipaṭṭhāna material. The (inevitable!) exception is the Prajñāpāramitā, which reverses the sequence of the body parts and elements; I take this as just an editorial slip-up.

56 Since the parts of the body is the only exercise mentioned in all versions, and since it virtually always comes at the start of this division, it has the greatest claim to authenticity, although the elements are not far behind. The two practices are very similar, for the elements, when taught in detail, are described by listing the appropriate body parts: earth element is head-hair, body-hair, etc., water element is blood, pus, etc. The charnel ground contemplations, too, appear in all the Sutta versions and always at the end. The other exercises are less important.[11]

57 These diverse exercises are treated in the Suttas in terms of both samatha and vipassanā. The central purpose of contemplation of the body parts is to abandon lust, which is samatha. Sometimes this samatha aspect is made explicit, as when one is said to reach an 'attainment of vision' such that, due to proper effort, one gains 'such a form of samādhi that, with the mind in samādhi, one contemplates this very body' by means of the body parts.[12] But the body parts, especially when subsumed under the elements, are also contemplated as 'not mine', etc., which is vipassanā.[13] The elements, as well as appearing in such vipassanā contexts, are frequently used as a basis for attaining samādhi, and can even be used as a shorthand reference to the four 'form' jhānas. The charnel ground contemplations, too, are a powerful ground for contemplating the impermanence of life; but the practice is described as 'guarding a subtle basis of samādhi' (*samādhinimitta*).[14] Thus all these practices have the potential for developing both peace and wisdom.

---

[11] Compare Sutta passages that describe the internal space element as the spaces where food is eaten, digested, and passed out. MN 140.18/MA 162; MN 62.12/EA 17.1.

[12] DN 28.7/DA 18.

[13] MN 28.6/MA 30.

[14] E.g. DN 33.1.11.10/DA 9.

58 In the body contemplation sections in the seven different versions of the satipaṭṭhāna material, three mention only this third division (Vibhaṅga, Dharmaskandha, Ekāyana Sūtra), while four mention all three divisions (Śāriputrābhidharma, Theravāda and Sarvāstivāda Satipaṭṭhāna Suttas, Prajñāpāramitā). Of these four long versions, the Śāriputrābhidharma and the Prajñāpāramitā are the best organized (leaving aside the reservations about the splitting of the exercises into 'internal' and 'internal/external'). Unlike the Theravāda Satipaṭṭhāna Sutta they keep the standard sequence of placing the 'awareness of movements' division first; and unlike the Sarvāstivāda they don't bring in unrelated practices.

59 There are good reasons for thinking that clear comprehension was not originally regarded as a meditation as such. For example in the Mahā Rāhulovāda Sutta, Venerable Rāhula asks the Buddha to teach him ānāpānasati.[15] The Buddha digresses with a long series of other meditations—the five elements, including the body parts, and culminating in space; then the divine abidings; then ugliness; then impermanence—before returning to ānāpānasati. Perhaps the reason for the Buddha's digression was that Rāhula's mind required preparation before it was mature enough to fully benefit from a subtle exercise like ānāpānasati.

60 The Meghiya Sutta is similar in that it presents a graduated series of dhammas for maturing the mind.[16] It culminates with four meditations: ugliness for abandoning lust; loving-kindness for abandoning anger; ānāpānasati for cutting off thinking; and impermanence for uprooting the conceit 'I am'. This has always struck me as one of the most sensible, balanced programs for meditation. Other variants occur, such as ugliness, ānāpānasati, and impermanence.[17] In these and other contexts we see ugliness, the elements, etc., treated alongside ānāpānasati as a straightforward meditation practice. But clear comprehension is conspicuously absent in such contexts—which is why those who promote such an approach to meditation rely so heavily on the Satipaṭṭhāna Sutta.

61 If, as the concordance of the texts suggests, the section on body parts, either alone or as the head of the third division, was the original body

[15] MN 62/EA 17.1.
[16] Ud 4.1.
[17] Iti 3.36.

contemplation, why were the other two divisions brought in, and why were they placed before the original section? I have suggested that the influence of the gradual training is sufficient to account for the intrusion of clear comprehension in first place. Another general consideration would have been to assemble in one digestible text the various texts on body contemplation scattered through the canon.

62 The relationship between the Dharmaguptaka Suttas and the Śāriputrābhidharma, so far as I know, still awaits detailed investigation. Cheng Jianhua, however, has done a comparative study of the versions of the Brahmajāla Sutta. This concludes that, while the Theravāda and Dharmaguptaka versions are very close, the Dharmaguptaka Sutta is even closer, in fact identical, with the Śāriputrābhidharma. It is therefore possible that the details of the list of body contemplations in the Śāriputrābhidharma reflect the form of a now-lost Dharmaguptaka version of the Satipaṭṭhāna Sutta. This is far from certain, as both the Theravāda and Sarvāstivāda display considerable variation between the Sutta and early Abhidhamma descriptions of satipaṭṭhāna (although not of most other doctrines). However if it were the case, it would suggest that the reversal of the positions of the first and second divisions in the Theravāda Satipaṭṭhāna Sutta occurred after the separation from the Dharmaguptaka, over 200 years after the Parinibbāna. Similar principles would apply to the other major differences between the Śāriputrābhidharma and the Theravāda, particularly the Theravādin insertion of the five aggregates into the contemplation of dhammas.

Chapter 14

THE SATIPAṬṬHĀNA SUTTAS

THERE ARE THREE COMPLETE VERSIONS of the Satipaṭṭhāna Sutta available, one in Pali and two in Chinese. There is also a fourth, incomplete, version in the large Prajñāpāramitā Sūtra.

14.1 Prajñāpāramitā

2 This is one of the foundational texts of the Mahāyāna, and is usually held to have been compiled roughly 500 years after the Buddha's passing away. This text is available in versions of varying length in Tibetan and Chinese, and a reconstructed Sanskrit text has been translated into English by Conze. This version was constructed from a conflation of Sanskrit fragments in comparison with Tibetan and Chinese translations. According to Conze, the different versions mainly vary in the quantity of repetitions, so as regards content we can treat it as one work.

3 A comparison with various versions of the Prajñāpāramitā literature in Chinese reveals a remarkable consistency in this passage. Since, as we shall see, the text is highly asymmetrical and unbalanced, almost certainly resulting from an abridgement of an earlier version of the Satipaṭṭhāna Sutta, it is likely that the Prajñāpāramitā passages on satipaṭṭhāna hark back to a single original source. This version of the satipaṭṭhāna material displays a refreshing simplicity that may indicate that it lies close to the early sources. In the Tibetan tradition it is said that there was a ver-

sion of the Prajñāpāramitā written in Prakrit belonging to the Pūrvaśaila and Aparaśaila schools.[1] These schools are branches of the Mahāsaṅghika, which suggests that the Prajñāpāramitā account of satipaṭṭhāna material was derived from a Mahāsaṅghika text. There is, however, no specially close relation between this version and the Ekāyana Sūtra.

4 Although the Prajñāpāramitā, like the Abhidhamma, is obviously later than the Āgama Suttas, I see no reason why the specifications of the common teachings should be less reliable as a guide to the early doctrines. It may seem strange to say that later literature preserves early features, but it is not such a mystery. All the traditions inherited the same mass of early Sutta material. The compilers of the Nikāyas/Āgamas arranged this material, and in doing so it is not surprising that they should tinker around the edges, filling out and expanding texts so that nothing is omitted. But the compilers of the Abhidhamma and the Prajñāpāramitā had a different agenda. They were evolving their own special concepts and procedures, so their attention was not on the early passages. In certain cases they may have simply left the early material unretouched. The additions and elaborations are extraneous and hence easily discerned. This is the case in the Prajñāpāramitā, where the teachings on satipaṭṭhāna have been basically 'cut-&-pasted' with minimal alteration.

5 Satipaṭṭhāna is treated in two separate places in the Prajñāpāramitā. These occurrences are widely separated and have no close textual relation. Both occur as part of a larger context treating the way of practice of a Bodhisattva, and treat satipaṭṭhāna as the first group of the 37 wings to awakening. As in the early Suttas, here the 37 are simply listed, with no attempt to synthesize the groups into an overall progressive scheme of practice, such as the Abhidhamma schools were to work out later.

6 The first passage begins by simply defining, as part of the Mahāyāna path of the Bodhisattva, the four satipaṭṭhānas.[2] Then comes a variation on the standard passage:

> 7 'There the Bodhisattva dwells, with regard to the inward body, feelings, etc., in the contemplation of the body, etc. But he does not form any discursive thoughts associated with the body, etc. He is

---

[1] DUTT, pg. 254.

[2] CONZE , pp. 153–155.

> ardent, clearly conscious, and mindful, after putting away all worldly covetousness and sadness. And that without taking anything as a basis. And so he dwells with regard to the outer body, the inner and outer body, to feelings, thought, and dhammas.'

8 All the familiar features are there: the reflexive repetition 'body in [regard to] body'; the four objects; contemplation; internal/external; and the standard auxiliary formula. The injunction not to think thoughts about the body is found in the Dantabhūmi Sutta, as well as the Mahāyāna Pratyutpannabuddhasammukhāvaṣṭhitasamādhi Sūtra. In that context the phrase serves as a springboard for a more characteristically Mahāyāna exposition of satipaṭṭhāna. Here the idea lies still in germ. The phrase rendered by Conze 'without taking anything as a basis' seems to be the phrase 'one dwells independent', found in the Sarvāstivāda Samudaya Sutta and the Satipaṭṭhāna Sutta.

9 The text goes on to ask how a Bodhisattva dwells with regard to the inward body in the contemplation of the body. Then a list of body contemplation practices is given: awareness of the four postures; clear comprehension in daily activities; ānāpānasati; elements; body parts; and charnel ground. This is identical with the body contemplation practices in the Theravāda Satipaṭṭhāna Sutta. Each practice is described in virtually exactly the same words and phrases, including the illustrative similes. Awareness of activities adds to the normal list the phrase 'and when retiring for meditation'. There are occasional, very slight, drifts in the sense of words. In the charnel ground contemplation, the Theravāda version says one should reflect 'This body, too, is of the same *dhamma*, the same *bhāva*...'. Here both *dhamma* and *bhāva* are non-technical words meaning simply 'nature'. But the Prajñāpāramitā translation has, instead of 'nature' for *bhāva*, 'own-being', obviously harking to an original *svabhāva*. This key technical term in Abhidhamma philosophy would have been more familiar to the compilers of the Prajñāpāramitā than the colloquial word *bhāva*.

10 While the differences in the phrasing of the particular exercises are miniscule, far more significant divergences occur in the structure. The Prajñāpāramitā lists the two 'awareness of postures' meditations first, before ānāpānasati. This is the same as every other exposition of the path in all schools, except the Theravāda Satipaṭṭhāna and Kāyagatāsati Suttas.

11 There is hardly any refrain. At the end of each meditation it is simply said, 'And that through non-apprehension.' I am not sure of the Sanskrit original, but this seems to be a Mahāyānist 'tag' added to identify with the special Prajñāpāramitā perspective on emptiness. It is similar to the earlier phrase 'not grasping at anything in the world'. This, and the substitution of 'bodhisattva' for 'bhikkhu', are the only Mahāyānist elements.

12 Given the Mahāyāna love of florid elaborations, it does seem odd that there is no real refrain supplied here. If the Mahāyāna authors were using a version of the Satipaṭṭhāna Sutta with a substantial refrain, like the existing versions, one would expect them to alter and expand it, rather than slough it off. This suggests that they had an early, bare-bones (if you'll excuse the pun!) version of body contemplation. It is quite remarkable that this version is very close to the Theravāda, even though the Mahāyāna in general owes more to the Sarvāstivāda and Mahāsaṅghika traditions.

13 It is a great shame that the text does not elaborate the remaining sections. It simply gives the standard formula for contemplating feelings, internally, etc. This asymmetry suggests editing irregularities. The statement of the basic passage at the start of the text gives the satipaṭṭhāna formula for all four satipaṭṭhānas. Then it gives the details of body contemplation, but does not repeat the relevant part of the satipaṭṭhāna formula. But for feelings, etc., the situation is reversed: it does not give the details of feeling contemplation, etc., but it does repeat the relevant part of the formula. It looks as though the detailed expositions were lost, then the basic formula was mechanically inserted to fill the gap.

14 Many years ago, Har Dayal commented: '...the Buddhist authors have written a great deal only about *kāyasatipaṭṭhāna* [body contemplation]; they dismiss the other three with a few words.'[3] Some therefore conclude that body contemplation was originally the only part of satipaṭṭhāna. However, this is an rash conclusion. Given the enormously repetitive nature of Buddhist texts in general, it is normal to find a text that deals with the first section in detail, then abbreviates the rest. In fact, if the remaining three satipaṭṭhānas were a later accretion, we might expect the reverse situation, that they should be explained in more detail. For example, in the Prajñāpāramitā literature we are currently considering, the basic

---

[3] DAYAL, pg. 90.

teachings such as satipaṭṭhāna are taught fairly briefly, but the special Prajñāpāramitā doctrines are elaborated at length. The lack of detailed explanations of the latter satipaṭṭhānas, then, can be understood as a later loss. This loss suggests that the authors of the Prajñāpāramitā were not overly concerned with satipaṭṭhāna as such; perhaps they simply assumed that their audience was already familiar with the basic teachings.

15 We may now consider the second exposition of satipaṭṭhāna in the Prajñāpāramitā. This defines satipaṭṭhāna, together with a list of other dhammas containing both early and late elements, as 'supramundane and not worldly'.[4] Then the basic passage on satipaṭṭhāna is given, with no detailed exposition of the various practices. The integrated internal/external contemplation is followed by: 'With regard to the body he dwells as one who reviews its origination, its disappearance, and both its origination and disappearance. He dwells as one who does not lean on anything, and as one who (does not) grasp at the world.' This is almost identical with the vipassanā refrain of the Theravāda Satipaṭṭhāna Sutta, although lacking the phrase 'Or mindfulness is established that "There is a body", only for the sake of a measure of knowledge and mindfulness.' It is also similar to the Sarvāstivāda version of the Samudaya Sutta, though lacking the specifications of the cause of each of the objects of satipaṭṭhāna.

16 There are a number of textual details that diverge from the earlier passage. The Bodhisattva is not mentioned. More important, the arrangement of the textual elements is different. In the earlier passage the order was: contemplate the internal body, feelings, mind, and dhammas; ardent, clearly comprehending, etc.; contemplate the external body, etc., and so on. Here the sequence is: contemplate the body internally, externally, then internally & externally; ardent, clearly comprehending, etc. In other words the auxiliary formula is added after each satipaṭṭhāna rather than being put at the end of the four. Of course, this variation has no significance of itself. But taken together with other features—the separation of the two passages in the text, the inconsistent use of 'Bodhisattva'—it suggests that the two passages are taken from different sources. That is to say, there is no reason to believe that the Prajñāpāramitā took an earlier, longer text integrating these two passages and broke it up into separate pieces.

---

[4] CONZE, pg. 580.

17 This reinforces one of our basic arguments about the formation of the Theravāda Satipaṭṭhāna Sutta. This contains two important aspects: the detailed list of meditation practices, and the vipassanā refrain. But there are at least three traditions that preserve these two aspects as independent textual entities. In the Sarvāstivāda, the list of meditation practices is found in the Satipaṭṭhāna Sutta, while the vipassanā refrain is found in the Samudaya Sutta. The Prajñāpāramitā is similar. Even the Theravāda preserves the meditation exercises in the Abhidhamma Vibhaṅga and the vipassanā refrain in the Saṁyutta Vibhaṅga Sutta and Samudaya Sutta. Thus the treatment of these two aspects separately represents an earlier tradition compared with the elaborated Satipaṭṭhāna Sutta.

14.2 Sarvāstivāda Smṛtyupasthāna Sūtra

18 The Smṛtyupasthāna Sūtra of the Sarvāstivāda school is preserved in the Madhyama Āgama of the Chinese Tripiṭaka, translated from Sanskrit into Chinese in 389 CE by the Chinese monk Sanghadeva.[5] The Smṛtyupasthāna Sūtra is more elaborate in some respects than the Theravāda Satipaṭṭhāna Sutta, and less elaborate in others. Hence it is probably neither earlier nor later, but stems from a slightly divergent tradition as the two new schools of the Theravāda and the Sarvāstivāda finalized the textual formulations of the teachings they had both inherited from the pre-sectarian period. This final editing followed the separation from the Sarvāstivāda, perhaps 200 years after the Buddha. I will ignore the various trivial differences in phrasing between the individual doctrinal units ('pericopes') in the various versions and concentrate on the significant differences in the choice of meditation exercises.

19 The Sarvāstivāda Smṛtyupasthāna Sūtra opens in the same way as the Theravāda Satipaṭṭhāna Sutta: the setting is at Kammassadamma in the Kuru country, and the teaching starts with the statement on the 'path leading to convergence'. After this, however, the Smṛtyupasthāna Sūtra introduces the statement that all Tathāgatas, past, future, and present realize enlightenment by being established on the four satipaṭṭhānas, abandon-

[5] MA 98.

ing the five hindrances, and developing the seven awakening-factors.[6] We have met such groupings frequently; this statement was likely brought in from SN 47.12/SA 498. As noted above, the extra emphasis on persistence through time suggests the sectarian bias of the Sarvāstivāda.

20 The satipaṭṭhāna formula is presented simply—one establishes mindfulness on the contemplation of the body, feelings, mind, and dhammas. We have established from the Sarvāstivāda Smṛtyupasthāna Saṁyukta that this abbreviated form was intended to be spelt out in full. In the Saṁyukta, the fact that there are many discourses, one after another, all featuring the same formula is a good reason for the use of such an abbreviation. But what of this Madhyama version? This discourse on satipaṭṭhāna stands alone, not in a series, and one who was not familiar with the Saṁyukta, when studying the Madhyama would not necessarily be aware of the longer formula. In this long discourse, why could the redactors not have found room to expand the formula? There is one simple answer to this puzzle: the Smṛtyupasthāna Sūtra was originally part of the Saṁyukta collection. There the formula was abbreviated along with the rest of the discourses; in fact the length of this discourse serves as a good reason to not spell out the formula in full, so that the length would not differ too much from that of the surrounding discourses.

21 Let us compare the body contemplation exercises to the Theravāda, first dealing with the factors in common. These are mostly in the same order in both the Theravāda and Sarvāstivāda texts. The exception is mindfulness of breathing, which in the Smṛtyupasthāna Sūtra appears in its usual position after clear comprehension. However, a swag of new practices is added, all somewhat uncomfortable in the context of body contemplation. This raises the question as to why these incongruous passages were inserted.

22 Part of the answer lies with the Kāyagatāsati Sutta, versions of which are found in both the Theravāda and the Sarvāstivāda Majjhimas.[7] The Theravāda version of the Kāyagatāsati Sutta centres on a list of 14 body contemplation exercises that is identical with the basic practices in the body contemplation section of the Theravāda Satipaṭṭhāna Sutta. This

---

6 Thích NHẤT HẠNH's translation refers in the plural to 'all Tathāgatas of the present (including myself)', which sounds very Mahāyānist; but the text is singular.

7 MN 119/MA 81.

specific set of practices is not found elsewhere in the Theravāda Nikāyas, and therefore indicates a strong relationship between these two texts.[8]

Table 14.1: Body in Sarvāstivāda & Theravāda

Sarvāstivāda Smṛtyupasthāna Sūtra	Theravāda Satipaṭṭhāna Sutta
1. Four postures	2.
2. Clear comprehension	3.
3. Cutting off thought	(see MN 20.3/MA 101)
4. Suppressing thought	(see MN 20.7/MA 101)
5. Ānāpānasati	1.
6. 1st jhāna simile	(Similes at MN 119.18/MA 81, etc.)
7. 2nd jhāna simile	
8. 3rd jhāna simile	
9. 4th jhāna simile	
10. Perception of light	(See SN 51.20)
11. Basis of reviewing	(See AN 5.28)
12. Parts of the body	4.
13. Six elements	5. (Four elements only)
14–18. Charnel ground	6–14.

23 However, the most significant difference between the Theravāda Satipaṭṭhāna and Kāyagatāsati Suttas is that the Satipaṭṭhāna Sutta, with its repeated refrain on investigating rise and fall, emphasizes vipassanā, while the refrain in the Theravāda Kāyagatāsati Sutta says:

> 24 'As he abides diligent, ardent, and resolute, his memories and intentions dependent on the household life are abandoned. With their abandoning his mind is settled internally, quieted, unified, and brought to samādhi. That's how a monk develops mindfulness of the body.'

[8] The Kāyagatāsati Sutta omits the simile for ānāpānasati: one observes the breath, long or short, like a skilled turner making a long or short turn. This simile is also absent from the Sarvāstivāda; thus the only place it occurs, so far as I know, is in the Theravāda Satipaṭṭhāna Sutta.

25 The Sarvāstivāda refrain says that diligent practice of this in a secluded place frees the mind from distress, brings samādhi, and brings knowledge according to reality. In both versions the body contemplation exercises then lead straight to the four jhānas, each of which is also said to be a practice of mindfulness of the body.

26 After the jhānas there is a substantial list of benefits of the practice, falling into four divisions. First, mindfulness of the body includes all dhammas that partake of realization, just as one who encompasses with their heart the entire ocean includes all the rivers that flow into it. Second, a list of three similes and their opposites (throwing a heavy/light ball, a sapless/sappy piece of wood, a full/empty water jug), illustrating whether Māra gains an opportunity or not. Both of these divisions are found in the Sarvāstivāda. Third, mindfulness of the body leads to the witnessing of all clear knowledges, illustrated with a further three similes—a brimful pot, a brimful pond, and a ready chariot. This division is absent from the Sarvāstivāda. Fourthly, mindfulness of the body, developed and cultivated, leads to ten benefits: overcoming discontent and delight; fear and dread; heat and cold, etc; one develops the four jhānas; one realizes the six kinds of clear knowledge. This list is also in the Sarvāstivāda, extended to 18 by the separate addition of the four jhānas and the four stages of awakening.

27 These four divisions are each of separate origin. There is substantial overlapping of the topics in this discourse, especially the jhānas and clear knowledges. The four jhānas were probably originally mentioned, not as a kind of mindfulness practice, but as a benefit of mindfulness practice. This is implied by the basic refrain and by the list of benefits in both versions.

28 The similes use a distinctive imagery—the ocean, the full pot, the full pond, the full water jug.[9] This is consistent with the simile for mindfulness of the body found in the Satipaṭṭhāna Saṁyutta (the bowl brimful of oil), as also the 'saturated' imagery of the jhāna similes:

> 29 **1st jhāna:** He makes the rapture and bliss born of seclusion drench, suffuse, fill, and pervade this body, so that there is no part of his whole body unpervaded by the rapture and bliss born of seclusion. Just as a skilled bath man, or bath man's apprentice heaps bath powder in a metal basin and, sprinkling it gradually with water, kneads it until

---

[9] ANĀLAYO, pg. 53*ff.*, discusses the various satipaṭṭhāna similes in more detail.

> the moisture wets the ball of bath powder, soaks it and pervades it inside and out, yet the ball itself does not ooze...
>
> 30 **2nd jhāna:** He makes the rapture and bliss born of samādhi drench, suffuse, fill, and pervade this body, so that there is no part of his whole body unpervaded by the rapture and bliss born of samādhi. Just as though there were a lake whose waters welled up from below, and it had no inflow from east, west, north, or south, and would not be replenished from time to time with showers of rain, then the cool fount of water welling up in the lake would make the cool water drench, suffuse, fill, and pervade the lake, so that there would be no part of the whole lake unpervaded by cool water...
>
> 31 **3rd jhāna:** He makes the bliss free of rapture drench, suffuse, fill, and pervade this body, so that there is no part of his whole body unpervaded by the bliss free of rapture. Just as in a pond of blue or white or red lotuses, some lotuses that are born and grow in the water thrive immersed in the water without rising out of it, and cool water drenches, suffuses, fills, and pervades them to their tips and their roots, so that there is no part of those lotuses unpervaded by cool water...
>
> 32 **4th jhāna:** He sits pervading this body with pure bright heart, so that there is no part of his whole body unpervaded by pure bright heart. Just as if there were a man covered from the head down with a pure white cloth, so that there would be no part of his body not covered by the pure white cloth...[10]

33 These beautiful images of embodied bliss complement the psychological jhāna formulas. The emphasis on immersion in the body no doubt prompted their inclusion in the Kāyagatāsati Suttas, and hence in the body contemplation section of the Sarvāstivāda Smṛtyupasthāna Sūtra.

34 It would be a mistake to think that 'body' here refers to the ordinary physical body, which completely disappears in jhāna. The Suttas use 'body' in an idiomatic sense to stress the immediacy of direct personal experience; the meaning is something like 'the entire field of awareness'.[11] Such abstract, almost mystical, usages of 'body'—note too the 'mind-made body', the 'body witness', the 'dhamma-body'—paved the way for the much later

---

[10] DN 2.76–82, etc.

[11] See SUJATO, *Swift Pair*, Appendix A.7.

doctrine of the 'Three-bodies' of the Buddha, a metaphysical and docetic reification of the Buddha and Nibbana.

35 The Sarvāstivāda Kāyagatāsmṛti Sutta, in addition to the variations mentioned above, presents a different list of basic exercises. These correlate exactly with the section on body contemplation in the Sarvāstivāda Smṛtyupasthāna Sūtra, just as the Theravāda Kāyagatāsati Sutta correlates with the Theravāda Satipaṭṭhāna Sutta. The Theravādins added the vipassanā refrain to the Satipaṭṭhāna Sutta, the three extra similes to the Kāyagatāsati Sutta, and reversed the sequence of ānāpānasati and clear comprehension in both. The Sarvāstivādins added the extra practices and padded out the final section on benefits. This shows that the specific details of these lists are sectarian. Each of the schools must have edited these paired discourses conjointly. This raises the important question: what was the main direction of influence, from the Kāyagatāsati Sutta to the Satipaṭṭhāna Sutta, or vice versa? To answer this question we must first examine in more detail the extra practices in the Sarvāstivāda.

36 Numbers 3 and 4, dealing with ways of controlling thoughts, are two of five methods advocated in both the Theravāda and Sarvāstivāda versions of the Vitakkasaṇṭhāna Sutta ('Discourse on the Quelling of Thoughts'), which is obviously a more appropriate home for them. The description in the Sarvāstivāda Smṛtyupasthāna Sūtra is, as expected, closer to that in the Sarvāstivāda version of the Vitakkasaṇṭhāna Sutta, and was no doubt taken from there. Both versions say that these practices are for one 'pursuing the higher mind', i.e. jhāna, and by means of them the mind becomes steadied internally, quieted, unified, and brought to samādhi. In the first practice, unskilful thoughts are replaced by thinking skilful thoughts. The Sarvāstivāda gives the simile of a carpenter who marks a piece of wood straight and then chops it with a sharp axe; the Theravāda simile, however, speaks of a carpenter knocking out a coarse peg by using a fine one, which is more appropriate. In the second practice one crushes and suppresses the mind with the mind, like two strong men would beat down a weaker. This violent approach to mental cultivation is unlike the Buddha's usual gentleness. This same practice is listed in the Mahā Saccaka Sutta among the useless byways the Bodhisatta mistakenly pursued before

his enlightenment.[12] Bronkhorst reasons from this that the practice must have been a Jain one, rejected by the Buddha, but later creeping back into the Suttas. However, the practice is the first and least ascetic of the Jain practices, and the last and most ascetic of the Buddhist, so maybe there is simply a slight overlap.

37 We have met number 10, the perception of light, together with some of the body contemplations, in the Iddhipāda-saṁyutta and the Aṅguttara Nikāya. Its inclusion in satipaṭṭhāna may also have been influenced by the standard passage on how one abandons the hindrance of sloth & torpor, being 'percipient of light, mindful & clearly comprehending'. There is no obvious reason in the passage itself why this should come under body contemplation. The emphasis on the perception of light in the Iddhipāda-saṁyutta, supported by other passages, suggests that here we are entering the exotic realm of psychic powers.

38 The 'basis of reviewing'[13] is mentioned in the Aṅguttara and the Dīghas as the fifth factor of noble right samādhi, the investigation of one who has emerged from jhāna 'just as if one standing should look at one lying down, or one lying down should look at one standing.'[14] Possibly the mention of the postures here, though obviously only a metaphor, prompted the inclusion under body contemplation. The situation with the jhāna similes is similar, the body in metaphorical or mystical sense merging with the literal physical body.

39 The internal sequence is obscure; why have the perception of light and the reviewing knowledge been inserted at this point? This has been influenced by the above-mentioned five-fold right samādhi. There are two variations of this: the Aṅguttara mentions the four jhānas (with similes) and the 'basis of reviewing' as fifth. The Dīgha mentions five factors: 'suffusion with rapture, suffusion with bliss, suffusion with heart, suffusion with light, basis of reviewing.' The first three of these obviously refer to jhāna, and are especially close to the descriptions of the jhāna similes. In particular the phrase 'suffusion with heart (*ceto*)' is quite unusual and distinctive

---

[12] MN 36.20.

[13] *Paccavekkhana nimitta*. Minh Châu has 'contemplating image', suggesting that the Chinese translation was influenced by the later meaning of *nimitta*. See discussion in SUJATO, *Swift Pair*, Appendix A.14–16.

[14] Cp. AN 5.28, DN 34.1.6/DA 10.

of this passage and the fourth jhāna simile. Then follow the perception of light and the basis of reviewing, all these in the same order in both the fivefold right samādhi and the Sarvāstivāda Smṛtyupasthāna Sūtra. The correspondence of these somewhat unusual passages is too close for coincidence.[15]

40 The identification of these structural influences on the Sarvāstivāda Smṛtyupasthāna and Kāyagatāsmṛti Sūtras allows us to make more sense of the overall structure of the body contemplation section of these texts. They start with the contemplation of body postures and movements through daily activities, the standard preparation for meditation. Another practice that acts both as a preparation for meditation and in meditation itself is the control of thoughts; this pertains to right intention of the eightfold path. Then follows the meditation proper, ānāpānasati, leading to the four jhānas. Next is the perception of light, associated with the development of psychic powers that regularly follow after jhāna. Finally the reviewing knowledge that investigates the whole process, especially the jhāna-consciousness, in terms of cause and effect.

41 This section so far makes perfect sense as a description of the normal course of practice in the Suttas. The problem lies, not in internal incongruities, but in its inclusion as part of body contemplation. Only some of the sections are body contemplation proper; the rest fleshes out the sequence of practice, and in the case of the jhānas the similes fit in with body contemplation. The incongruity is compounded by the addition of the body contemplations proper—parts of the body, elements, charnel ground—at the end of the body contemplation section. These have nothing to do with the progressive structure of the earlier part of the section. They were either tacked on at the end, or more likely were an early part of the text, which remained as the beginning was transformed into a comprehensive meditation program.

---

[15] The situation is complicated by a curious editing feature, which I was alerted to by Rod Bucknell. In the Aṅguttara, the fivefold right samādhi is followed by saying that one can then realize any of the clear knowledges, illustrated by 3 similes: a brimful pot, a brimful pond, and a ready chariot. This passage is in the Theravāda Kāyagatāsati Sutta, but not the Sarvāstivādin version. Thus from the fivefold right samādhi, the jhānas with similes are included in both Kāyagatāsati Suttas, the extra practices in the Sarvāstivāda only, and the 3 similes in the Theravāda only.

42 Here we see a tendency towards inflating mindfulness of the body until it encompasses the whole path. Satipaṭṭhāna provides an example of the same process on a larger scale. In fact the Satipaṭṭhāna Sutta covers much of the same ground in the later sections, the inclusion of samādhi being an obvious example; also the investigation into causes in contemplation of dhammas is similar to the 'basis of reviewing'. So the inclusion of these additional practices in the Smṛtyupasthāna Sūtra is largely redundant, suggesting that they were originally intended for the Kāyagatāsmṛti Sūtra, and the movement into the Smṛtyupasthāna Sūtra was a secondary development. If this is true for the Sarvāstivāda, it may hold good for the Theravāda too, although there, with leaving behind of the jhānas, the influence is not as strong.

43 Having considered in some detail the body contemplation section of the Sarvāstivāda Smṛtyupasthāna Sūtra, we may now move on to the remainder. The refrain in the Smṛtyupasthāna Sūtra speaks simply of contemplating internally and externally, then of establishing the mind on the body (feelings, mind, dhammas) and obtaining knowledge, vision, light, understanding (有知有見。有明有達; Pali equivalents are: *ñāṇa*, *dassana*, *vijjā*, *paññā*). There is no mention of impermanence.

44 The Theravāda Satipaṭṭhāna Sutta here has: 'One establishes mindfulness only for a measure of knowledge, a measure of mindfulness'. The word 'measure' (*matta*) here has always struck me as a bit odd. One can try to explain it away, but the normal meaning is 'mere' or 'limited'. Is it possible that there could have been an early confusion between *matta* 'measure' and *patti* 'attainment' or *attha* 'purpose'? It is also a bit clumsy to say that one is supposed to establish mindfulness (*sati*) in order to attain mindfulness (*patissati*). The Chinese term here means 'vision'. Could there have been a further confusion between something like *passati* and *patissati*? (Of course, *passati* is a verb and *patissati* is a noun, so this would have involved a syntactic and not merely a phonetic change.) Combining the two suggestions we could arrive at: 'One establishes mindfulness only for the sake of knowledge & vision.' This is a more straightforward meaning, but is not found in any existing texts.

45 The sections on feelings and mind in the Smṛtyupasthāna Sūtra are similar to the Theravāda Satipaṭṭhāna Sutta, but slightly more elaborate.

From here to the end the text refers to 'bhikkhus and bhikkhunīs', both as the audience of the discourse, and as the meditator in the discourse itself. This is quite extraordinary, and I don't know if it is representative of the Sarvāstivādin Suttas in general. There must have been nuns and laywomen present at many of the teachings, but the texts were put into the male voice. In the Theravāda, even when a discourse is addressed solely to nuns, the hypothetical practitioner of the discourse is usually a monk. Only rarely are the female practitioners acknowledged. This is rather a shame. The inscriptional evidence, according to Schopen, attests approximately even numbers of monks and nuns in the early schools. Many of the nuns are said to have been learned in a sutta, or in a Piṭaka, and so on, so they played their part in the transmission of the Dhamma. These inscriptions usually record substantial donations, of temples and suchlike. The Jains, unlike the Buddhists, made a census of their followers, and the figures consistently recognize far more nuns than monks. Given the patriarchal climate of the times, this is hardly a situation they would have invented, and the numbers of Buddhist nuns may also have exceeded the monks in India, as they do in some modern Buddhist countries.

46 The section on contemplation of dhammas compares as follows.

Table 14.2: Dhammas in Sarvāstivāda & Theravāda

Sarvāstivāda Smṛtyupasthāna Sūtra	Theravāda Satipaṭṭhāna Sutta
1. Internal & external sense media	
2. Five hindrances	1. Five hindrances
	2. Five aggregates
	3. Internal & external sense media
3. Seven awakening-factors	4. Seven awakening-factors
	5. Four noble truths

47 All of these exercises are described in virtually identical terms in both Suttas, as indeed in the Abhidhamma versions. The Sarvāstivāda omits the aggregates and truths, retaining the sense media as the only vipassanā practice. As we have seen, it shares this feature with the Dharmaskandha. There is one, possibly related, text in the Bojjhaṅga-saṁyutta that men-

tions the sense media.[16] There, the awakening-factors are said to be the 'one dhamma' for abandoning the 'things that fetter', namely the six sense media. The Satipaṭṭhāna Suttas, too, speak of the sense media in terms of fetters. But in the Bojjhaṅga-saṁyutta the awakening-factors, which chiefly pertain to samādhi, naturally precede the wisdom practice of the sense media. In the Sarvāstivāda Smṛtyupasthāna Sūtra, however, the sense media are displaced awkwardly to the beginning of the section, whereas in the Dharmaskandha they are in the middle. For this reason among others, I have no hesitation in concluding that this is a later interpolation, and that the original Satipaṭṭhāna Sutta included just the hindrances and awakening-factors.

48 The Sarvāstivāda Smṛtyupasthāna Sūtra omits the repetition of the 'way to convergence' statement at the end, but does include the guarantee of attainment in seven years, or as little as seven days; indeed, it goes further than the Theravāda and says one may see results in the evening if one practices in the morning. It also omits the final sentence of the Pali, 'This is what was said [i.e. satipaṭṭhāna is the 'way to convergence'] and this is the reason it was said [i.e. it leads to these results].' Since this sentence is found in no other version, it may be an attempt to tie together the loose assemblage of passages that the Satipaṭṭhāna Sutta had become.

49 The emphasis throughout the Sarvāstivāda Smṛtyupasthāna Sūtra is clearly on samatha. Like the Vibhaṅga, it omits virtually all the overtly vipassanā oriented material of the Theravāda Satipaṭṭhāna Sutta; and as well it adds much samatha material. It treats vipassanā solely as the contemplation of dhammas. Both schools were moving towards using the Satipaṭṭhāna Sutta as a compilation of meditation techniques; but for the Sarvāstivādins this was a samatha manual, while for the Theravādins it was a vipassanā manual.

14.3 Ekāyana Sūtra

50 The Ekottara Āgama, from which this discourse was taken, is the least congruent of the four Āgamas. It was translated, it seems, from Prakrit rather than Sanskrit. It is usually believed to belong to the Mahāsaṅghikas,

[16] SN 46.29.

the school that split from the ancestral Theravādins at the first schism. Thus, they are of particular interest, since textual and doctrinal material held in common between the Mahāsaṅghika lineage and the Theravāda lineage probably dates to the earliest pre-sectarian period. We have their Vinaya in Chinese, and some later texts, and recently a large number of sūtras or fragments in the original Prakrit have come to light, apparently from a monastery near Bamiyan in Afghanistan. The Mahāsaṅghika, like the Theravāda, proceeded to splinter into many sub-sects, with varying degrees of doctrinal development.

51 However, the affiliation of the Ekottara is far from certain and several scholars have raised serious objections to this identification. The main reason for ascribing it to the Mahāsaṅghikas is the inclusion of several references to Maitreya, and the school of the Ekottara may have had a special devotion for that Buddha of the future. This might be a trait of a Mahāsaṅghika school, but then again it might not. The doctrinal and other features that have been identified do not bear any specially close resemblance to known Mahāsaṅghika doctrines; but the collection is notoriously idiosyncratic, and presents many variations on even standard doctrinal formulas like the eightfold path. Given the very bad inconsistency of the text it might not be worth placing too much weight on doctrinal consistency as a guide to sectarian affiliation. Even the orthodox and rigorous Theravādins retain in their Suttas a number of passages that contradict tenets of the school (the in-between state; the gradual path; the necessity for jhāna; the primacy of Suttas over Abhidhamma; the primacy of practice over study, etc.). So we don't really know the school of the Ekottara, but we will follow the mainstream in treating it as Mahāsaṅghika.

52 The careless editing and divergence from the other sources suggests a later date than the Theravāda Satipaṭṭhāna Sutta and the Sarvāstivāda Smṛtyupasthāna Sūtra. The setting, in common with the Dharmaskandha, is the Jetavana at Sāvatthī rather than Kammassadamma. This could imply that it is actually a different discourse, delivered on a different occasion. However, it should be obvious to anyone familiar with the Suttas that they are set in the Jetavana far more frequently than anywhere else; the Jetavana was the 'default' setting for any Suttas whose provenance was unknown. This is supported by two passages mentioned by Schopen. One

passage from the Mūlasarvāstivāda Vinaya, has the Buddha telling Venerable Upāli that, if the setting or other details of a discourse or training rule is forgotten, one should declare that the setting was at one of the six great cities, or somewhere the Buddha stayed many times; if one forgets the name of the King, one should say it was Pasenadi; if one forgets the name of the householder, one should say it was Anāthapiṇḍika; and so on.[17] A similar statement is recorded in the Mahāsaṅghika Vinaya: in the rules concerning reciting the nine aṅgas, if a monk forgets the setting, he should say it was one of the eight famous places.[18] Schopen's discussion of this principle is sound, and, as he says, application of such principles would quickly result in the prevalence of settings at the Jetavana that is such a characteristic of the existing canons. We have seen in the Sarvāstivāda Saṁyukta that this kind of artificial ascription of setting is very prevalent. So when a discourse is said to have taken place at Sāvatthī, we should not take this too seriously. In cases like the Satipaṭṭhāna Sutta, where different versions of what look like the same text are set sometimes in the Jetavana, sometimes elsewhere, we should assume that the less common setting is likely to be authentic, and the shift to Sāvatthī happened as part of a later normalization. Thus the different settings do not imply that the texts had a different origin.

53 The Chinese here translates 'satipaṭṭhāna' by two characters that mean 'mind-tranquillity' (意止). The Indian original of this translation might be something like *manosamatha*. This term does not appear as such in the Pali, although the virtually identical *cetosamatha* does. It is an unusual rendering for satipaṭṭhāna; normally the Chinese has the more literal 'mindfulness-place' (念處). However, the rendering is found in several other places, such as T № 101 (the partial Saṁyukta SA[3]), an independant version of the Daśottara Sūtra (T № 13), the Dharmaguptaka Vinaya, and several versions of the Prajñāpāramitā literature. Thus it is not peculiar to the Ekottara.

54 After opening with the 'path leading to convergence' statement, the text says this path destroys the five hindrances. The mention of the hin-

---

[17] SCHOPEN 2004, pp. 395*ff.*

[18] SCHOPEN 2004, pg. 283, note 59. This note, unfortunately disconnected from Schopen's main discussion of the matter, gives a couple of further references.

drances here is in line with the mainstream understanding of satipaṭṭhāna, and in particular recalls the Sarvāstivāda Smṛtyupasthāna Sūtra. 'Path' is the eightfold path, here given in a typically eccentric form: right view, right prevention, right conduct, right livelihood, right skill in means, right speech, right recollection, right concentration.

55 The formula for the four satipaṭṭhānas treats each as internal/external; the internal/external formula is then omitted throughout the body of the discourse. The auxiliary formula is also omitted. The significance of this formula, however, is that satipaṭṭhāna is developed in the context of the path as a whole, and in the Ekāyana Sūtra this has already been stated.

56 In contrast with the consistency of the Theravāda Suttas, the refrains throughout vary considerably. Thus here in the introduction, body contemplation is said to lead to the ending of unwholesome thoughts and the removal of anxiety, while the remaining three contemplations lead to peace and joy. The refrain in the parts of the body section combines these two, saying to 'realize peace and joy, end bad thoughts, and remove anxiety and sorrow'. Elsewhere the refrains include one or other part of this phrase, which makes us suspect that this was the standard version, more-or-less garbled throughout the text. It is a similar kind of phrase to the standard auxiliary formula, but it is not easy to see a specific textual relationship. The end of the section on corpse meditation, after speaking of leading to peace, etc., speaks of understanding impermanence. Thus we see a combination of samatha and vipassanā aspects.

57 The text says it is the 'way to convergence' because it leads to oneness of mind. This saying is here given greater prominence than in the other versions: firstly, because it is explicitly explained in the text itself; second, because it is the title; and thirdly because the text is included in the 'Ones' of the Ekottara Āgama. I said in the GIST that the symbolic significance of number influenced the formation of the Aṅguttara/Ekottara. An important connotation of the 'one' in Buddhism is samādhi, and this is clearly reflected in the Theravāda Aṅguttara. So the Ekāyana Sūtra was included in the 'Ones', classified under the first word of the text, a word that encapsulates the primary spiritual purpose of the way of satipaṭṭhāna: the achievement of unification of mind.

58 Omitting ānāpānasati and awareness of activities, the section on body contemplations simply includes the parts of the body,[19] four elements, and charnel ground contemplations. It adds another practice—observing the openings of the body through which impurities flow. This is similar to the Śāriputrābhidharma. A simile is included for the elements (the butchered cow) and the orifices (like joints of bamboo or reeds), but is omitted for the parts of the body. Since the simile is found in all the other Sutta versions, this is a case of accidental loss.

59 The contemplations of feeling and mind are similar in their content to the other versions, but the refrains are different to both the other versions and to the refrains of the first sections in the same sūtra. They refer firstly to contemplating the principles of origination and ending so that, 'Regarding presently arisen feelings he has knowledge and vision, with awareness well-founded, with nothing to rely on, oneself has joy and happiness and does not give rise to feelings of attachment to the world.' The refrain here is difficult, and the translations I have vary widely. The above translation assumes that this phrase is similar to the Pali.

60 Then follow some slightly varying versions of formulas for attaining arahantship commonly found throughout the Suttas, which are obviously later additions. The refrain section has some affinity with the Theravāda Satipaṭṭhāna Sutta.

61 The contemplation of mind includes a further phrase that has confused the translators: 可思惟 · 不可思惟. This follows the phrase we have identified as referring to 'knowledge and vision'. Thích Nhất Hạnh says that this refers to knowing what is not knowable, and suggests that it is a Prajñāpāramitā style paradox. Pasadika translates 'from this it can be gathered whether one is really mindful or not'. But the phrase 不可思惟, which is peculiar to the Ekottara, elsewhere stands for *atakkāvacara* (beyond the sphere of reason) or *acinteyya* (unthinkable). This does not really tell us what the phrase means ('one considers that which is beyond thought'?), but it does suggest a connection with a phrase found occasionally in satipaṭṭhāna, 'one does not (or should not) think thoughts of the body'.

[19] 24 in number. Theravāda has 31. I have available to me three translations of the list of body parts from the same Chinese text of the Sarvāstivāda Smṛtyupasthāna Sūtra. They reckon the parts of the body at 29, 30, and 31 respectively.

62 Moving on to the dhammas section of the Ekāyana Sūtra, we find just the seven awakening-factors and the four jhānas. A measure of the text's difficulty is that Pasadika translates this section without even realizing that it refers to the awakening-factors. Bizarrely, the translation has 念, the normal rendering of mindfulness, here for both the awakening-factor of mindfulness and of rapture. The awakening-factors are presented very simply, omitting the inquiry into causes that is characteristic of the dhammas section in the other versions. It just says one develops each of the awakening-factors 'in reliance on initial application, on no-craving, on destroying the unwholesome mind, and abandoning the unwholesome dhammas'. This is a slightly garbled version of the common formula: 'dependent on seclusion, on fading of lust, on cessation, and ripening in relinquishment'. The Chinese seems to have read *vitakka* (initial application) for *viveka* (seclusion).

63 If we accept this reconstruction, then the description of the awakening-factors here becomes very much like the four modes of contemplation of dhammas in ānāpānasati: impermanence, fading of lust, cessation, and relinquishment.

64 The ending of the discourse with the four jhānas is similar to the Mahā Satipaṭṭhāna Sutta of the Dīgha Nikāya. It reaffirms yet again the function of satipaṭṭhāna to lead up to jhāna.

65 It is interesting that the inquiry into causes, prominent in the other expositions of the contemplation of dhammas, is absent here. While the Theravāda changed the samatha aspects of satipaṭṭhāna into vipassanā, the Ekāyana Sūtra changed the vipassanā aspects into samatha. Since this version is later than the Theravāda Satipaṭṭhāna Sutta and the canonical abhidhamma, perhaps it was deliberately formed in opposition to the vipassanā interpretation of satipaṭṭhāna favoured by the ābhidhammikas. The samādhi implication of the famous introductory phrase was drawn out and made explicit. Then the hindrances were rescued from obscurity in the contemplation of dhammas and placed at the beginning and the end, always the positions of greatest emphasis. This proclaims that abandoning the hindrances is not just one exercise among many, but is the main orientation of the whole practice. Then the four jhānas were brought in to culminate the contemplation of dhammas, rendering explicit what the

compilers may have felt was too ambiguous and subject to misinterpretation in the original version.

66 The Ekāyana Sūtra ends by repeating that satipaṭṭhāna is the 'way to convergence', and that it gets rid of the five hindrances. It omits the guarantee of attainment found in the other versions.

67 In conclusion, the Mahāsaṅghikas preserved a simpler version of the Satipaṭṭhāna Sutta for some time, resisting the trend to use it as a catchall repository of meditation techniques. Of course, they may well have had other texts fulfilling this function. The expansions, none of which are overtly sectarian, tended to be in the refrains rather than the content of the meditation exercises themselves. In accordance with all the early teachings on satipaṭṭhāna we have examined so far, the Ekāyana Sūtra strongly emphasizes the samatha aspect, while also giving due consideration to vipassanā.

14.4 Theravāda Satipaṭṭhāna Sutta

68 How might this text have been formed? Apart from the Satipaṭṭhāna Suttas, there are no texts in the Majjhima, or in the Dīgha for that matter, that deal with satipaṭṭhāna in detail. Desiring a full-length text on satipaṭṭhāna, the Majjhima redactors selected the *Vibhaṅga Mūla from the *vyākaraṇas* in the Satipaṭṭhāna-saṁyutta as the most promising. However, it was too short and needed filling out if it were to take its place in the Majjhima. This filling out involved expanding the list of meditation exercises in the contemplation of the body and of dhammas, and developing an extended refrain by adding the contemplation of rise & fall, taken from the Samudaya Sutta, to the internal/external refrain.

69 The evidence suggests that these 14 exercises appeared first in the Theravāda Kāyagatāsati Sutta and were later used to flesh out the Theravāda Satipaṭṭhāna Sutta. What change, if any, would the inclusion of these 14 exercises make?

70 We have seen that satipaṭṭhāna is normally seen as being very close or identical to ānāpānasati, so its inclusion here is unproblematic. The only question marks, as we have already commented, are whether it is valid to sever the first tetrad from the rest of the practice; and whether the simile

is authentic, since it is only found in the Theravāda Satipaṭṭhāna Sutta. Perhaps it was inserted under the influence of the strong prevalence of similes and imagery in both the Kāyagatāsati Suttas.

71 As regards the elements and death contemplations, we have noted that these occur grouped together elsewhere with the 31 parts, so again their inclusion is unproblematic.

72 The main change in the orientation of the practice is the inclusion of the sections on clear comprehension and body postures. Elsewhere these are clearly distinct from satipaṭṭhāna as meditation. In the Saṁyutta they are separated, in the Sarvāstivāda Smṛtyupasthāna Sūtra, the Śāriputrābhidharma, and the Prajñāpāramitā they come before ānāpānasati, and in the Vibhaṅga, the Dharmaskandha, and the Ekāyana Sūtra they are not found. Consistently, clear comprehension during daily activities is not treated as meditation, but as a precursor to meditation. Only in the Theravāda Kāyagatāsati Sutta and the Theravāda Satipaṭṭhāna Sutta is this practice placed after ānāpānasati.

73 In the context of the Suttas as a whole, this variation may have been intended to exalt ānāpānasati by granting it pride of place. But to one not familiar with the overall context of the teaching this could be taken to imply that clear comprehension of one's everyday activities is itself an alternative meditation, as powerful as ānāpānasati. This leads to the claim that the most important of the Buddha's meditation instructions was to be mindful whatever we do. But clear comprehension as part of the gradual training is part of the all-round mental training that was expected of those who had undertaken the monastic vocation. Thus from both the agreement of the texts, and from the broader consideration of how it fits in the Buddha's path, the sections on clear comprehension and body postures were not likely to have been in the *Satipaṭṭhāna Mūla. If they were, however, it is probable they were placed in the normal position at the beginning. There they naturally lead on, as in the gradual training, to the monk who has 'gone to the forest, to the root of the tree, or to an empty hut' to settle into meditation.

74 The refrain in the *Satipaṭṭhāna Mūla would have originally consisted of the internal/external contemplation and a simple exhortation to be mindful for the sake of understanding, independence, and letting go. But since

nowhere else in the Majjhima is any connection between satipaṭṭhāna and vipassanā mentioned, the Majjhima redactors wished to incorporate the section on impermanence from the Samudaya Sutta of the Saṁyutta. This became attached to the internal/external refrain at the end of each exercise, thus furthering the idea, already hinted at in the Theravāda Anuruddha-saṁyutta, that vipassanā may be undertaken from the start of practice. While this may reflect the orientation of the redaction school, it is possible that it was originally an unintended side effect of the purely formal evolution of the Satipaṭṭhāna Sutta.[20]

75 Another consequence of the extended refrain is that each section, ending with the phrase 'one abides independent, not grasping at anything in the world', leads all the way to arahantship. Thus the text has both a 'horizontal' dimension, a progressive deepening from one section to the next (as suggested by the phrase 'again & beyond' which prefixes each section), and a 'vertical' dimension, developing to liberation within each one of the exercises. This kind of structure is characteristic of the Suttas, and is no problem as long as it is understood holistically rather than divisively. That is, each meditation subject is complete, not because it replaces other approaches but because it includes them. As we have seen, this is brought out most clearly in the context of ānāpānasati. But this subtle point is easily overlooked, and historically it has contributed to the gradual neglect and marginalization of the progressive structure of satipaṭṭhāna.

76 The sections on feelings and mind are similar to all the other versions.

77 The section on dhammas is substantially lengthened; the main interpolations in the Majjhima version being the contemplations of the aggregates and the sense media. Although these occur frequently in the early texts, nowhere else do they appear as part of satipaṭṭhāna. Remember that the Samudaya Sutta of the Saṁyutta says that the origin of dhammas is 'attention'. It is impossible to understand, and clearly against the normal position of the Suttas, how attention could give rise to the aggregates

[20] The Theravāda Satipaṭṭhāna Suttas have a small spelling mistake in the refrain in the contemplation of dhammas section. The phrase is '"*Atthi dhammā*"*ti*' ('there is dhammas'), where *atthi* is singular and *dhammā* is plural. Presumably this was merely a reciters' glitch, as they mechanically repeated the phrase from the earlier sections, without noticing the change in number from singular to plural. Innocuous enough, but a reminder of the fallibility of the tradition.

and sense media. The commentary doesn't even try, simply agreeing that paying uncausewise attention gives rise to the hindrances and paying causewise attention gives rise to the enlightenment factors. This agrees with one of the outstanding themes of the Bojjhaṅga-saṁyutta.

> 78 'Monks, when one pays uncausewise attention, unarisen sensual desire arises, and arisen sensual desire increases and expands; unarisen ill-will... sloth & torpor... restlessness & remorse... doubt arises, and arisen doubt increases and expands.
>
> 79 'Monks, when one pays causewise attention, the unarisen awakening-factor of mindfulness arises, and the arisen awakening-factor of mindfulness goes to fulfilment by development; the unarisen awakening-factor of investigation of dhammas... energy... rapture... tranquillity... samādhi... equanimity arises, and the arisen awakening-factor of equanimity goes to fulfilment by development.'[21]

80 This is the same practice as in the Satipaṭṭhāna Sutta. Similar themes recur in more than a dozen texts in the Bojjhaṅga-saṁyutta.[22] In the Sarvāstivāda many of these texts are grouped right at the start of the chapter, emphasizing this theme even more. Even this alone would strongly imply that the aggregates and sense media were a later interpolation. These paradigmatic vipassanā exercises are suggestively placed *after* the abandoning of the hindrances but *before* the development of the awakening-factors. The normal position is that the awakening-factors, which are very close in meaning with samādhi, bring about the abandoning of the hindrances; but here it seems we can abandon the hindrances without developing samādhi and then do vipassanā straight away—an idea that was to prove highly influential in Theravāda meditation.

81 There are certain factors that suggest that the six sense media are more at home here than the five aggregates. Firstly, as we have seen, mindfulness is more characteristically mentioned with the sense media, and the sense media do occur one time in the Bojjhaṅga saṁyutta. Secondly, the sense media are included in the Sarvāstivāda versions and the Śāriputrābhidharma. Thirdly, the phrasing of the contemplation is more in line with with the sections on the hindrances and awakening-factors. I am still

---

[21] SN 46.35.

[22] SN 46.2, 5, 7, 23, 24, 33, 34, 37, 39, 40, 49, 51, 52, 53, 55, 56.

confident that both were later interpolations, but I am marginally less confident in the case of the sense media.

82 There is another incongruity, implicit elsewhere, but strongly evident here. In each of the other sections, as we have seen, there is no explicit mention of impermanence, causality, etc. Then impermanence is brought in with the vipassanā refrain that follows. While probably not original, this is perfectly coherent. But in the contemplation of dhammas according to the Theravāda, each meditation exercise speaks of impermanence. In the contemplation of the hindrances, enlightenment factors, and sense media, this is indicated by key words such as 'arising' (*uppāda*), which recurs through these sections. The contemplation of aggregates similarly speaks of 'origination' (*samudaya*). But then, having already discussed impermanence once, it is re-introduced in the vipassanā refrain, which also speaks of 'origination' (*samudaya*). Is one then to contemplate the 'arising of arising?' This unnecessary repetition might be explained away; but the most straightforward explanation is that it results from the editing together of two originally distinct texts.

83 The dhammas section in the Majjhima version closes with a brief enunciation of the four noble truths. This is then expanded greatly in the Mahā Satipaṭṭhāna Sutta of the Dīgha Nikāya.[23] Some of the recent Burmese recensions have re-incorporated this entire section from the Dīgha Nikāya back into the Majjhima Nikāya, and even acknowledge this provenance by re-titling it the 'Mahā Satipaṭṭhāna Sutta'. Perhaps a better title would be the 'Piltdown Sutta'. This canonical innovation is extraordinary. While it is common for a word or phrase to slip between the cracks, I don't know any other place where a large body of text has been moved, obviously in fairly recent times. No doubt this editorial innovation was designed to further exaggerate the already excessive status of the Satipaṭṭhāna Sutta. But the result is rather the reverse—such clumsy mishandling leaves all-too-obvious fingerprints at the scene of the crime. The altered version is found in the so-called 'Sixth Council' edition published by the Vipassanā Research Institute, but was inserted earlier, for the notes to the PTS Pali (edited in 1888) state that the Burmese manuscript includes under the four noble truths 'a passage of some length, borrowed from the Mahā

[23] DN 22.

Satipaṭṭhāna Sutta of the Dīgha Nikāya'.[24] This possibly refers to the Fifth Council edition.

84 There is a Pali work called Saṁgāyanapucchāvissajjanā which gives the questions and answers on the texts as spoken in the Council, although it doesn't say which Council—presumably it is the Fifth or Sixth. This also includes the 'Mahā Satipaṭṭhāna Sutta' in the Majjhima, and has the temerity to assert that because of its great usefulness to meditators this text was recited 'twice' 'in detail' by the redactors in ancient times. While most other discourses rate a bare mention in this work, the Mahā (sic!) Satipaṭṭhāna Sutta is distinguished by detailing the contents of the meditation exercises.

85 A similarly obvious bias is apparent in the Vipassanā Research Institute's (VRI) online version of the Tipitaka. Under the contents table of the Majjhima Nikāya, almost all discourses are simply listed by their title; but the Mahā (sic!) Satipaṭṭhāna Sutta is again singled out by individually listing all twenty-one sections. The meditative bias of those who have put together these recensions of the Tipitaka are well known: the questioner at the Sixth Council was Mahāsi Sayadaw, the founder of the main 'dry vipassanā' meditation system; and the VRI Tipiṭaka was put made by the followers of the Goenka tradition, the other main vipassanā school.

86 Such partisan manipulation of sacred scriptures has only one good consequence: no-one can reasonably insist that the Tipitaka must have remained unchanged for all time.

87 The Mahā Satipaṭṭhāna Sutta is the only significant discourse in the Dīgha Nikāya that is not found in the Dharmaguptaka Dīrgha Āgama. This is no mere oversight, for it is also absent from the Sarvāstivāda Dīrgha. I would therefore consider the Mahā Satipaṭṭhāna Sutta as a leading contender for the title of the latest discourse in the four Nikāyas, a lost waif straying over from the early abhidhamma. It is worth noting that this is the only discourse in all the existing collections to be duplicated in both the Majjhima and the Dīgha, further evidence of its anomalous character. It is obviously just the Satipaṭṭhāna Sutta padded out with further material, and again, the increase is not small.

[24] Majjhima Nikāya, Vol 1, PTS, pg. 534. The preface lists a number of similar interpolations from the Dīgha into the Burmese Majjhima, but none are of significance.

88 The Satipaṭṭhāna Sutta treats the four noble truths by merely stating them. In the Suttas this kind of formulation often indicates, not vipassanā, but the realization of stream entry; thus it could have been originally intended to express the results of the practice of the previous sections. But the Mahā Satipaṭṭhāna Sutta gathers much material from elsewhere in the Suttas, ending up with the longest of all expositions of the truths, virtually doubling the length of the Satipaṭṭhāna Sutta, and clearly presenting the four noble truths section as an extended course in vipassanā.

89 The new material is mainly identical with the Saccavibhaṅga Sutta.[25] The Mahā Satipaṭṭhāna Sutta adds a lengthy analysis of the second and third noble truths to the Saccavibhaṅga Sutta material. This is structured around the following series of dhammas, spelled out for each of the sense media: external sense media, internal sense media, cognition, contact, feeling, perception, volition, craving, initial application, sustained application. The Saṁyutta Nikāya includes a similar list, although it has the elements and the aggregates for the final two members of the list, rather than initial & sustained application. Several of the Saṁyuttas containing this series are missing from the Sarvāstivāda Saṁyukta.[26] Nevertheless, a similar list, again omitting the final two members, is found in the Sarvāstivāda Satyavibhaṅga Sūtra. The only place where the Mahā Satipaṭṭhāna list occurs verbatim in the four Nikāyas is in the 'repetition series' appended to the Aṅguttara sevens.[27] Such sections are late, and in the present case the whole passage is ignored by the commentary.

90 This list is an expanded form of the psychological analysis of the cognitive process first enunciated in the third discourse, the Ādittapariyāya Sutta, and repeated countless times subsequently. Eventually, this series would evolve into the *cittavīthi*, the final, definitive exposition of psychological processes worked out in great detail by the later ābhidhammikas. Thus the Mahā Satipaṭṭhāna Sutta stands as an important bridge to the Abhidhamma. We have already discussed the fact that almost all this four noble truths material is found in the Abhidhamma Vibhaṅga exposition of the truths.

---

[25] MN 141.

[26] SN 18, SN 25, SN 26, SN 27.

[27] AN 7.80*ff.*

91 Needless to say, most of the new material in the Mahā Satipaṭṭhāna Sutta is vipassanā oriented, continuing the trend we have consistently observed in the development of the satipaṭṭhāna texts within the Pali canon. Nevertheless, the exposition of the truths, and therefore the Sutta as a whole, ends with the four jhānas as right samādhi, restating the basic function of satipaṭṭhāna to lead to jhāna in the eightfold path.

92 The significance of the Mahā Satipaṭṭhāna Sutta can best be understood in light of the structure of the Dīgha Nikāya as a whole. The most authentic and often repeated teaching in the Dīgha sets out the very heart of Dhamma practice. In the discussion of the GIST we saw that, leaving aside the Brahmajāla Sutta, the Dīgha Nikāya starts off with a series of twelve discourses expounding the gradual training in detail, including the four jhānas. This would be pounded into the heads of the Dīgha students over and again as *the* way of training. In fact the GIST says that this section was the original core around which the Dīgha was formed. Thus the whole of the Dīgha may well have started out as a jhāna-manual.

93 There is little vipassanā material in the Dīgha. A striking example of this is the rarity of the five aggregates. Leaving aside the Mahā Satipaṭṭhāna Sutta, meditation on the aggregates is mentioned only in the legendary context of the Mahāpadāna Sutta. Elsewhere the aggregates receive but a bare enunciation in the proto-abhidhamma compilations such as the Saṅgīti and Dasuttara Suttas.

94 The compilers of the Theravāda Dīgha Nikāya wished to include more vipassanā material to balance the strong samādhi emphasis. Now, there are three texts treating mindfulness practice in detail in the Majjhima: the Satipaṭṭhāna Sutta, the Ānāpānasati Sutta, and the Kāyagatāsati Sutta. The latter two clearly emphasize samādhi, so in choosing which of the three to 'promote' to the Dīgha the compilers chose the most vipassanā oriented text and padded it out with further vipassanā material to redress the imbalance of the Dīgha Nikāya as a whole. And in context, this was most reasonable. But when the discourse is divorced from its context and treated as a blueprint for a meditation technique different from, even superior to, the mainstream samādhi practice, a shift of emphasis becomes a radical distortion of meaning.

95 We can pin down a little more precisely the date of the formation of the Mahā Satipaṭṭhāna Sutta. We have already noted that it is absent from both the Sarvāstivāda and Dharmaguptaka Dīrghas. These schools split after the time of Aśoka. The Sri Lankan mission arrived in the Aśokan period, and the Theravāda were based on the island from that time.[28] Given their doctrinal and textual closeness, the Theravāda and the Dharmaguptaka are really just the Northern and Southern, or Gandhāri and Sinhalese, branches of the same school.

96 This raises the possibility that the final editing of the Pali Nikāyas was carried out on Sri Lankan soil. This case was put by Oliver Abeynayake in his article 'Sri Lanka's Contribution to the Development of the Pali Canon.'[29] To summarize a few of his points, much of the Vinaya Parivāra was composed in Sri Lanka. In addition, the restructuring of the Vinaya Piṭaka, from the early form of the Bhikkhu Vibhaṅga and Bhikkhunī Vibhaṅga which is attested in all schools including the Theravāda Vinaya Culavagga itself, to the current division along the lines of the 'Pārājika Pali' and 'Pācittiya Pali' is unique to Sri Lanka, and may plausibly be regarded as a Sinhalese development. Several sections of the Khuddaka Nikāya, including the Khuddakapāṭha, are Sri Lankan. In the four major Nikāyas, Yakkaduwe Sri Pragnarama, the late principal of the Vidyalankara Pirivena in Sri Lanka, has identified, in the Theravāda Majjhima, eight sentences of the Mūlapariyāya Sutta and four verses of the Sammādiṭṭhi Sutta that are in Sinhalese Prakrit, not Pali. The Theravāda commentaries themselves assert that some of the material in the Dīgha was added by the Sinhalese elders, namely the closing verses of the Mahā Parinibbāna Sutta, starting with 'There were eight measures of the relics…'. This is plausible, since the verses are in a late metre; also they include, not merely worship of relics, but specifically the teeth relics, which is one of the most distinctive features of Sinhalese Buddhism. Moreover, the line preceding them is a catch-phrase in Pali (*evam'etaṁ bhūtapubbaṁ*, 'that is how it was') that refers to far-off events in the legendary past, like the English 'Once upon

[28] The headquarters of the Theravāda must have been in Sri Lanka from quite early, for an inscription at Nagarjunikonda in Southern India refers to a monastery belonging to the 'Theravādin teachers of Sri Lanka'. SCHOPEN 1997, pg. 5.

[29] ABEYNAYAKE, pp.163–183.

a time...'. The commentary even admits that this phrase was inserted in the Third Council, at the time of Aśoka.

97 However, despite this strong evidence, some of the verses are included in the Sanskrit version. This contains the verse 'There were eight measures of the relics...' and that on the teeth relics. It is most unlikely that a Sinhalese composition found its way into a Sanskrit text in the north of India, so perhaps these verses were added in India after all. But the later verses, starting with 'By their power this fruitful earth...', are absent from the Sanskrit, and may well have been added in Sri Lanka.

98 This last point may indirectly bear on the date of the Mahā Satipaṭṭhāna Sutta. The closing verses of the Mahā Parinibbāna Sutta are predominately late metres such as *vaṁsattha*. One of the few other places in the canon that contains *vaṁsattha* and other similarly late, elaborate verse styles is the Lakkhaṇa Sutta.[30] This hagiographical text is found in the Sarvāstivādin Majjhima and in the Theravāda, but not the Dharmaguptaka or Sarvāstivāda, Dīgha. It therefore must have been transferred from the Majjhima to the Dīgha after the Dharmaguptaka schism, at around the same time as the Mahā Satipaṭṭhāna Sutta was created. This shift was prompted by the large-scale expansion of the text. The Sarvāstivāda Madhyama version merely speaks of the two careers open to a Great Man, and lists the 32 marks. The Theravāda Dīgha version adds detailed prose explanations and verse elaborations of the workings of kamma and its fruits regarding the 32 marks.[31] The commentary says the verses were added by Venerable Ānanda. Although this cannot be accepted as literally true, it implies the commentators were aware that the verses were added later and by a different hand. They should be ascribed to monks following Ānanda's

[30] DN 30/MA 59.

[31] The doctrinal material of the Sarvāstivāda version is thus entirely stock formulæ, lacking all the unique material peculiar to the Theravāda version. But the setting is more complex: it has the monks sitting around discussing the 'wonderful and marvelous' qualities of the Tathāgata, then the Buddha entering and enquiring into the topic of conversation, etc. (as in the Mahāpadāna Sutta). So in the aṅgas it belongs to the *abbhūtadhammas*. The Theravāda just has the Buddha giving the discourse straight off, and so the identification as *abbhūtadhamma* is not explicit. The commentary explains the need for the discourse being the question of what kamma is it that gives rise to the marks, an issue that is not addressed at all in the Sarvāstivāda. All this raises the question of whether the two may be regarded as cognate texts.

devotional tradition. These verses are similar in style to the closing verses of the Mahā Parinibbāna Sutta, which the commentary says were added in Sri Lanka. Given this, as well as the verses' evident lateness and omission from the Sarvāstivāda, it is likely that they were also added in Sri Lanka. The verses were probably added to the Lakkhaṇa Sutta around the same time as the extra four noble truths material was added to the Satipaṭṭhāna Sutta, and so we suggest that the resulting Mahā Satipaṭṭhāna Sutta was composed in Sri Lanka.

99 We may then ask when these additions may have occurred. There is no direct evidence, but we can seek a convenient peg on which to hang them. After the introduction of Buddhist texts in the time of Aśoka, the first literary activity of major importance in Sri Lanka is during the reign of Vaṭṭagāminī. At that time, due to war with the Tamils, the lineage of oral transmission of the Tipitaka was nearly broken. The Sangha made the momentous decision to write down the Tipitaka, asserting that study and preservation of the texts was more important than practice of their contents (a decision that has set the agenda for the Theravāda until the present day). According to recent scholarly opinion this was around 20 BCE. I suggest that this was when the Mahā Satipaṭṭhāna Sutta was created.

100 There is an unfortunate side-effect of this kind of textual analysis. It's not hard to deconstruct ancient, heavily edited texts like the Buddhist scriptures. There are plenty of fault-lines, anomalies, and obscurities if one wishes to look. But what are we to do—demolish the palace and leave a pile of rubble? This too is not authentic to the texts, for, despite everything, the Nikāyas/Āgamas offer us a vast body of teachings springing from a remarkably uniform vision, a clarity and harmony of perspective that is unparalleled in any comparably large and ancient body of writings. To give the impression that the situation is hopelessly confused and problematic is to deny this extraordinary fact. While it is naïve and untenable to pretend there are no problems, throwing our hands up in the air in despair shows an excess of what the Satipaṭṭhāna Sutta calls 'spiritual depression' (*nirāmisa domanassa*). I think the lines of unity and consistency in satipaṭṭhāna are far more significant and powerful than the fractures. But in this book so far, the threads of connection and continuity are buried in the pages of analysis. The question is, how to make this unity vivid?

Chapter 15

THE SOURCE

MY SOLUTION IS TO PRESENT a reconstruction of what the authentic source material for the Satipaṭṭhāna Sutta. Of course this is problematic, but it's no more problematic than simply walking away and leaving the job undone. None of the scriptural traditions offer us a pile of meaningless, deconstructed rubble. Reading a reconstructed text gives a more immediate impression of what the satipaṭṭhāna teachings were like.

2 The following table summarizes the contents of satipaṭṭhāna. It shows the strands of continuity and discontinuity between the recensions. The table does not differentiate between the Theravāda Dīgha and Majjhima.

3 The basic principle in editing the *Satipaṭṭhāna Mūla is simple. We have seven early texts that teach satipaṭṭhāna in detail. These have much in common. The best explanation for this is that they are descended from a common source. The most likely content of this source is the shared material found in each of the texts.

4 However, we cannot mechanically assume that unshared material is late. For example, the Abhidhamma always omits similes, so their absence from the Vibhaṅga does not imply they were absent from the source. Another case is the Ekāyana Sūtra, which is late and erratically edited. Generally, then, the *Satipaṭṭhāna Mūla includes material found in all texts, but will occasionally allow phrases found only in four or five.

Table 15.1: The Satipaṭṭhāna Material

	Vibhaṅga	Dharmaskandha	Śāriputrābhidharma
Body	Parts of the body	Parts of the body 6 elements	4 postures Clear Comprehension Ānāpānasati Parts of the body 4 elements Food Space (5th element) Oozing orifices Charnel ground
Feelings	Happy/pain/neutral Carnal/spiritual	Happy/pain/neutral Bodily/Mental Carnal/spiritual Sensual/Non-sensual	Happy/pain/neutral Carnal/spiritual
Mind	Greedy Angry Deluded Contracted Exalted Surpassed Samādhi Released	Greedy Angry Deluded Contracted Slothful Small Distracted Quiet Samādhi Developed Released	Greedy Angry Deluded Contracted Exalted Surpassed Samādhi Released
Dhammas	5 hindrances 7 awakening-factors	5 hindrances 6 sense media 7 awakening-factors	5 hindrances 6 sense media 7 awakening-factors 4 noble truths
Refrain	Internal/external	Internal/external Shortcomings	Internal/external Shortcomings Rise/fall Knowledge Independence

Theravāda Satipaṭṭhāna Sutta	Sarvāstivāda Smṛtyupasthāna Sūtra	Ekāyana Sūtra	Prajñā-pāramitā
Ānāpānasati 4 postures Comprehension Parts of the body 4 elements Charnel ground	4 postures Comprehension Cutting off thought Suppressing thought Ānāpānasati 4 jhāna similes Perception of light Basis of reviewing Parts of the body 6 elements Charnel ground	Parts of the body 4 elements Oozing orifices Charnel ground	4 Postures Comp. Ānāpānasati 4 elements Body parts Charnel
Happy/pain/neutral Carnal/spiritual	Happy/pain/neutral Bodily/Mental Carnal/spiritual Sensual/Non-sensual	Happy/pain/neutral Carnal/spiritual No mixed feelings	——
Greedy Angry Deluded Contracted Exalted Surpassed Samādhi Released	Greedy Angry Deluded Defiled Contracted Small Lower Developed Samādhi Released	Greedy Angry Deluded Affection Attained Confused Contracted Universal Exalted Surpassed Samādhi Released	——
5 hindrances 5 aggregates 6 sense media 7 awakening-factors 4 noble truths	6 sense media 5 hindrances 7 awakening-factors	(5 hindrances in intro & conc.) 7 awakening-factors 4 jhānas	——
Internal/external Rise/fall Knowledge Independence	Internal/external Knowledge	(Internal/external in introduction only. Body: refrains vary. Feelings, mind, dhammas:) Rise/fall Knowledge Independence Arahantship	Internal/ external Independence

5 By taking just the common material, we end up with a text that, in effect, is much like the Theravāda Abhidhamma Vibhaṅga, minus the special Abhidhamma material. I have shown in the discussion of this text that it is refreshingly free of the anomalies and problems found elsewhere.

6 The *Satipaṭṭhāna Mūla is not mechanically produced by assuming that the concordance of the texts 'must' be the original core. I have considered the internal coherence of the material, intertextual relationships with the rest of the scriptures, cultural and philosophical contexts at the time of the Buddha, evolution of sectarian positions, and so on. Using the concordance of material from all the sources we end up with a text that is internally logical and consistent, fits neatly with the satipaṭṭhāna teachings in the rest of the canon, and closely resembles an existing text.

7 The tradition supplies us with a rational explanation of how the Satipaṭṭhāna Suttas came to be in their current form; that is, they were spoken by the Buddha and preserved word for word by the traditions. That may be so. However, I find it implausible, since the traditional explanation cannot account for the divergences between the existing texts. If I wish to offer an alternative, I should supply a demonstration of how the Satipaṭṭhāna Suttas could have evolved that: 1) is rational; 2) accords with historico-critical methodology; 3) accounts systematically for the existing texts on satipaṭṭhāna; 4) enhances understanding of the subject; 5) allows us to draw inferences about the evolution of doctrine in early Buddhism that may be tested by comparison with other texts; and 6), most important, is useful for practice of Dhamma-Vinaya. I believe this analysis fulfils these criteria.

8 I present my reconstruction in full, without the customary elisions, in order to make it as explicit as possible. First, though, I will briefly run over my reasons for inclusion or exclusion of some particular sections.

9 **Setting:** I think the original setting was at Kammassadamma, but I leave the setting out of the *Satipaṭṭhāna Mūla to emphasize that this material is not really part of the discourse, but was added by redactors.

10 **Audience:** I follow the lead of the Sarvāstivāda and have the discourse addressed to monks and nuns. While the textual support for this is slim, this is a little effort to redress the efects of 2500 years of male redactors.

However, for convenience I retain the male pronoun, despite the slight incongruity that results.

11 **Path to Convergence:** I have doubts about this, as I think the evidence of the Saṁyuttas implies that it was meant for a specifically Brahmanical context, and that is lacking in the *Satipaṭṭhāna Mūla. However, I bow to the agreement of the three main Suttas and include it.

12 **Auxiliary formula:** Although absent from two of the Suttas, I include it because of the agreement of the Abhidhamma texts and the Prajñāpāramitā, and assume that its loss in the Sarvāstivāda and Mahāsaṅghika Suttas was due to abridgement, as indicated in the Sarvāstivāda Saṁyukta.

13 **Internal/external:** I bow to the weight of sources and present the integrated version, rather than following each exercise.

14 **Body contemplation:** I include the simile, which is found in most of the Sutta versions, including the Prajñāpāramitā, and assume its absence from the Ekāyana Sutra is accidental.

15 **Refrain:** All the refrains have their problems, but there is sufficient agreement among the Sutta versions to indicate a common ancestor, though perhaps none exactly reflect that source. The most distinctive common elements are that one establishes mindfulness for knowledge and vision; and one dwells independent, not grasping.

16 **Ending:** I repeat the 'path to convergence', but omit the guarantee of attainment, which is only found in two versions, and could easily have been imported from elsewhere in the canon.

*Satipaṭṭhāna Mūla

17 This is the path to convergence, monks & nuns, for the purification of beings, for surmounting sorrow & lamentation, for ending bodily & mental suffering, for understanding the way, for witnessing Nibbana: that is, the four satipaṭṭhānas. What four?

18 Here, a monk or nun abides contemplating a body in the body internally, he abides contemplating a body in the body externally, he abides contemplating a body in the body internally & externally—ardent, clearly comprehending, mindful, having removed desire & aversion for the world. He abides contemplating a feeling in the feelings internally, he abides contemplating a feeling in the feelings externally, he abides contemplating a feeling in the feelings internally & externally—ardent, clearly comprehending, mindful, having removed desire & aversion for the world. He abides contemplating a mind in the mind internally, he abides contemplating a mind in the mind externally, he abides contemplating a mind in the mind internally & externally—ardent, clearly comprehending, mindful, having removed desire & aversion for the world. He abides contemplating a dhamma in the dhammas internally, he abides contemplating a dhamma in the dhammas externally, he abides contemplating a dhamma in the dhammas internally & externally—ardent, clearly comprehending, mindful, having removed desire & aversion for the world.

19 And how, monks & nuns, does a monk or nun abide contemplating a body in the body?

20 Here, a monk or nun reviews this very body up from the soles of the feet and down from the tips of the hair, bounded by skin and full of many kinds of impurities thus: 'In this body there are head-hairs, body-hairs, nails, teeth, skin, flesh, sinews, bones, bone-marrow, kidneys, heart, liver, spleen, lungs, diaphragm, large intestines, small intestines, contents of the stomach, faeces, bile, phlegm, pus, blood, sweat, fat, tears, grease, spit, snot, oil of the joints, and urine.' Just as if there was a bag with an opening at both ends, full of various sorts of grain, such as hill rice, red rice, mung beans, peas, millet, and white rice, a man with good eyes were to open it up and review it thus: 'This is hill rice, this is red rice, these are mung beans, these are peas, this is millet, this is white rice.' In just the same way, a monk or nun reviews this very body up from the soles of the feet and down from the tips of the hair, bounded by skin and full of many kinds of impurities thus: 'In this body there are head-hairs, body-hairs, nails, teeth, skin, flesh,

sinews, bones, bone-marrow, kidneys, heart, liver, spleen, lungs, diaphragm, large intestines, small intestines, contents of the stomach, faeces, bile, phlegm, pus, blood, sweat, fat, tears, grease, spit, snot, oil of the joints, and urine.'

21 Mindfulness of the body is well established for the sake of knowledge & vision. One abides independent, not grasping at anything in the world. That is how a monk or nun abides contemplating a body in the body.

22 And further, monks and nuns, how does a monk or nun abide contemplating a feeling in the feelings?

23 Here, when feeling a pleasant feeling a monk or nun understands: 'I feel a pleasant feeling.' When feeling an unpleasant feeling he understands: 'I feel an unpleasant feeling.' When feeling a neither pleasant nor unpleasant feeling he understands: 'I feel a neither pleasant nor unpleasant feeling.'

24 When feeling a carnal pleasant feeling he understands: 'I feel a carnal pleasant feeling.' When feeling a spiritual pleasant feeling he understands: 'I feel a spiritual pleasant feeling.'

25 When feeling a carnal unpleasant feeling he understands: 'I feel a carnal unpleasant feeling.' When feeling a spiritual unpleasant feeling he understands: 'I feel a spiritual unpleasant feeling.'

26 When feeling a carnal neither pleasant nor unpleasant feeling he understands: 'I feel a carnal neither pleasant nor unpleasant feeling.' When feeling a spiritual neither pleasant nor unpleasant feeling he understands: 'I feel a spiritual neither pleasant nor unpleasant feeling.'

27 Mindfulness of feelings is well established for the sake of knowledge & vision. One abides independent, not grasping at anything in the world. That is how a monk or nun abides contemplating a feeling in the feelings.

28 And further, monks and nuns, how does a monk or nun abide contemplating a mind in the mind?

29 Here a monk or nun understands mind with lust as 'mind with lust'. He understands mind without lust as 'mind without lust'.

30 He understands mind with anger as 'mind with anger'. He understands mind without anger as 'mind without anger'.

31 He understands mind with delusion as 'mind with delusion'. He understands mind without delusion as 'mind without delusion'.

32 He understands contracted mind as 'contracted mind'. He understands distracted mind as 'distracted mind'.

33 He understands exalted mind as 'exalted mind'. He understands unexalted mind as 'unexalted mind'.

34 He understands surpassed mind as 'surpassed mind'. He understands unsurpassed mind as 'unsurpassed mind'.

35 He understands mind in samādhi as 'mind in samādhi'. He understands mind not in samādhi as 'mind not in samādhi'.

36 He understands released mind as 'released mind'. He understands unreleased mind as 'unreleased mind'.

37 Mindfulness of the mind is well established for the sake of knowledge & vision. One abides independent, not grasping at anything in the world. That is how a monk or nun abides contemplating a mind in the mind.

38 And further, monks and nuns, how does a monk or nun abide contemplating a dhamma in the dhammas?

39 Here, when there is sensual desire in him, a monk or nun understands: 'There is sensual desire in me'. When there is no sensual desire in him, he understands: 'There is no sensual desire in me'. And he understands how the arising of the unarisen sensual desire comes to be. And he understands how the abandoning of the arisen sensual desire comes to be. And he understands how the non-arising in the future of the unarisen sensual desire comes to be.

40 When there is anger in him, he understands: 'There is anger in me'. When there is no anger in him, he understands: 'There is no anger in me'. And he understands how the arising of the unarisen anger comes to be. And he understands how the abandoning of the arisen anger comes to be. And he understands how the non-arising in the future of the unarisen anger comes to be.

41 When there is sloth & torpor in him, he understands: 'There is sloth & torpor in me'. When there is no sloth & torpor in him, he understands: 'There is no sloth & torpor in me'. And he understands how the arising of the unarisen sloth & torpor comes to be. And he understands how the abandoning of the arisen sloth & torpor comes to be. And he understands how the non-arising in the future of the unarisen sloth & torpor comes to be.

42 When there is restlessness & remorse in him, he understands: 'There is restlessness & remorse in me'. When there is no restlessness & remorse in him, he understands: 'There is no restlessness & remorse in me'. And he understands how the arising of the unarisen restlessness & remorse comes to be. And he understands how the abandoning of the arisen restlessness & remorse comes to be. And he understands

how the non-arising in the future of the unarisen restlessness & remorse comes to be.

43 When there is doubt in him, he understands: 'There is doubt in me'. When there is no doubt in him, he understands: 'There is no doubt in me'. And he understands how the arising of the unarisen doubt comes to be. And he understands how the abandoning of the arisen doubt comes to be. And he understands how the non-arising in the future of the unarisen doubt comes to be.

44 When there is the awakening-factor of mindfulness in him, he understands: 'There is the awakening-factor of mindfulness in me'. When there is no awakening-factor of mindfulness in him, he understands: 'There is no awakening-factor of mindfulness in me'. And he understands how the arising of the unarisen awakening-factor of mindfulness comes to be. And he understands how the fulfilment through development of the arisen awakening-factor of mindfulness comes to be.

45 When there is the awakening-factor of investigation of dhammas in him, he understands: 'There is the awakening-factor of investigation of dhammas in me'. When there is no awakening-factor of investigation of dhammas in him, he understands: 'There is no awakening-factor of investigation of dhammas in me'. And he understands how the arising of the unarisen awakening-factor of investigation of dhammas comes to be. And he understands how the fulfilment through development of the arisen awakening-factor of investigation of dhammas comes to be.

46 When there is the awakening-factor of energy in him, he understands: 'There is the awakening-factor of energy in me'. When there is no awakening-factor of energy in him, he understands: 'There is no awakening-factor of energy in me'. And he understands how the arising of the unarisen awakening-factor of energy comes to be. And he understands how the fulfilment through development of the arisen awakening-factor of energy comes to be.

47 When there is the awakening-factor of rapture in him, he understands: 'There is the awakening-factor of rapture in me'. When there is no awakening-factor of rapture in him, he understands: 'There is no awakening-factor of rapture in me'. And he understands how the arising of the unarisen awakening-factor of rapture comes to be. And he understands how the fulfilment through development of the arisen awakening-factor of rapture comes to be.

48 When there is the awakening-factor of tranquillity in him, he understands: 'There is the awakening-factor of tranquillity in me'. When there is no awakening-factor of tranquillity in him, he understands: 'There is no awakening-factor of tranquillity in me'. And he understands how the arising of the unarisen awakening-factor of tranquillity comes to be. And he understands how the fulfilment through development of the arisen awakening-factor of tranquillity comes to be.

49 When there is the awakening-factor of samādhi in him, he understands: 'There is the awakening-factor of samādhi in me'. When there is no awakening-factor of samādhi in him, he understands: 'There is no awakening-factor of samādhi in me'. And he understands how the arising of the unarisen awakening-factor of samādhi comes to be. And he understands how the fulfilment through development of the arisen awakening-factor of samādhi comes to be.

50 When there is the awakening-factor of equanimity in him, he understands: 'There is the awakening-factor of equanimity in me'. When there is no awakening-factor of equanimity in him, he understands: 'There is no awakening-factor of equanimity in me'. And he understands how the arising of the unarisen awakening-factor of equanimity comes to be. And he understands how the fulfilment through development of the arisen awakening-factor of equanimity comes to be.

51 Mindfulness of dhammas is well established for the sake of knowledge & vision. One abides independent, not grasping at anything in the world. That is how a monk or nun abides contemplating a dhamma in the dhammas.

52 This is the path leading to convergence, monks & nuns, for the purification of beings, for surmounting sorrow & lamentation, for ending bodily & mental suffering, for understanding the way, for witnessing Nibbana; that is, the four satipaṭṭhānas.

*
**

53 If this is coming close to the original form of the Satipaṭṭhāna Sutta, what does it tell us about the satipaṭṭhāna method? Textual analysis only takes us so far; the real test is whether the teachings make sense as a way of practice. I've been using this understanding of satipaṭṭhāna in my own practice, and here is how I apply it.

54 Start with the body. This is where we're bound to our most basic drives: sex and food. We try to meditate, but can't stop thinking about our body and its desires. What to do? Walk fearlessly into the lion's den. Plunge into the guts and sinews, the blood and the bones, making the body itself the first object of our meditation. This is not being gruesome or morbid, but trying to understand, accept, and let go of this our fleshly home. We contemplate both the principle of life—the fragile, delicate breath—and the principle of death—a decomposing corpse. The body is a solid and familiar ground of consciousness, less changeable than thought is. So it is an ideal basis for stabilizing the mind. Bring attention to the breath, an image of the parts of the body, or the inner experience of physical properties such as hardness, softness, heat, and cold. Awareness is continually refocused and refined, and the mind sinks deeper and deeper into the chosen object, seeing as if for the first time this body that is habitually obscured beneath our desires, aversions, and fears.

55 The image of the body in our mind becomes very subtle; so subtle that the *mental* aspect of *physical* experience becomes prominent. It was always there, but we didn't notice it. We are moving into the contemplation of feelings. Feelings are notoriously nebulous and changeable: physical feelings tend to be overpowered by the physical impact that stimulates them, and mental feelings are enigmatic and complex. But by treating the contemplation of feelings as emerging from the tranquillising process of body contemplation these problems are minimized. For a time our feelings become more stable, simple, and clear: a subtle and cool sense of rapture and bliss welling up from within the meditation subject. If we are watching the breath, the blissful feeling transforms the breath from lifeless air into a silken, gorgeous flow. If we're contemplating the body parts or elements, they too will become clear, glowing, strangely beautiful.

56 The mind settles further into this bliss, becoming ever more comfortable and trusting. Gradually awareness opens up: the mind *knows* better. In

the contemplation of mind we see how awareness operates under different conditions: burnt up by lust, withered by bitterness, darkened and compressed by sloth. We see how the mind opens up, blossoms, and expands under wholesome influences, so our knowing has more clarity and focus. We become acutely aware of the mind as awareness itself, soft and tender as a flower or a baby, yet at the same time possessed of incredible strength and resilience. At this level of development the mind becomes a thing of unparalleled sensitivity.

57 All this time we have a clear-eyed awareness of the various contrasting feelings and mind-states that are directly present in consciousness. In the contemplation of dhammas we become aware not just of presence, but also of absence; and this is a deeper matter, for in seeing absence one sees impermanence. But then the practice digs deeper still. Investigate *why* the mind like the way it is. What is helpful to meditation, and what is obstuctive? How do these qualities appear, why do we get caught up in unskilful patterns, how can we let go of them?

58 In body contemplation, we apply ourselves to the meditation object. Here, we are basically just following the meditation instructions. Gradually we see the more subtle feelings and mind-states more clearly, and as the practice matures one enters jhāna. At first this will be a hit-and-miss affair. But as we repeat the practice over and over we understand why the mind is sometimes peaceful and sometimes not. As wisdom deepens, samādhi becomes more reliable. These are the central, most clearly and powerfully realized processes in our spiritual consciousness, so they naturally lead to understanding the nature of conditioned experience in general. In the contemplation of dhammas, samatha matures into vipassanā. The whole process is so natural it's misleading to call it a 'method'. One is not deliberately applying an artificial, preconceived scheme; the stages simply signpost the unfolding of meditation.

Chapter 16

SARVĀSTIVĀDA & THERAVĀDA

We now broaden the focus, considering a claim made earlier, that this analysis of satipaṭṭhāna allows us to make testable inferences about doctrinal developments. In this chapter we may consider some unshared, possibly sectarian, material in the discourses of the two main schools whose texts are largely available to us, namely the Sarvāstivāda and the Theravāda, as well some developments in the Abhidhamma period. Historically, then, we are here interested in the Aśokan and following period. The effort is made to incorporate some perspective on how the religion as a whole was evolving in this time. The next chapter will look at the later period of Indian Buddhism.

16.1 Theravāda and Vipassanā

2 We have suggested that the difference in character of the emerging schools is reflected in the different orientation of their versions of the Satipaṭṭhāna Sutta. The Mahā Satipaṭṭhāna Sutta is moving to a proto-abhidhammic stance, where vipassanā is conceived as the systematic analysis of a comprehensive array of phenomena. A similar idea occurs in the Anupada Sutta,[1] which is one of only a few discourses in the Majjhima Nikāya that has not so far been discovered in the existing Āgamas. There, the Buddha praises Venerable Sāriputta, who is especially associated with

1 MN 111.

the Theravāda school, for his practice of analytical insight based on the eight attainments. In addition to the usual jhāna factors, the discourse contains a unique long list of mental factors in strikingly Abhidhammic style; indeed, the Anupada Sutta is one of the key texts which has been invoked by the ābhidhammikas to support the notion that the Buddha, even if he did not actually teach the Abhidhamma Piṭaka itself, at least taught in Abhidhamma style. But the Anupada Sutta is clearly late. It consists chiefly of stock phrases and technical terms; if these are left out there are only a few lines that make up the characteristic vocabulary of the Anupada Sutta. These lines include at least three words suggestive of a late idiom (*anupada*, *vavattheti*, and *pāramī*). In addition, the text is poorly edited. The jhāna factors are listed, as per the usual Sutta idiom, with the conjunctive particle *ca*. But the remaining factors are listed in the Abhidhamma style with no *ca*; they have clearly been inserted from another source.

3 Another example is furnished by the Chachakka Sutta.[2] The Theravāda version is one of the most incisive texts dealing purely with insight in the canon. The elegance of form and profundity of content argue for its authenticity. The six groups of six dhammas that gives the discourse its title are similar to the exposition of the second and third noble truths in the Mahā Satipaṭṭhāna Sutta, suggesting an Abhidhamma leaning. The Theravāda version celebrates the discourse by having 60 monks attain arahantship at the conclusion. This detail is missing from the Sarvāstivāda, which is unsurprising, since the traditions seldom agree in their accounts of attainment while listening to a discourse. Both the setting and the contents of the Sarvāstivāda version display considerable divergence, especially the inclusion of many groups of dhammas dealing with meditation and samādhi practice, thus altering the pure insight orientation of the Theravāda version. The text is far less balanced and elegant, and shows all the signs of a gradual accretion. In fact it has been pointed out by Watanabe that the added factors show strong similarities to the mātikā of the Dharmaskandha.[3]

4 We have referred to the Mahā Hatthipadopama, acknowledging the significance of its mode of presenting the four elements through focussing

---

[2] MN 148/MA 86.

[3] WATANABE, pg. 54.

finely on one aspect of the four noble truths. As one of the weightiest discourses given by Venerable Sāriputta, hailed by the Theravāda and others as the first ābhidhammika, we are not surprised to see that, as with the Anupada Sutta, certain aspects of the teachings suggest an affinity with the Abhidhamma.[4] This discourse is one of the most detailed treatments of the elements in the early Suttas. While the Theravāda and Sarvāstivāda versions are very similar, there are slight sectarian differences. There are some editing anomalies in the Theravāda that imply that the Sarvāstivāda, especially in its general treatment of the external elements, may be a little more reliable. In our current context, we are interested in what appears to be a subtle shift in the samatha/vipassanā balance. Where the Theravāda has Venerable Sāriputta saying that each element is to be contemplated as 'this is not mine...' etc., the Sarvāstivāda lacks this detail.[5] And where both versions encourage one to avoid anger by reflecting on the simile of the saw, the Sarvāstivāda complements this by adding the passage on spreading universal loving-kindness, a detail lacking in the Theravāda.[6] So while both versions acknowledge both samatha and vipassanā there is a slight difference in orientation.

5 Another slight difference may be noticed in the details of how the perceptual process is described.[7] Each gives three conditions for the arising of cognition; but the Sarvāstivāda presents all three as either present or absent together, while the Theravāda presents cases where certain conditions may be either present or absent. This is a unique passage, often quoted, and the elaboration suggests a later, Abhidhammic, development, although the evidence is less strong than in the case of the Anupada Sutta. It would be interesting to see if the specific differences are worked out in the respective Abhidhammas.

6 The sectarian perspectives further emerge in the ending. The Theravāda ends simply by speaking of the ending of greed, anger, and delusion regarding the five aggregates. But the Sarvāstivāda emphasises that such detachment must be towards the aggregates past, future, and present, thus emphasizing continuity in time, the basic thesis of this school.

4 MN 28/MA 30. The following information is from Bhikkhu Anālayo (unpublished essay).

5 MN 28.6.

6 MN 28.9.

7 MN 28.27.

7 Such discourses indicate a growing trend. Not only is there a shift in emphasis from samatha to vipassanā, but the nature of vipassanā itself is changing. The early discourses treat vipassanā as understanding the principles of dhamma, not as accumulating information. They do not treat vipassanā in terms of a comprehensive analysis of an objectively defined set of mind/body phenomena—that is why the ābhidhammikas have supported this idea by invoking these texts. In time, this idea would grow alongside the idea of a path of pure insight that could dispense with jhāna. But here we have merely the beginnings of a long slow process. In fact the Anupada Sutta treats the jhanic experience as intrinsic to the ability to clearly and precisely define each mental factor; in this it preempts the compilers of the Dhammasaṅgaṇī.

8 Such texts were formulated by the Theravādins specifically to authorize their new direction. That is to say, it is not that Theravādin 'dry vipassanā' meditation is authentic because it is taught in the Satipaṭṭhāna Sutta, but that the Satipaṭṭhāna Sutta was assembled in order to authenticate the move towards dry insight. Of course, we should give the teachers of old the benefit of the doubt. They presumably believed they were 'drawing out' the implications of the embryonic Sutta material that they were editing.

9 Having identified this trend, and having pinpointed it to the nascent Theravāda, it can then be used as a precedent. Teachings within the Suttas that are highly analytic and display the Theravādin Abhidhamma style of pedantic, systematic repetitions may be late. Thus our analysis provides us with further interpretive tools.

16.2 Sarvāstivāda and Samādhi

10 If the Theravādin emphasis on vipassanā as evidenced in their recension of the Satipaṭṭhāna Sutta is subtly discernable elsewhere in the Pali canon, so too the Sarvāstivādin emphasis on samādhi is apparent in their Madhyama Āgama. A number of interesting discourses with no Pali cognates deal with jhāna. These texts are so little known that it is worth summarizing them here.

16.2.1 Dependent Liberation

11 MA 44, MA 54, and MA 55 present versions of the doctrinal framework that I call 'dependent liberation', known elsewhere as 'transcendental dependant origination'. The Sarvāstivāda Saṁyukta Āgama includes a saṁyutta comprised of discourses on this theme, most of which in the Pali have been shifted to the Aṅguttara Nikāya. The elements of the framework occur in a whole range of central teachings, yet a full exposition is lacking from the Theravāda Majjhima. It does seem as if this important teaching found less favour among the Elders of the Mahā Vihāra in Sri Lanka. Each of the various versions of the dependent liberation presents a series of factors unfolding in a conditional sequence that culminates in Nibbana. The sequences here are very similar to the Pali, yet have no exact cognate.

12 **MA 44:** Mindfulness & clear comprehension[8] → protection of sense faculties → protection of precepts → non-remorse → gladness → rapture → bliss → samādhi → knowledge & vision of things as they have become → repulsion → fading of lust → liberation → Nibbana.[9]

13 **MA 54:** Honouring and attending upon → approaching → listening to the good Dhamma → giving ear[10] → consideration of the meaning of the Dhamma → learning the Dhamma by heart[11] → recital → reflective acceptance[12] → faith → right consideration[13] → mindfulness & clear comprehension → protection of the sense faculties → protection of precepts → non-remorse → gladness → rapture → bliss → samādhi → knowledge & vision of things as they have become → repulsion → fading of lust → liberation → Nibbana.[14]

---

[8] To help comparison, where the parallels with the Pali are close and obvious I have substituted my own preferred renderings of technical terms for those given by Minh Châu. Here and elsewhere the Chinese regularly has 'right knowledge', evidently reading *sammā ñāṇa* instead of the Pali *sampajañña*.

[9] Cp. AN 5.24, 5.168, 6.50, 7.61, 8.81, 10.3–5, 11.3–5.

[10] Chinese has 'the ear-sphere'.

[11] Chinese has 'receiving and hearing the dhamma'.

[12] Chinese has 'consideration of patience', evidently a mistranslation of *nijjhānakkhanti*. *Khanti* in this sense seems to be misunderstood throughout the Chinese tradition, leading to a distinct shift in meaning in many passages.

[13] Probably *yoniso manasikāra*, 'paying attention to the root'.

[14] Cp. MN 95.

14 **MA 55:** Ignorance → conceptual activities → cognition → name & form → six senses → contact → feeling → craving → grasping → existence → birth → aging & death → suffering → faith → right consideration → mindfulness & clear comprehension → protection of sense faculties → protection of precepts → non-remorse → gladness → rapture → bliss → samādhi → knowledge & vision of things as they have become → repulsion → fading of lust → liberation → Nibbana.[15]

16.2.2 The Teachings of Anuruddha

15 In the Theravāda Majjhima Nikāya, Venerable Anuruddha appears in a few discourses, typically dealing with samādhi, but he only delivers one full-length discourse. The inclusion of three major extra discourses by Anuruddha, the archetypical reclusive meditating sage, suggests that his mode of teaching was more popular in the Sarvāstivāda than in the Theravāda. We have already seen that the two Anuruddha-saṁyuttas differ in this regard, too: the Sarvāstivāda emphasizes samādhi where the Theravāda has vipassanā.

16 **MA 80 (*Kaṭhinadhamma Sutta):** Although this charming story is not found in the Nikāyas, the background events are included in the commentary to Dhammapāda 93. At Venerable Anuruddha's request, Venerable Ānanda organized a group of monks to sew replacements for Anuruddha's worn-out robes. The Buddha noticed the monks sewing, and asked Ānanda why he had not informed him so that he could help in sewing the robes. The Buddha then joined in with the monks to help sew Anuruddha's robes. When they were finished, the Buddha lay down to ease his sore back and asked Anuruddha to speak on *kaṭhina* to the monks. Anuruddha spoke of how he embraced the monk's life, observed the precepts, abandoned the hindrances, developed meditation, attained the four jhānas, and finally the six clear knowledges culminating in arahantship. The Buddha sat up, praised Anuruddha, and encouraged the monks to practice these *kaṭhina* dhammas.

17 **MA 218:** Venerable Anuruddha is asked how a monk is said to die as a noble one. He explained that if one attained the four jhānas one would die

---

[15] Cp. SN 12.23.

as a noble one, but not as absolutely noble. However if one developed the six clear knowledges culminating in arahantship one was said to die with a noble mind that was supreme and absolute.

18 **MA 219:** Similar, but here the question is how to die without distress. Venerable Anuruddha then taught that one who had correct view and the precepts beloved of the noble ones, the four satipaṭṭhānas, the four sublime abidings, and the four formless attainments would die without distress. However, only one who could eliminate the bodily touch (?)[16] and through understanding end the defilements would die absolutely without distress. Here the mention of 'correct view' and 'precepts' echoes the Satipaṭṭhāna-saṁyutta. The four satipaṭṭhānas occur here in place of the four jhānas, as occasionally in the Nikāyas too.

16.2.3 Miscellaneous

19 **MA 176:** Describes four people: one whose meditation was regressing but they thought it was progressing; one whose meditation was progressing but they thought it was regressing; one whose meditation was regressing and they thought it was regressing; and one whose meditation was progressing and who thought it was progressing.

20 **MA 117:** Describes another four kinds of meditators. The following scheme is repeated for each of the eight attainments.

> 21 1) Attained first jhāna but does not hold on to the practice, does not pay attention to the basis,[17] but harbours thoughts connected with desire. They would not stand fast, nor progress, but would regress.
> 2) Attained first jhāna, holds on to the practice, pays attention to the basis, establishes their mind on that dhamma and makes it one-pointed. They would not regress, nor progress, nor become repulsed, but would stand fast with long-lasting samādhi.
> 3) Attained first jhāna but does not hold on to the practice, does not pay attention to the basis, but inclines their mind to the second jhāna, wishing to progress further. They would not regress,

[16] Probably a confusion stemming from the idiom *kāyena phusati*, 'one personally contacts'.
[17] Chinese has 'think of its characteristic', evidently from *nimittaṁ manasikaroti*.

nor stand fast, nor become repulsed, but before long would progress to the second jhāna.
4) Attained first jhāna but does not hold on to the practice, does not pay attention to the basis, but inclines their mind to extinction, calmness, absence of desire. They would not regress, nor stand fast, nor progress, but before long they would experience repulsion and evaporate the defilements.

22 **MA 222:** To understand each of the 12 links of dependent origination one should develop: the four satipaṭṭhānas; the four right efforts; the four bases of psychic power; the four jhānas; the five spiritual faculties; the five spiritual powers; the seven awakening-factors; the noble eightfold path; the ten spheres of totality;[18] the ten dhammas of the adept.

23 So the difference in emphasis, however slight, between the Theravāda and Sarvāstivāda versions of the Satipaṭṭhāna Sutta may also be discerned elsewhere in the early texts. I have been looking for indications in the Nikāyas/Āgamas to support this contention, and as you can see, I have not come up with much. If the difference is genuine, it is minimal. It is a mere shadow of the divisions that were to vex later Indian Buddhism.

24 We might consider whether this divergence reflects something of the religious and philosophical orientations of the emerging schools. There is a range of hints that suggest something of the different characters of the Theravāda and Sarvāstivāda schools: the Theravāda was a more intellectual, scholarly, urban movement, while the early Sarvāstivāda emphasized devotion, meditation, and forest dwelling. It is worth mentioning some of these points, for the scholarly discussion of the Sarvāstivāda has focussed on their later Abhidhamma works and has thus tended to see them as a scholastic movement, which was perhaps not so true for the early school.[19]

25 **1) Patriarchs:** The root patriarch of the Sarvāstivāda is Venerable Mahā Kassapa, who is the archetypal charismatic forest sage, rejecting settled monastic life in favour of the austere life in the jungle. The Theravādins, however, regard as their root patriarch Venerable Sāriputta, renowned for his subtle analytic wisdom, and as a Dhamma teacher second only to

---

[18] *Kasiṇāyatana.*
[19] Most of these points are discussed more fully in MINH CHÂU.

the Buddha himself; the Jains evidently saw him as encouraging the move from the jungle to the village monasteries. This difference is evident even in the Suttas. In the Theravāda version of the Mahā Gosiṅgavana Sutta,[20] Sāriputta and Mahā Kassapa refer to each other with the familiar term *āvuso* ('respected friend'), but in the Sarvāstivādin version[21] Sāriputta addresses Mahā Kassapa as *bhante* ('venerable sir'). This distinction is maintained in the later patriarchs of the Aśokan era. Moggaliputta Tissa of the Theravāda was a master dialectician, skilled in subtle logic and doctrinal niceties, whereas Upagupta of the Sarvāstivāda was a reclusive and eccentric forest sage renowned for his unpredictable teaching methods and his meditative attainments. Time after time, his countless disciples are said to have realized the Dhamma after developing the four jhānas.[22]

26 **2) Sitting cloth:** The sitting cloth is a small mat originally used for sitting meditation in the forest. The Sarvāstivāda Madhyama Āgama frequently describes the monks taking the sitting cloth, folding it, placing it over the shoulder, and going into the forest to meditate. The Theravāda almost always omits this detail; however it is mentioned, interestingly enough, in the famous episode where the Buddha claims he could live on for an aeon.[23] Since this kind of idea is absolutely characteristic of the Sarvāstivāda it is possible that this is evidence of Sarvāstivāda influence on the Theravāda canon. But, as so often, the texts don't allow any simplistic conclusions: the complete Sarvāstivāda version of the Mahā Parinirvāṇa Sūtra in Sanskrit omits to mention the sitting cloth, but the shorter Sanskrit fragment does. Be that as it may, the references to the sitting cloth indicate that the Sarvāstivāda had a preference for forest dwelling and meditation.

27 **3) Compassion:** The four divine abidings are mentioned frequently in both schools, but there are several discourses in the Majjhima where these are mentioned in the Sarvāstivāda but absent in the Theravāda.[24]

28 **4) Miracles:** The Sarvāstivāda Madhyama tends to emphasize the miraculous more than the rather sedate Theravāda discourses. For example, the

---

[20] MN 32.

[21] MA 184.

[22] See e.g. LI , Chapter 8.

[23] DN 16.3.1.

[24] MN 31/MA 185 Cūḷagosiṅga; MN 25/ MA 178 Nivāpa; MN 99/MA 152 Subha.

Theravāda depicts Venerable Raṭṭhapāla as walking from his home to the forest, whereas the Sarvāstivāda have him flying through the air.[25]

29 **5) Devotion:** In the Theravāda texts the monks usually address the Buddha simply as 'bhante', but the Chinese has 'World Honoured One' (*lokanātha*). It is possible, however, that this change occurred with the translation into Chinese. Some of the Sarvāstivāda discourses include exuberant descriptions of the Buddha's appearance, 'reverberating with light like a golden mountain', etc.[26] Also the Bodhisattva theory was at a slightly more developed stage.

30 **6) Early Abhidhamma:** The early strata of the Sarvāstivāda Abhidharma, such as the Dharmaskandha and the Saṅgītiparyāya, retain a more archaic, less specialized mode of analysis than the Theravāda Abhidhamma.

31 This difference reflects the orientation of these emerging schools. The Theravādins, with their vipassanā emphasis, were more scholastic and urban. The Sarvāstivādins were faith-orientated, emphasizing the unpredictable charisma of the forest sage. A similar distinction is recognizable within the modern Theravāda, with the forest monks devoting themselves to samādhi, while their brothers in the city monasteries do dry vipassanā. But it is inevitable that the rugged earnestness of the forest tradition will become tamed and civilized, and will turn away from practice towards study. Sometimes this only takes a generation or two. And so the later Sarvāstivādins went on to develop a vast Abhidhamma commentarial literature, in which, as we shall see in the next chapter, satipaṭṭhāna became just vipassanā.

16.3 The Demon of Time

32 The differences between the Theravāda and Sarvāstivāda Satipaṭṭhāna Suttas, and to a lesser degree the Saṁyuttas, reflect the fundamental schismatic issue that divided these schools—time. The Sarvāstivādins, preferring the evenness and constancy of samatha, shied away from the contemplation of impermanence in satipaṭṭhāna, while the Theravādins emphasized watching the successive passing away of phenomena in experience.

[25] MN 82/ MA 132 Raṭṭhapāla.

[26] MN 75/MA 153 Māgandiya, MN 99/MA 152 Subha.

Vipassanā sees discontinuity in time, samatha sees continuity: taken together, one realizes the relativity of continuity and discontinuity; taken separately one would tend to reify either continuity or discontinuity into an absolute. In these incipient stages the differences were a mere matter of emphasis, not yet consciously articulated. The need for clear and cogent justifications for these divergent approaches was a driving force in the formulation of the metaphysics of time. The Theravādins went on to develop a radical version of the theory of momentariness, holding that each dhamma arises, stays, and passes away in an instant, leaving no remainder in the following instant. The Sarvāstivādins accepted a version of the theory of moments, but they also held the tenet, from which they derived their name, that 'all dhammas—past, present, and future—exist'. The present moment was seen as the manifest or effective mode of phenomena. Thus impermanence is marginalized; ultimate reality is becoming changeless. We have seen hints of this perspective emerging in their Smṛtyupasthāna Sūtra and Dharmaskandha; the Kośa applies the fully-fledged Sarvāstivādin metaphysic of time to satipaṭṭhāna.[27]

33 The origins of this arcane idea should be sought in the emotional response of the Buddhist community to the acute sense of pain and loss with the passing of the Buddha. The Sarvāstivādins keenly felt that they lived in a diminished age, that the glory days of the religion were inexorably passing. As an emotional rather than intellectual issue, it is articulated on the mythic and symbolic level. Their patriarch Venerable Upagupta's role was to halt the passage of time by sustaining the religion.

34 The key myth had him binding Māra, the God of Death, with a rotting carcase slung around his shoulders. Māra could do nothing to remove the stinking corpse, and all his begging left Upagupta unmoved. 'The Buddha,' whinged Māra, 'He never did anything nasty to me like this! All those terrible things I did to him, and never once did he punish me or try to hurt me. You know, he wasn't such a bad guy after all.' And so Māra gained faith in the Buddha. Immediately, Upagupta released his hold and the corpse vanished. Māra, with the fervour of the newly converted, offered to do whatever he could in service of Upagupta, unsurpassed in skilful means. Upagupta said that his only regret was that he had not lived in

[27] Kośa 6.19d.

the time of the Buddha, and had never gazed upon that glorious visage, so sadly passed away. 'But you, Māra,' he said, 'You were alive in the Buddha's time. You saw him often, and must remember his appearance well. And, you are an unequalled master in changing your form. Now may you, out of gratitude to me for releasing you from the ways of evil, assume the appearance of the Supreme Buddha!' Māra was shocked. 'I couldn't do such a presumptuous thing!' he protested. But Upagupta implored and insisted, until finally Māra agreed, on one condition: that when he changed his shape into the Buddha, Upagupta was not, under any circumstances, to bow to him. After all, he's still Māra. Upagupta agreed; but when he beheld the splendour of the Buddha's form created by Māra he could not help himself—overwhelmed with rapture he fell to the ground and bowed before Māra.

35 This brilliant myth relates the poignant dilemmas tearing apart the Buddhist community: the ambiguity of the Buddha-cult, with its worship of idols; and the paradox of longing to preserve forever the Buddha's precious dispensation, a dispensation whose essential message is that all things must pass under the sway of the god of Death and illusion. This ambiguity emerges in the contrast between the Jātakas' emphasis on continuity of character in time, with their yearning for return and personal connection to the 'golden age' of the Buddha, and the atomic, seemingly nihilistic, theories of momentariness in the Abhidhamma schools. There is a widening fracture in consciousness between the popular and scholastic forms of Buddhism.

36 It was in the pan-sectarian folk Buddhism, far removed in spirit from the combative sectarianism of the Abhidhamma scholars, that the Bodhisatta doctrine slowly emerged, with all its momentous implications for Buddhist history. But the Theravāda Abhidhamma scholars, for all their insistence on radical momentariness, betray a nervousness, amounting almost to neurosis, in their obsessively repetitive texts, a massive attempt to freeze the Dhamma in a matrix of abstract, contextless, changeless, and bloodless dhammas.

16.4 The Vibhaṅga's Abhidhamma Exposition

37 We have already examined the treatment of satipaṭṭhāna in the Sutta Exposition of the Vibhaṅga, an early stratum of the Abhidhamma Piṭaka. Now we turn to the second part of the Vibhaṅga's treatment, the Abhidhamma Exposition.

38 This treats satipaṭṭhāna purely as it occurs in the abhidhammic 'transcendental jhāna'. Note that the idea of 'transcendental jhāna' is presented here, quite correctly, as a peculiarly abhidhammic doctrine. So it would be a mistake, according to the Abhidhamma Piṭaka itself, to interpret the Suttas in this way. It has its interest, however, in showing how closely the Theravāda school, at this early stage, equated satipaṭṭhāna with their conception of jhāna. The basic passage is an adaptation of the standard description of transcendental jhāna in the Dhammasaṅgaṇī.

> 39 'How does a monk abide contemplating a body in the body? Here, on the occasion when a monk develops transcendental jhāna—which leads out [of samsara], brings dispersal [of rebirth], for the abandoning of pernicious views, for the attainment of the first stage [i.e. stream-entry]—quite secluded from sensual pleasures, secluded from unskilful qualities, he enters and abides in the first jhāna, which has initial & sustained application and the rapture & happiness born of seclusion, on the painful way of practice with sluggish clear knowledge contemplating a body in the body; on that occasion the mindfulness, recollection ... right mindfulness, awakening-factor of mindfulness, path-factor, included in the path—this is called satipaṭṭhāna. Remaining dhammas are associated with satipaṭṭhāna.'[28]

40 This is repeated with appropriate variations for the various jhānas, stages of enlightenment, etc. Most of the variations are not spelt out in the text. The whole thing is then taken through two rounds—one for the path, one for the fruit. The phrasing is as clumsy in the Pali as in the translation, since the passage is essentially just a conglomeration of technical terms from various sources.

41 There are a number of both continuities and discontinuities with the earlier accounts. The basic descriptions of jhāna and satipaṭṭhāna are identical to the Suttas. The close relation between the two is also characteristic

---

[28] Vibhaṅga pg. 374.

of the Suttas, although they do not equate the two quite as comprehensively as here. The mention of the painful way of practice is clumsy. In the Suttas this is contrasted with jhānas; while it would be a mistake to see this in the context of the Suttas as implying a separate path than jhāna, it is incongruous to call the jhāna itself 'painful'. 'Satipaṭṭhāna' itself is defined just as *sati*; that is, satipaṭṭhāna is simply the subjective act of mindfulness. Other dhammas are 'associated with satipaṭṭhāna'. This seemingly innocuous phrase reveals an underlying tension in the development of a strictly abhidhammic interpretation of satipaṭṭhāna; for 'association' (*sampayutta*) is a technical abhidhamma term that only applies to interdependent mental phenomena, and yet here it is supposed to include the body as well. More on this below.

42 The Theravāda came to interpret the 'transcendental jhāna' discussed here and throughout the Abhidhamma Piṭaka as a single 'mind moment' (*cittakkhaṇa*) flashing by immediately before enlightenment. However, this text should not be read in terms of the atomic theory of moments that came to dominate the later metaphysics. The theory of moments was not yet developed at the time of the Abhidhamma Piṭaka. The only reference to 'moments' in the Abhidhamma Piṭaka is to the 'moment of rebirth' in the Vibhaṅga.[29] There are plenty of contexts in the Abhidhamma that treat time in an everyday sense.[30] As always with the historical method, we should try to interpret, not by looking back through the lens of later tradition, but forward through the lens of earlier tradition. The Abhidhamma Piṭaka was written by and intended for those who were already familiar with the thought-world of the early teachings. The Vinaya Piṭaka begins each passage with 'On that occasion...' (*tena samayena*); the Sutta Piṭaka has 'On one occasion...' (*ekaṁ samayaṁ*); and the Abhidhamma Piṭaka uses 'On whatever occasion...' (*yasmiṁ samaye*). All these idioms treat time in a vague, common sense manner. The difference is not in the duration of time that they envisage, but in that the Suttas and Vinaya are contextual while the Abhidhamma is universal. The Sutta and Vinaya idioms are intended to ground the teachings in time and place, to lend them concreteness and historicity, emphasizing how they are true and useful relative to context. The

---

[29] Vibhaṅga pp. 411*ff*.

[30] E.g. Dhs 597, 636, 642–646, 1115, 1366.

Abhidhamma wants to universalise, de-contextualise as it moves towards a conception of abstract, absolute truth.

43 There is nothing in the description of transcendental jhāna to suggest that it was meant to be applied purely to the moment immediately preceding enlightenment, which was the developed interpretation. On the contrary, the language clearly implies duration; the Pali verb of duration, *viharati* (abides), is mentioned twice. Time is treated in the transcendental jhāna in just the same way as the normal jhāna leading to rebirth. For the Vibhaṅga, 'during' the transcendental 'path', one 'abides' 'contemplating the body', 'cultivating, developing, making much of' a 'way of practice' that may be either 'sluggish' or 'swift', and which 'leads' to enlightenment.

44 'Transcendental jhāna' is not contrasted with 'non-transcendental jhāna' in terms of time, but in terms of object and result. The treatment of result is straightforward—non-transcendental jhāna leads to rebirth, transcendental jhāna leads to enlightenment and dispersal of rebirth.

45 The treatment of object is trickier. For the Dhammasaṅgaṇī, normal jhāna is based on one of the various meditation subjects such as *kasiṇas*, divine abidings, corpses, etc.[31] Transcendental jhāna on the other hand is based on emptiness, signlessness, or desirelessness.[32] But the Vibhaṅga confuses that distinction. The problem arises because the Vibhaṅga wants to apply the idea of transcendental jhāna to the various wings to awakening. Of those groups, satipaṭṭhāna is the only one to specify the object of meditation. It would be difficult to explain how, in the transcendental path and fruit, one was 'contemplating the body', since the object of the transcendental jhāna is supposed to be Nibbana. The later traditions hesitated over this one; the sub-commentary to the Vibhaṅga suggests that the mention of the body, feelings, mind, and dhammas here distinguishes the various satipaṭṭhānas by way of approach.[33] This implies that one is not literally contemplating the body at this point, but that the contemplation

---

[31] Here we see the move towards elevating kasiṇas from obscurity in the Suttas to primacy in the Visuddhimagga.

[32] We have already encountered above a Sutta passage where the signless concentration is clearly distinguished as different from satipaṭṭhāna (SN 22.80), although it is not clear whether these things have the same meaning in the Abhidhamma; the treatment of these meditations in the Suttas is somewhat obscure and variable.

[33] Mūla Ṭīkā Be (1960) to Vibh-A 287; quoted at GETHIN pg. 323.

of the body has been the predominant preparatory factor. This, however, is not what the passage says. The Visuddhimagga addresses the issue thus.

> 46 'When they [i.e. the 37 wings to awakening] are found in a single consciousness in this way [i.e. at the path-moment], just the one mindfulness that has Nibbana as its object is called the "four satipaṭṭhānas" by virtue of its accomplishing the function of abandoning the notions of beauty, etc., with regard to the body, etc.'[34]

47 This is neat; but again, it is not what the Vibhaṅga is talking about. The Vibhaṅga is caught in an awkward developmental stage. It is not clear whether transcendental jhāna is a kind of 'vipassanā samādhi' (if we may borrow still later terminology) where one is absorbed in the contemplation of the body as empty of self, or as an awakening experience. The Dhammasaṅgaṇī has forced a wedge between the non-transcendental jhāna and the transcendental jhāna and identified the path with the latter. But the Abhidhamma Piṭaka remains close enough to the thought-world of the Suttas that it struggles to apply this conception consistently. Not until the fully-fledged metaphysics of the mature commentarial phase of abhidhamma were the implications of this breach made explicit.

48 It hardly needs saying that, apart from the discrete mention of the word 'emptiness', vipassanā is entirely in the background during this exposition. Even 'emptiness' cannot really mean vipassanā here, for it applies just as much to the fruit as to the path. In fact this presentation emphasizes how jhāna is as intrinsic to the very idea of satipaṭṭhāna as it is to the path itself. The compilers of the Abhidhamma seem to have taken to heart the Sutta saying that 'samādhi is the path'.

49 So much the stranger then, that the later idea of transcendental jhāna, which was orthodox from the time of the Visuddhimagga, in time became one of the key conceptual tools used to wriggle out of the necessity for practicing jhāna as part of the eightfold path, substituting dry insight meditation based on satipaṭṭhāna: one only need enter the mind-moment of jhāna at the time of realization itself. This is not only a grave distortion of the Suttas; it is a misunderstanding of the transcendental path. This is simply the perfected path, the culmination and consummation of the various practices that make up our spiritual journey. Transcendental jhāna

[34] Vsm 22.40.

is not a non-jhāna, it is not something else that can be substituted for jhāna; it is the ideal, the quintessence of jhāna, which emerges as the practice of jhāna matures in harmony with the rest of the path.

16.5 Other Abhidhamma Texts

50 To my knowledge, the idea that jhāna might be superfluous from the path is first suggested in the Puggala Paññatti.[35] Although most of the material in this minor Abhidhamma work is derived from the Aṅguttara Nikāya with only slight modifications and is therefore early, here the use of purely abhidhammic doctrines shows that the ideas underlying the Dhammasaṅgaṇī must have been already current when this passage was composed. It describes four people who are mentioned in the Aṅguttara Nikāya.[36] One gains 'samatha of the heart within' but not 'vipassanā into principles pertaining to the higher understanding'. A second person has vipassanā but not samatha, a third has neither, and a fourth has both. The Aṅguttara describes samatha here as steadying, settling, unifying, and concentrating the mind in samādhi, which is similar to the Puggala Paññatti's description as one who gains the form or formless attainments. But whereas the Aṅguttara describes vipassanā as the seeing, exploring, and discerning of activities, the Puggala Paññatti speaks of one who possesses the transcendental path and fruit. This is incongruous—the discourse is quite clearly speaking of the contemplative investigation of conditioned phenomena. For the Suttas, both samatha and vipassanā should be developed and only then will the one enter the path.[37] But if one already has the transcendental attainments, why bother developing mere mundane jhāna? A further incongruity is that the transcendental path and fruit, as we have seen, is invariably described in the Abhidhamma in terms of jhāna, yet here one is able to get the path and fruit without having 'samatha of the heart within'. The passage does not clarify just how one can gain the transcendental jhāna without non-transcendental jhāna; and this omission is made even more pointed when we notice that this short passage follows close behind

[35] PP 4.187.

[36] AN 4.94.

[37] AN 4.170.

a full exposition of the gradual training, presenting jhānas right in the heart of the path, just as in the Suttas.[38]

51 The next discussion of satipaṭṭhāna is in the Kathāvatthu, a polemical work of the Theravāda school dedicated to refuting the wrong views of other schools of Buddhism. This is the latest book of the Abhidhamma Piṭaka. A controversy arises, seemingly due to the ambiguity we noted above between the normal, subjective meaning of satipaṭṭhāna ('the act of establishing mindfulness') and the objective sense in one discourse dealing with vipassanā ('things on which mindfulness is established'). The heretic asserts that all dhammas are satipaṭṭhāna. This view is attributed to the Andhakas (Mahāsaṅghikas), and was also held by the Sarvāstivādins and Mahīśāsakas. The Theravādin quite properly shows the incoherence: the four satipaṭṭhānas only manifest with the arising of a Buddha; if there were no Buddha would all dhammas disappear? If everything is satipaṭṭhāna, then do all beings practice satipaṭṭhāna?

52 The next book to consider is the Paṭisambhidāmagga. This is a treatise on the path of practice from the Theravādin perspective. The style is similar to the Abhidhamma Piṭaka, but it is included in the Khuddaka Nikāya of the Sutta Piṭaka. However its final compilation was around 100 BCE, which makes it later than the bulk of the Abhidhamma Piṭaka. Bhikkhu Nyanatiloka concurs in placing the Paṭisambhidāmagga later than the Abhidhamma. And indeed, the treatment of satipaṭṭhāna bears this out.

53 The section on the body gives a unique list: earth, water, fire, air, head hair, body hair, outer skin, inner skin, flesh, blood, sinew, bone, and bone-marrow. Feeling is simply pleasure, pain, and neutral feeling; thus the 'spiritual feelings' associated with jhāna are not mentioned. Mind is as in the Satipaṭṭhāna Sutta, with the addition of the six kinds of sense cognition; we have already seen that the treatment of *citta* in terms of *viññāṇa* in satipaṭṭhāna signals the shift from samatha to vipassanā. In the corresponding section on ānāpānasati, however, mind is defined with a list of synonyms lifted from the Dhammasaṅgaṇī. Dhammas are all dhammas except body, feeling, and mind; or, in the ānāpānasati section, a list of 201 dhammas derived from the beginning of the Paṭisambhidāmagga. Both of these are similar to the developed conception of dhamma found in

[38] PP 4.177*ff.*

the Mahā Satipaṭṭhāna Sutta, the Dharmaskandha, and the Śāriputrābhidharma. The position of the Paṭisambhidāmagga is thus curiously similar to the heretical view that had been refuted in the Kathāvatthu.

54 The Paṭisambhidāmagga wriggles out of the dilemma by means of an obscure argument. The body (etc.) is an establishing, but is not mindfulness; mindfulness is both an establishing and mindfulness. The solution is a way of avoiding having to admit that the idea of considering the satipaṭṭhānas as objects is really incoherent. It glossess over the fact that 'establishing' and 'mindfulness' are quasi-synonyms;[39] and it runs aground in the context of the fourth satipaṭṭhāna: at least one dhamma is mindfulness, i.e. the awakening-factor of mindfulness. Notice that the contexts that emphasize the samatha aspect of satipaṭṭhāna—most of the Suttas and the Abhidhamma Vibhaṅga—treat satipaṭṭhāna purely as subjective, whereas contexts that emphasize the vipassanā aspect—the Saṁyutta Vibhaṅga Sutta and the Paṭisambhidāmagga—spell out the objective interpretation.

55 The Paṭisambhidāmagga virtually brings to completion the process of 'vipassanizing' satipaṭṭhāna. At first satipaṭṭhāna was primarily samatha, the way of getting jhāna. Then vipassanā was seen to emerge through understanding the process of samādhi in contemplation of dhammas only. Then, for one already well established in all four satipaṭṭhānas, vipassanā was introduced as an advanced mode of contemplating them.[40] The next step was to insert vipassanā after each of the four sections.[41] In the Theravāda Satipaṭṭhāna Sutta it became affixed at the end of each exercise within the four sections. Finally in the Paṭisambhidāmagga, each item in each section ('earth', 'water', etc.) is contemplated from the start in terms of impermanence, suffering, not-self, repulsion, fading away, cessation, and relinquishment. The ultimate outcome of this process would be to marginalize or discard the original four objects of satipaṭṭhāna altogether, abstract the vipassanā aspect of satipaṭṭhāna as constituting the essence of the practice, and treat satipaṭṭhāna purely as contemplation of impermanence, etc., on any miscellaneous phenomena. This step was taken in the next strata of abhidhamma/commentarial literature.

---

[39] See Vsm 20.120.

[40] SN 47.40.

[41] SN 52.2, and to some extent MES.

56 There are a few references to satipaṭṭhāna in the paracanonical work the Peṭakopadesa. This is a treatise on exegetical technique, parallel to the Netti, and of equally uncertain date. Satipaṭṭhāna is regularly treated as vipassanā, using the method of opposing the four satipaṭṭhānas to the four perversions. However, satipaṭṭhāna, or more precisely the second element of the compound, *upaṭṭhāna*, is mentioned under the definition of samatha. The word *paṭṭhāna* is also included; although this is not etymologically the second element of the word 'satipaṭṭhāna', the commentaries treat it as such, so it was probably intended to evoke satipaṭṭhāna here. This is not one of the standard definitions as found in the Dhammasaṅgaṇī or the Paṭisambhidāmagga, and seems to be unique to the Peṭakopadesa. It starts with a series of words formed from √*sthā*, 'to stand'. Here is an attempt to represent the effect in English:

57 > 'Whatever, of the mind, is standing, steadiness, stability, stasis, standpoint [*paṭṭhāna*], establishment [*upaṭṭhāna*], samādhi, concentering, non-distraction, non-dispersal, tranquillity of the heart, one-pointedness of mind; this is samatha.'[42]

58 I'll briefly mention here the Vimuttimagga, a commentarial treatise that was a model for the Visuddhimagga. It only mentions satipaṭṭhāna under ānāpānasati, adding nothing new. However, it introduces a new concept, the path of 'dry vipassanā', which is conspicuous by its absence from the Suttas and its prominence in contemporary meditation. However, this is not connected with satipaṭṭhāna.

---

[42] Peṭakopadesa 6.64.

Chapter 17

LATER BUDDHISM

LET US FINISH OUR JOURNEY with a brief survey of some statements on mindfulness in the later Buddhist texts. The primary interest lies in the lines of continuity between the perspective on satipaṭṭhāna developed in this essay and later traditions.

17.1 The Theravāda Commentaries

2 Material on satipaṭṭhāna is found in the commentaries for the Satipaṭṭhāna-saṁyutta as well as the Satipaṭṭhāna Sutta in the Majjhima and Dīgha, and also the Vibhaṅga. The Satipaṭṭhāna Sutta received an extensive commentary, but since this has been translated into English and the ideas are found in many modern books, I will treat it only briefly here.[1]

3 But first I will glance at the Saṁyutta commentary. Like the material in the Saṁyutta Nikāya/Āgama itself, this is much briefer than the Satipaṭṭhāna Sutta commentary, and has received much less attention. But for this very reason it is of interest.

4 Often the Saṁyutta commentary will give a brief explanation for a particular word or phrase. The Majjhima will repeat exactly the same phrase, but then offer a much more lengthy elaboration. This suggests that the Majjhima commentary represents a later phase of development. Both com-

---

[1] The discourse and commentary, together with extracts from the sub-commentary, have been published in translation by SOMA Thera under the title *The Way of Mindfulness.*

mentaries mention places or people in Sri Lanka, but the Saṁyutta does so less often, leading me to wonder whether it lies closer to the Indian commentary from which the tradition claims it is derived.

5 One passage has a number of Elders giving different opinions as to what 'satipaṭṭhāna', 'awakening-factors', and 'supreme awakening' mean. All the Elders equate satipaṭṭhāna there with vipassanā; but vipassanā is not mentioned in the definition of satipaṭṭhāna at the start of the commentary.

6 The Satipaṭṭhāna-saṁyutta's references to samādhi are explained away using the convenient commentarial terms 'momentary samādhi' and 'threshold samādhi'.

7 Moving on to the Majjhima Nikāya Satipaṭṭhāna Sutta commentary, it subjects each of the aspects of satipaṭṭhāna to a detailed exposition utilizing the fully developed apparatus of the mature abhidhammic and commentarial systems. Similar versions are given for both the Satipaṭṭhāna Sutta and the Abhidhamma Vibhaṅga. The Vibhaṅga commentary offers no explanation as to why the satipaṭṭhāna material there is so much shorter than the Satipaṭṭhāna Sutta; sometimes it refers to Sutta material, as for example when it speaks of the '14 kinds of body contemplation', which probably indicates borrowing from the Sutta commentary.

8 There is strong emphasis on vipassanā throughout; nevertheless, the samatha perspective is not completely neglected. When recommending approaches for different character types, body and feelings are suggested for samatha yogis, while the mind and dhammas are appropriate for vipassanā yogis.[2] But it goes on to contradict itself by asserting that, while the contemplation of the body concerns both samatha and vipassanā, the remaining three deal with pure insight only. The mention of the contemplation of mind as vipassanā-only is incongruous, for the commentary itself agrees that many terms in the contemplation of mind refer to jhāna.

9 In one place, the commentary says that 'mindfulness' means samatha while 'clear comprehension' means vipassanā.[3]

---

2 Pg. 30.

3 Pg. 40.

10 In the discussion on ānāpānasati it says that 'the four jhānas arise in the sign of breathing. Having emerged from the jhāna, he lays hold of either the breath or the jhāna factors [for developing vipassanā].[4]

11 The section on clear comprehension has an interesting piece of advice for over-enthusiastic yogis:

> 12 In this matter, a person who experiences pain in every moment due to standing long with bent or stretched hands or feet does not get concentration of mind, his subject of meditation entirely falls away, and he does not obtain distinction (jhāna and so forth). But he who bends or stretches his limbs for the proper length of time does not experience pain, gets concentration of mind, develops his subject of meditation, and attains distinction.[5]

13 The Sub-commentary adds some interesting points:

> 14 Mindfulness denotes samādhi, too, here on account of the inclusion of mindfulness in the aggregate of samādhi.[6]

> 15 Confusion is the state of mind which, because of the whirling in a multiplicity of objects, is jumping from thing to thing, diverse of aim, and not unified.[7]

> 16 If wisdom is not very strong in the development of concentration there will be no causing of contemplative attainment.[8]

17 Thus the commentary and sub-commentary, although emphasizing vipassanā, recognitize the samatha aspects of satipaṭṭhāna.

17.2 Developments in Sarvāstivāda

18 Venerable Śāṇakavāsin, the preceptor of Venerable Upagupta, the most famous of the Sarvāstivāda patriarchs, was a forest meditator:[9]

---

[4] Pg. 54.
[5] Pg. 97.
[6] Pg. 39.
[7] Pg. 165.
[8] Pg. 166.
[9] Śāṇakavāsin is mentioned in the Pali; Upagupta is unknown. They were regional heroes of Mathura, who were later honored by the Mahāsaṅghika and Sarvāstivādin schools that flourished in the region.

19 'Clothed in hempen robes,
I have attained the five stages of jhāna.[10]
Seated in jhāna among the mountain peaks,
And lonely valleys, I meditate.'[11]

20 Upagupta himself took over Śāṇakavāsin's monastery at Mount Urumuṇḍa, which was called 'the foremost of the Buddha's forest domains, where the lodgings are conducive to samatha.'[12] These sages embodied the austere forest tradition—clad in unkempt hempen rags, living in remote mountains and jungles, unpredictable, sometimes depicted with long hair and beard: feral monks. This lifestyle inspired the early Mahāyāna, which began as a 'back-to-nature' movement of unconventional forest yogis who, as 'bodhisattvas', took as their chief inspiration the ascetic, meditative lifestyle of *the* Bodhisattva. Such reform movements spring up from time to time in reaction to the tendency of religions to urbanize and ossify.

21 A difference in the attitude towards mindfulness in the Sarvāstivāda and Theravāda is evidenced in their respective Abhidhammas. For the Theravādins, mindfulness was an exclusively skilful mental quality; it cannot coexist with unwholesome states of mind. This leaves an inconvenient gap. Despite its claim to systematically list all mental factors, the Theravāda Abhidhamma has no term for memory. If *sati* meant memory, this would mean that one could have no memory of unskilful states of mind, which is, alas, all too obviously not the case. Venerable Nyanaponika was perhaps the first ābhidhammika to notice this anomaly; he suggests *saññā* could perform the role of memory. But while *saññā* has some connection with memory, it is not used in the required sense of 'recollection'. *Saññā* is always present in consciousness, recollection is not.

22 This problematic position of the Theravādins developed out of their wish to exalt the role of mindfulness. The Sarvāstivādins, with no such agenda, were happy to take the Sutta references to 'wrong mindfulness' at their face value and treat *sati* as both good and bad. In general agreement with the Indian traditions, they treat *sati* as the 'not-forgetting' or 'retention' of the object, the, as it were, 'repetition' of the object leading

[10] The 'five stages' of jhāna are the normal four, plus a separate stage between the first and second jhāna that is with *vicāra* but without *vitakka*.

[11] Aśokarājavadāna 1206 [PRZYLYSKI 1923 a:363–364].

[12] Aśokarājavadāna pg. 3 [Strong 1983b:174; PRZYLYSKI 1923 a:363].

to non-distraction. These descriptions suggest the samatha dimension of mindfulness.

23 We have already discussed in some detail the treatment of satipaṭṭhāna in the Dharmaskandha, noting the connections and divergences from the Sarvāstivāda Smṛtyupasthāna Sūtra. While the Dharmaskandha forms the basis for the canonical Abhidhamma of the school, the massive Jñānaprasthāna forms its culmination.[13] This work encompasses all the fields of Abhidhamma within its very broad purview; in this sense it does not have a close analogy in the Theravāda Abhidhamma. It was composed around the close of the canonical Abhidhamma period.

24 The chapter on satipaṭṭhāna contains some verbatim quoting and some commentary. The section on body contemplation is mainly devoted to the four jhānas. This is curious, and certainly shows that this passage is dependent on the Sarvāstivāda Smṛtyupasthāna Sūtra, rather than any pre-sectarian text, or even the Dharmaskandha. The sections on feelings and the mind are also similar to the Sarvāstivāda Smṛtyupasthāna Sūtra. Contemplation of dhammas includes the five hindrances, six sense media with fetters, and seven awakening-factors. Here the content is the same as both the earlier Sarvāstivāda sources, but the sequence is shared only with the Dharmaskandha, while the Sarvāstivāda Smṛtyupasthāna Sūtra places the sense media at the start of this section, which is less convincing. Anyway, we can confirm that the Jñānaprasthāna is based on the existing Madhyama Āgama, which adds another detail to the evidence that this is indeed a Sarvāstivādin collection. Also the Sarvāstivādin emphasis on jhāna as a central part of satipaṭṭhāna, especially body contemplation, continued through this period.

25 This makes the position of our next text somewhat surprising. Frauwallner has an interesting discussion of a Sarvāstivāda text, the Abhidharmasāra of Dharmaśrī. This post-canonical treatise is one of the earliest Abhidharma philosophical systems, and many of its features were taken over by the later Abhidharmakośa and even the Mahāyāna. Here are some of Frauwallner's comments.

> 26 If we now compare these [Sutta descriptions of the satipaṭṭhānas] with Dharmaśrī's description, it is striking that even taking the

---

[13] T26, № 1023.

> concision of the latter into account, there are no individual correspondences. The contemplation of the body as impure, impermanent, suffering, and non-self is important in Dharmaśrī's account as preparation for what follows, but it has no counterpart in the Satipaṭṭhāna Sutta. The treatment of the contemplation of dhammas is also completely different...There is no question [in the Satipaṭṭhāna Sutta] of uniting the objects of all the satipaṭṭhānas and their contemplation as impermanent, empty, non-self, and suffering as in Dharmasri's work. It is, however, important in the latter as preparation for what is to follow. Under these circumstances it would seem justified to regard the use of the satipaṭṭhānas in the new doctrine merely as a means of gaining a canonical starting point with which the new doctrine can be linked and from which it can as far as possible be derived.
>
> 27 ...In the canon, the attainment of the liberating cognition and thus of the elimination of the defilements is premised by entry into the state of jhāna.
>
> 28 In Dharmaśrī's version of the new doctrine there is no mention of this. Without interruption the satipaṭṭhānas, the skilful roots, and the path of vision follow one another without any mention being made of entry into meditation [jhāna]... This is a radical innovation.[14]

29 The only mention of jhāna in the system of the Abhidharmasāra is the 'peak non-transcendental dhamma' (*laukikagrādharma*). This occurs, as 'non-return', 'jhāna-interval', or the four 'root jhānas' for one moment only, immediately prior to the enlightenment experience. Thus, despite the opposing labels, this 'peak non-transcendental dharma' fulfils the same function in the Sarvāstivāda system as the 'transcendental jhāna' of the Theravāda: to maintain a terminological continuity with the old Suttas while teaching a radically new doctrine.

30 It is hard to understand how the treatment of satipaṭṭhāna could have changed so much in such a short time. The major canonical work the Jñānaprasthāna treats body contemplation mainly as the four jhānas; then the earliest strata of post-canonical literature, composed in roughly the same period, treats body contemplation as straight vipassanā. I suspect that the answer lies in the manner and role of the presentation of satipaṭṭhāna within the overall framework, and must be sought in a more detailed contextual study of these works.

---

[14] FRAUWALLNER (1995), pp. 179*ff.*

17.3 The Abhidharmakośa

31 Vasubandhu's classic Abhidharmakośa (4th century CE) presents a clear and thorough description of the field of Sarvāstivāda Abhidharma from the point of view of an author who is not committed to that school, but is a Sautrāntika.

32 The Kośa defines satipaṭṭhāna not as 'mindfulness', but as 'understanding' (*paññā*). The Sarvāstivādins arrive at this definition through taking the term *anupassanā* to express the essence of satipaṭṭhāna. We have seen that the Theravādins agree in taking *anupassanā* as 'understanding', but they still treat satipaṭṭhāna itself as mindfulness, not wisdom.

33 Here the Sarvāstivādins run smack into absurdity. They must conclude that satipaṭṭhāna belongs, not with the path factor of right mindfulness, but with right view; not with the spiritual faculty of mindfulness, but with understanding.[15] The same problem must arise for anyone who equates satipaṭṭhāna with vipassanā—satipaṭṭhāna as faculty, power, awakening-factor, or path factor is always distinguished from understanding, and when the factors are grouped together, it is included with samādhi.

34 However, a closer look suggests that mere terminological confusion is part of the problem. The description of the path according to the Sarvāstivāda, which was later adapted by the Mahāyānists too, falls into five stages: the paths of preparation, reaching, vision, development, and the adept. A very simple summary is sufficient for our purposes. The path of preparation includes all the early stages of the gradual training from learning the teachings, ethics, etc., up to jhāna; the path of reaching is vipassanā; vision is stream-entry; development is the further development of the eightfold path by the noble ones; and the adept is the arahants. In the path of preparation the approach to meditation is exemplified with ānāpānasati for cutting off thinking and the ugliness of the body parts for dispelling lust.[16] These are treated primarily as samatha; ugliness is specifically said to be *not* impermanence, etc.[17] Nevertheless, ānāpānasati is defined as 'understanding'.[18] The definition of ānāpānasati and satipaṭṭhāna

---

[15] Kośa 6.68.

[16] Kośa 6.9.

[17] Kośa 6.11.

[18] Kośa 6.12.

as 'understanding' reflects the very broad treatment of understanding in Sarvāstivādin theory. Jhāna itself is also defined as 'understanding', and is said to have samatha and vipassanā yoked together.[19] Evidently in such contexts we are to take 'understanding' in the sense of 'clear awareness', which we have seen is a prominent theme in these contexts in the Nikāyas/Āgamas too.

35 Strangely, the Kośa says that ānāpānasati is cultivated with neutral feeling, because:

> 36 ...pleasant and painful feelings are favourable to thinking; thus ānāpānasati, which is the opposite of thinking, cannot be associated with pleasure or pain. On the other hand, the two agreeable sensations [rapture & bliss of the jhānas, apparently] form an obstacle to the application of the mind to any object, and ānāpānasati can only be realized by this application.[20]

37 I have no idea how Vasubandhu can come to this conclusion, which seems so different from both the Suttas and from meditative experience.[21] The next section is just as odd. Whereas for the Nikāyas/Āgamas ānāpānasati and body contemplation were part of satipaṭṭhāna, here they are supposed to be just preliminaries.

> 38 We have spoken of the two teachings, the visualization of ugliness and ānāpānasati. Having attained samādhi by these two portals, now with a view to realizing insight... Having realized stilling, he will cultivate the satipaṭṭhānas.[22]

39 Thus satipaṭṭhāna is identified exclusively with insight developed on the basis of jhāna. In this the position of the Kośa is quite different from the Abhidharmasāra, which omits jhāna altogether in favour of vipassanā. This satipaṭṭhāna vipassanā proceeds by seeing each of the four satipaṭṭhānas in terms of their 'intrinsic essence', and also in terms of their general

---

[19] Kośa 8.1.

[20] Kośa 6.12.

[21] The commentary to the Arthaviniścaya, however, evidently takes him seriously enough to offer an explanation: although ānāpānasati is accompanied by equanimity, the meditator turns back the awareness that has air as its object and experiences rapture and bliss. This does not interrupt the practice, since the purpose of the practice is not given up, or since he can regain his object quickly. (See SAMTANI, pg. 102.)

[22] Kośa 6.13–14.

characteristics as impermanent, etc. However the text dwells little on the intrinsic essence, merely defining the body as primary elements and derived materiality, and dhammas as everything that is not the other three; strangely, feelings and mind are omitted. The focus is clearly on the general characteristics, and these are often talked of just in terms of dhammas.[23] Thus satipaṭṭhāna in the Kośa virtually ignores the basic exercises of the Suttas and treats satipaṭṭhāna entirely in terms of the vipassanā aspects. However this is partly a mere change in the expression, for this satipaṭṭhāna vipassanā is undertaken only after samādhi based on ānāpānasati or contemplation of body parts, and so is not 'dry insight'.

40 We can discern echoes of the earlier significance of satipaṭṭhāna too. The four satipaṭṭhānas are said to be undertaken in sequence, for:

> 41 ...one sees first that which is the coarsest. Or rather: the body is the support for sensual desire, which has its origin in the lust for feeling; this feeling occurs because the mind is not calmed, and the mind is not calmed because the defilements are not abandoned.[24]

42 Or in the context of the spiritual faculties:

> 43 In order to obtain the result in which one has faith, one rouses energy. When striving, there is the establishing of mindfulness. When mindfulness is set up, one fixes the mind [in samādhi] in order to avoid distraction. When the mind is fixed, there arises a consciousness that conforms to the object [*paññā*].[25]

44 The exposition on the way of practice in the Kośa falls into confusion when it tries to treat various frameworks such as satipaṭṭhāna and the other wings to awakening as distinct stages along the path, rather than as each offering complementary perspectives on the path as a whole. The Kośa gives two alternative explanations of the progressive development of the 37 wings to awakening. Both of these sequences, however, place the satipaṭṭhānas before samādhi, thus preserving a significant thread of continuity with the early teachings.[26]

---

[23] Kośa 6.14, 15b, 16, etc.

[24] Kośa 6.15; cp. 6.2.

[25] Kośa 6.69.

[26] Kośa 6.70. Similar explanations occur, e.g. Arthaviniścaya commentary (SAMTANI, pg. 99).

45 The Arthaviniścaya Sūtra is an Abhidharma work from a Sautrāntika/Sarvāstivāda affiliation like the Kośa, organized around the now-familiar saṁyutta-mātikā. The Sanskrit has been published together with its commentary. The text presents a straightforward integrated internal/external version of the satipaṭṭhāna formula, without mentioning impermanence.[27] Later, right mindfulness is described in terms of contemplating the impurities of the body, internally and externally.[28]

46 The commentary presents the common scheme of opposing the four satipaṭṭhānas to the four perversions of beauty, happiness, permanence, and self.[29] Contemplating the body, etc., is explained, as in the Kośa, as seeing both the individual and the general characteristics. The general characteristics are impermanence, suffering, emptiness, and not-self (the Sarvāstivāda, from the Āgamas onwards, adds emptiness to the three more familiar in the Theravāda). The individual characteristics are as follows:

Table 17.1: Arthaviniścaya Sūtra

Satipaṭṭhāna	Individual Characteristic
Body	Primary and derived materiality (*bhūtabhautikatvā*)
Feelings	Experientiality (*anubhāvatvā*)
Mind	Beholding (*upalabdhitvā*)
Dhammas	All except those three

47 'Internal' is defined as pertaining to one's own continuum (*santati*), while 'external' pertains to others. The repetitive idiom 'body as body' is explained by saying that it serves to avoid the perverted mind that would arise from seeing 'body' as 'feeling', 'mind', or 'dhamma'. Following the Sarvāstivādin precedent the text says that understanding (*paññā*) is the intrinsic essence (*svabhāva*) of the satipaṭṭhānas. The sequence of the satipaṭṭhānas is explained as the order in which they arise. All in all, the text and commentary add little to our understanding of satipaṭṭhāna, except by showing the influence and consistency of the interpretations of the schools.

[27] SAMTANI, pg. 48.
[28] SAMTANI, pg. 52.
[29] SAMTANI, pp. 96–97.

17.4 Other Early Schools

17.4.1 Bahuśrutīya

48 Richard Gombrich mentions that Harvarman's Satyasiddhiśāstra of the Bahuśrutīya school uses the Susīma Sutta to justify a path requiring a degree of concentration short of jhāna. In this they agree with the Theravāda commentaries; but their position is not justified by the Susīma Sutta itself, in either the Theravāda or Sarvāstivāda versions. The name of this school ('The Very Learned', or 'The Followers of the Very Learned') confirms the correlation between the move towards dry insight and the move out of the forest hermitages into the urban scholastic universities.

49 Nevertheless, it appears that they did not base their conception of the path of dry insight on satipaṭṭhāna. The Satyasiddhiśāstra analyses the 37 wings to awakening as either samatha or vipassanā. It says the first three satipaṭṭhānas are samatha and the contemplation of dhammas is vipassanā. Mindfulness in the faculties, powers, and awakening-factors is also treated under samatha. In this respect this text agrees with the early Suttas, the *Vibhaṅga Mūla, and perhaps, in spirit if not in letter, with the Sarvāstivāda too.

17.4.2 Puggalavāda

50 The Puggalavāda ('Personalist School') was another important early school, whose distinctive doctrine was that there is a 'person' who exists, neither identical with or separate from the five aggregates, who undergoes rebirth, experiences the results of kamma, and who attains final Nibbana. They were condemned by the other schools, who alleged they were reverting to the 'self' of the non-Buddhist teachings. However, they rebutted such claims with vigour, and survived to exert considerable influence on the doctrines of the schools for over 1000 years.

51 Thích Thiện Châu has published a detailed study, *The Literature of the Personalists of Early Buddhism*. Only four of their works survive, all in Chinese translation; one of these is on Vinaya, one deals specifically with their special doctrine of the person, and the remaining two are very similar versions of an Abhidhamma treatise. Effectively, then, we are limited to

one work, known as the Tridharmakaśāstra.[30] This is attributed to a certain Giribhadra of the Vātsiputrīya sub-school of the Puggalavāda, and possibly dates from around the start of the Common Era. It comes together with a commentary of perhaps a few centuries later, and the whole was translated into Chinese by Gautama Sanghadeva in 391 CE.

52 The work first deals with the classic triad of good acts: generosity, ethics, and meditation, the latter being described as the jhānas, divine abidings, and formless attainments. Then it goes on to deal with the skilful roots, acceptance, learning, right thoughts, practice, ascetic practices, sense restraint, and 'access samādhi'. This last term is familiar from the Theravādin commentaries in the sense of an approach to jhāna; but for the Puggalavādins it denotes rather the approach to insight. All these topics are, of course, familiar to all the schools. The next section is on 'means', (*upāya*), which here is a term for the triad of ethics, samādhi, and understanding. Samādhi (here the Chinese translation suggests a Sanskrit original *uttaraśamatha*, 'exalted tranquillity') is said to include three factors of the eightfold path: energy, mindfulness, and wisdom. Mindfulness is defined as the absence of forgetfulness regarding the four satipaṭṭhānas of body, feelings, mind, and dhammas—internal, external, and both internal & external. 'Internal' means 'kammically acquired' (*upadinna*), a mainly abhidhammic technical term denoting this set of aggregates, elements, and sense media that has been acquired as a result of past actions. 'External' refers to others. This practice eliminates greed, anger, and delusion. All of these teachings on satipaṭṭhāna are in perfect accord with the Suttas and the schools.

53 The sectarian perspective of the school, however, is brought out when the text argues that when the Buddha said that 'he contemplates a body in the body', the word 'he' (*so*) refers to the ineffable person.[31]

54 Next the text deals with samādhi, focussing on the triad of 'emptiness samādhi', 'undirected samādhi', and 'signless samādhi'. This set replaces the normal four jhānas here, probably because it is a triad; the title of the work means the 'Treatise of Threefold Dhammas', and the work does indeed subsume much of its subject matter within groups of three. The

[30] San-fa-tu-lun, T 25, № 1506, pp. 15c–30a.
[31] DUTT, pg. 187.

four jhānas were dealt with earlier, where they were listed with the divine abidings and formless attainments, thus making up an extended set of three groups of four dhammas. So the substitution of the three samādhis for the four jhānas here is dictated by the purely formal exigencies of the context (an application of the aṅguttara-principle), rather than a genuine doctrinal shift.

55 Next is the section on wisdom; this is where the sectarian emphasis on the 'person' is prominent. The rest of the work deals with various matters unrelated to our present purpose. However, it is interesting to note that under the topic of 'doubt', there is a comprehensive list of samādhi attainments, all familiar from the early Suttas, and conspicuously lacking the commentarial innovations of 'momentary' and 'access' samādhi.

17.4.3 Chinese Commentaries

56 Leon Hurvitz has published a translation of some Āgama sūtras on satipaṭṭhāna together with cognates from the Pali canon, and Chinese commentaries by Fa Sheng and others. The text gives the first vagga of ten Sūtras in the Sarvāstivāda Smṛtyupasthāna-saṁyukta (Hurvitz adds Pali cognates, not all of which are correct), and then has a discussion that has little to do with the particular texts at hand. The commentaries for the most part agree with the Kośa. Vipassanā is a strong theme throughout, with a special emphasis on dependent origination (which recalls the Śāriputrābhidharma), as well as Abhidhamma-style analysis into 'atoms' and 'moments'. However, one of the commentators is careful to note that right knowledge is produced by samatha.

57 Body contemplation exercises mentioned are ānāpānasati, ugliness, and elements. Initially one is to concentrate one's mind on these internally only; according to one commentator only the perception of ugliness can be developed on the bodies of others.

58 The other objects of satipaṭṭhāna are not specified, except 'dhammas', once more, are defined as perception and conceptual activities. The satipaṭṭhānas as objects is again discussed; the text claims that the Buddha said that 'all dhammas' refers to the four satipaṭṭhānas; since this statement is not found in the existing Nikāyas/Āgamas, it may be discounted. But the text rightly warns of the dangers in this approach:

59 > ...though it is all-inclusive, its fields of perception tend to get out of hand and a certain restriction is needed if the same goal, severance of the defilements, is to be achieved.

60 Here the commentators, more explicitly than the other texts we have seen, treat the contemplation of dhammas as including the other three:

61 'Having entered into the dhammas, he takes a general look,
Beholding identically the marks of the dhammas:
"These four [objects of satipaṭṭhāna] are impermanent,
Empty, not-self, suffering." '

17.4.4 Mūlasarvāstivāda

62 The Mūlasarvāstivāda were said by Warder and others to be a late offshoot of the Sarvāstivāda (*circa* 200 CE), although recent scholars have questioned this.[32] It is difficult to isolate specific doctrinal differences

[32] ENOMOTO suggests that Sarvāstivāda and Mūlasarvāstivāda are really the same. Although this is certainly the case in some of the passages he quotes, his argument is not really convincing. One of his passages, quoted from the Ārya-sarvāstivāda-mūla-bhikṣunī-pratimokṣa-sūtra-vṛtti, says: ' Sarvāstivāda also has the root (*mūla*) and the branches. Of them the root is one, namely Sarvāstivāda. The branches derived from it are seven, namely Mūlasarvāstivāda, Kaśyapīya, Mahīśasaka, Dharmaguptaka, Bahūśrutīya, Taṁraśātiya, and Vibhajyavāda.' This is obviously polemical, aimed at exalting one school over another, and its historical value is diminished accordingly. As it stands, the passage clearly distinguishes between Sarvāstivāda and Mūlasarvāstivāda. What it seems to be claiming is that the Sarvāstivāda is the real root (*mūla*) school, and those Mulasarvāstivādins, who pretend to be the root, are just a branch. Enomoto goes on to say that the Mūlasarvāstivāda Vinaya, which is different from the other Sarvāstivāda Vinayas, should be recognized as not belonging to a distinct school, but to a sub-sect of the Sarvāstivādins. This distinction between a sub-sect of a school and a closely related derived school is arbitrary, and we need to simply accept that the notion of what constitutes a 'school' is not clear-cut. There is also much textual evidence left unconsidered by Enomoto. For example, the mātikā of the Mulasarvāstivādins mentioned in their Vinaya, while also based on the saṁyutta-mātikā, has no specially close relation with the topics of the Dharmaskandha. Others suggest that the Mūlasarvāstivāda is really the same as the Sautrāntika. This, too, I find implausible, though I have not examined the arguments in detail. The Mūlasarvāstivāda Vinaya has Mahā Kassapa reciting the mātikā at the First Council. It is implausible that the Sautrāntikas, whose primary tenet was that the Suttas alone represent the word of the Buddha, should have thus endowed the Abhidhamma with mythic authority, something even the Theravāda Vinaya does not do. Moreover, another of the Sautrāntika's key doctrines was to deny the existence of dhammas in the three times, insisting on a radical version of the momentariness theory. Again, it is

from the Sarvāstivāda, and it may be that their main innovations were literary rather than doctrinal. They composed long and elaborate texts in the fashionable style of the contemporary Mahāyāna sūtras. Their Saddharmasmṛtyupasthāna Sūtra (sometimes called the Mahā Smṛtyupasthāna Sūtra) takes advantage of the trend towards expansiveness that had already begun in the treatment of satipaṭṭhāna by the early schools.[33] As well as offering much doctrinal and meditative material it includes various descriptions of heavens and hells and also refers to the arts, painting, and theatre. Thus it popularises the topic, placing satipaṭṭhāna within the contemporary cultural movements of the day. Indeed, some scholars have seen in one of the late Chinese translations of this work the influence of the Kasmirean version of the Rāmāyana. I have not been able to locate the Sanskrit text, but in a cursory survey of the Chinese I cannot find the satipaṭṭhāna pericope or any of the special features of the Satipaṭṭhāna Sutta. I have found the following interesting passage.

> 63 When the time of death is approaching, he sees these signs: he sees a great rocky mountain lowering above him like a shadow. He thinks to himself: 'The mountain might fall on top of me', and he waves with his hand as though to ward off this mountain. His brothers and kinsmen and neighbours see him do this; but to them it seems that he is simply pushing his hand out into space. Presently the mountain seems to be made out of white cloth and he clambers up this cloth. Then it seems to be made out of red cloth. Finally, as the time of death approaches, he sees a bright light, and being unaccustomed to it he is perplexed and confused. Because his mind is confused he sees all sorts of things such as are seen in dreams. He sees his future father and mother having sex, and seeing them a thought crosses his mind, a perversity arises in him. If he is going to be reborn as a man, he sees himself having sex with his mother and being hindered by his father; or if he is going to be reborn as a woman, he sees himself having sex with his father and being hindered by his mother. At that moment the intermediate existence ends, life and consciousness arise, and

---

implausible that anyone calling themselves Sarvāstivāda, whether 'Mūla-' or otherwise, should reject the chief tenet of the school.

[33] T № 721/T № 722.

> causality begins once more to work.[34] It is like the imprint made by a die; the die is then destroyed, but the pattern has been imprinted.[35]

64 While the style and subject matter might seem far removed from the early Satipaṭṭhāna Suttas, the passage still retains an urgent interest in the questions of life, death, and causality. In fact the connection between satipaṭṭhāna and understanding rebirth is already implicit in the Saṁyutta Nikāya, where the causes of the four satipaṭṭhānas may all be explained in terms of dependent origination. Probably the key link is the term 'confusion'. Mindfulness, the antidote for confusion, prepares us for death, the most important moment of our life. The whole process sounds remarkably similar to samādhi experiences. The bright light appears like a samādhi *nimitta*; this unexpected and unknown experience often causes confusion and fear in inexperienced meditators. Then various signs and visions appear. If the dying person or the meditator loses mindfulness and becomes distracted, the hindrances such as desire and anger arise, here exposed in their most stark, Oedipal form. As far as I know, Buddhism is the only religion that explicitly recognizes the Oedipal situation. This and other aspects of this passage are found in the 'Tibetan Book of the Dead', and was possibly a source text for that work. The illustration of rebirth with the simile of the die is also found in Visuddhimagga 17.166, which is interesting, since by the time of the compilation of these texts, the two traditions had already been separated for seven hundred years.

17.5 The Mahāyāna

65 It will be fitting to conclude this survey with some details from the treatment of satipaṭṭhāna in the main Indian schools of Mahāyāna. First, however, we may briefly look at how the pair of samatha and vipassanā is treated in Mahāyāna meditation in general. The Mahāyāna texts emphasize the complementary nature of samatha and vipassanā, where the

[34] So the translation; but no school of Buddhism, to my knowledge, has ever taught that causality does not operate during the period between lives. Presumably the original referred to the start of a new cycle of dependent origination, or something of that sort.

[35] Saddharmasmṛtyupasthāna Sūtra 34 (quoted in *The World's Great Religions*, pg. 63, published by Time Inc., 1957). French translation by LIN.

Theravāda emphasizes their difference. This reflects the difference in philosophical orientation between the schools. The Theravāda, emphasizing the method of analysis, tends towards an ontology of pluralistic realism, and thus sees samatha and vipassanā as essentially different 'things', while the Mahāyāna, emphasizing the method of synthesis, tends towards a monistic (or 'holistic') idealism, and thus sees samatha and vipassanā as contributing to a greater whole.

66 Here are some quotes from a collection of essays edited by Minoru Kiyota under the title *Mahāyāna Buddhist Meditation* .

> 67 ...[some speak] of a 'dry vipassanā', in other words, a vipassanā without samatha, even though the presence of samatha is held to be an indispensable condition for all vipassanā. (pg. 47)
>
> 68 The perfect union of these two, mental stabilization and higher vision (*samathavipassanāyuganaddha*) is the immediate aim of Buddhist meditative practice, for all the paths of Buddhism—whether Hīnayāna or Mahāyāna including Vajrayāna—depend on this coupling. (pg. 47)
>
> GESHE SOPA
>
> 'Śamathavipaśyanāyuganaddha: The Two Leading Principles of Buddhist Meditation.'

> 69 From the very beginning, it has been generally accepted that the higher reach of wisdom (*paññā*) is attained either through or accompanied by meditation (jhāna, samādhi, and so on). Examples of this idea can be seen in various formulæ such as 'the pairing of quietude and insight' (*samathavipassanāyuganaddha*), and in the last two of the 'three disciplines' (*sīla-samādhi-paññā*), the 'five faculties' (*saddhā-viriya-sati-samādhi-paññā*), and the 'six perfections' (*dāna-sīla-khanti-viriya-jhāna-paññā*).
>
> GADJIN M. NAGAO
>
> ' "What Remains" in Śunyatā: A Yogacāra Interpretation of Emptiness', pg. 66.

> 70 Meditation, the basis of the third kind of wisdom, is practiced in the following way: (1) by mastering samatha or the tranquillization of the mind through the observation of moral and yogic rules, nine stages of samatha, four jhānas, and so on; then (2) by vipassanā (analysis of the object of meditation from the point of view of what has been studied by investigation).
>
> YUICHI KAJIYAMA
>
> 'Later Mādhyamakas', pg. 135.

71 > ...this cognition, nonerroneous and free from conceptualization with respect to an ultimately real object, depends on a principal cause, which is samatha intimately conjoined with vipassanā.
>
> CHARLENE MCDERMOTT
> 'Yogic Direct Awareness', pg. 149.

72 > Now, in Indian Buddhism, vipassanā is an exercise in the close scrutiny of the characteristics of the skandhas, dharmas, and other compounded elements, and it is supposed to be done in conjunction with exercises in tranquillity (samatha) or stilling the externally directed activities of the mind. (pg. 178)
>
73 > In commenting on the [Heart] sūtra passage, "O Sāriputta, form is not different from emptiness, emptiness is not different from form", he [Fa-tsang] first says that when one sees form as identical with emptiness, one perfects the practice of samatha, and when emptiness is contemplated as identical with form, one perfects the practice of vipassanā, and he concludes that when the two are practiced together, they are ideal. (pg. 179)
>
> FRANCIS H. COOK
> 'Fa Tsang's Brief Commentary.'

74 > ...the practice of transferring merits is guided by insight (vipassanā), and insight by meditation (samatha). In the Upadeśa, worship and praise [earlier identified as samatha] are the instruments to purify the mind; vow and meditation [= vipassanā] refer to the state which has realized pure mind. The two are not distinct and apart.
>
> MINORU KIYOTA
> 'Buddhist Devotional Meditation', pg. 259.

75 Thus most of the essays in this collection speak of the harmony of samatha and vipassanā. These fundamental aspects of meditation are reinterpreted in accord with the particular perspective of the school.

76 A good example of this is in the treatment of the Heart Sūtra above. The Heart Sūtra boldly confronts us with a series of statements that, on the face of it, appear paradoxical. In order to make sense of these enigmas, the commentator brings in the more familiar, readily comprehensible teachings on samatha and vipassanā. This does a number of things: it explains the new and radical by showing connections with the already known; it invokes basic Buddhist concepts, thus reassuring us that the Heart Sūtra does not really mean to destroy Buddhism; and it points out that the Heart

Sūtra is meant to inspire practice, not philosophical speculation. Perhaps most importantly, the presentation of the commentator is clearly intended to demonstrate at length that the relationship between samatha and vipassanā is integrative, rather than divisive, and he works from this basis to show the integrative nature of the Heart Sūtra teachings as well. (The text does this with much more thoroughness than the short quote above.)

77 Several of the passages quoted above speak of 'samatha conjoined with vipassanā', a phrase derived from a discourse by Venerable Ānanda.[36] This says that all those who say they are enlightened do so in one of four ways: samatha preceding vipassanā; vipassanā preceding samatha; samatha conjoined with vipassanā; or else the mind is seized with restlessness, but later becomes settled in samādhi. Practicing in each of these ways, the path is born, then cultivated to enlightenment. These four options all involve a balance of samatha and vipassanā, and rule out any approach that would try to dispense with samatha altogether. Yet the passage treats each option as equal and does not, as the Mahāyāna interpretations above do, praise 'samatha conjoined with vipassanā' as superior to the other options. So these interpretations emphasize the integrative approach even more than the early Suttas.

78 Let's continue with some sayings from a few Mahāyāna writings.

79 The persevering practice (of satipaṭṭhāna) is called 'samādhi'.

NĀGĀRJUNA
Letter to a Friend.

80 He who has established mindfulness as a guard at the doors of his mind cannot be overpowered by the passions, as a well-guarded city cannot be overcome by the enemy.

AŚVAGHOṢA[37]
Saundarānanda Kāvya.

81 ... constant mindfulness
Which gains in keenness by devoted zeal
And zeal arises if one comes to know
The greatness that lies in inner stillness.

ŚANTIDEVA
Śikṣāsamuccaya, Kārikās 7–8.

---

[36] AN 4.170/SA 560.

[37] Aśvaghoṣa was probably not a Mahāyanist, but his works were renowned in the schools.

82 If an excessive preoccupation with external activities has been avoided with the help of mindfulness & clear comprehension, then, thanks to them, the mind can steadily keep to a single object as long as it wishes.

Śantideva
Śikṣāsamuccaya.

83 Thus these great teachers all acknowledge the samādhi aspect of mindfulness. We have already seen that the great Prajñāpāramitā Sūtra, the cornerstone for all Mahāyāna philosophy, contains an exposition on satipaṭṭhāna inserted almost unchanged from the Satipaṭṭhāna Sutta of an early school. We may now examine a few other Mahāyāna Sūtras in their treatment of satipaṭṭhāna.

84 One of the important early collections of Mahāyāna Sūtras is the Mahā Ratnakūṭa (translated as *A Treasury of Mahāyāna Sūtras*). One of the discourses contained therein, translated under the title 'Sūtra of Assembled Treasures', has a short passage on satipaṭṭhāna, included as part of a long list of various dhammas.

85 The four mindfulnesses cure clinging to body, feelings, mind, and dhammas. One who practices the Dharma and contemplates the body as it really is will not be trapped by the view of a real self. One who contemplates feelings... mind... dhammas as they really are will not be trapped by the view of a real self. These four mindfulnesses, therefore, cause one to abhor the body, feelings, mind, and dhammas, and thereby open the door to Nibbana.[38]

86 Here the vipassanā aspect is emphasized. The passage is not directly derived from the early satipaṭṭhāna pericope. The emphasis on not-self is familiar from the Suttas, although not in the context of satipaṭṭhāna. The attitude of abhorring (*nibbidā?*) comes across as over-strong, although this may be just the translations. The early Suttas have a more balanced approach, embracing both the attractive (breath, pleasant feelings, purified mind, awakening-factors, etc.) and unattractive (charnel ground, painful feelings, defiled mind, hindrances) aspects of experience within satipaṭṭhāna. This strong negativity is surprising given the Mahāyāna's reputation for a non-dualistic approach, but this is just one passage.

[38] Chang, pg. 399.

87 The Avataṁsaka Sūtra is one of those vast, sprawling Mahāyāna Sūtras that finds a place for almost everything. The 26th chapter, in a discussion of the ten stages of the Bodhisattva's progress, describes the fourth stage as 'Blazing', and includes a list of dhammas, including our familiar 37 wings to awakening, starting as usual with the satipaṭṭhāna formula.[39] This is the integrated internal/external formula, with the standard auxiliary formula. It is identical with the pericope at SN 47.3/SA 636/MA 76*, the only change being the substitution of 'bodhisattva' for 'bhikkhu'. Again we see the use of straightforward 'cut-&-paste' insertions from the early Suttas even in such an advanced Mahāyāna scripture.

88 Santideva's Śikṣāsamuccaya, which I have quoted from briefly above, includes many powerful statements on satipaṭṭhāna, in part collected from other Mahāyānist works. Many of the passages are collected in Nyanaponika Thera's widely available *The Heart of Buddhist Meditation*, so there is no need to repeat them here in detail. Suffice to note the inclusion of sectarian material, continuing the trend of using the prestige of satipaṭṭhāna to buttress one's position in the energetic doctrinal debates that characterize much of Buddhist history. The text quotes the Ārya Ratnacūḍa Sūtra, giving a characteristically Mahāyānist slant on the internal/external contemplation of feelings.

> 89 When experiencing a pleasant feeling he conceives deep compassion for beings whose character is strongly inclined to lust, and he himself gives up the propensity to lust. When experiencing an unpleasant feeling he conceives deep compassion for beings whose character is strongly inclined towards hatred, and he himself gives up the propensity to hatred. When experiencing a neutral feeling he conceives deep compassion for beings whose character is strongly inclined to delusion, and he gives up the propensity to delusion.

90 The contemplation of body includes a very powerful passage from the Dharmasaṅgīti Sūtra. This includes an attack on the Sarvāstivāda doctrine of time:

> 91 This body did not come from the past and will not go over to the future. It has no existence in the past or the future except in unreal and false conceptions.

[39] CLEARY, pg. 729 (one-volume edition), V^OL 2, pg. 41 (two-volume edition).

17.5.1 The Samādhi of Meeting the Buddhas of the Present

92 A more interesting development is found in the Pratyutpannabuddhasammukhāvaṣṭhitasamādhi Sūtra, which means 'The Discourse on the Samādhi of the Direct Encounter with Buddhas of the Present'. I will refer to it more economically as the 'Buddhas of the Present Sūtra'. Here I condense the main passages dealing with satipaṭṭhāna.[40]

93 [18B] 'Further, Bhadrapāla, Bodhisattvas who dwell contemplating a body in the body, but do not think any thoughts (*vitakka*) connected with the body, and who dwell contemplating feelings... mind... dhammas, but do not think any thoughts connected with feelings... mind... dhammas—those Bodhisattvas obtain this samādhi [i.e. the samādhi of the sūtra's title]. Why is that, Bhadrapāla? It is because if Bodhisattvas and Mahāsattvas [practice satipaṭṭhāna in the way described], then they do not objectify any dhammas... they do not conceptualize or think discursively... they do not see any dhammas... that is known as unobscured cognition. Bhadrapāla, it is precisely unobscured cognition that is called samādhi. Bhadrapāla, the Bodhisattvas who possess this samādhi see immeasurable and incalculable Buddhas, and they also hear the True Dhamma. On hearing it they master it. They also obtain the unobscured cognition and vision of liberation and the unimpeded cognition of those Tathāgatas, Arahants, Perfect Buddhas.

94 [18C] 'Further, Bhadrapāla, Bodhisattvas dwell contemplating a body in the body, and in doing so do not see any dhammas whatsoever. Not seeing them they do not conceptualize or think discursively, even though they are neither blind nor deaf. Similarly as regards feelings, mind, and dhammas. Not seeing them they are not dependent; not being dependent they cultivate the path; by virtue of having cultivated the path they have no doubts with regard to dhammas; and being without doubts they see the Buddhas. And in seeing the Buddhas, by virtue of the fact that all dhammas are unproduced, liberation occurs.

95 [18D] 'Why is that, Bhadrapāla? If Bodhisattvas should adopt the perception of dhammas, that itself would be for them the false view of an object of apprehension (*upalambhadṛṣṭi*). That itself would be the false view of existence, of a self, a being, a soul, a person. That itself would be the false view of aggregates, elements, sense media,

[40] The Sanskrit of the satipaṭṭhāna formula from this sūtra is at chapter 11.67.

> signs, existing things, causes, conditions, and the seizing of an object of apprehension.'[41]

96 The basic formula is adapted from the Dantabhūmi Sutta,[42] including the special phrase, 'does not think thoughts connected with the body, etc.' Readings vary between 'body' (*kāya*) and 'sensual desires' (*kāma*). In the Dantabhūmi Sutta the context does not clarify the meaning; even though the interpretation might change, still both readings make sense. But in the Buddhas of the Present Sūtra the text unambiguously depends on the meaning 'body' (etc.). The fundamental purpose of practicing in this way is to attain samādhi, just as, in the Dantabhūmi Sutta, the practice leads on to the jhānas.

97 Here it is emphasized that one with such samādhi does not 'objectify' or become 'dependent' on any dhammas. As we saw in the discussion on satipaṭṭhāna in the Prajñāpāramitā, the idea of lacking 'dependence' suggests the 'independence' of the Satipaṭṭhāna Sutta. The argument is a standard Mahāyāna criticism of the Abhidhamma schools, who took the dhammas as being really existent 'things'. Thus wrong views about dhammas are said to be just as mistaken as wrong views about a self. The implication here is that one who merely thinks about dhammas will misconstrue them, mistaking the intellectual understanding of the teachings for true wisdom into the emptiness of all phenomena. Satipaṭṭhāna is enjoined in order to overcome the thinking mind so that one can 'see' without 'views'.

98 It is fascinating to see how the schools can take the same texts and develop them in quite opposite ways. For in the Theravāda, satipaṭṭhāna was to become more and more a matter of seeing these ultimately existing dhammas, and one is instructed to 'think thoughts connected with the body [etc.]' through the habit of mental noting.

99 Another intriguing aspect of the Buddhas of the Present Sūtra is the statement that one in such a samādhi will see immeasurable Buddhas. This is a new innovation in satipaṭṭhāna, and is the central theme of the discourse. The meditation on the Buddha in the early discourses is one of the six 'recollections' (*anussati*), and the use of this term shows the connection with satipaṭṭhāna. The seeing of the Buddhas appears to be a

---

[41] Harrison, pp. 144, 145.

[42] MN 125/MA 198.

kind of meditation vision or *nimitta*. The text then says that one will 'hear the True Dhamma. On hearing it they master it.' This points to the belief that one can, in a state of meditative concentration, hear the Buddhas teach the authentic Dhamma, a Dhamma which is to be learnt by heart.

100 Here we have evidence on the disputed question of the origin of the Mahāyāna Sūtras. The Mahāyāna Sūtras claim to have been spoken by the Buddha, although this is historically impossible. Are we to believe that the Mahāyanists were so unscrupulous as to deliberately forge new texts and palm them off as authentic? There are a number of general things to be kept in mind here: the ancient world, including the early Buddhists, did not have such an individualistic insistence on ownership and authorship of works; editing of the early Suttas had been ongoing, thus making people accustomed to a somewhat fluid idea of what the canon was; and, most pertinently for this context, the Mahāyāna philosophy was breaking down the distinction between the inner, subjective world and the outer, objective world, thus paving the way for imagination to be considered as moreor-less on a par with historical facts. The desire to include new Sūtras as authentic developed hand-in-hand with this anti-historical world view, hence the mythic settings of the Mahāyāna Sūtras. According to the Buddhas of the Present Sūtra, the Mahāyāna monks were inspired by meditative visions and interpreted these as stemming from the Buddha in some mystical sense. Even the title of the Sūtra suggests this. It has the word *sammukha*, literally meaning 'face to face', which is a familiar early idiom emphasizing that one has heard a teaching in the immediate presence of the Buddha himself: 'Face to face with the Blessed One have I heard this, face to face I have learnt it.'[43]

101 It is not uncommon today, even among Theravādins, for meditators to see a vision of the Buddha, hear his teaching, accept it as authentic, and to teach it to others as the Buddha's teachings. Such 'inspired' teachings can be straightforward re-statements of Buddhist doctrines, insightful elaborations, or mildly eccentric reformulations; but sometimes they are just mumbo-jumbo.

102 The status and meaning of meditative visions is further explained elsewhere in the Buddhas of the Present Sūtra, again relying on satipaṭṭhāna,

[43] E.g. MN 123.3/MA 32.

here the exercises in charnel-ground contemplation. The passage is not exactly the same as the Satipaṭṭhāna Sutta, yet it clearly depicts the same practice.

> 103 [3J] For example, Bhadrapāla, when a monk performing the meditation on ugliness sees in front of him corpses—bloated... livid... putrefied... bloody... gnawed... with the flesh peeled off... with no flesh and blood... white... shellcoloured... become skeletons—then those corpses have not come from anywhere, nor have they gone anywhere, they are not made by anyone, nor are they made to cease by anyone. Yet, Bhadrapāla, by that monk's mastery of mental focussing he sees the skeleton lying in front of him.
>
> 104 In the same manner, Bhadrapāla, in whatever quarter Tathāgatas, Arahants, Perfect Buddhas might dwell, those Bodhisattvas who are supported by the Buddha and established in this samādhi concentrate their minds on that quarter in order to obtain a vision of the Buddhas. By concentrating their minds on that quarter they see the Tathāgatas, Arahants, and Perfect Buddhas in that quarter. Why is that? Namely, Bhadrapāla, this obtaining of a vision of the Buddhas is a natural outcome of this samādhi. Bodhisattvas who are established in this samādhi see the Tathāgatas, and they appear to them through the combination and concurrence of these three things: the glory (*ānubhāva*) of the Buddha, the application of the force of their own wholesome potentialities, and the power from attaining samādhi.[44]

105 The visualization of the Buddhas is said to be an imaginative exercise just the same as the visualization of a corpse. The shocking analogy between the Buddha and a rotting corpse might be an accident of the text; the corpse meditation may have been chosen as example merely because it is one of the clearest examples of a meditative exercise in visualization. Yet there is a poignancy to the juxtaposition, for by the time the Buddhas of the Present Sūtra was written, the historical Buddha had long since become the Buddha of the Past; the living presence had become a corpse, combusted in the flames of impermanence. The meditative visualization of the Buddha was perhaps the most potent of the many means developed by the Buddhist faithful to resurrect the Buddha, to preserve the vital force of the Teacher and his Teachings. In this way the meditation on the transience of life is transformed.

---

[44] HARRISON, pg. 41.

17.6 Yogacāra

106 Now let's examine mindfulness in some of the methodical treatises, starting with the Yogacāra school. They were a meditative school whose distinctive philosophy is usually said to be the assertion that 'mind only' exists, all else is illusion. This opens them up to the criticism that they are reverting to the Upaniṣadic position of postulating consciousness as the ground of being, which is equated with Nibbana; however the early Yogacārins such as Vasubandhu and Asaṅga stated that even the underlying 'storehouse consciousness' ceases in Nibbana.[45] Actually, the early Yogacārins were not idealists; they emphasized how the mind forms the world as experienced, but didn't say that nothing exists outside the mind.

17.6.1 Asaṅga

107 A key figure was Asaṅga, who lived in the 4th century CE in North-West India.[46] He was Vasubandhu's brother and converted him from Sautrāntika to Yogacāra. Asaṅga was inspired by Maitreya, the Bodhisattva currently dwelling in Tusita heaven awaiting rebirth to become a Buddha. His major work was the massive Yogacārabhūmiśāstra, but here we will consider the more manageable Abhidharmasamuccaya. This was described as 'an extremely important work of the Mahāyāna Abhidharma. It contains nearly all the main teachings of the Mahāyāna, and can be considered a summary of all the other works by Asaṅga. The method of treatment of subjects in this work is the same as the traditional method found in the texts of the Pali Abhidhamma which preceded it by several centuries, such as the Dhammasaṅgaṇī, Vibhaṅga, and Dhātukathā: posing a question and answering it.'[47] It is not just the 'Q & A' format that is reminiscent of the early Abhidhamma: the first part treats the aggregates, elements, and sense media, using Abhidhamma methods such as *saṅgaha* ('grouping') and *sampayoga* ('conjunction'); the second part treats the four noble truths, including the path in detail; so these two parts together are similar to the

---

45 Nevertheless, Vasubandhu makes a couple of casual references to Nibbana as the true Self. Viṁśatikā-kārikā-vṛtti 10c (ANACKER pg. 166).

46 BOIN-WEBB, pg. xvii.

47 BOIN-WEBB, pg. xviii.

saṁyutta-mātikā. Although the text is strongly defensive of the Mahāyāna perspective, it mostly deals with matter familiar from the early Suttas, strongly influenced by the Sarvāstivāda/Sautrāntika.

108 Mindfulness is first mentioned under a general list of 52 mental factors described under the umbrella of the aggregate of activities. While the list is fairly ad hoc, the sequence just at this point is reminiscent of the Suttas: mindfulness, samādhi, understanding. I give the definitions for mindfulness and samādhi:

> 109 'What is mindfulness? It is non-forgetting by the mind (*cetas*) with regard to the object experienced. Its function is non-distraction.
>
> 110 'What is samādhi? It is one-pointedness of mind on the object to be investigated. Its function consists of giving a basis to knowledge (*jñāna*).'[48]

111 These are the most useful succinct definitions of these terms I have come across. 'Non-forgetting' regarding an object that has already been experienced emphasizes the sustained observation of *anupassanā*. 'Nondistraction' is the basic function of samatha; here it recalls such contexts as satipaṭṭhāna as the 'path to convergence', the 'basis for samādhi', and so on, and particularly ānāpānasati in its function of non-distraction. And while mindfulness gives rise to samādhi, samādhi in its turn has the proper function of giving rise to wisdom.

112 The path is described, in a way similar to the Kośa, as starting with the gradual training: ethics, sense control, moderation in food, putting forth effort, clear comprehension, etc., and also the wisdom from hearing, thinking, and meditating. Samatha and vipassanā are mentioned without explanation. Next is a lengthy analysis, again leaning heavily on the Sarvāstivāda, of the process leading to the vision of the four noble truths. Then the 'path of development' is explained, largely consisting of the 37 wings to awakening, treated exclusively as applying to the noble disciples (in Theravāda terminology the 'transcendental path'). The explanations of satipaṭṭhāna are clear and straightforward, offering some interesting new perspectives. I will summarize the key aspects.[49]

---

[48] BOIN-WEBB, pg. 9.
[49] BOIN-WEBB, pp. 160–162.

113 **Objects:** Body, feelings, mind, dhammas; 'things relating to oneself'.
Intrinsic essence: Understanding and mindfulness.
Companion: Associated mind and mentality.
Development: Contemplation of a body in the body, etc., internally/externally/internally-externally.
Internal: Internal material sense media.
External: External material sense media.
Internal-external: The external sense media, which are the seats of the sense faculties, and which are linked to the internal sense media; and also the internal material spheres pertaining to others.

114 The first explanation for internal-external relates the internal to the external, and suggests a synthetic interrelationship. The second half of this explanation suggests that the internal spheres of others are external for oneself, and so taken together they are 'internal-external'. These explanations differ somewhat from the Theravāda.[50] Internal-external feelings, etc., are described as feelings, etc., produced by the internal-external body. The most interesting aspect is the contemplation of the 'body in the body': 'contemplation of the identity (or similarity, *samatāpaśyanā*) of the natural image of the body (*prakṛtibimbakāyasya*) with the imagined counter-image of the body (*vikalpapratibimbakāyena*).' This refers to the development of a visualized reflex-image in meditation, known in Theravāda as the 'counterpart sign' (*paṭibhāganimitta*). This appears as a reflective mirror-image of the body, or of a part of the body such as the breath, in the period immediately preceding full absorption. Although this is readily comprehensible, it is not at all clear how a similar explanation would apply to the other satipaṭṭhānas. The text offers no help, merely saying that the contemplation of feelings, etc., should be understood the same way.

115 The treatment of the five spiritual faculties and powers acknowledges that each factor supports the next, including mindfulness as support for samādhi.[51] In the discussion of the noble eightfold path it is said that 'right effort is the factor that dispels the impediments of the [major] defilements

[50] See CDB, note 1, pg. 1397.
[51] BOIN-WEBB, pg. 166.

(*kleśa*), right mindfulness is the factor which dispels the impediments of the minor defilements (*upakleśa*), right samādhi is the factor which dispels the impediments to the qualities of distinction.'[52] In this the text demonstrates its close reliance on the early texts, visible even among the many later elements.

116 There is another interesting passage on satipaṭṭhāna in Asaṅga's Śrāvakabhūmi, which is the section of the Yogacārabhūmiśāstra that deals with the training of the 'disciples', in other words, early Buddhism. We have already seen that the contents of the contemplation of mind here is identical with the Sarvāstivāda Śrāmaṇyaphala Sūtra. The contemplation of the body is, however, very different from the Suttas, listing 35 of the most diverse kinds of 'body'. As usual, the satipaṭṭhānas are said to be opposed to the four perversions. Then the text offers an original reflection on the differences between the four satipaṭṭhānas:

117

> Another method is: where one does the action; the purpose for which [one acts]; who does the action; and by what does one act. Comprising all that in brief, the four satipaṭṭhānas are established. Therein: in the body one acts; for the sake of feeling; by the mind; by way of skilful and unskilful dhammas.[53]

118 The 'skilful and unskilful' dhammas can only be the hindrances and awakening-factors, not the aggregates and sense media, so this passage harks back to the original content of contemplation of dhammas.

17.6.2 Vasubandhu

119 Stefan Anacker's 'Commentary on the Separation of the Middle from the Extremes' offers a translation of the Madhyāntavibhāgabhāṣya, which is, according to the translator, 'one of the most striking works in the Mahāyāna literature'. It is a commentary by Vasubandhu[54] on verses attributed to 'Maitreyanātha'.

---

[52] BOIN-WEBB, pg. 168.

[53] WAYMAN, pp.97–98.

[54] Frauwallner's postulation of 'two Vasubandhus' has been vigorously contested by ANACKER (pp. 7*ff.*), but defended by others; suffice to note that Vasubandhu's Abhidharmakośa is from the Śrāvakāyana (Sarvāstivāda/Sautrāntika) perspective, while the Madhyāntavibhāgabhāṣya is Mahāyāna (Yogacāra).

120 Following the Sarvāstivādin precedent the text tries to rationalize the traditional order of the wings to awakening as a progressive sequence (whereas for the Suttas the order is not essential to the groups and simply organizes the sets according to numbers for the sake of convenience). There is an attempt to equate the four satipaṭṭhānas with the respective noble truths; this section has a refreshingly simple description of the contemplation of dhammas: 'lack of confusion as regards dhammas that serve to afflict and dhammas that serve to alleviate.'[55] This is identical with the conception of contemplation of dhammas we have seen in the early material. Having accomplished this, one is supposed to undertake the four right efforts, and then develop samādhi through the four bases of psychic power. There is considerable discussion on various obstacles to meditation and antidotes; mindfulness is defined in agreement with the schools as 'the lack of loss of image, etc. of the meditation object.'[56] Elsewhere the function of mindfulness is as antidote to 'secondary afflictions' because of 'the absence of slackness and excitedness in mindfulness which is well-established in the preparatory causes for samatha, etc.'[57] Next, continuing the sets of the wings to awakening, arise the five spiritual faculties:

> 121 Having taken hold of faith, one undertakes energy, the result of this cause. Having undertaken energy, mindfulness occurs, and through mindfulness having occurred, the mind enters samādhi. When the mind is in samādhi, one knows as it is.[58]

122 Here we are firmly in Sutta territory. The difference between the spiritual faculties and spiritual powers is explained in terms of progressive stages of the path according to the Sarvāstivāda system; and then the awakening-factors and the noble eightfold path arise in due order.

---

55 MVB 4.1. Anacker has published an earlier, partial translation of this work in under the title 'The Meditational Therapy of the Madhyāntavibhāgabhāṣya' in Kiyota, and a revised full translation under the title 'Commentary on the Separation of the Middle from the Extremes' in ANACKER. In order to assist readers who may have access to one or other of these works, I give references to the divisions of the text rather than page numbers; these are, however, not quite consistent in the two versions. The references usually refer to the commentary on the numbered verses.

56 MVB 4.5b.

57 MVB 4.11a.

58 MVB 4.7.

123 Although the above treatment is basically similar to the Kośa, now the text asserts three features distinguishing Mahāyānist satipaṭṭhāna:[59]

> 124 1) The object of meditation for disciples is their own bodies, etc., while the bodhisattvas' is both their own and others.

125 This is wrong; as we have seen, all texts from the Suttas on acknowledge both internal and external contemplation.

> 126 2) Disciples contemplate the impermanence, etc., of the body, etc., while bodhisattvas practice non-apprehension [of bodies, etc.].

127 This refers to the fundamental philosophical division between the Abhidhamma schools and the Mahāyāna: the ābhidhammikas, especially the Sarvāstivādins, tended to treat the dhammas as real entities that possessed the characteristics of impermanence and so on. But the 'Emptiness School' (to which the author belonged) held that a dhamma, like a magical illusion, 'does not exist as it appears, with the state of possessing apprehended [objective] and apprehendor [subjective] aspects, but yet it doesn't not[60] exist, because of the existence of the illusion itself.'[61] This is the most important and complex philosophical dispute in later Indian Buddhism. Suffice to say here that, in my opinion, the ābhidhammikas ventured significantly beyond the Suttas in their ontological reification of dhammas; but the 'emptiness' reaction by and large did not distinguish between the doctrines of the Suttas and the ābhidhammikas, and hence tended to stigmatise all of the followers of early Buddhism as naïve realists. So this criticism, while it may have been pertinent in a certain context, does not apply to those simply following the Suttas.

> 128 3) Disciples cultivate satipaṭṭhāna for the sake of non-attachment to their bodies, etc., while bodhisattvas practice neither for lack of attachment nor for non-lack of attachment, but for Nirvana which has no abode.

129 This requires some interpretation, for of course all schools of Buddhism practice for 'Nirvana which has no abode'. Presumably this is intended to refer to Buddhahood, the ultimate goal of the Mahāyāna schools. Mere

---

[59] MVB 4.12b.

[60] ANACKER's earlier translation omits the second 'not'.

[61] MVB 5.17.

non-attachment is perhaps thought to lack compassion. No doubt a similar point is being made here as when the text says that studying, reflecting on, and teaching the sūtras of the Great Vehicle only is of great fruit, not of the Inferior Vehicle, since the Great Vehicle is distinguished because of its kindness to others.[62] It is the old cliché about the selfishness of the disciples. Given how emphatically the Mahāyāna stigmatized the early schools as selfish, there must have been some truth to the accusations, in certain places and times. But it is naïve to apply this to all early Buddhists; I can do no better than to quote the words of the Master.

> 130 'I will protect myself,' monks: thus should the satipaṭṭhānas be practiced. 'I will protect others,' monks: thus should the satipaṭṭhānas be practiced. Protecting oneself, monks, one protects others; protecting others, one protects oneself.
>
> 131 And how is it, monks, that by protecting oneself one protects others? By the cultivation, development, and making much [of the four satipaṭṭhānas]. It is in such a way that protecting oneself one protects others.
>
> 132 And how is it, monks, that by protecting others one protects oneself? By patience, harmlessness, loving-kindness, and sympathy. It is in such a way that protecting others one protects oneself.[63]

17.7 Mādhyamaka

133 The other main Indian Mahāyāna school was the Mādhyamaka. They arose earlier than the Yogacāra, but here I treat them later, as the only relevant work of theirs that I have access to is later than the Yogacāra works discussed above. Whereas the Yogacāra were better known as a contemplative school, the Mādhyamaka were renowned for their witheringly sophisticated dialectic. However, they did not neglect meditation; the Bhāvanākrama of Kamalaśīla was a meditation manual of the Mādhyamaka school of Śantarakṣita that seems to have been prepared for introducing meditation to the newly converted Tibetans. This work was studied in an essay by Yuichi Kajiyama titled 'Later Mādhyamakas'.

---

[62] MVB 5.9, 10.
[63] SN 47.19.

17.7.1 Bhāvanākrama

134 The general path is described in the usual way as first mastering the scriptural and theoretical aspects, then developing samādhi culminating in jhāna and formless attainments before undertaking vipassanā. As in the Yogacāra account it is acknowledged that only on the vipassanā level is there any significant divergence from the early schools. What is truly remarkable is that the course of vipassanā is derived from the doctrinal evolution of the schools through history. One is to meditate on ultimate reality as conceived by each of the main schools, then to realize that this level of reality is empty, and pass to higher, more subtle perspectives, culminating, of course, in the ultimate emptiness of the Mādhyamaka. Thus one's individual consciousness evolves in reflection of the collective consciousness. Even more remarkable, these stages of evolution clearly parallel the four satipaṭṭhānas, even though the satipaṭṭhānas are not invoked. Here I will quote from Kajiyama's summary.

> 135 In the foregoing sections taken from Kamalaśīla's Bhāvanākrama, four stages are plainly distinguishable:
>
> 136 1) The preliminary stage in which external realities admitted in the systems of the Sarvāstivāda and Sautrāntika are presented as the object of criticism;
>
> 137 2) The stage in which only the mind with manifested images is admitted—the system of the Satyākāravāda-Yogacāra school forms the object of meditation;
>
> 138 3) The meditation stage in which the objects of cognition as well as the duality of subject and object are condemned as unreal and in which the knowledge without duality is proclaimed to be real—this being the standpoint of the Alīkākāravāda-yogacārin.
>
> 139 4) The stage in which even the non-dual knowledge or the pure illumination of cognition is declared to be empty of an intrinsic nature. This latter stage is the highest one proclaimed by the Mādhyamaka.'

140 The first stage sees the dhammas as substantial entities, paralleling the contemplation of the body. The second stage admits the 'features' or objects of the mind, paralleling the contemplation of feelings, which are the most prominent properties of the mind. The third stage only admits cognition itself, corresponding to the contemplation of the mind. And the last sees only pure emptiness, which is defined as 'dependent origination',

just as the contemplation of dhammas focuses not on seeing the dhammas in and of themselves, but as a matrix of conditions.

141 The parallelism is both undeniable and significant. The sequence of the four satipaṭṭhānas embodies a natural progression, from coarse to fine, that can be discerned in experience. Like so many other Buddhist teachings it is a simple but extremely subtle paradigm that is reflected in any number of manifestations. As such, for those steeped in the teachings there is a tendency, whether conscious or not, to assimilate the principles, abstract them, and apply them in contexts quite removed from the original. This helps to discern continuities and relationships, but it demands a corresponding re-assertion of the original context if we are not to be cut adrift from our mooring.

17.7.2 Meditation on Emptiness

142 To examine the role of mindfulness in later Tibetan Buddhism, which is primarily derived from the Mādhyamaka, I will rely on the modern scholarly work *Meditation on Emptiness* by Jeffrey Hopkins. This is based on a variety of sources, including Indian Buddhist texts, Tibetan treatises, and oral teachings by contemporary Tibetan monks. Here, mindfulness is treated exclusively in the mode of samatha. The basic descriptions of mindfulness expand on Asaṅga's definition given above.

> 143 Mindfulness is non-forgetfulness with respect to a familiar phenomenon; it has the function of causing non-distraction. Mindfulness has three features:
>
> 144 **1) Objective feature:** a familiar object. Mindfulness cannot be generated towards an unfamiliar object.
>
> 145 **2) Subjective feature:** non-forgetfulness within observation of that object. Even though one might have become familiar with that object previously, if it does not presently appear as an object of mind, mindfulness cannot occur.
>
> 146 **3) Functional feature:** causing non-distraction. Since the stability of the mind increases in dependence on mindfulness, non-distraction is specified as the function of mindfulness.
>
> 147 ...all achievements of samādhi in Sūtra and tantra are attained through the power of mindfulness.[64]

[64] HOPKINS, pg. 247.

148 > 'Right mindfulness: constant attentiveness to objects of awareness and to modes of perception of those objects necessary for ascending the paths.'[65]

149 Hopkins presents some charts summarizing the Tibetan conception of the stages in the development of samatha. Here is a list of five faults in samatha together with their remedies.[66]

Table 17.2: Faults and Remedies of Samatha

Faults	Remedies
Laziness (*kausīdya*)	Faith (*śraddhā*), desire (*chanda*), effort (*vyāyāma*), tranquillity (*prasrabdhi*)
Forgetting the instructions (*avavādasammoṣa*)	Mindfulness (*smṛti*)
Slackness (*laya*) and restlessness (*auddhatya*)	Clear comprehension (*samprajanya*)
Lack of application (*anabhisaṁskāra*)	Application (*abhisaṁskāra*)
(Over-)application (*abhisaṁskara*)	Equanimity (*upekṣā*)

150 Most of these are sensible enough, although tranquillity as remedy for laziness is a bit incongruous. Mindfulness appears in its old sense of 'memory'.

151 The following list, which is to be read from the bottom up, also places mindfulness among the factors developing samatha.[67]

152 1) Concentration (*samādhāna*)
2) One-pointedness (*ekotikaraṇa*)
3) Strong peace (*vūpaśamana*) *saṁsāra*)
4) Peace (*śamana*)
5) Control (*damana*)
6) Close setting (*upasthāpanā*)
7) Re-setting (*avasthāpanā*)
8) Continuous setting (*samsthāpanā*)
9) Setting the mind (*cittasthāpanā*)

---

[65] HOPKINS, pg. 289.
[66] HOPKINS , pg. 72, chart 2.
[67] HOPKINS , pg. 81, chart 3.

153 The nine aspects of samatha are identical to the definition of samatha in the Abhidharmasamuccaya, and have obviously been taken from there or from a related source.[68] However, in the early source there is no implication that sequence of the terms are meant to describe the progress in meditation. They are simply a list of synonyms for samatha in typical Abhidhamma style. Some time later they were re-interpreted as stages in mediation by reading arbitrary meanings into the terms.

154 The most interesting are the four terms at the basis of the nine aspects of samatha. They culminate with *upasthāpanā* (= *upaṭṭhāna*), the second member of the compound satipaṭṭhāna (*smṛtyupasthāna*). The first three terms are all from the same root, and have been derived from *upasthāna*.[69] Little can be inferred from the prefixes used to distinguish these terms. The emphasis is on the root meaning of 'standing, stability, steadiness', three English words also ultimately derived from the same Indo-Aryan root √*sthā*. 'Setting', or 'establishing', or 'placing' the mind on the object, firmly, repeatedly, continuously, is the way to unification.

---

[68] BOIN-WEBB, pg. 170.

[69] The Theravāda Abhidhamma definition of samatha similarly includes a series of terms derived from √*sthā*; this has the same prefixes in the same order (*ṭhiti*, *saṇṭhiti*, *avaṭṭhiti*).

AFTERWORD

I WOULD LIKE TO FINISH by recapping a few important areas where the GIST and the history of mindfulness intersect.

2 The first thing to notice is the value of seeing the Buddhist scriptures in their historical and cultural context. In some cases this leads us to secure conclusions, which we could not have reached relying on the Buddhist sources alone. A good example of this is the analysis of *ekāyana*, where both the Pali and the Chinese sources seem to be unsure of the meaning, but the Upaniṣadic context is very revealing.

3 This case also reaffirms the necessity to examine the Saṁyutta as the prime source. From the Satipaṭṭhana Sutta itself we would have no idea that the phrase *ekāyana* had any Brahmanical connection, but the Saṁyutta clearly suggests this.

4 Our studies have also emphasized the crucial importance of a holistic approach to study of the Dhamma. We cannot treat individual limbs as if they have nothing to do with the greater organism. The holistic paradigm must stem from the four noble truths, and the dhamma categories that are most directly derived from the four noble truths. Any serious study along such lines will inevitably end up back at the Saṁyutta before too long, since this is where most of the core doctrines are found. Thus we have treated satipaṭṭhāna, not as the 'only way', but as the *seventh* factor of the *eightfold* path. The Satipaṭṭhāna Sutta is no more—and no less—than an elaboration of this stage of the path.

5 While the doctrinal centrality of the Saṁyutta must force itself upon the student, we have also made the more radical claim, following Yin Shun, that the Saṁyutta also constitutes the historically oldest strata

of Buddhist scriptures, and have even suggested that this collection was current during the Buddha's lifetime, and was the prime work codified at the First Council. This does *not* mean that everything in the Saṁyutta is early and authentic and everything else is late and inauthentic. It simply means that the saṁyutta material is likely, on average, to be early, and the accretions are mainly restricted to editorial repetitions, etc., rather than doctrinal expansion. Nevertheless, we have noted several instances where the Saṁyutta shows slight sectarian influence.

6 This holistic approach also reaffirms the necessity for comparative studies. When we turn attention away from the more obvious sectarian differences and look more closely at the central teachings, the similarities between the traditions are outstanding. We have mostly dealt with the Pali and Chinese sources, since this is where most of the early scriptures are found. However, the Tibetan canon, though lacking the actual texts, is still based on the Āgama sūtras, which are regarded as canonical within that tradition. It is rather a shame that those inspired by the Tibetan tradition remain largely unaware and unappreciative of the historical sources from which their teachings and practices ultimately stem.

7 We have used our appreciation of the central role of the Saṁyutta to reassess the Satipaṭṭhāna Sutta. A cursory examination of the various versions shows that there is a real problem to be resolved. While we can certainly go a long way with straight comparative study of the existing versions, at several points the saṁyutta connections give crucial assistance. Thus, in deciding whether the satipaṭṭhāna auxilliary formula was standard in the Sarvāstivāda as in the Theravāda, the Satipaṭṭhāna Suttas are useless, and the key is only provided by a little footnote in the Chinese translation of the Saṁyutta. Again, it is the Saṁyutta that confirms the original specification of contemplation of dhammas.

8 While stressing the importance of the pre-Buddhist environment, we have also acknowledged the significance of considering the later sources. The pre-Buddhist sources tell us of the Buddha's audience, his language, the kinds of issues and ideas he was addressing. But we can't forget that the fact that the early Suttas exist at all is due to the efforts of the schools; and the ideas and agendas of the schools can hardly be expected to leave no imprint at all on the scriptures. In some cases this is merely the echoes

of the technologies and languages of the times; in other cases we find significant doctrinal developments.

9 It is the later accretions in the Satipaṭṭhāna Sutta—specifically, the vipassanā refrain and the addition of the aggreggates, sense media, and truths to the contemplation of dhamma—that are most emphasized in later works, almost to the point of ignoring the authentic material. Nevertheless, we repeatedly find, across the schools, that important aspects of satipaṭṭhāna are remembered and explained accurately. Thus we cannot agree fully with the traditionalists, who assert that the commentarial tradition of their own particular school has got it all wrapped up, nor with the radical modernist reformers, who opine that the traditions are just a mass of error, better disposed of. Rather, a careful evaluation of the traditions in the light of the Suttas shows they have much to teach us about the Suttas, and even when they are in error they show us how the living communities adapted the Dhamma to their situation.

10 Dhamma never lives in a vacuum. Differences in meditation techniques, divided precisely along the lines of samatha versus vipassanā, are among the most divisive issues in Buddhism. We invest a lot in our meditation, a lot of time, a lot of effort, a lot of pain; and so we attach, much more deeply than to mere theory. Differences in approach and emphasis to meditation hardens into dogma as to who's got the right 'system', and the interpretation of doctrine is then shaped to suit, with a strident insistence on one's own take on 'ultimate reality'.

11 This being so, an approach to meditation that emphasizes the essential harmony and complementariness of samatha and vipassanā should be a healing force. We can appreciate the various approaches to meditation without insisting on any one of them as absolute and sufficient for everyone. In this we would be following in the tolerant footsteps of the Buddha.

> 12 'What, Bhante, does "one who abides in Dhamma" refer to?'
>
> 13 'Here, a monk studies the Dhamma—*sutta, geyya, vyākaraṇa, gāthā, udāna, itivuttaka, jātaka, abbhūtadhamma, vedalla.* He does not waste his days with that Dhamma he has studied, he does not neglect retreat, he is devoted to tranquillity (*samatha*) of the heart within. Thus, monk, a monk is "one who abides in Dhamma".

14 'Thus, monk, I have taught you the monk who studies a lot, the one who teaches a lot, the one who thinks a lot, and the one who abides in Dhamma. I have done for you what should be done by a Teacher seeking the welfare of his disciples out of compassion. Here, monk, are roots of trees, here are empty huts. Practice jhāna, monk! Do not be negligent! Do not regret it later! This is our instruction to you.'[70]

[70] AN 5.73.

ABBREVIATIONS

AN	Aṅguttara Nikāya
BU	Bṛhadāraṇyaka Upaniṣad
CDB	Connected Discourses of the Buddha (Saṁyutta Nikāya translation)
CU	Chāndogya Upaniṣad
DA	Dīrgha Āgama
Dhp	Dhammapāda
Dhs	Dhammasaṅgaṇī
DN	Dīgha Nikāya
EA	Ekottara Āgama
Iti	Itivuttaka
Kośa	Abhidharmakośabhāṣya
LDB	Long Discourses of the Buddha (Dīgha Nikāya translation)
MA	Madhyama Āgama
MBh	Mahā Bhārata
MLDB	Middle Length Discourses of the Buddha (Majjhima Nikāya translation)
MN	Majjhima Nikāya
MVB	Madhyāntavibhāgabhāṣya
PP	Puggala Paññatti
PED	Pali-English Dictionary (Pali Text Society)
SA	Saṁyukta Āgama
SED	Sanskrit-English Dictionary (Monier-Williams)
Skt MPS	Sanskrit Mahā Parinirvāṇa Sūtra
Skt CPS	Sanskrit Catuṣpariṣat Sūtra
Skt SPS	Sanskrit Śrāmaṇyaphala Sūtra
SN	Saṁyutta Nikāya
Sn	Sutta Nipāta
T	Taishō edition of the Chinese Tripiṭaka
U	Udāna
Vsm	Visuddhimagga
YS	Yoga Sūtra

BIBLIOGRAPHY

For Pali texts the references are to discourse and section of LDB and MLDB; saṁyutta and discourse of CDB (this varies from earlier texts and translations, especially in SN 35); nipāta and discourse for the Aṅguttara Nikāya and the Itivuttaka; vagga and discourse for the Udāna; and verse number for the Dhammapāda and Sutta Nipāta. For other Pali texts I used the Vipassana Research Institute CD and/or the listed translations.

ABEYNAYAKE, Oliver. 'Sri Lanka's Contribution to the Development of the Pali Canon', in *Buddhism for the New Millennium*, London: World Buddhist Foundation, 2000. Available online.

AKANUMA, Chizen. *The Comparative Catalogue of Chinese Āgamas and Pali Nikāyas,* Sri Satguru Publications, 1990.

ALLON, Mark. *The Mahā Parinirvāṇa Sūtra*, Honours sub-thesis, Australian National University 1987 (translation of WALDSCHMIDT 1950, 1951).

ANACKER, Stefan. *Seven Works of Vasubandhu*, Motilal Barnasidass, 1984, etc., corrected edition 1998.

ANĀLAYO. *Satipaṭṭhāna: The Direct Path to Realization*, Buddhist Publication Society, 2003.

ANESAKI, M. 'The Four Buddhist Āgamas in Chinese: A Concordance of their Parts and the Corresponding Counterparts in the Pali Nikāyas', *Transactions of the Asiatic Society of Japan*, XXXV (1908), pp. 69–138.

ASAṄGA. Śrāvakabhūmi, (Sanskrit text edited by the Śrāvakabhūmi Study Group, The Institute for Comprehensive Studies of Buddhism, Taishō University), The Sankibo Press, Tokyo 1998 (Taishō Books).

BEAL, Samuel. *Buddhist Literature in China*, (second edition) Sri Satguru Publications, 1988.

———. *The Romantic Legend of Śakya Buddha*, first edition Trubner & Co., 1875, reprinted Motilal Barnasidass, 1985.

BODHI, Bhikkhu (trans.) *The Connected Discourses of the Buddha—A New Translation of the Saṁyutta Nikāya*, Wisdom Publications, 2000.

BOIN-WEBB, Sara. (English trans. from Walpola RĀHULA's French trans. of the Sanskrit.) *Abhidharmasamuccaya: The Compendium of the Higher Teaching (Philosophy)* by ASAṄGA, Asian Humanities Press, 2001.

BRONKHORST, Johannes. 'Dharma and Abhidharma', *Bulletin of the School of Oriental and African Studies* 48, 1985.

———. *The Two Traditions of Meditation in Ancient India*, Motilal Barnasidass, 2000.

BUCKNELL, Roderick S. 'The Structure of the Sagāthāvagga of the Saṁyutta Nikāya', unpublished essay.

CARR, David M. *Reading the Fractures of Genesis: Historical and Literary Approaches*, Westminster John Knox Press, 1996.

CHANG, Garma C.C. (ed.) *A Treasury of Mahāyāna Sūtras: Selections from the Mahāratnakūṭa*, (translated from the Chinese by the Buddhist Association of the United States), Motilal Barnasidass, 1991.

CHOONG Mun-keat. *The Fundamental Teachings of Early Buddhism*, Harrassowitz Verlag Wiesbaden, 2000.

CLEARY, Thomas (trans.) *The Flower Ornament Scripture* (Avataṁsaka Sūtra), Shambala, 1986, 1993, etc.

CONE, Margaret. *A Dictionary of Pali, Part 1*, Pali Text Society, 2001.

CONZE, Edward. *The Large Sūtra of Perfect Wisdom* (Prajñāpāramitā Sūtra), Motilal Barnasidass, 1990.

COUSINS, L.S. 'The "Five Points" and the Origins of the Buddhist Schools', included in Pollamure Sorata Thera, etc. (ed.), *Buddhist Essays: A Miscellany*, Sri Saddhatissa International Buddhist Centre, 1992.

———. 'The Origin of Insight Meditation', included in Tadeusz Skorupski (ed.), *The Buddhist Forum IV*, School of Oriental & African Studies, University of London, 1996.

———. 'Pali Oral Literature', included in Philip Denwood and Alexander Piatigorsky (eds.), *Buddhist Studies, Ancient and Modern*, Curzon Press, 1983.

———. 'Samatha-yāna and vipassanā-yāna', included in DHAMMAPALA, GOMBRICH, NORMAN (eds.), *Buddhist Studies in Honor of Hammalava Saddhatissa*, Buddhist Research Library Trust, 1984.

CRANGLE, Edward Fitzpatrick. *The Origin and Development of Early Indian Contemplative Practices*, Harrassowitz Verlag Wiesbaden, 1994.

DAYAL, Har. *The Bodhisattva Doctrine in Buddhist Sanskrit Literature* (1932), Motilal Barnasidass, 1978.

DIETZ, Siglinde. *Fragmente des Dharmaskandha*, Gottingen Vandenhoeck & Ruprecht, 1984.

DUNDAS, Paul. *The Jains*, Routledge, 1992, 2001.

DUTT, Nalinashka. *Buddhist Sects in India*, Motilal Banarsidass, 1978, reprinted 1998.

ENOMOTO, Fumio. '"Mūlasarvāstivādin" and "Sarvāstivādin"', included in CHOJNACKI, HARTMANN, and TSCHANNERL, *Vivadharatnakarandaka*, Swisttal-Odendorf, 2000.

———. 'On the Formation of the Original Texts of the Chinese Āgamas', included in *Buddhist Studies Review*, V^OL 3, № 1, 1986.

FRAUWALLNER, Erich. *The Earliest Vinaya and the Beginnings of Buddhist Literature*, 1956.

———. *Studies in Abhidharma Literature and the Origins of Buddhist Philosophical Systems*, State University of New York Press, 1995.

GETHIN, Rupert. *The Buddhist Path to Awakening*, Oneworld Publications, 2001.

———. 'The *Mātikās*: Memorization, Mindfulness, and the List', included in Janet GYATSO, *In the Mirror of Memory*, Albany SUNY, 1992.

GOMBRICH, Richard. *How Buddhism Began: The Conditioned Genesis of Early Buddhism*, Synergy Books International.

GNANARAMA, Pategama. *The Mission Accomplished: A Historical Analysis of the Mahāparinibbāṇa Sutta of the Dīgha Nikāya of the Pali Canon*, Ti-sarana Buddhist Association, 1997.

GNOLI, Raniero (ed.) *The Gilgit Manuscript of the Sanghabhedavastu (17th section of the Mūlasarvāstivāda Vinaya), Part II*, Istituto Italiano per il Medio ed Estremo Oriente, 1978.

HARRISON, Paul (trans.) *The Samādhi of the Direct Encounter with the Buddhas of the Present* (Pratyutpanna-Buddha-Sammukhāvaṣṭhita-Samādhi-Sūtra, T № 416), The International Institute for Buddhist Studies, Tokyo, 1990.

HEIRMANN, Ann. *The Discipline in Four Parts: Rules for Nuns According to the Dharmaguptakavinaya*, Motilal Barnasidass Publishers, 2002.

VON HINÜBER, Oskar. *A Handbook of Pali Literature*, Munshiram Manoharlal Publishers, 1997.

HOPKINS, Jeffrey. *Meditation on Emptiness*, Wisdom Publications, 1983.

HURVITZ, Leon. 'Fa Sheng's Observations', included in KIYOTA.

JAYATILLEKE, K.N. *Early Buddhist Theory of Knowledge*, G. Allen & Unwin,1963.

JIANHUA, Cheng. *A Critical Translation of Fan Dong Jing, the Chinese Version of Brahmajāla* Sūtra.

JONES, J.J. (trans.) Mahāvastu, V^OL 1–3, Pali Text Society, from 1949.

KAJIYAMA, Yuichi. 'Later Mādhyamakas', included in KIYOTA.

KEENAN, John P. (trans.) *The Scripture on the Explication of Underlying Meaning* (Saṁdhinirmocana Sūtra, T № 676), Numata Center for Buddhist Translation and Research, 2000 (BDK English Tripitaka 25-IV).

KIYOTA, Minoru (ed.) *Mahāyāna Buddhist Meditation*, University Press of Hawaii, 1978; Motilal Barnasidass, 1991.

KLOPPENBORG, Ria (trans.) *The Sūtra on the Foundation of the Buddhist Order*, Religious Texts Translation Series Nisaba, VOL 1, Leiden, E J Brill, 1973.

LAMOTTE, Étienne. *History of Indian Buddhism*, Peeters Press, 1976.

———. 'The Assessment of Textual Authority in Buddhism', included in *Buddhist Studies Review*, VOL 1, № 1, 1983–4.

LI Rongxi (trans.) *The Biographical Scripture of King Aśoka* (A-yu-wang-jing, or Aśoka-rājasūtra, T № 2043), BDK English Tripitaka, Numata Center for Buddhist Translation and Research, 1993.

LIN Li Kouang (trans.) *L'Aide Mémoire de la Vraie Loi* (Saddharmasmṛtyupasthāna Sūtra), Paris, Adrien-Maisonneuve, 1949.

MASEFIELD, Peter. 'Mind/Cosmos Maps in the Pali Nikāyas', included in Nathan KATZ (ed.), *Buddhist and Western Psychology*, Prajñā Press, Boulder, 1983.

MATSUMURA, Hisashi. *Four Avadānas from Gilgit Manuscripts*, PhD thesis at Australian National University, Oct. 1980.

MEISIG, Konrad. *Das Śrāmaṇyaphala Sūtra*, Otto Harrassowitz-Wiesbaden, 1987.

MINH CHÂU, Bhiksu Thích. *The Chinese Madhyama Āgama and the Pali Majjhima Nikāya*, Motilal Barnasidass, 1991.

MONIER-WILLIAMS, Monier. *A Sanskrit-English Dictionary* (SED), Motilal Barnasidass, 2002. (First published by Oxford University Press, 1899.)

NAKAMURA, Hajime. *Indian Buddhism*, Motilal Barnasidass, 1996.

ÑĀṆAMOLI, Bhikkhu and Bhikkhu BODHI (trans.), *The Middle Length Discourses of the Buddha*, Wisdom Publications, 1995.

ÑĀṆAMOLI, Bhikkhu (trans.) *The Path of Purification* (Visuddhimagga), Buddhist Publication Society.

———. *The Life of the Buddha*, Buddhist Publication Society, 1992.

———. *The Piṭaka-Disclosure (Peṭakopadesa)*, Pali Text Society, 1964.

NHẤT HẠNH, Thích. *Transformation and Healing*, Parallax Press, 2006.

NORMAN, K.R. 'Magadhisms in the Kathāvatthu', included in Dr A.K. Narain (ed.), *Studies in Pali and Buddhism*, B.R. Publishing Corporation, 1979.

NYANAPONIKA Thera. *The Heart of Buddhist Meditation*, Buddhist Publication Society, 1973.

POUSSIN, Louis de la Vallée and Leo M. PRUDEN (trans.) Abhidharmakośabhāṣyam, Asian Humanities Press, 1988.

PRASAD, Sital. *A Comparative Study of Jainism and Buddhism*, Sri Satguru Publications, 2003 (first published 1932).

PRZYLYSKI, J. *Le Concile de Rājagaha.*

RAHULA, Bhikkhu Telwatte. *A Critical Study of the Mahāvastu*, Motilal Banarsidass, 1978.

RHYS DAVIDS, T.W. and William STEDE. *Pali-English Dictionary* (PED), Pali Text Society, 1921–1925, etc.
ROCKHILL, W. Woodville. *The Life of the Buddha*, (1884), reprinted Asian Educational Services, 1992.
SENEVIRATNE, H.L. *The Work of Kings*, The University of Chicago Press, 1999.
SAMTANI, N.H. *The Arthaviniścaya Sūtra and its Commentary*, Kashi Prasad Jayaswal Research Institute, Patna, 1971.
SCHMITHAUSEN, L. 'Die vier Konzentration der Aufmerksamkeit', *Zeitschrift fur Missionwissenschaft und Religionwissenschaft*, 60, 1976.
SCHOPEN, Gregory. *Bones, Stones, and Buddhist Monks*, University of Hawai'i Press, 1997.
———. *Buddhist Monks and Business Matters*, University of Hawai'i Press, 2004.
SMITH, Norman Joseph. 'The 17 Versions of the Buddha's First Discourse.' www.archive.org/details/The17VersionsOfTheBuddhasFirstDiscourse
SOMA Thera. *The Way of Mindfulness*, Buddhist Publication Society (reprinted by WAVE, 1999).
SUJATO, Bhikkhu. *A Swift Pair of Messengers*, Santipada, 2011.
———. *Sects & Sectarianism*. Santipada, 2011.
ṬHĀNISSARO Bhikkhu. *The Wings to Awakening*, Dhamma Dana Publications, 1996.
THIỆN CHÂU, Bhikṣu Thích. *The Literature of the Personalists of Early Buddhism*, Motilal Barnasidass, 1999.
TIN, Pe Maung (trans.) *The Expositor* (Aṭṭhasālinī), Pali Text Society, 1976.
VELKAR, Neela. *Upāsana in the Upaniṣads*, unpublished PhD thesis, University of Bombay, June 1969.
WALDSCHMIDT, Ernst. *Das Mahāparinirvāṇa Sūtra* (in 3 parts), Akadamie-Verlag, 1950, 1951 (Complete reconstructed Sanskrit Mahāparinirvāṇa Sutta).
———. Drei Fragmente Buddistischer Sūtras aus den Turfanhandschriften, 1968 (Sanskrit fragment of Mahāparinirvāṇa Sutta).
WALSHE, Maurice (trans.) *The Long Discourses of the Buddha—A Translation of the Dīgha Nikāya*, Wisdom Publications, 1995.
WARDER, A.K. *Indian Buddhism*, Motilal Barnasidass, 3rd revised edition, 2000.
WATANABE, Fumimaro. *Philosophy and its Development in the Nikāyas and Abhidhamma*, Motilal Barnasidass, 1983.
WAYMAN, Alex. *Analysis of the Śrāvakabhūmi Manuscript*, University of California Press.
WILLIS, Michael. 'Buddhist Saints in Ancient Vedisa', *Journal of the Royal Asiatic Society*, Series 3, II, 2, pp. 219–28.
WYNNE, Alexander. 'How Old is the Sutta-Piṭaka? The relative value of textual and epigraphical sources for the study of early Indian Buddhism', St John's

College, Oxford, 2003.
http://www.budsas.org/ebud/ebsut056.htm

YIN Shun. 'A Sixty Years' Journey in the Ocean of the Dhamma'.

———. *Yuanshi Fojiao Shengdian zhi Jicheng* (*The Formation of Early Buddhist Texts*), Zhengwen Chubanshe, Taipei, 1971.

———. *Za-ahan Jing-Lun Huibian* (*Combined edition of Sūtra and Śāstra of Saṁyuktāgama*), Zhengwen Chunbanshe, Taipei, 1991.